Horoscope Symbols

HOROSCOPE
SYMBOLS
Robert Hand

Para Research
Rockport, Massachusetts

To Pat, who made this book possible.

International Standard Book Number: 0-914918-16-8

Edited by Pat White
Typesetting by Barbara Kassabian, Marah Ren
Illustrations by Barbara Kassabian
Graphics by Louisa Hamachek

Printed by R.R. Donnelley & Sons Co.
on 54-pound Warren Sebago paper

Published by Para Research, Inc.
Whistlestop Mall
Rockport, Massachusetts 01966

Manufactured in the United States of America

First Printing, January 1981, 10,000 copies
Second Printing, September 1981, 10,000 copies

Contents

ANGULAR RELATIONSHIPS

ZODIACAL POSITION

MUNDANE POSITION

PREFACE

Preface

This book was originally conceived as the opening chapters of a single book on synthesizing the horoscope. It seemed to me that in order to synthesize, that is, to produce a coherent, unified reading of a birth chart, one first needs to have a thorough understanding of each of its separate symbols. Only by grasping their essential meanings can one combine these symbols in the creative and intuitive way that good astrology demands.

The section on symbolism soon grew both large enough and important enough to stand on its own. The actual process of putting the symbols together is now relegated to another book, *Horoscope Synthesis*, which is to be published separately.

The present book examines in depth each symbol in the birth chart. Not only does it include the factors I find indispensable, it also discusses and evaluates most of the other horoscope factors that are in use today. Thus it is a fairly comprehensive survey of astrological symbolism, omitting only some hypothetical planets and sensitive points with which I have had absolutely no experience or which I regard as completely crackpot.

Although I hope to give new insights to those who have done much astrology, I have written this book so it can be understood by the intelligent and only slightly knowledgeable beginner. If you have taken a beginner's course or have read a basic book or two, you should be able to get something useful out of *Horoscope Symbols*.

A few words are in order concerning my approach to astrological symbolism. Ever since I first began to study astrology, I have been impressed by its symbolic richness, but I have also been disturbed by some of its features. Perhaps my greatest source of unease has been the obvious superficiality of the interpretations given to many astrological symbols. The houses in particular are often given a seemingly random grab-bag of meanings having to do with the outward details of life. Few authors seem to have tried to understand the unifying principles behind these interpretations.

Another thing that disturbed me was that many of the meanings have been oriented toward fortunetelling. Events in the external world are described with little or no understanding of their psychological roots and the role a person may have played in bringing them about. I believe that the primary value of astrology is as a symbolic description of the human psyche. To me, astrology best describes what we are like inside. It relates to external events only insofar as they arise out of what we are and how we behave. For these reasons, in this book I try to:

1. Unify the symbolism of each astrological factor so that its various significations can all be derived from the understanding of a single essence.

2. Understand this essence in internal, psychological terms.

3. Explain how the essential symbolism gives rise to the traditional symbolism.

In doing the above I have had to jettison much of what has been said recently about astrological symbols. Many modern attempts to do what I have done in this book have contradicted some of the traditional meanings and ended up clouding rather than clarifying things. I often prefer the older descriptions because, despite their superficial and fatalistic style, they seem closer to the archetypes that I believe are embodied in astrology. Only their superficiality must be overcome.

I request one thing of you. There are a number of ideas presented here that may seem radical. Please suspend judgment until you have had the opportunity to apply these ideas. My own perceptions have gone through transformations because of the ideas of others. I hope you will allow yours to do the same.

I do not expect what I say in this book to be regarded as final. It is certainly not so from my point of view. As long as one lives, one's ideas should be in a state of growth. Unfortunately, books tend to trap and preserve ideas at a particular state of development. This book is the result of many years of study and reflects my understanding at this time, but I reserve the right in the future to contradict anything I have said should new material and experience present new understanding.

I hope that this book will spur you on to similar efforts to understand the basic symbols of astrology. In this way, we can arrive at a collective view that is more profound and useful than any we now have. Though I hope to contribute to that end result, I do not expect that this will be even close to the last word.

October, 1980

INTRODUCTION

INTRODUCTION

1

The Horoscope:
A Map of the Psyche

The horoscope or birthchart is the basic tool of astrology nowadays, but it has not always been so. Originally, in Mesopotamia, the land from which astrology as we now practice it was derived, astrology was a system of celestial omens by which the fate of the king and his people was judged. If any individual was involved, it was the king alone. Even he was involved only as he represented the fortunes of his people. Not only was the individual considered too unimportant for astrological investigation, there was also no technique by which the indications of the heavens could be personalized to the individual.

By the late Babylonian period, however, just before Alexander invaded the East, astrologers were beginning to use factors that can be applied to individuals. One of these was the rising degree, or at least the rising constellation. What is rising can change more rapidly than any other astrological indication in the heavens, and hence can mark the particular moment in time (and place on Earth) of the birth of a single individual. The rising sign or degree was called the "watcher of the hour," or *horoscopos* in Greek. "Horoscope" thus originally meant only what we now call the Ascendant; much later, in the Renaissance, it came to mean the entire chart erected for a specific time and place. This usage stands today.

The horoscope has been from the very beginning a tool for the study of *individuality*. Without relating the motions of the heavenly bodies to a specific time and place on Earth, you have no personal indication at all, only a general one that applies to everyone on the planet born on a particular day.

Astrology still deals with historical cycles and the fates of nations, but what this book treats is the study of individuals and what they are, with all that implies. Individual astrology is not merely a study of what will happen to people in the course of their lives. It is a study of the whole human life and everything about it: birth, childhood, relationships throughout life, self-image, the images projected onto others, the calling (in both the highest and most mundane sense of the word), the feelings, and the patterns of energy that one generates around oneself. In the final analysis, the study of the horoscope is the study of almost everything about human beings with which one could possibly be concerned.

No one astrologer can be expected to master all of this, but even with some degree of specialization, astrology is obviously a study that requires the greatest possible depth and breadth of knowledge, wisdom, and experience. Do not let this discourage you: what else were you planning to do with your life, anyway? Besides, the needed knowledge, wisdom, and experience are not learned in school. Rather, they are acquired from living life consciously and with understanding. They may also be acquired from doing astrology: the study of astrology feeds itself. Studying astrology can bring the higher perceptions that life requires.

But acquaintance with astrologers reveals there are at least as many unenlightened and unconscious people in this field as in any other. Astrology by itself does not lead to understanding. One has to start from a viewpoint that will enable one to create a greater understanding of life. To do this, one must be willing to suspend belief in some concepts by which one has been structuring the world, and to look at the world and one's involvement in it in a different light. One must be willing to stop playing certain games that one has been playing, and instead to deal with the world as honestly and as openly as possible. Also, one has to be willing to expand one's view of the individual human being.

The Author's Viewpoint

The conventional view of the individual is that he or she is a body, containing a mind, an emotional nature, muscles, and all the other parts of a person. Most people feel that they end at their skins and that everything outside belongs to a world that is other than themselves. This basic division of the universe into self and not-self is important in understanding the individual world-view and the ways most people structure their experience. But if you are studying astrology it is not an adequate understanding of the structure of existence.

I do not wish you to accept what I am about to say blindly on faith, nor do I want you to reject it out of hand. I want you to try it as a working hypothesis and see whether it makes sense for you and improves your understanding of life. After you have done much study of astrology you may or may not agree with what I am about to say, but the very act of suspending your current belief system about what you are and what constitutes an individual will enable you to come to a much higher level of realization than you may have had before. Instead of simply providing a new way of playing old ego games, your study of astrology will have expanded your understanding.

Here are the basic ideas I ask you to entertain as working hypotheses. You are, as an individual, the sum total of all your actions, all your experiences, and everything and everyone that is in your life. There is no split between the self and the not-self. As will be explained on pages 263-266, whatever split you may feel changes location within your field of consciousness according to where your attention has turned and what kinds of issues you are dealing with. In other words, the apparent split that you feel is only relative, not absolute.

Equally important is a second principle: you are, in the totality of what you are, the creator and focus for divine energy within your universe. This is not to say that there is no God higher than you as an individual. More accurately, you are the channel for that entity's energy coming into your world.

Before challenging this, you should recognize that you do not experience the universe as it is in the ultimate sense, but as it is channeled through your senses and modified by the sum total of your previous conceptions and past experiences. What you create, therefore, is really your experience of the universe, and your experience is yours and uniquely yours.

Now comes a point even harder to accept: you create not only the experiences of events involving you with others, but also the experiences of events involving others with others. If such experiences were not appropriate to you at the time when you experienced them, you would not be in the place that allows you to experience them. Events of which you are unaware may or may not exist on the level of absolute reality, but unless you are aware of such events, they are not real for you and do not exist for you. If you have trouble with this idea, remember it is only a working hypothesis. Even I have trouble applying it consistently.

Before you can deal with the idea that you create events, there is something else to understand. To say you create something, let us say something "evil," is not to say you are guilty of it. You must look at events and things without making value judgments, either positive or negative. You are only concerned with what is so in your life, not what ought to be. Most people in their normal consciousness of life are not ready to make judgments about what ought to be.

Here is where the horoscope is useful. We have said you are the creator of your own experience and the true source of all intentions in your universe. For one reason or another, however, you will often mislay within consciousness some fact or truth about your universe, and get into the habit of no longer seeing it. This is usually because recognizing such a truth will bring you into conflict with some other aspect of your universe: events that you experience or participate in, or desires and intentions that have taken hold of your awareness. Or you may have created such a conflict in the past, and now you have fallen out of the habit of dealing with issues related to that conflict. In these ways you can get lost in your own universe and need some kind of map or compass. All systems of divination, including astrology, really have the same purpose: to find where one is within one's own universe. One can then get back in touch with the creative process of making one's universe work. None of these techniques, be it palmistry, Tarot, numerology, astrology, or any other, should be used for telling what is going to happen to people as if they were only passive spectators in a universe beyond their control. If one forecasts events, one should make it clear that they will only result from energies that the individual is currently manifesting, should these energies go on to their logical conclusion without change.

This brings us to another point, which to rationalists and materialists may seem like a dodge. Astrology and all other divinatory techniques require the active participation of the person being counseled, so that both client and counselor can apply the symbols of astrology or whatever system is being used to the individual's own life. A good astrologer can get something out of the chart without the client's active participation, but it is not really useful to do so. Far too many people go to an astrologer expecting to sit back passively and be told something about themselves. Usually the astrologer can amaze and astound with facts and insights, but the client then receives no benefit from the process except entertainment.

Totally apart from whether any real influences come from the planets, an individual can gain simply by focusing on astrological symbols. Just as by making up stories suggested by inkblots one can reveal to oneself aspects of life that are not otherwise apparent, one can also gain insight by studying one's horoscope. There is evidence that there is considerably more going on with astrology than with an inkblot test, but I am willing to admit there may be certain parts of astrology that function entirely in such a way. Unlike the Rorschach test, however, in which the same inkblots are shown to every individual, horoscopes are peculiar to each person. For whatever reason (and several have been suggested, including Jung's concept of synchronicity), the horoscope seems to act as a schematic diagram of one's intentions in life. It only shows what one is going to experience because one intends to experience it. It is a description not of what is going to happen (that is, destiny), but of what one is and what shape one is going to give to one's life. Though many critics have said so and many astrologers have made it seem that way, astrology is in no way a retreat from individual responsibility. Rather, it acknowledges responsibility on the highest level.

In everything said so far, the following is implicit: if you are in touch with whatever you are doing and know your responsibility for what is happening (and are therefore operating from a position of choice), you are going to be happier and more fulfilled than if you feel out of touch (and therefore constantly a victim of forces beyond your control). You will always *be* what you are in the deepest sense of that idea, but you may not be *aware* of what you are and of what should be done in life as a result. The aim is not to change yourself, but to make yourself more conscious of what you are at a particular point in time.

Levels of Manifestation

A concept I will refer to frequently is that of level of manifestation. Every symbol in the chart can and often will manifest at all levels of the personality and environment. But some symbols work better at certain levels than at others. Every indication in the chart has a positive role to play, yet it can also be made to play a difficult one. As I have often said in my lectures, it is hard to drive a nail with a screwdriver. Every symbol in the horoscope, every indication about the self, has a level where it is a screwdriver trying to drive a nail, and some people manage to get their entire lives operating at that level. The astrologer strives to eliminate this kind of activity by giving the client self-understanding.

All difficult astrological indications have a level of manifestation in which they can be made to work out properly. This often requires the individual to go into a tightly defined existence in which there are few alternatives that work easily. The alternatives that do work, however, often do so very well. In astrology there are no indications that are absolutely "bad," there are only those that are often mishandled.

Astrology and Religion

One last point. There are religious sects and philosophies that consider astrology to be somehow immoral, or at best a deviation from the path one should follow. The Bible, interpreted literally, occasionally condemns astrology, though in books like Daniel, Ezekiel, and Revelation the symbols of astrology and numerology are rife. The condemnations are either general condemnations of divination (that is, fortunetelling, not divination in the sense it has been used here) or statements to the effect that if a genuine prophet of God is available, one should heed the prophet rather than an astrologer. I am inclined to agree with this: genuinely enlightened teachers are indeed better sources of guidance than most astrologers.

Christianity has been ambivalent about astrology both because of the Biblical criticism and because of its own theological emphasis on free will. One must be free in order to choose whether or not to accept salvation. Salvation becomes a cruel joke if the position of the planets at birth determines whether one achieves it. Both the Biblical and the Christian criticisms are in fact concerned with the doctrine of the planets as absolute determinants of one's fate. Most astrologers would not accept this doctrine.

From what has been said already, it should be clear that horoscope symbols only indicate certain aspects of one's style of being, and that these are only indications, not causes. One still has the responsibility for determining one's destiny, even if one is not aware of this. One has complete responsibility for achieving one's own salvation, enlightenment, or whatever one's religious tradition chooses to call it.

Some might object that I am giving the individual too much power. I believe the individual is powerful, but also that the individual is the route through which the will of the universe is made manifest. I do not separate humankind from the divine and oppose the two. That, I feel, may be a fundamental error in philosophy and religion, especially in the West. This error has been the root of many evils. Only by believing in the opposition of the will of human beings to that of the universe can one create the sense of evil with which many approach the world. This belief has created Satan, who has no existence beyond the consciousness of those who give him power by believing in him.

The Role of the Symbols

Turning to the horoscope symbols themselves, now, we will look at the range of patterns associated with each. We must understand that we are dealing not with forces that coerce us, but with psychological, spiritual, and metaphysical energies that lie both within ourselves and within the universe. In every aspect of our lives we will manifest these forces: in our bodies, our minds, our ways of life, our relationships with others, and even in what we see around us.

It is our sharing of these energies with the universe that ties us to it, makes us part of it, and ensures that it is our home. Within these patterns our creativity and responsibility are not diminished, but only given a form from which infinite possibilities can emerge.

2

The Symbol
Systems of Astrology

The horoscope describes an individual through the interaction of several symbol systems or categories of symbols. The most-used categories are the planets, horoscope angles, aspects, houses, and signs. This book examines these categories and each of their members in great detail. Less-used categories, like asteroids, hypothetical planets, planetary nodes, fixed stars, midpoints, planetary pictures, antiscia or solstice points, and Arabian parts are also looked at, but more briefly.

I call these categories "symbol systems" because besides being collections of symbols with something in common, these groupings have an internal structure. Each separate symbol is related to all the others in the system in a definite way. Thus, in addition to discussing each symbol, I will in this book discuss the structure of the symbol system as a whole. I will often compare and contrast the individual symbols with each other, and sometimes symbols in other systems. In this way I hope to give you a feeling for the overall structure of the horoscope as well as for the symbolism of its individual factors.

The above symbol systems can be grouped in various ways. In this book they are divided into four overall classes: points in the chart (planets, nodes, etc.), angular relationships (aspects, midpoints, etc.), indicators of zodiacal position (signs), and indicators of mundane position (houses). In this chapter I will attempt to sketch in the astronomical basis for each system and then indicate how each system fits into the overall symbolic structure of the horoscope.

Points in the Chart

The horoscope contains several categories of point-like symbols, chief among which are the planets. These and the horoscope angles—the Ascendant, Midheaven, Descendant, and I.C.—are by far the most important points in the chart.

The Planets   To modern astronomers, a planet is one of the larger bodies orbiting a star. It is something other than a self-luminous body (a star), a small orbiting body (a planetoid, asteroid, or comet), or a body (a moon or satellite) orbiting a larger non-luminous body. According to this definition, the Earth is a planet, but the Sun is a star and the Moon is for most purposes a satellite.

To astrologers, however, the Sun and Moon are planets, along with Mercury, Venus, Mars, Jupiter, Saturn, Uranus, Neptune, and Pluto. The Earth is not usually listed as a planet at all. This is because astrology is interested not in an abstract astronomical picture, but in the way things are seen from Earth, that is, from a human perspective. The ancient Greeks gave us the word "planet" from their verb *planetein*, "to wander." For astrologers, too, planets are those major heavenly bodies that, alone among the thousands of objects visible in the sky, appear from Earth to move against the background of the fixed stars.

When seen from Earth, the planets all travel in a fairly narrow belt of sky known as the zodiac. This is because, when seen from the Sun, all the planets including the Earth and the Moon have orbits in approximately the same plane. Because the orbital planes are very nearly the same, astrologers find it convenient to measure the progress of all the planets along one plane. For this purpose, they have chosen the plane of the Earth's orbit around the Sun, which from the Earth appears to be the Sun's yearly path through the sky. This plane is known as the ecliptic. The terms "zodiac" and "ecliptic" are often used interchangeably, though strictly speaking the ecliptic appears to us as a line and the zodiac is the area surrounding that line. In order to measure the progress of the planets, the ecliptic is divided into 360°, or twelve signs of 30° each. The circle of the horoscope that we draw on paper represents the circle of the ecliptic, and the degrees and minutes of the planets and other points are degrees along the ecliptic, or degrees of celestial longitude. (If we want to measure how far a body is above or below the ecliptic, we do this in degrees of celestial latitude, which are at right angles to degrees of celestial longitude.)

If you live in the Earth's Northern Hemisphere and you view the Sun or Moon at the same hour day after day, they appear to be moving steadily counterclockwise, or from west to east, against the background of the fixed stars. The Sun takes a year to go around the zodiac, while the Moon takes about 28 days. The other planets move mainly counterclockwise, but from time to time they appear to stop and move clockwise or retrograde before continuing their generally forward progress in the zodiac. (The reasons for retrogradation are given in Chapter 3.) Each planet takes a different amount of time to go once around the zodiac, and so the spatial relationship between the planets is constantly changing, giving each day a unique pattern of planets arranged in space.

For this reason, in astrology the planets have come to represent those factors that vary in time and which thus relate to the dynamic components of one's life. Planets are the most basic astrological symbols. They represent the energies of the personality, all dynamism and process within the psyche, body and environment. They describe change, events, and the living energies within us. They signify growth and development, as well as energies that we use to deal with a particular set of circumstances. In a real sense, planets can be likened to the verbs in a sentence.

Often astrologers speak as if planets can also symbolize specific entities, saying, for example, that the Moon signifies women, or Saturn signifies hard objects, crystals, and the like. Strictly speaking, this is erroneous: planets do not signify actual entities. But there is some truth in the idea. When certain planetary energies are active, one may attract people, things, or situations that embody those planetary energies. It is really the energies that are signified, not the entity embodying those energies. For example, if a woman receives a strong Mars influence, she may encounter strong, domineering males. But she may also encounter domineering females, be domineering herself, or encounter other entities that embody Mars energy. The real issue is ego energies, not the entities that embody them. So even though certain kinds of entities usually go with certain planets, planetary energies will often show up in other ways. This is one of the things that makes astrological prediction difficult.

There is one branch of astrology in which planets are routinely spoken of as things. This is horary astrology, the astrology of answering specific questions. This is the part of astrology closest to fortunetelling, and it relies heavily on the intuition of the interpreter. But even in horary, planets only represent objects insofar as the objects exhibit the particular energy patterns of the planets that signify them. It is only the speech and writing habits of horary practitioners that make it seem otherwise.

Another essential point: the planets as representations of energies do not signify the objective reality of what one encounters. They signify the energies as they are experienced. Thus if, due to conditions in the natal chart, a man tends to attract women who seem strong-willed, he may experience even a relatively weak-willed woman as strong-willed. And he may be the only one who does so with a particular woman. In such a case, his observations about this woman will not be reinforced by other people's observations. In most cases, a person's experience of another will be shared by others—but not always. Astrology is a guide to the nature of a person's experience, and knowing what that experience is is absolutely essential to a psychological understanding of the individual.

Other Points   Some of the other point-like categories of symbols are much like planets. The asteroids, planetoids like the newly-discovered Chiron, and even the hypothetical planets of the Uranian and other schools of astrology behave like planets in that they are bodies orbiting against the background of the fixed stars. Like the principal planets, these represent various kinds of energy.

Fixed stars, though they do not travel in orbits, are also bodies in space. According to most authorities they are at least somewhat planet-like in the role they play in the horoscope.

But points like the Ascendant, Midheaven, Vertex, East Point, 0° Aries, and the lunar and planetary nodes are not bodies in space. Rather, they are places where another important plane crosses the plane of the ecliptic. These points are less like energies and more like places where energies can manifest. In Chapter 5, I discuss these symbols as points, but I bring up the Ascendant and Midheaven again later in the book because they, along with the houses, are also indicators of the planets' mundane positions, or positions in relation to a specific point on Earth. The East Point and Vertex reflect mundane position, too, but are discussed only under "Other Points" because they are not basic markers of mundane positions in the way that the Ascendant and Midheaven are.

There are also points in the horoscope that are derived from the angular relationships of the points mentioned above. All of these can be grouped under the heading "planetary pictures." They include midpoints, Arabian parts, and antiscia or solstice points. These points could also be discussed in the section on angular relationships, and, in fact, in the main text of this book I do discuss midpoints more fully there.

Angular Relationships

As mentioned above, the position of every point is usually projected onto the plane of the ecliptic and expressed as a particular degree and minute of celestial longitude. The horoscope is usually represented as a circle, with the person as the center, and the planets and other points discussed above are ranged around the circumference. Thus every point lies in some angular relationship to every other point in the chart.

Some of these angles are considered significant, and others are not. When the angle separating two points is not significant, there is supposed to be no relationship between the symbols. When two points are separated by a significant angle, the symbols interact in some way: two planetary energies combine or come into conflict, or, when a planet forms a significant angle with one of the crossing points described above, a planetary energy finds a certain area of life in which to manifest.

There are two cases when an angle can be significant: when it is an aspect or harmonic, and when it is part of a planetary picture.

The Aspects Among the angular relationships possible in a horoscope, aspects are the most well-known and important. Two points are considered by most astrologers today to be in aspect to each other if the angle between them is exactly, or within a few degrees of being, 180°, 150°, 135°, 120°, 90°, 60°, 45°, 30° or 0°. These aspects all come from dividing the 360° of the ecliptic by the numbers one, two, three, four, six, eight or twelve.

It is also possible, though less common, to divide the circle by other whole numbers, such as five, seven, eleven, thirteen, fourteen, fifteen, sixteen and so forth. Astrologers such as Johannes Kepler in the seventeenth century and John Addey in the twentieth have found validity in these less-used angles. As will be explained in Chapter 6, all aspects are harmonics of the circle, but to distinguish them from each other, the more usual whole-number divisions of the circle are called aspects and the less-used ones are called harmonics.

As with the other symbolic categories, each aspect angle has its own symbolism. The type of angle signifies the type of relationship between planets or other factors. The angle can have a considerable effect on the way two planets interact. Nevertheless, as one might expect, certain planetary energies are compatible or not compatible regardless of the angle between them.

Though we are usually concerned with aspects between two planets or other points, it is also proper to speak of a sign aspecting another sign or a house aspecting another house. In fact, as I will show in later chapters, both the signs and houses may well derive their meanings from the aspects they form among themselves. In the case of the houses, these aspects are not in the plane of the ecliptic. Aspects can be formed in other planes, but with the exception of the parallel and contraparallel aspects described in Chapter 6, non-ecliptic aspects are beyond the scope of this book.

Midpoints and Other Planetary Pictures   An angular relationship between points does not, however, have to be a whole-number division of the circle in order to link the points together. An arc of any size whatsoever between two points can become significant if there is an arc of the same size between two points elsewhere in the chart. For example, if planets A and B are separated by 17° along the ecliptic and planets C and D are also separated by 17°, all four planets are considered to be linked together, even though 17° is not an aspect. Angular relationships like this involving equal openings between pairs of points are called planetary pictures. As I will explain further in Chapter 5, Arabian parts and antiscia or solstice points are also forms of planetary picture.

The special case of planetary picture that I find the most useful is the midpoint configuration. This only needs to involve three points instead of four. The opening between planets A and B is the same as the opening between planets B and C. In other words, planet B is at the midpoint between planets A and C.

Using nothing but planets, the Ascendant and Midheaven, aspects, and midpoints, it is possible to do an accurate and detailed reading of a horoscope. I have put these symbol systems in the first half of the book because they are so fundamental. They usually speak the loudest and yield the most reliable results, and for this reason they make a good starting point for interpreting the chart.

There are, however, two other widely used symbol systems that can round out one's interpretation. These are the signs and the houses. In contrast to the point-like symbol systems discussed earlier, both of these are field-like. That is, they are not specific points, but ranges of position. The twelve signs are all 30° divisions of the ecliptic, and the twelve houses divide the ecliptic into segments of varying length. Signs and houses are not energies in the sense that planets are. Rather, they are modifiers of planetary energies, or backdrops against which planetary energies can be viewed.

The signs and the houses each measure a different type of planetary motion. The signs mark where the planets are in their apparent progress through the zodiac, which is caused by the planets' and the Earth's orbiting the Sun. This is the long-term, mainly counterclockwise type of motion described above in the section on the planets. The houses, on the other hand, mark where the planets are in their apparent daily circling of the Earth, which is caused by the Earth's rotation on its axis. When seen from the Northern Hemisphere, this short-term motion is clockwise: looking south, you can see the Sun and other planets rise in the east and set in the west. In fact, the reason our clock hands go clockwise is that they are imitating this heavenly progress: the hour hand, representing the Sun, reaches its highest point at noon. In older texts, the counterclockwise, long-term motion is called secondary motion, whereas the clockwise, daily motion is called primary motion. Secondary motion is what gives planets their zodiacal position, or position in relation to the beginning of the zodiac. Primary motion is what gives them their mundane position, or position in relation to the horizon of a specific place on Earth.

Zodiacal Position

There are two ways of measuring the progress of a planet through the zodiac. One is to use the so-called sidereal zodiac, which is a measure of a planet's relation to the background of the fixed stars. The other is to use the so-called tropical zodiac, which is a measure of a planet's relation to the point in the sky where the Sun is on the first day of spring. This point, known as the vernal equinox, or 0° Aries of the tropical zodiac, moves clockwise or backwards in the zodiac in relation to the fixed stars at the rate of about 1° every 72 years. About 2,000 years ago, the signs of the tropical zodiac lay in approximately the same part of the heavens as the constellations of the same name, but now 0° of tropical Aries has moved 24° to 25° back into the constellation of Pisces. This movement of the vernal point is called the precession of the equinoxes.

There are several reasons why I prefer to use the signs of the tropical zodiac rather than the constellations of the sidereal zodiac, which bear the same names but have different locations. For one thing, the tropical zodiac reflects the seasons of the year more clearly than does the sidereal zodiac. In the tropical zodiac, 0° Aries marks the beginning of spring, 0° Cancer the beginning of summer, 0° Libra the beginning of fall, and 0° Capricorn the beginning of winter. Thus the position of the Sun in the tropical signs is a clear indicator of the time of year. The seasons are phases in one of the most obvious astronomical cycles, and have a powerful effect on the Earth and its inhabitants.

Another reason for using the tropical zodiac is that its beginning is a matter of clear-cut astronomical fact, whereas the beginning of the sidereal zodiac is a matter of debate. Tropical 0° Aries marks the intersection of two fundamental planes: the plane of the ecliptic, along which secondary motion takes place, and the plane of the equator, along which primary motion takes place. As defined above, the ecliptic is the plane of the Earth's orbit around the Sun, or, as seen from the Earth, the plane of the Sun's apparent path through the fixed stars. The equator, on the other hand, is the plane of the Earth's daily rotation on its axis. Tropical 0° Aries marks the beginning of the Sun's yearly cycle: on the first day of spring, the Sun is directly overhead at the Earth's equator, midway between its extreme north and south declinations. (Declination, the angular measure of a body's distance north or south of the equator, is discussed more fully in the section on parallels at the end of Chapter 6.) On the first day of the Northern Hemisphere's summer, the Sun reaches its northernmost declination. This is the summer solstice (from the Latin for "Sun standing"), when the Sun stops its northward progress. On the first day of fall the Sun is directly over the equator again, marking the autumnal equinox. And on the first day of winter the Sun reaches its southernmost declination, marking the winter solstice. This Sun-Earth cycle defines the four seasons, which in turn are each divided into three parts by the signs of the tropical zodiac.

The tropical signs thus express something very real about one of the main cyclical relationships of the Sun to the Earth. They are, however, not so clearly connected to the cycles of the other planets, which take either more or less than a year to complete a circuit of the zodiac, and which have orbital planes that cross the equator near, but not right at, 0° Aries. Nevertheless, the degrees of the tropical signs are used by most astrologers as the scale by which to measure the position along the ecliptic not only of the Sun, but of all factors in the chart. And most astrologers believe that each sign modifies in its own characteristic way the energies of all the planets and other points that fall within it.

The Signs   The signs of the tropical zodiac are the most familiar part of astrology. Even non-astrologers know "their sign," which is the sign their Sun is in. This is because the Sun sign can be determined from the birthday alone without even knowing the year. The result is an excessive emphasis on zodiacal signs.

Popular texts attribute effects to signs that signs simply do not possess. For example, two people's Sun signs will not be the principal determinant of whether or not they will get along. The Sun signs are only one relatively minor factor among many.

An apt metaphor likens the signs to the colored glass in the rose window of a cathedral. The Sun shines through the glass and takes on different colors according to the part of the window it shines through. The signs have this effect on the planetary energies "shining" through them. As such, signs may assist or inhibit the easy expression of a planet's energies, but they cannot fundamentally change the energies.

Signs can symbolize behavioral quirks that give a person a great deal of individuality. But the mere fact that a planet is in a certain sign does not usually reveal an individual's greatest strength or weakness, whereas combinations of that planet with another planet may do so. If planets can be likened to verbs, signs can be likened to adverbs.

Even though signs and planets do not signify the same kinds of thing, each planet has an affinity with certain signs, and works less well in other signs. This has given rise to the doctrine of rulerships. Rightly or wrongly, astrologers have developed a scheme whereby each planet "rules" a sign, and they have used this scheme to link a planet to a house when the sign the planet rules is on the house's cusp. This procedure is discussed further at the end of Chapter 10.

Mundane Position

The word "mundane" comes from the Latin *mundus*, meaning "world," and it is used by astrologers in two senses. Mundane astrology is the astrology of world and other public events, as opposed to the astrology of the individual that I am presenting here. Mundane position, on the other hand, applies to any horoscope, whether public or individual. It is the part of the horoscope that refers to the turning of the world, as opposed to the celestial part that refers to the orbiting of bodies in space. Mundane position tells you which planets are above, and which are below the horizon at any particular point on the surface of the Earth. It also describes what stage of its daily cycle a planet is in: how far it has traveled between rising and culminating (reaching its highest point in the sky), or culminating and setting, or setting and anticulminating (reaching its lowest point in the sky), etc. As with the year cycle, most astrologers divide the day cycle into twelve parts, which in the case of the day cycle are nowadays called the houses. Because it allows you to relate celestial events to the local horizon, mundane position makes it possible to set up an astrological chart for a particular event on Earth, be it the birth of a nation or the birth of an individual.

Mundane position involves the interaction of four different planes:

the horizon of the birthplace, the meridian of the birthplace, the equator and the ecliptic. Of these four, the horizon is the principal mundane plane of reference. Every point on the surface of the Earth has its own horizon plane. If you are standing on the Earth holding a weight on a string, that string will point down, in the direction of gravity, approximately to the center of the Earth. The horizon plane will be perpendicular to the string. For you, the horizon separates above from below. The heavens above the horizon are visible to you, but the heavens below are blocked from view by the Earth you are standing on.

The local meridian is perpendicular to the horizon. It goes from the point due south of you on the horizon, up directly overhead, down through the point north of you on the horizon, under your feet, and back to the south point on the horizon. Whenever a planet reaches the upper part of your local meridian, it has reached its highest point in the sky, from your point of view. When a planet reaches the lower part of your local meridian, it has reached its lowest point in the sky. The meridian separates planets that are on their way up from those that are on their way down.

Your local meridian is also perpendicular to the equator, or plane of the Earth's daily rotation. In fact, all meridians are by definition perpendicular to the equator: a meridian is any great circle that passes through the north and south poles, which are at right angles to the equator. Meridians divide up the sphere of the Earth and the heavens like the sections of an orange. Your local meridian is the one that happens to be passing overhead.

As the Earth turns in the plane of the equator, the relation of the meridian to the fixed stars changes. It is from the motion of your local meridian relative to the fixed stars and other bodies in the sky that you can tell that the Earth is turning. The local meridian is our reference point for telling the time of day. Noon (Latin *meridiem*) is the time the Sun is near the meridian, and we divide our day into AM (*ante meridiem*, "before noon") and PM (*post meridiem*, "after noon").

The ecliptic is important in measuring mundane position chiefly because astrologers have chosen to project mundane positions onto it for the sake of convenience. In this way, the position of everything in the horoscope can be expressed in degrees of celestial longitude. Having one measuring scale for all the symbols greatly simplifies the job of relating one horoscope symbol to another.

Unfortunately, however, projecting mundane positions onto the ecliptic results in a certain degree of distortion. This is because the plane of the ecliptic is rarely perpendicular to the plane of the horizon or of the meridian.

The Horoscope Angles   Astrologers generally use the term "aspect" for the angular relationships between factors in the horoscope, and reserve the term "angle" for one of the four principal mundane points, the

Ascendant, Descendant, Midheaven, and I.C. These are the "horoscope angles," and planets near them on either side or anywhere in the house immediately counterclockwise from them are often called "angular."

The horoscope angles are in part a device for expressing the horizon and meridian planes in terms of degrees along the ecliptic. The Ascendant and Descendant are the two points where the ecliptic crosses the horizon. Planets rise, or pass from below the horizon to above it, at or near the Ascendant. They set, or pass from above the horizon to below, at or near the Descendant. These two points are always exactly 180° from each other.

Similarly, the Midheaven and I.C. are always exactly opposite each other. These angles are where the ecliptic crosses the local meridian. The Midheaven (English for the Latin *medium coeli*) is where these two circles cross above the horizon, and the I.C. (short for *imum coeli*, or "lowest heaven") is where they cross below the horizon.

In the case of the Sun, which is always exactly on the ecliptic, and of any other planet that happens to be right on the ecliptic at the moment of birth, the horoscope angles are accurate indicators of the body's mundane position. If the body's ecliptic longitude is a half degree above the Ascendant, the body will be a half degree above the horizon. But if the body has any celestial latitude (that is, if it is not exactly on the ecliptic), the body's longitude may be above the horizon while the body itself is below the horizon, or vice versa. And something similar is true of the Midheaven. If the body has latitude, it can actually reach its highest point in the sky before or after its degree on the ecliptic reaches the Midheaven.

The greater a body's celestial latitude, the less reliable its ecliptic relation to the horoscope angles is likely to be as an indicator of mundane position. The worst case among the planets is Pluto, which can reach a latitude of over 17°. Pluto can appear by ecliptic longitude to be a whole house below the horizon when in reality it is above. And the distortion with fixed stars, which can have latitudes up to 90°, can be extreme. The only times this distortion does not occur with a body that has latitude are those occasional moments when the ecliptic is perpendicular to the horizon or meridian.

If you are interested in the geometry of all this, you can refer to Figure 1. But it is not necessary to do so. Just remember that if a planet is near an angle or an intermediate house cusp and its latitude shows it to be far from the ecliptic, you should not base your whole interpretation on the fact that it is in the house it appears to be in, or is actually rising, culminating, setting or anticulminating. Handily, some ephemerides and computerized chart calculations list celestial latitudes so you can check them and thus decide how well a planet's degree on the ecliptic expresses its true relation to the horizon or meridian.

Fortunately, the horoscope angles are for most purposes fairly good indicators of how close a planet is to the horizon or meridian. As such, the angles are extremely important. The two points where a planet crosses the horizon (rises and sets) and the two points where it crosses the meridian (culminates and anticulminates) appear to be at or near four peaks in the daily cycle of a planetary energy's intensity. Both the experience of countless astrologers and the findings of formal research confirm this. Thus a planet close to an angle can stand out from all the other planets and become a dominant theme in a person's life.

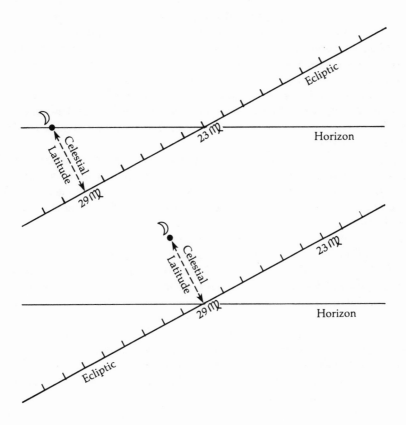

Figure 1. The actual rising of a planet that is not on the ecliptic

In figure 1, the Moon is shown at 29° ♍ , but several degrees north of the ecliptic. It crosses the horizon when the Ascendant is 23° ♍ . By the time the Ascendant becomes 29° ♍ , the Moon is well above the horizon.

The horoscope angles not only bestow intensity on planetary energies, they also seem to exert a qualitative effect. This effect is strongest when planets are conjunct (right next to) the horoscope angles, but it also works when planets are in other aspects or in planetary-picture types of relationship to the angles. So far in this section, I have been talking about the angles as ecliptic-based indicators of mundane position, but as you will recall from the earlier section in this chapter, "Other Points," the Ascendant and Midheaven also appear to have validity in their own right as sensitive points along the ecliptic. Like other forms of node, they indicate specific areas where planetary energies can manifest, and like all points in the horoscope, they work in aspects along the ecliptic, seemingly independently of the true mundane position of the planets they are aspecting.

These two ways of using angularity come from different schools of astrology. Today some astrologers, mainly those who use the sidereal zodiac, downgrade the importance of the ecliptic in favor of true mundane positions. For them, "angularity" is simply a measure of planetary strength, and it means closeness to the horizon or meridian, rather than to the point along the ecliptic that is the Ascendant, Midheaven, Descendant, or I.C. To them, mundane position does not affect planets qualitatively, and so it makes no sense to use houses.

Most tropical astrologers today, however, including followers of the Uranian and Cosmobiological schools, work almost entirely along the ecliptic and consider the horoscope angles to have specific meanings. The Uranians and Cosmobiologists see the horoscope angles almost exclusively as sensitive points, and measure the angles' relationship in ecliptic longitude to everything else in the chart. So extensive is their use of angular relationships among points, that they are usually able to derive sufficient information without using houses. Traditionalists, on the other hand, often de-emphasize the angles as sensitive points, and see them mainly as the cusps of houses one, four, seven and ten, carrying the meanings of those houses.

In my present approach to astrology, I draw something from all these views. I use the horoscope angles as approximate indicators of whether a planet is on the horizon or meridian, as sensitive points making aspect and planetary-picture-type relationships, and as the fundamental divisions from which the houses are derived.

The Houses   The horoscope angles divide the chart into four quadrants much as the cardinal points (0° Aries, Cancer, Libra, and Capricorn) divide the year and the zodiac into seasons. And as in the zodiac, each of the four main divisions of the mundane cycle is usually further divided into three parts, making a total of twelve. In most house systems the horoscope angles are the same as the cusps of the first, fourth, seventh and tenth houses.

Unlike the divisions of the signs, however, the four mundane quadrants and twelve mundane houses are rarely an equal number of degrees apart when measured along the ecliptic. This is because we are projecting mundane divisions onto the plane of the ecliptic.

I said above that there can be some question as to whether a planet whose longitude is the same as an angle's is actually on the horizon or meridian, but at least there is no question as to the location of the Ascendant, Midheaven, Descendant, and I.C. themselves. There is, however, a great deal of debate over the position of the house cusps subdividing the quadrants. There are literally dozens of methods of dividing up the ecliptic to represent twelve stages in the mundane cycle, and none of these methods is ideal from all standpoints.

The horoscope angles seem to have some validity as sensitive points that can make aspects, but the intermediate house cusps are not treated by most astrologers in this way. The main exceptions to this seem to be 1) astrologers of the Uranian or Hamburg school, who use aspects to cusps in the Meridian house system and 2) the old formulas for Arabian parts, many of which involve house cusps. I prefer to think of the houses as approximate indications of mundane position, and to use only the horoscope angles as definite points.

Like the horoscope angles, the houses represent areas in life where planetary energies can manifest. Although nothing in the chart really represents actual entities that may be experienced in life (persons, objects, etc.), houses come somewhat closer than planets. They are the closest thing to nouns in the chart. Houses represent compartments of the self, the psyche, and the environment as it is acted upon and experienced. They represent the orientation that the energies of the planets have in the individual's life. They describe, at least in part, where energies will surface. If they are somewhat noun-like, they are also much like prepositional phrases that designate from whence, to which, and by whom a planetary energy may be experienced.

The problem is that, like planets, houses operate at different levels, and it is difficult to determine exactly which level will be the level of manifestation. Levels of manifestation have little to do with the horoscope itself, but rather with the way the individual is handling it. This subject will be brought up again in Chapters 13 and 14.

Now let us turn to a detailed investigation of each symbol system and the symbols within it.

POINTS IN THE CHART

3

The Planets: Introduction

As a prelude to the individual discussions of the planets in the next chapter, I introduce the solar system here as a whole, showing how it is a framework for the symbolism of the individual planets. When you come to the longer planet discussions, you will then have a better idea of how each planet fits into the overall symbolic structure of the solar system. We will view the solar system from a broad perspective, considering both the astronomical and the symbolic realities: not only the objective structure, but also the manner in which the human psyche perceives it.

Inner versus Outer Planets

The planets can be classified into two main groups according to the distance of their orbits from the Sun. Going in order outward from the Sun, there are Mercury, Venus, the Earth-Moon system, and Mars. These are the inner planets. Beyond Mars is a gap filled with asteroids (discussed in Chapter 5), and then there are the outer planets: Jupiter, Saturn, Uranus, Neptune, and Pluto. Not only are the outer planets set off from the inner by the asteroid belt, most of them also differ greatly from the inner in size and chemical composition. With the likely exception of Pluto, the outer planets are many times larger than the inner, and whereas the inner planets are dense and rocky, the outer are much lighter, being composed of substances that on Earth would be gaseous or liquid.

Perhaps the most important difference from an astrological point of view is in the length of time it takes the various planets to go once around the zodiac. As seen from Earth, the Sun, Mercury, and Venus all complete the circuit in about a year, and Mars takes about two years, whereas the orbital periods of the outer planets range from about twelve years for Jupiter to two-and-a-half centuries for Pluto.

Astrologers usually call the inner planets the "personal planets." Because they move quickly, their position helps to distinguish one birthchart from another of nearly the same date. Each of these planets is also personal in that its symbolism has to do with the development of the individual ego. Even Venus, the most socially oriented of the group, refers to intimate encounters, which define and clarify the position of the ego in the world.

While both the Sun and Moon are personal planets, each also has a transpersonal side. The Sun says much about an individual's ego development but it is also the basic universal energy of which the other planets are particularized reflections. The Moon, in addition to symbolizing perhaps the most personal and intimate parts of one's life, links the individual to another kind of fundamental energy deeper than the level of ego consciousness.

In contrast to the personal planets, the outer planets relate to the social world and beyond. Jupiter and Saturn describe one's attitudes toward the collectives of which one is a part, and sometimes say more about one's social milieu than about one's personal life. Uranus, Neptune, and Pluto describe one's attitudes toward the greater universe as a whole and one's relationship to the transcendent levels of human experience.

Though the outer planets are not "personal," they can have powerful effects on individuals when they aspect or make midpoints with fast-moving factors like the inner planets, the Ascendant, or the Midheaven. In fact, they are often the major key to those patterns of living with which the individual has the most trouble. This is not because all except Jupiter are considered malefic, but because the greatest problem for most people is the integration of the self into the various aspects of the universe while maintaining a viable individuality.

Even when the outer planets only aspect each other, they may affect the individual. For example, they may signify a period in history like a war, which is bound to affect even those who have no personal planets connected to the outer-planet configuration.

Pairs of Planets

It is also fruitful to view the planets as pairs of polar opposites or energies that complement one another, with the outermost three planets forming a trio.

The Sun and Earth: Dual Centers of the Solar System   The solar system has an objective center, the Sun, and a subjective center, the Earth. The Sun is the center from an objective viewpoint because it is the dynamic focus of the solar system, providing almost all the radiant energy and holding the system together in its powerful gravitational field. And from a god-like perspective far above in outer space, the Sun is at the approximate spatial center of the solar system.

From our subjective viewpoint, however, the Earth is the center. Human consciousness and ability to experience the solar system is centered here, not on the Sun. All the energy put out by the Sun and reflected in various ways by the planets is experienced by us on Earth. Experience by its very nature requires awareness, and the Earth is our center of awareness. If a tree falls in the forest, and there is no one to hear it, is there a sound? My answer is no: a sound is an experience, and if there is no one to do the experiencing, the experience does not exist. If there were sentient beings on another planet, their planet would be their subjective center. Subjectivity, unlike objectivity, can have a number of centers simultaneously.

The symbolism of the Sun and Earth is closely bound up with the symbolism of yang and yin. The Sun provides energy and heat, and the Earth provides matter that is animated by the Sun's energy. Thus the solar system has a yang center and a yin center. The Sun is also one of the planets associated with the father, and the Earth with the mother.

The other planets derive their significance from their relation to these two centers. As we will shortly see, there is a special relation between the Earth and the Moon.

Mercury and the Moon: The Two Modulators   In physical terms, the body closest to the Sun is Mercury, and the body closest to the Earth is the Moon. And in symbolic terms, Mercury modulates the energies of the Sun, while the Moon does the same for the Earth. The concept of modulation is explained more fully in the next chapter's section on Mercury, but in short, a modulator imposes a pattern on energy so that what started out as raw and undifferentiated becomes a meaningful arrangement. Modulation turns energy into information, as a radio turns electrical energy into speech or music.

Mercury, the planet that rules speech, communication, and indeed all forms of transferring information from one medium to another, is the more obvious modulator. It is the first step in a stepping-down process from the raw energy of the Sun into the more particularized energies of the other planets.

But in its way the Moon modulates also. You may wonder why I just discussed the Earth, because in the traditional horoscope the Earth has no place as a symbol. The Earth is implied by the presence of houses in the horoscope, but it is not explicitly there as a symbol like the other planets. It is as if the Earth is too much a part of us for us to be aware of it. In astrology the Moon has taken on much of the Earth's symbolism: its position as the primary yin force among all the celestial bodies, and its connection with nurture and the mother. The Moon modulates the symbolic energies of the Earth in that it takes energies that are a part of us and puts them out away from us so we can perceive them consciously.

Thus Mercury gives the raw energy of the Sun an order that can be perceived, and the Moon makes the Earth's reception of those energies into a form that can be perceived. Mercury modulates the Sun's energy, and the Moon modulates the Earth's experiencing of that energy. If Mercury's modulation turns energy into information, then the Moon's modulation produces a context without which the information cannot be received.

Mars and Venus: The I-Thou Dichotomy   Continuing out from the Sun past Mercury, we encounter Venus, and continuing out from the Earth past the Moon, we encounter Mars. Whereas the Earth-Moon system defined awareness and the Sun-Mercury system defined what there is to be aware of, Mars and Venus signify two kinds of *relationship* between the experiencer and the experienced.

Mars relates by emphasizing the experiencer, the "I." It defines the experiencer, gives the experiencer a definite form and shape, and makes sure there is a separate entity to do the experiencing. Venus emphasizes the relationship or the "thou." It strives to create relationships among experiencers so that higher levels of being can arise out of the interaction of individuals. When Venus is working well, however, no one individual loses definition or becomes a less perfect expression of what it is.

A balance between Mars and Venus energies is necessary for continued relationships between subject and object. If either planet's energy becomes excessive, relationship ceases. If Mars gets the upper hand, the entity tries to destroy the realm of the object, which the entity needs to give its own existence meaning. If Venus gets the upper hand, the entity loses the ability to survive as a separate experiencing entity.

Jupiter and Saturn: The Social Planets   Jupiter and Saturn are so far away from both centers of the solar system that their positions viewed from the Earth are not that different from their positions viewed from the Sun. With this pair of planets, the distinction between subject and object, experiencer and experience is no longer so important. Whereas the bodies from the Sun out to Mars dealt with the individual's personal existence and personal experience of the universe, Jupiter and Saturn introduce a larger area of reality, that of the world in which one lives.

Jupiter is an archetype of support, and Saturn, of resistance. After you have achieved a certain degree of definition so you know who you are, you need to be integrated into a larger system. Whereas Venus integrates you into intimate relationships, Jupiter integrates you into the world. Jupiter represents an energy that causes you to grow and to leave the infantile matrix into which you were born. Jupiter signifies a kind of nurture related to, but different from, that of the Moon. Whereas the Moon supports an individual's being, Jupiter supports an individual's becoming, reaching out, and doing more and more with life. The individual is propelled toward and supported in becoming a member of the larger world, of the social order, the theater in which we work out our various characters in the drama of life.

With Saturn we encounter the rules of the drama: our obligations, what we must do to get others to play their roles with us on the same stage. It tests us, makes demands, and ultimately defines our reality for us, at least until we are ready to break free of the play. Rather than supporting us in our efforts to grow, it represents a resistance that we must overcome in order to take our place in the world.

Saturn is the outermost planet visible without a telescope. As such, it represents the limits of the reality that can be perceived by ordinary consciousness. After Saturn, something else must come into play, something that transcends ordinary reality and even sometimes destroys it so a new reality can be born.

Uranus, Neptune, and Pluto: The Transcendental Planets Just as they require a telescope to be seen, Uranus, Neptune, and Pluto require an expanded consciousness to be dealt with constructively. All break the system of rules represented by Saturn. From the perspective of ordinary consciousness they are disruptive: Uranus brings unpleasant surprises, Neptune confuses us with what we perceive as false realities, and Pluto brings about disintegration and decay. But these are not the primary effects of these planets, they are only the result of our involvement with ordinary reality.

Viewed from an expanded perspective, these planets represent pathways out of the limitations of normal consciousness. Uranus releases us from the over-structuring of Saturn and grants us the opportunity for freedom. Neptune is a channel for other realities to come through to us, offering the possibility of truly new creations. All we need do is understand the role of Saturnine reality, give it no more than its due, and remain flexible despite Saturn's tendency to harden us. Pluto brings the breakdown that precedes rebirth. Its sole demand is that one be willing to die so one can be reborn.

All three bodies symbolize the fact that even though the Sun is a mighty star, there are billions more like it, and each bears the promise of other modes of being and consciousness. These other modes are available to us from the galaxy, and the transcendental planets are their channels. Just as Mercury modulates the Sun's energy, giving it form, and the Moon modulates the manner in which we experience, so the outer three planets modulate what comes to us from beyond the solar system. Through them, we are potentially more than the children of the Sun and the students of Saturn.

Retrograde Planets

Often in a horoscope or an ephemeris you will see a planetary symbol followed by the letter "R" or " ℞." This means that on the day of the birth or of the ephemeris entry the planet was retrograde. That is, from the viewpoint of Earth it appeared to be traveling backward in the zodiac. Periodically every planet except the Sun and the Moon appears to do this.

The literature on retrograde planets is conflicting. Ideas range from the belief that they are cursed, totally incapable of turning out well for an individual, to the belief that they have no effect at all. Some astrologers feel that retrogradation inverts or diverts a planetary energy so it is not expressed as directly and forthrightly as it might otherwise be. Others feel retrogradation makes a planet act more slowly. Still others think it causes a planet to operate more on the subjective level. (My only problem with this is that I believe horoscope symbolism always operates on a subjective level first, and only afterward is it projected onto what others would call an objective level of reality.)

The fact that astrologers have been unable to agree on retrogradation used to make me suspect that retrogradation is insignificant. But I have since changed my views. What follows is an examination of others' ideas about retrogradation, along with my own theory about what it means.

First, it is clear that in a natal chart, at least, retrogradation does not destroy a planet's influence or make it incapable of doing good. This extreme view derives from horary and electional astrology, special procedures for answering specific questions and picking favorable times for action. In horary and electional charts, if the planet symbolizing the activity that is of main concern is retrograde, it is supposed to signify that the matter can come to no good. This may be true in these branches of astrology, but not necessarily because retrogradation hopelessly blights the planet. I believe that retrogradation does not signify any kind of intrinsic disability for a planet, except insofar as anything that affects a planet will make it better suited to some situations than to others. No astrological energy is well-suited to every occasion. Further on, I will show why I think retrogradation might adversely affect the significator planet in a horary or electional chart.

I also reject the idea that retrogradation weakens a planetary energy or makes it less capable of manifesting. Astrologers who believe that it does forget that the outer planets are retrograde a large proportion of the time. For example, almost half the population has Pluto retrograde. And when the Sun and Jupiter are in trine, a very positive aspect according to most astrologers, Jupiter is usually retrograde.

I can, however, accept the possibility that retrogradation alters or diverts the energy of a planet from its normal paths. And I find it reasonable that a retrograde planet does not as often manifest on an external plane. To see why, it is necessary to examine what retrogradation is in astronomical terms.

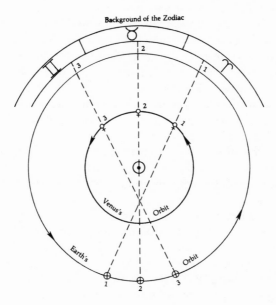

A. Direct motion

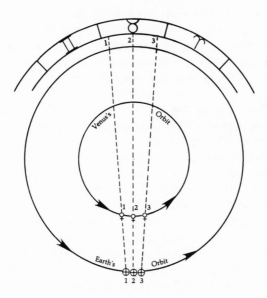

B. Retrograde motion

Figure 2. Direct and retrograde motion of the inner planets

When a planet is retrograde, it is actually closer to the Earth than when direct. This is easy to see with Mercury and Venus, whose orbits lie between the Sun and the Earth's orbit. In Figure 2A, Venus is on the far side of the Sun. From the Earth's viewpoint, Venus here appears to be traveling forward in the zodiac, just as the Sun always appears to. Venus appears to be in Aries at instant 1, in Taurus at instant 2 and in Gemini at instant 3. In Figure 2B, however, Venus is between the Earth and the Sun. As you can see, Venus is traveling forward in its orbit the way it always does, but from the viewpoint of Earth it looks as if it is going backward against the background of the fixed stars. In Figure 2B, Venus appears to be in late Taurus at instant 1, in middle Taurus at instant 2 and in early Taurus at instant 3. It will appear to turn direct when it starts to go around behind the Sun.

Retrogradation is also easy to see with the rest of the planets, from Mars on out to Pluto. Because these planets are all farther from the Sun than the Earth is, they move more slowly in their orbits than does the Earth. When the Earth overtakes them, it is like a faster-moving car overtaking a slower-moving car on a highway. Seen from the faster-moving car, the slower-moving car appears to be going backward, even though it is only going forward more slowly. In Figure 3A, the Earth and Mars are on opposite sides of the Sun. As seen from Earth, Mars appears to be going forward in the zodiac, from Aries at instant 1, to Taurus at instant 2, and Gemini at instant 3. In Figure 3B, the Earth is overtaking and about to pass Mars, and so from Earth's viewpoint Mars appears to be going backward in relation to the background of the fixed stars from late Taurus at instant 1, to middle Taurus at instant 2 and early Taurus at instant 3. Note that Mars and the Earth are on the same side of the Sun and hence closer to each other than they would otherwise be.

The fact that planets are closer to the Earth when they are retrograde makes it seem absurd to say that retrograde planets are weaker. If there is any connection at all between distance and strength in astrology, you would expect retrograde planets to be stronger.

My observations suggest, however, that a retrograde planet is not so much stronger as it is closer to a person's center. I feel that its closeness to Earth symbolizes the person's lack of distance or lack of perspective in dealing with what that planet stands for. Someone with a retrograde planet is less able to be objective about that planet's energies.

This has its strong and its weak points. The advantage is that one sees the planet's energies at close range, and is deeply, intensely, and intimately involved in them. But when one is too close to something, it is hard to gain perspective. One tends to take the relatively unimportant seriously and to overlook what is truly significant in the long run. Being deeply involved in something, one runs the risk of losing perspective, but to get an accurate perspective one must sacrifice close-range, intimate experience. Clearly, a balance is necessary.

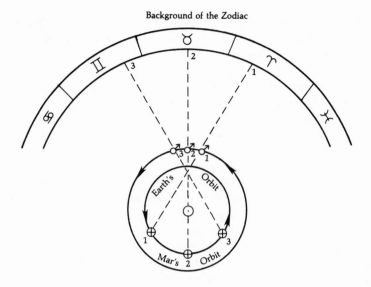

A. Direct motion

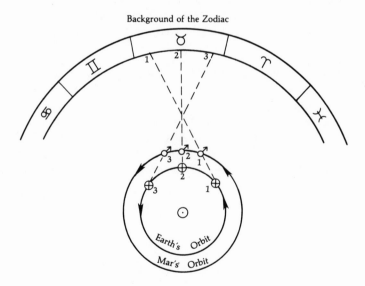

B. Retrograde motion

Figure 3. Direct and retrograde motion of the outer planets

I am not suggesting an introversion-extraversion split. I believe that direct and retrograde planetary energies are each capable of being experienced as either external or internal. But I do suspect that retrograde energies are harder to experience as separate from oneself. If they are experienced as separate, they represent issues so close to one's daily involvements that one is not easily able to stand back and get a clear view of how they operate. By contrast, it is easier both to objectify and to detach oneself from the energies of planets in direct motion, and thereby one is better able to take control of them.

It is this feature that makes retrogradation such a bad thing in horary and electional astrology. Retrograde significators of the issue in question suggest that the individual is not detached enough from the matter to manipulate it with any skill. If one is too involved, one tends to act as the result rather than the cause of the energies that are around one. Unable to see clearly, one tends to act ineffectively.

When reading a natal chart, the astrologer can help the client to gain a perspective on any retrograde planets by exploring what they mean from a detached, objective viewpoint. In this way, the person with a retrograde planet can combine the intimate knowledge based on experience with the wisdom that comes from seeing with a sense of proportion.

The foregoing is just a hypothesis that helps to account for my experience of retrograde planets. Keep this in mind when you apply these principles, and always remember that much more work needs to be done concerning retrograde planets and their effects.

The next chapter takes up the individual planets in detail. Though the categories outlined in the present chapter are useful for understanding the interrelation of the planets, there will necessarily be facets of each planet that do not completely conform to these patterns. Rather than making all the planets fit in, you should concentrate on getting the feel of each planet in its own right. When you fully comprehend the nature of each planet, the basis of the schema will become clear wherever it is presently obscure.

4

The Planets: Core Meanings

The following descriptions discuss, as much as is possible in limited space, the various levels at which planetary energies can manifest: in one's psyche, emotions, thoughts, body, and one's experience of others and the outer world.

The planets as they affect one's health will not, however be handled in depth, first, because this is a highly specialized subject in its own right, and second, because I think the lore of astrological medicine is not sufficiently clear or standardized to permit the same in-depth discussion we can make of astrological psychology. But where appropriate and where there is some agreement I will mention physiological effects of planetary energies.

By the very nature of writing books, what follows is only words. But it is the understanding beyond words that you ultimately attain. It will take years of experiencing the planets before you can really say you know what they mean. But the first step is to use texts like this as a guide, and then consciously experience the planetary energies in your own life. When you can feel what the planets mean, you will truly understand them.

The Sun

One of the most important points in the chart, the Sun represents the energy that enables everything else to exist. It is the basic energy of Being. Just as the physical Sun shines and enables all the other bodies to shine by reflecting its light, so the symbolic astrological Sun is the basic energy of which all the other planetary energies are specialized reflections.

The Sun represents light, consciousness, and day. It is the ultimate planetary symbol of yang, yang being the active energizing principle that is the source of all motion. The Sun, as yang, is the polar counterpart to the Moon, as yin. The Sun and Moon are one of the horoscope's most important manifestations of this primary duality.

As yang, the Sun is the archetype of will, power, and desire, but not necessarily sexual desire. It has the meaning of "wanting to." It represents the energy that exerts itself upon and influences whatever may exist. The energy of the Sun does not simply accept, but always seeks to change, and, if possible, to improve. Above all, it seeks room for the greater expression of itself.

The Sun is also the energy that gives an entity its integrity as a being. It represents the entity's will to exist. As such, it counters pressure from the environment that seeks either to make the entity something that it is not, or to destroy it completely.

The Sun is the archetype of the hero. The hero sets out into the world and attempts to bring order out of chaos through imposing his will. He undergoes severe trials in order to prove his strength and worthiness, especially against the powers of darkness. At sunset the hero, like the Sun, descends into the underworld and is challenged by the monsters of darkness. After proving his right to be born again the following dawn, he manifests triumphant in the world.

This is not just poetry. The pattern described here can be seen in the personality of someone with a strongly placed Sun. (The idea of strong versus weak placements is dealt with at the beginning of Chapter 12.) These people have great vitality, are tireless both emotionally and physically, and work relentlessly to bring into the world their vision of what ought to be. But their efforts are not wholly selfless. They always have a personal dimension. Solar people work to express who they are and seek to make an impact in terms of their own identity. Consequently, they are at the forefront of any activity where they can be recognized. They do not work behind the scenes. Solar-dominant personalities are able to make others notice them: simply by their demeanor, they turn heads when they enter a room. They are also people who seem to be at the center of a number of other people's lives. Like the Sun, they provide light and energy so that others can live and act. But the solar type needs always to be acknowledged by others for having done this.

For these reasons, the Sun has traditionally been said to "rule" persons in authority, like employers, important government officials, the government itself, and, of course, kings and nobles. But keep in mind that planets do not symbolize actual persons or things. The relationship exists only insofar as an actual person manifests the energies of the Sun. Not all kings or presidents act in a solar manner.

There is a negative side to all this. Solar people are not especially modest. They may even be boastful and arrogant, totally wrapped up in themselves. Sometimes they may overestimate their own worth, not feeling it necessary to do anything to justify their high self-opinion. However, in truth this is not really in the character of the Sun, which is an active force concerned with accomplishment. When a solar personality exhibits this kind of problem, there is usually something else wrong.

It is often difficult to get solar types to cooperate with others in a team effort. They often feel that they have to be at the forefront or they would rather have nothing to do with the project. There is also the solar type who would rather do nothing than risk compromising his or her integrity. A strong solar type who has indications elsewhere of severe ego weakness is the most likely to have this kind of problem.

On the psychological level, the Sun represents the Jungian libido: that is, the basic psychic energy that drives all psychological functions. Like the libido, the Sun often acts non-specifically, simply providing the energy for which another symbol will provide a specific shape. In predictive astrology, the action of the Sun is usually simply to set off or to time an event or development in the individual's life. It brings energy to whatever symbol complex represents the event. Symbolism that is specific to the Sun is often absent in such cases.

The Sun is also physical energy, and if it is weakened through contact with a symbol that denies energy, there will be a decline in the individual's physical energy level. This is most marked with Sun-Neptune contacts. Difficulties with solar energy in the chart can indicate periods of physical illness. Many astrologers even consider the Sun to represent the physical body. Here again, we have the planet-as-thing fallacy, but the Sun certainly can be an index to physical vitality.

Archetypally speaking, masculinity is an aspect of yang. Therefore, the Sun, along with Mars, represents masculinity. Traditionally, the Sun was considered as having to do with persons of the male sex, but again this is using a planet to represent an entity. Now that sex roles are shifting, a growing number of women exhibit solar personalities, and thereby serve as representatives of solar energy in the lives of others. If one were to have a female employer, for example, her role would be as solar as if she were male. And, of course, a male who is not very yang in temperament will not manifest strong solar symbolism despite his sex. The archetypal sexuality that an individual will manifest is only partly connected with a person's gender. Most people are mixtures of the two energies.

Nevertheless, it is still observable that women as a group have a greater tendency than men to experience their solar energies as coming through males. In fact, a common difficulty with women is being cut off from the masculine elements in their own nature. They project it onto their men, thereby depriving themselves of initiative and independence. (And men often do a corresponding thing with their lunar energies.) In most cases, difficulties that women consistently have with men are best handled by getting the women in touch with the masculine side of their own personality rather than by doing anything about a particular relationship that they may have with a man. The trend is clearly toward women gaining their inward masculinity consciously for themselves.

One classic male function that is associated with the Sun is fatherhood. The Sun shares this function with Saturn, but the two represent very different facets. The situation of the Sun in the birthchart often relates to the individual's experience of the father—not necessarily the actual father, but all the people who played that role. Often the mother will actually play the father role, in which case it is that relationship which will be symbolized by the Sun. A key concept is that the Sun represents the experience of being fathered, not the objective truth about one's father. In fact, the relationship with all authority figures will be shown by the Sun. As a component of the father archetype, the Sun represents the father's function as a shaper of the will, particularly the will to be a free, independent source of power and energy in one's own right.

From what has been said, it should be clear that a weakly placed Sun in a horoscope signifies weak vitality, and in some way an inability to fend for oneself. On the psychological side it may indicate an individual who is too subject to another's will, or who cannot defend and protect what he or she values, at least through direct confrontation. On the physical side, a weak Sun can indicate bodily weakness, a tendency to illnesses and allergies, or simply a lack of muscle strength. A full understanding of the Sun in a horoscope is an important step toward understanding the person.

The Moon

Along with the Sun and Ascendant, it is agreed that the Moon is one of the centers of the chart. But when one reads astrological descriptions of the Moon, the core meaning is hard to grasp. Surface manifestations are given, but the central idea remains elusive.

The Moon represents two basic archetypes. First, it is the archetype of the medium or container in which an energy may become manifest. It is also the archetype of the matrix, source, or origin of all things. Fundamentally, as we shall show, these two archetypes are really one.

The glyph (the character by which a symbol is represented) of the Moon is a bowl on edge, facing either left or right (depending on whether one represents the Moon as waxing or waning). The glyph is obviously derived from the crescent-shaped form the Moon takes between the third quarter and the new moon, or the new moon and the first quarter. The bowl shape also suggests a container, which gives form to, limits, and helps define whatever it contains. This idea is central to an understanding of the Moon, but we must understand "container" in an expanded sense. We refer to the principle of containment, the idea of providing a surrounding, a location, a place, or an environment—a set of circumstances in which something may take place.

Containment can be viewed as purely passive, and passivity has low esteem in this culture. But one must go beyond the limits of one's culture to understand this principle. The Moon is the planetary archetype of yin. It is the equal of yang, which is indicated by the Sun. The yin principle defines the circumstances and conditions under which the yang energy can manifest. The nature and situation of the Moon in the horoscope can limit, curtail, or assist the operation of vital energies. The final manifest form of anything is as much due to the yin principle of containment as it is to the energies that drive or motivate it. The Moon's yin nature gives place and form to the action of the Sun's yang. It is the root and foundation of that which can experience existence. It does not itself signify action or experience, but without it there can be neither.

But the principle of containment, of providing a medium for life, gives rise to another factor that is even more relevant to an understanding of the Moon. Every entity, especially every living entity, goes through a period prior to mature manifestation in which it is developing and growing, not yet ready to appear and to exert itself in the world. During this time the entity exists in some kind of container that both protects it and gives it structure and form. It may be an egg, a womb, the Earth's soil, or a seed, to name but a few of the possibilities. This is the principle of the container as the nurturing matrix. It is another of the central themes of the Moon. For this reason, the Moon is connected to all forms of motherhood, both literal and metaphorical. The Moon in the chart affects humans most strongly just before and after birth, when they are most dependent on the mother. The Moon also symbolizes our experience throughout life of being nurtured, protected, and supported. The Moon's energies are manifest not only in the home in which we were raised as children, but also in the home to which we retire in the evening in order to regain our strength after the day's activities.

In a larger sense, the physical universe is the ultimate medium in which much of our life takes place. (I do not count introspection, meditation, and other forms of purely internal mental, psychic, or spiritual activity as taking place in the physical universe.) Consequently, the state of the Moon in the horoscope indicates our attitude toward being incarnate in the physical universe. Certain difficulties with the natal Moon indicate that one feels alone, alienated from, and a stranger to, the physical universe—that one does not belong within it. A well-situated Moon, on the other hand, signifies an individual who feels at home on the planet Earth. If you have a poorly situated Moon you may often feel that you are justified only by what you do, not by what or who you are. The ideas "I am at home," "I am all right," and "I belong here" are a function of the Moon's energy.

This leads us directly into the second of the Moon's primary meanings, which can now be seen to be related to the first. It is the idea we have of where we have come from: the source, the womb, the Great Mother. It is our past, childhood, heredity, or family (both current and ancestral). It is also bound up with our ideas of country and native land.

Interestingly, there is a common tendency to treat the homeland as mother: witness the feminine endings on the names of many nations.

An individual's attitudes toward the home and family of childhood are often represented in the chart by the Moon. People with a poorly placed Moon will often want to get away from the past, to deny and obliterate its influence upon their lives. They will often feel that the past weighs them down, smothers them, limits them so that they cannot be free. As adults, they will often have difficulty with any kind of intimacy, especially if it requires making a commitment.

The ideas of containment, matrix, and source give rise to yet another psychological facet of the Moon. While yang energy is conscious energy, the limitations and forms imposed upon it by the matrix or medium in which it operates are not usually conscious (unless, of course, the individual makes an effort to look within at the internal structure of the self). In addition, the Moon as nurturing principle affects one most strongly at a time of life when one is not very conscious. For both reasons, the action of the Moon tends to be unconscious. Either it is part of the structure of the self that has not been examined (though it influences our thinking and perception every minute of the day), or it relates to experiences that were very early, even prenatal, and which are therefore not conscious. The Moon relates to unconscious assumptions that we have made about life from the beginning—attitudes that we learned from our parents without realizing it, hereditary mental patterns such as instincts, and, very important, psychological patterns that arise from infantile experiences, both positive and negative.

Although it is not quite accurate to say that the Moon is the unconscious mind, it does *operate* largely unconsciously. We are not used to examining its processes, and tend either to overlook them or to be unable to look at them without a great deal of training. Certainly those aspects of ourselves that are lunar cannot be understood by purely rational means: they must be understood through feelings and emotions.

In most astrological literature, the Moon is considered the primary indicator of the emotions. Perhaps now you can see why. Emotions are one of the principal manifestations of the part of the self that is either hereditary or structured at a very early age. Emotions are one of the strongest signs that something deep within the self, the part that is most likely to be dominated by lunar energies, is being activated. Emotions are neither more nor less right than the rational mind in making judgments. It is only that the rational mind does not have ready access to the power of the emotions and therefore mistrusts them. This is all the more true the more one consciously identifies with one's rational mind. In someone who does not make a split between the rational and emotional natures, there may be a greater ability to make judgments using every faculty of the self.

The Moon-dominated parts of the mind often act like computer programs—completely mechanical patterns that are set off automatically and completely by the appropriate stimulus. On the physical level, this is known as a reflex. We have emotional reflexes, too, which are hard to modify by rational consideration. Also, because they are either instinctual or originate in earliest life, such reflexes often result in behavior that is not appropriate in adults.

And yet a great deal of our behavior requires instantaneous judgment and quick response. When a car is rushing at us, we have no time to consider what to do. Similarly, we do not have time to think about exactly what we are doing when we are walking, what muscles to move when, and so forth. These are all lunar patterns within the mind. They govern a larger portion of our activity than rational thought does, and they are indispensable. The Sun (and Mars, as we shall see) represent the energy that the muscles use, but the patterning of that energy is usually lunar.

There is another facet of the Moon that arises from its association with the unconscious mind. The unconscious mind does not deal with the patterns and restrictions that consciousness imposes. In particular, it does not recognize separateness. All is one, and everything takes place in a continuum. At a certain level, the lunar parts of the mind are in touch with everything, everywhere. The Moon, then, becomes one of the indicators of psychic ability, a mode of perception in which everything is in some way connected.

The female sex, at least in its traditional role, is more yin than the male sex. Consequently, the Moon has always been associated with womanhood. Of course, the connection of the Moon with motherhood and the Sun with fatherhood would also assign these planets to the respective sexes. Even today, the Moon does seem more often to symbolize women than men. I believe, however, that the Moon has more to do with the roles that women have played (wife and mother) than with women themselves. Both sexes have masculine and feminine psychological elements within them, and it is not clear at this point how much of a woman's sexuality is conditioned and how much is innate.

In traditional astrology, the Moon is said to indicate the people of a country as opposed to its rulers, who are supposed to be solar. There is much truth in this, even to the extent that an individual with a strong and well-placed Moon is able to appeal to large groups of people and make them feel that he or she is one of them. This is a requirement for politicians and salesmen. But a part of the idea also comes from the assumption that the-people are largely passive in relation to their rulers. This is less true now than it was, although clearly in times of relative tranquility when rulers have little resistance from the people, it still holds. In times of social turmoil when the people of a country are conscious of what they want and oppose the interests of their rulers, however, the people are not lunar at all.

To conclude this description of the Moon's symbolism, there is an important point to be made. We have already said that astrologers have seemed not to understand the Moon as well as the Sun, and not to accord it quite the same importance. This is due to something within our culture that has manifested as sexism, but which is in reality much deeper. Our culture has lost touch with the power of yin. We strive to go out into the world, to grab it by the throat, and thus to master it. We do not understand the way of waiting and of learning to fit in to become a part of the whole. The only role we completely respect is that of mastery: of the universe, of nature, of circumstances, or of ourselves. The Moon represents the energy of an alternative path, that of becoming a part of, of belonging, of creative submission to that which we will gain nothing by mastering. It is not enough that the female sex gain political equality with the male if the yin principle does not also gain equality with the yang. Man as well as woman is yin, and both are yang. As long as we act as if the yin is not an equal principle, we face life as half-beings, incomplete and out of touch with nature. Through the study of astrological symbols it is possible to gain some appreciation of what being whole means.

Mercury

Mercury is often underplayed in astrological writing. In part, this may be because it is not often an obvious source of difficulty to people. Also, I suspect, people find its symbolism less exciting than that of some other planets. Yet it is a symbol of immense importance. It is connected to the mind, especially the logical and reasoning capabilities, and to all forms of communication. Likewise, Mercury (along with Uranus) signifies the nervous system, because the nerves enable the organs to communicate among themselves. In the world, Mercury is connected to all forms of transportation and movement. But, important as these traditional ascriptions are, they do not make the real importance of the planet clear.

Mercury's importance comes from two sources. The first lies in the function Mercury serves, and the second in the mechanism by which the symbolism operates.

Mercury signifies the power to overcome the gap that exists between separate entities. The world as seen in normal human consciousness is a world of divisions. The first of these is the division between subject and object, I and Thou. I cannot experience what you experience and you cannot experience what I experience. We can never fully occupy another's point of view, yet we are not wholly cut off. We can communicate, and communication is one of the chief Mercurial functions.

As we grow out of the infantile state of consciousness in which everything appears more or less one, we become aware that we are separate from the universe around us. At the same time, we gain the ability to speak, to share what we know and experience, and also to allow others to do so with us. This faculty is peculiarly human. With it, we can hand culture down from generation to generation, without having to wait for nature to create new kinds of programed behavior through instinct, which develops very slowly.

In this way, Mercury is an aspect of consciousness itself: it creates the relationship between subject and object that is necessary in order for consciousness to exist. The child begins to speak (a Mercurial function) just at the time that its consciousness is beginning to grasp the fact that people are indeed separate from one another, in particular the child from the mother. Also, it is about this time, usually sooner, that the child begins learning to walk, which is another Mercurial function. In learning physically to move through our surroundings we are also learning how to overcome the gaps between ourselves and others.

The second source of Mercury's importance is that it represents the power of symbol-making. By extension, this includes all forms of data transfer.

All our knowing, experiencing, sensing, believing, or disbelieving is done through signs which represent actual facts, experiences, or entities in our minds. For example, our visual impression of a tree is not the thing itself. It is the brain's experience of the impact of a pattern of light waves focused on the retina of the eye. What we see as a tree is only our experience of an aspect of the total reality of the tree. All other sense impressions are also patterns of this kind created by the brain's receiving data from the sense organs.

One remarkable fact about nerve impulses is that in general they are identical. What varies is the portion of the brain that receives each set of impulses. Thus it is the brain that creates sensory experiences such as sights, smells, sounds, tastes, textures, and the like. In this way we are quite literally the creators of our own experience. Every sense experience is a brain-created sign that corresponds (at least most of the time) to a physical reality.

We habitually identify our sense experiences with the physical universe, such that we cannot even conceive of the physical universe apart from the signs created by the brain to represent it. Modern physics is difficult to grasp precisely because it requires that we go beyond the sign systems of the brain in order to deal with what the science has shown us. What the brain perceives has a reliable but not inevitable correspondence with reality. You can create the experience of light in total darkness: simply press gently for a time on your closed eyelids, and you will see light. No electromagnetic radiation is involved. It does not matter what is stimulating the optic nerves: as long as something is stimulating them, the optic centers of the brain will interpret it as light.

We make the brain's signs for experiences stand for the physical reality. Experience of the outer world, no matter how profound, consists only of such signs: the outer world itself is beyond being directly experienced. But, using the signs for experiences, we create complex systems, mental maps that we call reality. If our map enables us to interact with the universe effectively, we act "realistically." If our map does not, we are victims of illusion.

We are assisted in this process by memory, which enables us to call up the signs of experiences at will. And memory is assisted by another tool, language. Language consists of signs of signs. If we call the signs created directly from experience primary signs, then language consists of secondary, tertiary, and even higher orders of signs. We translate the primary signs of experience into higher-order signs of language which have the virtue of being able to be written down. In preliterate societies, the same function was served by poetry (with the rhythm, rhyme, and meter serving to assist the memory).

Language also allows us to close the gap between us and others—to transmit to another some understanding of our personal map of reality. Something is always lost in translation, of course, because the primary signs of experience are much more powerful than the higher-order signs of language. This is one reason we have created something more powerful than verbal language—something that can carry more of the immediate power of primary signs. This is art in all its forms. While not as precise as verbal language for some purposes, art is much more powerful in conveying certain kinds of experience. Insofar as art is communication, it is signified by Mercury (though the act of creation is Venusian).

The translation of immediate experience into language does not proceed on a one-to-one basis. Not only must the experiences themselves be translated into language, the relationships among those experiences must also be translated. The language itself must contain rules for doing this, and such rules do not arise directly out of experience. Thus language, both in speech and thought, gains in the mind a life of its own, apart from experience. Concepts arise which are not directly derived from experience, but they help form our memories of experience, and may in turn influence later experiences. And we create even higher-level concepts that stand for groups of concepts and experiences.

It happens, then, that we constantly have to translate ideas and signs from one level to another, creating several different maps of reality according to whether we are thinking, speaking, imagining, or simply having an experience directly. The mind must be able to shift quickly from one level of signs to another, and ideally it must be able to communicate to others as well. In this way intelligence is like physical dexterity, which is also Mercurial. Both relate to speedy and efficient manipulations which may or may not have to do with a meaningful context.

Creating maps or sets of signs that correspond either to reality or to other groups of signs is a Mercurial function. And very often the signs by which things are represented may be found operating in several different media simultaneously. It is obvious that written and spoken language are closely parallel sign systems. But it is not so obvious that radio waves modified so as to communicate sound and video images also constitute a set of signs which can parallel language.

The conversion is done by a process known as modulation. Anything that is modified from its normal state so it can be used as a medium for data transmission can be thought of as modulated. Devices that translate data from one medium to another are known in languages as translators, and in mechanical terms as transducers. Translation and transduction are important functions of Mercury. Spoken language is a translation of experience into sound waves, and written language a translation of experience into visual patterns, while a tape recording system transduces sounds into magnetic patterns and back again.

Mercury is neither the maps themselves, nor the languages, nor the mechanical media in which data is stored, nor is it any of the representational signs themselves. It is the *process* of creating the maps or the languages, of storing the data or the signs, and of making sure that maps created in one medium correspond to the original set of experiences, ideas, or signs that the map represents.

Mercury manifests in the action of the nerves, which are the physical channels by which these processes are carried out in the body, and in the action of the brain, where the mapmaking takes place. (Actually, the brain is related to several different planetary energies. It is solar in that it governs the body, lunar in that it is a seat of feelings and behavior patterns, and it is related in various ways to the other planets as well.)

Intelligence is the ability to handle all the functions and processes we ascribe to Mercury. People of higher intelligence are better able to handle several levels of abstraction in the signs by which the brain works, and are better able to make translations from one sign system to another.

Consciousness, on the other hand, is different from intelligence. Consciousness is related to wisdom, in that both have to do with keeping the mind clear about how far removed from direct experience a set of signs may be. People who are intelligent but not wise or conscious may confuse high-level concepts with the things they represent and allow the structure of their concepts to modify the way they deal with truth. The wise person always keeps in mind that concepts are no more than representations and that they are somewhat arbitrary representations at that. One can be relatively low in intelligence and still be wise. The symbol-making processes of the wise are less likely to get in the way of their experiencing.

Mercury is connected with travel because travel is a means by which one fills in the details of one's map of reality. Mercury signifies travel of the routine, day-to-day variety, however, not long journeys, which are discontinuous with normal experience and hence expand the mind.

Mercury has also been associated with youth, but I do not believe that this is intrinsic to the symbol. The association probably arises because Mercury has its strongest effects during early life, when basic mental patterns are set, and thus remains connected in the mind with youth. From this, Mercury also derives its androgynous, presexual quality.

Mercury's nature often produces restlessness, an appetite for input. Mercurial energies can cause the mind to try to move on to a new experience before it has digested and integrated an old one. Thus people of a Mercurial nature run the danger of being superficial learners unless they discipline themselves.

Mercury also tends to be concerned with details. This comes from its function of putting many signs together into maps which must be as clear as possible. Consequently, the details of the signs themselves must also be very clear. Sometimes this habit can turn into nitpicking, in which the concern for details replaces the concern for actual experience. This side of Mercury is most associated with Virgo. A Mercurial person can also become more concerned with the elegance of an idea than its usefulness. This side of Mercury is more of the nature of Gemini.

On the highest level, Mercury is associated with the Logos or Word, the aspect of divinity in which the will of God is translated into the particular forms and structures of the created universe. Occultists have always considered the physical universe itself to be nothing more than a set of signs or a map corresponding to the divine nature. All knowledge and wisdom come through the Logos, whose planetary symbol is Mercury. Thus, as long as the process of knowing is recognized to be less important than that which is to be known, Mercury is one of the highest symbols of all.

Venus

In the universe there are two kinds of force that bring things together. One is coercive, trying to bring elements together regardless of their individual natures or inclinations. Such a force, working from without, does not express the natures of the elements themselves. It creates a conflict when the intrinsic natures of the elements involved resist the energy of coercion from without. The external force must be maintained, or the elements forced together will break apart and try to resume the free expression of what they are. Depending on conditions, such a coercive force may be represented by various combinations of Mars, Saturn, and Pluto.

The second force works differently. It arises from *within* the entities that bond together as an expression of their intrinsic natures rather than a violation of them. In anthropomorphic terms, the union is voluntary, not involuntary. The entities come together because their differences are complementary. Together they can create a new whole that is higher—more perfect, complete, and stable—than the state of separation in which they previously existed. This is the power that is manifested in the bonding of subatomic particles into atoms, of atoms into molecules, molecules into molecular complexes, cells, organisms, and so forth.

Although the essence of this non-coercive bonding energy is constant at all levels of being, the particular manifestations are different. At one level it might be called electrostatic attraction, at another, molecular binding energy, or at another, gravitation.

In human beings, this force is experienced as love. Of all the forces that bind people together, love produces the most stable groupings. I am not referring to romantic love between the sexes, which is a temporary narcotic state produced by people projecting onto others the creations of their own minds. I mean being fond of people, liking them for what they really are. The unions produced by love are stable because such relationships allow people to express what they are, better than they could if the union were absent. This kind of voluntary union holds people together more tightly than any union based on coercion or even on mutual benefit.

Venus is the planetary significator of this second type of binding force in general, and of love in particular. Venus also signifies beauty and creation. Beauty arises when a set of relationships between different entities allows them to express themselves more completely, to be more perfectly themselves.

Creation is the act of combining separate elements to form a more nearly perfect whole, often revealing facets that were not apparent when the entities were separate. An artist is one who sees these potentials and is able to actualize them.

One should not confuse "beautiful" with "pretty," even though the beautiful is often also pretty. Much beautiful art is also grotesque—the gargoyles on medieval cathedrals, for example. Truly beautiful art, however, always expresses a truth that was not apparent before, and this is what makes it beautiful. Keats's line,"Beauty is truth, truth beauty," is literally true.

Wherever Venus operates, one can clearly see the harmony produced by something moving in accordance with nature and itself. In its highest manifestations Venus always expresses a beauty that is not only aesthetic but also somehow functional. That function can be something like making people more aware of themselves and more in tune with their world. The materialist is not wrong when he demands that everything must justify its existence by being useful; he is only wrong in giving the word "useful" too narrow a meaning. Giving people a sense of harmony in their world is just as useful as making sure they have material resources.

All Venusian forces are experienced as spontaneous attractions. For this reason, Venus is often associated with attraction itself. But Venus only rules spontaneous, self-expressive attractions, in which neither entity has to violate its nature in order to be involved.

Venus and Mars, the next planet to be discussed, operate as a polarity. Whereas Venus is a planet of merging, Mars helps one establish one's separate identity. Unless you have established yourself as an individual, Venus cannot operate properly in your life. You have to express yourself, be what you really are, before you can love or be truly loved. If love is an attraction that comes about through true self-expression, there must first be an individuality to express. Those who have given up their individuality in what they think is a love relationship often wonder why the partner loses interest in them. It is hard to love someone whose individuality has been submerged, even if it has been submerged into oneself. Many who fail at positive love relationships do so because they lack faith in their own individuality. Even people who do have relationships will often compromise their needs in order to get along with the other. Then their real nature comes into conflict with the role that they have taken on, and the relationship becomes strained. At some point, the relationship will either have to be adjusted to let the real individuality of the partners come out, or it will end.

The symbolism of Venus is particularly important to astrology as a study of human individuality that strives to get people in touch with their own true selves. A well-developed Venus energy is essential in any type of counselor, because the client-counselor relationship must not only express the natures of both individuals, it must also allow both to develop themselves and their self-expression more completely. Any relationship that causes people to become more fully realized is Venusian.

It has been often said that as a molecule is composed of atoms, and the body of cells and tissues, so society is composed of individuals. Indeed, that is implicit in what we have been saying. Some claim, however, that society is the next level of organic evolution, and use this to justify totalitarian systems which repress individual liberty. According to this thinking, the individual is less important than the state and must live to serve it. I hope it is clear that this is not really a manifestation of Venus energies, and also that this does not truly represent the kind of evolutionary energy found in nature. A state that demands far more from the individual than it gives is a manifestation of the first, or coercive, kind of energy discussed earlier, which relies on external force to maintain itself. Such a state must eventually disintegrate, as all such states have done. No state has ever come close to fulfilling the ideal of a creative union of fully individualized beings coming together for mutual fulfillment and gratification. The state is in no way a forward step in biological evolution: something new must come along.

Before we conclude our discussion of Venus, there is another important point that follows from the idea of Venus as love. Venus is also associated with nurturing mother-love in particular. Together with the Moon, Venus forms the planetary part of the mother complex of symbols. Because of the self-expressive aspect of Venus, it is not necessary for someone to be anything in particular in order to be loved. I do not love you because you do this and that; I love you simply because you exist and I exist and it is in my nature to love what you are. The most profound example of this, and the example that provides the basis for our giving and experiencing love later in life, is the experience of being loved by one's parents, especially one's mother (but this is by no means restricted solely to the female parent).

Venus is like the Moon in that it is not overly concerned about distinctions and details. It gives what it gives freely and without worrying as to whether it is appropriate or whether the object of one's affections is worth it. This should be fairly obvious from looking at the kinds of people with whom other people fall in love.

Venus has become too closely associated with Taurus, one of the signs it traditionally rules. Because of this, many modern commentators have begun to overlook the connection between Venus and love and have begun to see Venus only as the planetary manifestation of the negative side of Taurus. They see Venus as passive, excessively fond of luxury and comfort, and unwilling to exert itself. There is some basis for this in that Venus, being a yin energy, is not especially assertive, and in that it attracts things to you rather than going out after something you want. Also, Venus's love of the beautiful can work out to be a fondness for the cheap and flashy. This is not intrinsic to Venus, however; it is a perverted manifestation caused by interference from other planetary energies or from inharmonious sign placement. Although there is clearly some affinity between Venus and Taurus, I am not entirely sure that Venus "rules" Taurus. One should not simply assume that Venus and Taurus are identical. Taurus is much more earthy and less watery than Venus. (For a discussion of the meanings of the elements, see pages 184-196.)

Normally, Venusian people are warm and loving as well as socially adept. They enjoy being with their loved ones and are often at a disadvantage when alone. More than any other planetary type, the Venus type recognizes the power that being with a loved one gives one to cope with life creatively.

Mars

One does not merely exist; one must exist as something or someone in particular. And one must also be able to maintain one's individuality in the face of pressures from the world and other members of society—pressures that threaten to violate one's true nature or even survival itself. Nothing exists in nature without the energy of Mars enabling it to survive. Everything maintains its true nature through Mars energy. Mars energy is extemely individualistic, causing one to emphasize differences rather than similarities. This is one trait that Mars shares with Saturn.

In excess, Mars may cause one to attempt to survive by eliminating others who might compete. Thus, one person's Mars may be a threat to another's. This is the source of conflict: the inability of two people's Mars energies to operate in the same space. Excess aggression is nothing more than an overabundance of survival energy, which feels it must control everything nearby. As we shall see, this is not really typical of Mars when it is functioning in a healthy manner.

Like the Sun, Mars is a yang energy that enables one to get things done. But it is only effective when it works for an entity's survival and self-expression. Mars's energy is self-centered, not altruistic, but it can be transmuted to appear selfless. In war, for example, people may be willing to sacrifice themselves for the good of the state. But for this to happen, they must identify their own survival and their need to be whatever they are as a people with the survival of the nation. When the people become aware that a war is being fought solely for the benefit of the rulers, they will not fight with the same kind of selfless energy.

This brings us to one of the most peculiar attributes of Mars, its faculty of identification. In its crudest form, the energy of Mars is concerned with biological survival, but purely biological functions can become metaphorized in the human mind. Aspects of life that have nothing to do with the original biological functions of an energy pattern, but which have symbolic structural parallels with the original function, become involved. An example of this (which has nothing to do with Mars) is the way in which the energies of orgasm, originally related to biological sexuality, become translated and metaphorized in the experience of religious ecstasy. Religious ecstasy is not orgasm, but the mind uses the vocabulary of orgasm in the experience. Similarly, Mars energy will be applied by the mind to matters that have little to do with pure survival, although they may have to do with survival on a psychological level.

The mind identifies its existence with the existence and survival of other entities around it or with things that the mind might be doing. In war, people individually and collectively identify with the state and transfer their Mars energies to it. By the same means, Mars energies may be transferred to one's possessions, social status, career, credibility, reputation, or any number of other possible entities. In each case, however, one acts as if the entity in question were oneself in a concrete, biological sense. It is the "as if" aspect of the matter that leads me to use the term "metaphorization."

When one's Mars energies are challenged, one reacts with the fight-or-flight syndrome. Adrenalin is released, and the body begins to react to a stressful situation in which it must either defend itself or run away. In ancient mythology, Mars (or Ares as he was called in Greek) was accompanied by Phobos and Deimos, fear and panic, which are now the names of the planet Mars's moons. Fear and panic are aspects of the fight-or-flight syndrome, and are thus attributes of Mars. One only has to realize that all it takes to activate this side of Mars in many people is to put them up before a large group of people to speak. The body reacts to the crowd as if it were a predator. This makes clear the level of primitivism that may creep into our actions when we behave according to Mars's energies.

Although fear and panic are aspects of Mars's energies, they do not represent its normal functioning. Mars normally is more fight than flight, and only when it is weakly placed in a chart is it likely to come out as fear. Fear comes from insecurity. Insecurity comes with a poorly operating Mars or Sun. Note, however, that a very strong-seeming Mars may disguise a weak one. Domineering or bullying behavior is not the normal style of an adequately strong Mars. Those who thrill to the glory of competition and enjoy testing their courage are really the ones in whom Mars is strong. They like to see how far they can go in any endeavor, and how strong they are with respect to others. The strongest Mars types of all have little desire to compare themselves to others. They prefer to improve on their own performance, constantly becoming better and stronger.

Thus the Mars type is an individualist. Mars people do not want to compromise their own integrity by following a path set by another, so this type is often the first to go where none have gone before. The true Mars type wants neither to dominate nor be dominated, but wishes to be left alone, free to pursue whatever path is desired. For this reason, however, the Mars type may have difficulty in relationships, especially work relationships. In love relationships the Mars type needs a partner who is an independent equal, capable of going his or her own way when necessary.

Women will often experience their own Mars energies through men. Hence Mars, like the Sun, is said to rule males. This is also changing as women become more in touch with their own yang energies. But anyone can experience Mars through other people who are associated with force, strength, and vigor. Thus Mars traditionally signifies athletes, military people, police in their forceful aspect, and the like, and also, less obviously, things like iron and steel (used by military people and in powerful machines) and those who work with them.

In a healthy body, Mars represents the vigor and vitality of movement, and especially the muscles. But it can also manifest as irritations, inflammations, infections, and fevers. Mars can be one of the principal significators of operations and accidents. These difficulties only manifest when for some reason the normal psychological channels for Mars's expression are blocked.

As we have already mentioned in connection with Venus, Mars has a vital role to play in love. Obviously, as the planet of conflict, it does not symbolize love itself. But it is necessary for love: only people who have realized their Mars, who have formed and defined their individuality and learned to maintain it in the face of resistance, can truly love and be loved. Love has a self-expressive quality as much as a quality of merging with another. In fact, in many animals, including human beings, there is a strong connection between sexual behavior and fighting. The intensity of sexual passion is the result simultaneously of the expression of selfish energies (Mars) and an experience of merging (Venus). Keeping the balance between these two energies is one of the difficulties in sexual relationships. Men in particular, who traditionally are more identified with the Mars facet of sexuality, may act selfishly in love relationships, exploiting and using women. Women, on the other hand, who have traditionally been identified with the Venus aspect of sexuality, may demand too little of a relationship and may allow themselves to be exploited. This, too, is changing, as both sexes are becoming increasingly aware of the need to experience both Venus and Mars in sexual expression.

This brings us to an important point which has not been made clear in older texts. Neither Venus nor Mars alone is the planet of sexuality. It is the combination of the two that rules sexual passion. And other planets, including Pluto, have lesser roles to play. It is not correct to describe Mars as masculine sexuality and Venus as feminine sexuality, except with respect to very primitive notions of sexuality. Ideally, both sexes should manifest both energies. The complete human being will always have a strong Mars balanced by a strong Venus, and will be able to avoid extremes of conflict and passivity.

Jupiter

Tradition regards Jupiter as the planet that most signifies success and achievement, good luck, and every conceivable benefit that life can offer. Jupiter has been called the greater benefic (Venus being the lesser), and it has always been considered the sign of positive results in every endeavor.

More recently, there has been a reaction against the old view, and the feeling has grown that Jupiter is overrated. Now there is talk of its tendency toward excess, arrogance, waste, and sloppiness. Nevertheless, people usually enjoy the energies of Jupiter, and in most cases it is a genuinely constructive influence.

Neither view of Jupiter gets to the heart of the matter, however. It is not enough to know that Jupiter can bring about one thing or another, or that people feel good or not good in reaction to its energies. The question is, what *are* Jupiter's energies?

Jupiter, in my experience, relates to two apparently different but closely related sets of energies: the energy of expansion and the energy of integration. We will take up both of these in turn and show how one or the other or both lead to the ideas that people have had about Jupiter. More importantly, we shall come to a clearer understanding of the role Jupiter plays in our lives.

First of all, what do we mean by expansion? Expansion of what? As all planets are fundamentally psychological in action, Jupiter is that energy which expands something in the psyche. Specifically, Jupiter symbolizes the energy that expands the sphere of action and experience in which the individual lives and moves.

Each person is born into a relatively narrow range of action and experience. In the beginning, one's world is the crib and its immediate environs, one's immediate family and their friends. This is not a problem for the individual as long as there is a sense of being at one with the world. Newborn children are probably not aware that they are distinct persons, separate from their mother and environment. Experience soon shows them, however, that they are separate, and that they have little control over the environment or the people in it. This dawning awareness of separation and lack of control must inevitably lead to a desire to expand one's world, go out into it, and make it a part of oneself again.

Thus, in its earliest form, Jupiter represents the reaching out of people to reincorporate as much of the external world as possible into themselves, possibly in order to re-create the feeling of oneness felt in the earliest period of life. This includes the desire and need to grow both physically and psychologically.

The initial stages of the Jupiter energy, then, consist of the individual growing on a physical level, going out into the world and learning about it, gaining control and autonomy, and increasing the scope of his or her action and experience. This is the facet of Jupiter that gives it its association with consciousness expansion, learning, the desire for travel, the love of freedom and independence. It is also the side of Jupiter that gives rise to its association with excessive growth, waste, and sloppiness. In the desire to grow, the need to handle details and deal with the minor aspects of living tends to get overlooked or deemed unworthy of one's attention.

Jupiter is associated with incorporation, the bringing of entities external to one's self into one's world and making them part of the self. There is a strong connection between the Moon and Jupiter in this regard. On the physiological level, for example, both are associated with digestion. Jupiter is usually regarded as the energy leading to obesity.

There is yet another connection between the Moon and Jupiter. Both are part of the support system needed in growing up. The Moon, as we have pointed out, relates to nurture and the creation of an individual's sense of emotional well-being. Whereas the Moon is part of the mother complex of symbols, Jupiter is more connected with the father complex. It is the part of parenting where the parents give the child encouragement and support in its efforts to grow and expand its world. For every challenge with which the child is presented in its education, there should be a corresponding encouragement that allows the child to believe that it can learn to overcome the challenge. This is an aspect of Jupiter as the planet of growth.

In strongly Jupiterian people, the growth aspect of this planet can lead down either of two paths. One type of Jupiterian personality may live life reaching out to comprehend and experience as much of the universe as possible. This type is interested in all kinds of learning, knowledge, and experience. Breadth of experience prevents this person from taking narrow-minded positions based on short-term goals at the expense of long-range objectives. Knowing that the self's own interests are best furthered by furthering those of the greater world of which one is a part and of which one has seen and experienced so much, such a person usually has a strong sense of social consciousness.

The other type of Jupiterian personality manifests the lunar side of Jupiter and cannot let go of what is seen and experienced. This person tries to own everything and to become more important than anyone, more grand and more arrogant. This type is never satisfied with anything gotten in life and is always on the move.

What is the difference between these two types? I believe it lies in other energies that have to do with the security of the ego. Both types are restless and always on the move, but one is never happy and the other usually is.

There is always a limit to growth, and that limit is imposed by two factors. One is that every entity has a certain built-in capacity for growth, and when that capacity is exceeded, growth stops. The other factor is that the external world can only support so much growth. There is a limit, for example, to food and resources. Room is also needed for growth because no one entity can grow beyond a certain point without trespassing upon others' rights. Whatever the source, the limit is imposed by the energy of Saturn, as we shall see in the next section.

Jupiter as the energy of integration arises from encountering the limits of Saturn. Put simply, if the extent to which one can grow, absorb the external universe, and make it one's own is limited, then maybe there is another way to overcome one's littleness, one's feeling of isolation and lack of control. One can integrate oneself into the prevailing social order. This allows one to connect with others by becoming part of them. If one cannot control the social order around oneself, maybe one can represent what it stands for.

This integrative side of Jupiter is also connected with the father complex of symbols. It is the function of the father symbols not only to cause one to grow through constant challenges and to provide support to help one meet those challenges, but also to assist one in finding a place in the world, a role to play, a sphere in which one can be effective.

The integrative side of Jupiter expresses itself most typically in its association with religion. Religion is (at least one hopes) a consciousness-expanding system. But even more, it is a system for giving one a relationship to the universe. The most common etymology of the word "religion" is that it comes from the Latin *religere*, "to bind back"—that is, to bind oneself back to the universe. Religion is a powerful device for attempting to overcome one's feeling of separateness. Jupiterian religion is not the religion of the ascetic alone on a mountain top, however, but rather the religion of elaborate social rituals in which all may play a part. It is the religion of the priest rather than the mystic.

Jupiter's connection with the law is also a function of its integrative side. Insofar as the law is a set of rules and restrictions, it is Saturnine, but insofar as it is the fabric of formal agreements that bind a society together, it is Jupiterian. Jupiter also rules the informal, implicit agreements by which we get along as a society.

Jupiter has also been associated with medicine and healing, the reintegration of the body after illness or prevention of bodily disintegration.

The desire of the mind for the grand overview also stems from the integrative side of Jupiter. The Jupiterian mind is more interested in seeing how everything relates to everything else than it is in examining any one thing in detail. Details are simply not as important to the Jupiterian as the understanding of what it is that integrates things. From this we get the Jupiterian's love of philosophy.

Just as an aggressive personal overexpansiveness can lead to arrogance, so, too, can overidentifying with that with which one feels integrated. One may feel, for example, that as a representative of the social order, one has the right to act as if one were its embodiment. Here we get a colossal arrogance, such as can be seen clearly in the chart of Adolf Hitler with his Moon conjunct Jupiter. This aspect is usually positive, but in Hitler's case it shows the power of Jupiter perverted.

Most people like to grow. Most like to feel a part of something greater than themselves. Most enjoy having increased opportunities in life. As a result, most enjoy Jupiter. But this is not the result of Jupiter's being *inherently* good. Jupiter seems to get along with more different planetary energies than most other planets, yet it is not unusual for its energies to work out badly. Unlimited growth may leave no room for further growth. Too many available resources can lead one to waste what one has. And the waste, in turn, as is all too clear at this point in history, can become a barrier to further growth. At the same time, every organism must grow and must have a place in the scheme of things. All of this is Jupiterian.

Saturn

Saturn is central to an understanding of the individual and his awareness, though its importance is of a different kind from that of the Sun, Moon, and other personal points. Since Saturn is so slow-moving, its position in the zodiac does not distinguish one individual very well from another. Yet Saturn is an energy that concerns collectives, and the relationship of an individual to the collective aspects of life is one of the most important things we can know about a person.

One matter must be dealt with immediately. Saturn is undergoing a great rehabilitation nowadays, and most modern writers agree that it is not as malefic as was once thought. Just as Jupiter, once called the "greater benefic," can indicate difficult energies at times, it is also now recognized that Saturn can play a positive role. Yet its power for destruction is still great, not because it is intrinsically destructive, but because in many cases we do not know how to handle Saturn energy. Those who have studied planetary energies have learned to handle what is traditionally described as "Saturn's malefic effects," but few have learned that Saturn's greatest threats to happiness come at precisely those times when it seems to be operating positively. In order to understand this, we must first understand Saturn's basic meanings.

In the course of this text we shall see that Saturn can be seen as the opposite pole of several planetary energies. This stems from the all-pervasive nature of Saturn. Before we look at Saturn's polar relation to Jupiter, let us examine the concept of polarity.

The experience of the universe that we share with each other is founded directly upon the principle of polarity: up-down, left-right, male-female, backward-forward, I-thou, I-it, good-evil, and so forth. In every pair of polar opposites, each member of the pair derives its meaning from the opposite member: each would be meaningless without the other. We all have noted that anything, no matter how pleasurable it might be at first, in excess becomes cloying and even unpleasant. We enjoy cooling off when it is too hot, warming up when it is too cold. And it is not just a matter of finding a balance. Most people need to go back and forth at least to some degree in order really to appreciate one or the other side of any polarity. This is true even of good and evil. At times, most of us enjoy doing what might be considered evil, but few appreciate unalloyed evil. Similarly, most people find those who are too good rather trying. I believe, along with the various schools of Eastern philosophy, that polarity is intrinsic to the nature of the universe, and that it is proper for humanity to follow the shifting paths between polar opposites. This is the path of the Tao.

Reality itself gains its varied nature from the interweaving of polar opposites. Without them, there would be no reality that we could relate to, in fact, no existence. Even existence is polarized by nonexistence.

In the Jupiter-Saturn polarity, the individual pursuing a Jupiterian path reaches out to incorporate as much of the universe as possible. But if this were carried to completion, all existence would be incorporated within the individual. And if the individual were to be everything, in experience as well as fact, there would be nothing to experience outside of the self. Yet one's awareness of oneself is with reference to that which is not part of one.

Not-self creates awareness of self; awareness of self creates not-self. When there is only self, the game of existence comes to an end.

For this reason, the universe resists the individual's reaching out. At some point, it says, "No! You cannot come any further." This is the energy of Saturn. It is the energy that maintains reality as we understand it. It makes the rules, sets the limits, creates the structure, and defines the nature of the game.

Saturn energy affects collectives because it represents that aspect of reality which arises from a consensus among human beings. Saturn energy does not represent truth or absolute reality. It represents a reality that is created socially, operates within a social universe, and has its greatest effects upon an individual in a socially defined context. Those aspects of reality that are purely personal are not so strongly affected by the Saturn archetype.

Saturn tends to direct the attention of an individual outside the self. It may represent others' opinions, others' needs, others' ideas of the truth, others' law, or more accurately, collective law, collective truth, and so forth.

The difficulty with Saturn comes from two sources, only one of which is widely understood. That is the one that has given Saturn its reputation as the "greater malefic."

It is not pleasant when reaching out to grasp something to be told it is not attainable. It is not pleasant to encounter one's limitations the first time (although it is pleasant to know them and live according to them without resistance). It is not pleasant to encounter rules that thwart one. Nor is it pleasant to encounter the natural but unlovely consequences of one's mistakes. Sometimes one's collisions with the rules of the game are so violent that they can kill, or at least destroy what one has painfully wrought over the years.

These, the well-known difficulties with Saturn energy, result from not understanding either one's own limitations or the rules of the game. While Saturn permits and even strengthens certain aspects of personal reality, such reality cannot come into conflict with social, collective, or consensus reality. When it does, the rules of collective reality work with an almost automatic quality, such that one seems to be only suffering the consequences of one's actions. From this come the ideas that Saturn brings what one deserves, or that Saturn is the Lord of Karma. This side of Saturn can be handled simply by becoming adequately conscious of the nature of the given situation. In fact, it is such encounters with situations that cause one to mature. Although Saturn here is often painful, it is actually quite creative and is necessary in human experience. This positive side of Saturn's energies has been brought out strongly in recent literature.

The truly serious problem of Saturn lies in the idea of reality itself: namely, the equation of reality with truth. Reality seems immutable, orderly, and eternal. Yet life is so short that we cannot see whether or not at some fundamental level the rules of the game are slowly changing. But they may be. What we with our limited perspective think of as reality is not necessarily truth.

Nevertheless, we need this reality: the experience of living in a universe where everything is in flux, where no rule can be counted on, or where an understanding of yesterday provides no clue for understanding tomorrow, would be enough to send most of us to the madhouse. We depend on a reality system for support, and even if we are at times unfamiliar with its rules, we are grateful for its existence.

Reality is structure, and so is Saturn. Reality is limitation, and so is Saturn, for everything is as much defined by what it is not as by what it is. If I took a chair and said "Let the essence of this chair fill this room," and it were to do so, we would lose the ability to perceive the chair. The chair is defined both by the fact that it occupies whatever space it occupies, and the fact that it does not occupy whatever space it does not occupy. Reality is created by a process of exclusion, of eliminating other possible realities. This aspect of exclusion is one of Saturn's most important attributes.

The existence of reality as we have described it is not the problem, however. The problem is our addiction to reality. I believe that there are many possible realities and that the world we share is only one of them. Even if you do not agree, it is obvious that within this reality there are many situations where it is possible to define reality in several ways.

Yet we cannot live with this: we create realities where there are none, simply for the sake of having structure. We exalt belief systems to the level of reality and then persecute others who do not share them. And even more important for ourselves as individuals, we needlessly limit our lives and our growth by excluding possibilities that might bring new life.

This is why aging is ruled by Saturn. As we get older we actualize more and more and thus have less and less potential. We run the risk of rigidity and premature death. Death ultimately can be understood as the time when all is actualized (at least in this life) and there is no more potential. One can come very close to this state without actually undergoing physical death. This is the real and very serious danger of Saturn.

Structure becomes rigidity, discipline becomes narrowness, order becomes a straitjacket, and too much patterning kills spontaneity. On another level, an individual's conformity to the consensus of any particular time in history comes to limit, define, and ultimately to strangle that person's creative potential. And this creative potential is the only hope for the future progress of culture. Every time we do what is untrue to our nature, acting not from a real necessity but rather to fulfill what others may expect of us, we commit a crime against ourselves that is peculiarly Saturnine. We move a bit more toward death, more of our potential becomes actual, and what is actual does not express what we are.

Like all energies, Saturn energy has its time and place. But, because Saturn issues are so central to social existence, we are likely to apply Saturn principles to situations where they are inappropriate. Being mature and able to accept responsibility is Saturnine; so is being guilt-ridden about one's inadequacies. Having a clearly defined image of who and what one is is Saturnine; but so is being so isolated from others that one cannot relate successfully. Alienation and one's sense of having a separate self are the same energy in different degrees in different situations. Knowing one's limitations is Saturnine; so is settling for too little in life. Being realistic is Saturnine; but so is compromising one's integrity and denying one's self-expression for fear of seeing what is really possible in the world.

As the planetary embodiment of the forces that shape our lives and give them form in the context of a social universe, Saturn is strongly connected to the symbolism of the father. Indeed, Saturn's symbolism is most clearly seen in myths about father-gods. The closest mythological representation of Saturn is not the Saturn-Kronos of Greco-Roman myth, but the Yahweh-Jehovah of the most ancient parts of the Old Testament. This god hands down commandments and demands obedience to them. He is just and righteous in a peculiarly rigid way that lacks mercy: to this god, obeying the letter of the law is more important than acting in gentleness or peace.

A strong Saturn often indicates a particularly powerful experience of the father principle (sometimes, but not necessarily, embodied in one's biological father). This father principle is experienced in all situations that call for learning a discipline, growing into a social role, or learning the rules. School is Saturnine. So are teachers and guide figures, and often one's boss or employer.

Saturn tends to focus one's concern on areas of life that need work— not only in the natal chart, but also as Saturn transits and progresses through the natal chart after birth, highlighting various areas of the chart and forcing growth in those directions. Many of the major crises of adulthood are represented at least in part by Saturn transits. These are times when one has to make decisions and pass up one path in favor of another. In this way Saturn energies actualize our lives and at the same time limit future possibilities. Such a process is necessary, though it can have dangerous consequences.

Saturn only deals with normal, day-to-day kinds of consciousness. It cannot anticipate the unprecedented, nor can it deal with the energies through which new life and creative powers enter the universe. If Saturn is too strong, it will even deny the emergence of such energies. Herein lies another of the deadlier attributes of Saturn. It is the function of the next planet in the solar system, Uranus, to create disruptions in the orderly world of Saturn so that creative energies can flow.

Uranus

Uranus is an antidote for many Saturn problems. Unfortunately, however, its action is drastic. Whereas Saturn creates a neat and orderly but sometimes oppressive universe in which one feels one knows what is happening, Uranus intrudes with an energy that is unexpected and often disruptive. Uranus energies strive to break one out of patterns that have become too rigid, even though one may wish to stay within them. Or, if one has already recognized that some Saturnine aspect of life has one in a stranglehold, Uranus can represent the desire to break free of it. It is an energy that strives to keep the universe flexible by preventing too much order. Uranus represents the random element of mutation that is necessary for creative innovation.

Although Uranus is the first of the outer planets that are normally invisible to the naked eye, it can be seen under ideal conditions when in opposition to the Sun. Uranus's position on the periphery of awareness symbolizes the way its energies tend to peep in and out of the world of normal consciousness, and how they often seem to be alien to the concerns of normal consciousness. Its energies operate suddenly and with extreme eccentricity. Whatever it may affect or symbolize takes the form of something unusual, far different from the everyday world. Uranus can therefore be more truly consciousness-expanding than Jupiter. Whereas Jupiter represents expansion into worlds that are at least similar to those with which one is already familiar, Uranus can bring about encounters with totally alien worlds. Along with Neptune, it is associated with alternative states of consciousness. It is said to rule enlightenment. It is the lightning flash that illuminates a dark landscape, the flash itself being totally discontinuous with the darkness that preceded it.

Uranus is often experienced as malefic—that is, difficult. Most of us are sufficiently comfortable in our reality systems so that we do not welcome elements that violate it. The problem with Uranus is being ready for it, and most people are not. To the extent that one is dominated by the negative side of Saturn, Uranus will be experienced as traumatic. But if one is ready for change and new experiences, Uranus can be life-restoring.

In order really to take advantage of Uranus, however, one must have grown to a certain point in the manner of Saturn. One must have created a certain amount of structure in life and gained a certain degree of maturity. In order for the Uranian alteration of structure to be useful, there must be a structure to alter. Uranus energies coming too soon in life can cause a chronically erratic quality that prevents any kind of maturation and produces an individual incapable of taking part in the social contract. Such people are automatic rebels: they rebel simply to negate order, even when order is still useful.

This is not to decry the rebellions of the young against their elders. Such rebellions are natural and proper Uranian crises which prevent any generation from getting a stranglehold on the next. To some extent each generation must form a structure that embodies its own nature. Uranus assists the young in breaking free of their parents so they can create their own order. All people must eventually create some kind of order in their lives so they can achieve what they wish. Then, when they have attained their goals, the power of Uranus can return to transform and restructure their lives. Thus achievements become not ends in themselves but only steps on a longer path. Left alone, Saturn causes people to stop at some point and be totally satisfied with the status quo. When this happens, life becomes a downward process, and one begins to perceive life as being less and less of what it once was. The individual who learns to handle Uranus is able to continue growing throughout life.

In order to deal with Uranus, detachment is necessary. One must not be wedded to any status quo. One must be ready to experience anything and to give up anything. Those who have given up possessions, social position, and cherished ideas are not held hostage against creative change by what they have. Most people cling to a Saturnine security even when this causes much pain and a diminished sense of being alive. As Uranian energies threaten, these people hold on harder, and Uranus becomes even more threatening and painful. The more easily one can let go, the more easily one can use the energies of Uranus positively.

When I was young, everyone in my town was amazed when a native son came back home after being vice-president of a large corporation. He was tired of being in business and wanted to do something else. He completely changed his life in order to reestablish touch with being alive. This is the Uranian way.

This detachment can be another source of difficulty with Uranus because it does not care about individual concerns. Uranus is a force of nature that operates outside human culture. It often takes the form of revolutions, natural disasters, and other disruptions that break down Saturnine order. Many people suffer when this happens. Uranus at these times is terrifying, and it is not clear that it is a force for aliveness. The destruction seems gratuitous, and most individuals do not benefit. Uranus has a ruthless side: Uranian people often have no concern for individuals at all, but only for a process of revolutionary change with which they have identified. In this identification one can see the transpersonal quality of Uranus as individuals completely bury their own egos in a cause.

It is best not to worry about or resent the ruthless side of Uranus. It is simply the way nature works. Nature is not completely reliable and predictable, and it does not always conform to our Saturnine expectations. In the face of this fact, one must be prepared to take advantage of Uranus's structure-annihilating powers, powers that can re-create aliveness and reestablish touch with the living self that has been buried by Saturn's structure. Interestingly, in times of natural disaster many people feel more alive than they ever do in normal times. Dealing with disaster brings out something creative in human nature, even in the midst of suffering.

Some people embody Uranian energies for society as a whole. They exist to challenge society's outworn structures and bring about change. Depending on the orientation of those who view them, they may be feared as dangerous revolutionaries or admired as reformers. Clearly, the more Saturnine elements of society, the reactionaries and conservatives, will feel threatened. Society can be like the individual who exacerbates a Uranian crisis by trying to prevent it from manifesting. If society resists too successfully, the Uranian element goes underground and bides its time. Meanwhile, the culture goes into a period of stagnation, only to erupt later on. The peculiar apathy of the nineteen fifties came partly from stifling Uranian energies during the early fifties' anti-Communist hysteria. But the Uranian energies then erupted much more strongly in the sixties. In the seventies another period of deadness settled over America. Was this also the result of stifling Uranian energies, and will it cause more violent eruptions in the future?

Astrologers have long associated Uranus with innovative technologies like electronics, computers, aeronatics and astronautics, and also with sciences such as chemistry, physics, and mathematics—all fields that have brought radical change in our world. But when scientists become spokesmen for the social order and try to determine what people shall and shall not believe, it is questionable whether they are still Uranian. Science in all its forms is both Uranian and Saturnine, but some scientists are predominantly Saturnine. It is worth noting that Saturnine scientists have seldom been the most creative, and when they have, their creative work has usually been done in youth, before the Saturnine hardening of their attitudes. Uranus represents the intuitive flash that leads to new discovery and the overturning of old ideas, while Saturn represents the systematic plugging away involved in testing ideas. Science requires a balance between these energies.

Other fields with revolutionary potential are also Uranian. Though individual astrologers may project the energies of Saturn, Neptune, or other planets, astrology itself is plausibly Uranian. This is because astrology works with flashes of intuition gained directly from a symbolic study of the cosmos. The student of astrology can gain direct knowledge of religious, metaphysical, and spiritual truths without having to be guided by priests or other representatives of the established philosophical order. Here is the real reason why astrology has gone in and out of favor. Unlike most of the orthodox (the very word "orthodox" is Saturnine) sciences, what astrology teaches has profound social implications, a fact obscured by the conservatism of many astrologers. In this respect, astrology is more like a social science, which often has controversial things to say about the world. But at the time astrology fell out of favor there were no social sciences to speak of, and I doubt that any would have been tolerated. The physical sciences became acceptable once it became clear that they would have little to say about social realities, and that they were useful for military purposes.

One of the essential features of Uranian fields of study is that they are very mind-oriented. Uranus does not touch the feelings the way that, say, the Moon, Venus, or Neptune do. While it does not necessarily follow traditional canons of logic or reason, the Uranian mind does operate in ways that reason can relate to. In fact, Uranian people will often carry an idea out to an extent that is positively inhuman. This is another aspect of the ruthlessness of Uranus. The engineer who can only think of increasing the power of his or her technology, regardless of the human cost, is a true negative Uranian type. The positive consequences of his or her activities must be integrated into society without letting the negative side run rampant.

Uranus may signify death through accident, injury, or natural disaster, but at least it never signifies the death-in-life that is characteristic of Saturn. Thus, although Uranus energies can be extremely difficult to live with, the measure of chaos that they introduce is essential for life. Life is to a great extent a balancing of the orderly forces of Saturn with the chaotic forces of Uranus. Each has its place, and each needs to be kept in check by the other.

Neptune

Neptune is probably the most difficult planetary energy to understand. Its nature eludes definition because it is associated with aspects of the universe that are unclear, illusory, delusory, ill-defined, and even imaginary.

But Neptune can be understood in part by defining what it is not. Even more than Uranus, it is an energy that negates everything that Saturn stands for. If Saturn is reality, Neptune is unreality. If Saturn is an aspect of the ego, Neptune is denial of the ego. If Saturn is our notion of time and space, Neptune is outside time and space, in either a non-dimensioned or an infinitely dimensioned universe. Neptune symbolizes the truth and divinity perceived by mystics. (Keep in mind that the planet is an agent or a representation of an energy, not the source of the energy.) At the highest level, Neptune represents Nirvana, where all individuality is merged into an infinite oneness of being and consciousness.

The planet is probably misnamed from an astrological point of view, since it has little similarity to the boisterous Roman sea-god. It is more like the Hindu goddess Maya, who is really a philosophical principle. Like the planet Neptune, Maya is both illusion (especially the illusion that is the physical universe) and the way through illusion to absolute truth. Unlike Maya, however, Neptune has little to do with the physical universe. Its illusions usually involve a departure from the physical universe's commonly accepted rules. As we have seen, the idea that the reality of the physical universe is also the truth comes from Saturn, not Neptune. Thus Maya in the philosophical sense is represented in its different aspects by both of these planets.

Neptune energies are extremely hard for most people to deal with, simply because to be successful in the mundane universe, one must be able to deal effectively with Saturn, and it is hard to deal effectively with both planets at once. Saturn represents the apparent reality of reality, giving what we call reality the appearance of truth. The universe of Neptune is one of unlimited possibilities, in which there are no rules except for those created arbitrarily at certain points in time-space so that the divine dance we call reality can take place.

To be able to handle Neptune and Saturn at once is difficult. One must be able to play the game of reality completely and with total conviction, exactly as if it were real in the ultimate sense, while at the same time knowing in one's heart that it is not. One must be able to live in the universe of Saturn, being responsible and aware of its laws, while at the same time not requiring it for support. The addiction to structure that we referred to under Saturn is not permissible with Neptune. This is what is called detachment: playing the game for real yet knowing that it is not.

One cannot even be attached to oneself, because the ego, the form of one's being that one calls oneself, is also not ultimately real. This is why Neptune is an ego-denying energy. In the presence of Neptune, the illusion of the ego becomes clear. The illusion is not so much the awareness of *having* an ego, as it is of *being* an ego. On a low level, Neptune represents experiences that becloud the ego, which, in order to function, needs a sense of a secure ultimate reality. Thus Neptune symbolizes illusion, mystery, confusion, and crises in which one's ego is severely defeated.

Neptune may also signify both an ideal and an illusion of the perfectly ideal. Though Saturn also has an ideal of perfection, Neptune's ideal transcends physical reality. Neptune's ideal of perfection is positive when it is held as something to strive for, but illusory when it is believed already to be true on this plane.

When one is relatively at ease with Neptune, higher manifestations come forth. The awareness Neptune gives—that the ego is not ultimately what one is—grants us the ability to sacrifice ourselves for that in which we believe, for higher causes and truth. The catch here is that, if we really understand Neptune, we realize that what we are likely to sacrifice ourselves for is as much an illusion as our own ego. It is the awareness of the game that is important in such a case. Simply as a kind of statement about what one may be in the course of playing the divine game, one may, in the full awareness of its ultimate unreality, choose to sacrifice heavily for that in which one believes. Or one may sacrifice oneself while not knowing this, and waste one's life for nothing. The difference between a high martyr and a simple victim is hard to establish; both are Neptunian.

Unfortunately, Neptune may indicate severe ego weaknesses in people who really do have to deal with the physical universe in order to play the game of life. In such cases, Neptune gives rise to covert or dishonest actions, to people who act behind the scenes because they do not have the strength to confront life directly. Poisoning, often called the weapon of the weak, is Neptunian. Many Neptunian people have a severe lack of confidence in themselves. The most desperate will attempt to withdraw from life into drugs or alcohol or even insanity, although all of these difficulties require a considerable contribution from other planets such as Pluto and Saturn.

Some who have a relatively weak ego structure due to Neptune manifest a positive characteristic as well. Because they are not as bound up in the definitely structured world that comes with a strong ego, they may be more sensitive to energies that others have ruled out of order in their systems of reality. Neptune is therefore connected with psychic people of all kinds.

Neptune can be a great source of difficulty in relationships. This is because relationships require a clear idea of what one is: a clearly defined ego. When Neptune affects relationships there is not only a lack of clarity about what the other person may be by himself or herself, but also no clarity about which aspects of the relationship are really the other person and which are actually oneself. Neptunian people are prone to create projections in which there is no correspondence between the energy projected upon the other person and what that person may really be. All relationships are to some extent based on projection, but with Neptune the fit between the projection and the person may be very poor indeed.

As with every other planet, there are times when Neptune manifests creatively and times when it is inappropriate. Neptune energy best comes when one has learned somewhat to play the game of life, at a time when the structures one has created threaten to take away the sense of aliveness. Its peculiar kind of enlightenment is best left to those who are relatively advanced in years or who have otherwise gained wisdom and maturity.

But many try to go on to a Neptunian state too soon, usually because of the kind of ego weakness that we have already mentioned. Many young people become involved in spiritual movements, not because they have mastered the game of life and are ready to leave it, but because they are either afraid of life or disgusted by it without really understanding it. The question here is one of motivation: why does one choose to leave the ordinary world? The individual's answer to this will determine whether or not the spiritual quest is appropriate. For many, it is perfectly proper to retire from the routine of ordinary living to a contemplative, spiritual life in an ashram or monastery. Such people understand at a very early age that of various realities, the one that a given society creates with its laws, customs, and expectations for its members is one of the most illusory. (Even in an ashram, however, one does not leave the physical universe, only the social one to some extent.) It is a radical idea for many to realize that it is not always or even usually good for everyone to follow the spiritual path. We are here to do what must be done, and this requires an ego. Neptune can be quite damaging in this way.

Along with Venus, Neptune signifies artistic creativity. Whereas Venus represents the physical aspect of creation, Neptune is the inspiration that must take place before a thing can be brought into the physical world. A creative person with a strong Venus but little Neptune is more craftsman than artist. Such people will have elegant taste and design sense, but little imagination, imagination being one of the most important benefits of Neptune. By the same token, an individual who has much Neptune but little Venus will be able to conceive creative ideas but not be as good at bringing them into physical reality. Those arts that are the most abstract are the most Neptunian, such as music (primarily composition) and poetry. Painting and sculpture require a good deal of Venus because of the physical nature of the creation.

In the scheme of planets presented here, Neptune is the next stage beyond Uranus in the encounter with the transcendent aspects of existence. If Saturn represents normal reality and the consciousness that deals with that reality, and Uranus represents those energies that break through normal reality so its structures cannot become too deadening, then Neptune represents the total negation of all the principles of normal reality. Neptune is often described as illusion, while Saturn is said to represent truth. The relation is actually the reverse: Saturn is the illusion that there is a reality that is truth; Neptune is the truth that there isn't. In some respects, Neptune is more truly chaotic than Uranus, in that Neptune can be the formless void before any structure is imposed upon it. Yet on closer examination we could say that Neptune symbolizes the universe in which all truth is simultaneously true, even the contradictions!

I have said we create Saturnine reality by a process of elimination and exclusion: the selection is made from the overwhelming array of realities symbolized by Neptune. In its manifestations in ordinary life, Neptune can represent either illusion or mystical illumination, depending on one's level of spiritual evolution. For this reason, Neptune can represent the highest and lowest aspects of human experience, the most beautiful and painful of human emotions. The task of mastering Neptune's energies is one of the most difficult, and very few do it completely. I suspect this is so because to master the energy that Neptune represents requires being able to accept all its truth at once. To do this means that one cannot perform the acts of exclusion and selection that are required in order to create—that is, to incarnate into—a physical universe under Saturn. If one really masters Neptune, one probably does not incarnate into this world. The mere fact of such incarnation suggests that Neptune has not been mastered and probably will not be in this lifetime, except for the occasional bodhisattva who incarnates totally realized for the sake of guiding others to the truth. We should not be sorry about this; we should simply go about doing what is to be done and learning what is to be learned.

It is important to learn that all the energy that comes with being alive has its origin in the universe of Neptune, and that if we cut ourselves off from Neptunian energy with walls of Saturn, we ultimately cut ourselves off from life. Uranus makes the break in what armors us against the ultimately real, while Neptune gives a glimpse of the ultimately real itself.

Pluto

As the outermost known planet, Pluto symbolizes the end of the process Uranus began: that of breaking down the reality structure of normal consciousness. If Uranus breaches the normal reality structure and Neptune exposes us to the ultimately real, then Pluto symbolizes the radical transformation of consciousness and being that must result. Pluto is the archetype of death and resurrection: it breaks down the old and outworn entities into their component parts, and then reassembles them into new being.

It does this at every level of life. As with Uranus and Neptune, Pluto may be experienced by people of any level of consciousness, but, also like these other planets, Pluto is hard to handle if one is bound up in the universe of Saturn. Pluto operates with extreme power, and, being a force beyond the ego, when it manifests it usually causes one to feel out of control. While Uranus interrupts normal reality and Neptune confuses ordinary reality by exposing one to other realities, Pluto can symbolize a complete breakdown in ordinary reality. Such a breakdown forces one not only to deal with an alternate reality, but even to build a new day-to-day reality out of it.

When faced with the breakdowns of Pluto, people often draw on all their reserves to hold together what is disintegrating. But this only makes the breakdown difficult and even deadly, and frustrates the new birth. Mental illness is often an example of this: psychotic episodes have been observed in people's lives when the power of Pluto is strong. There comes a time when the mind's old structures no longer work and the only hope is to destroy them and build new ones. But people who experience psychotic breakdowns, and even more often those around them, tend to be overwhelmed by the pain of the situation. They panic and resort to tranquilizing drugs. The breakdown is slowed and the confrontation that must occur cannot. The rebuilding process is delayed or even prevented. The sick individual then falls into a state of arrested development hovering between madness and sanity, and never completely builds a structure that can work. This is typical of the ways in which many people react to Plutonian crises in general. It is best to let go of whatever must go at such times and work to hasten the birth of the new. Like Uranus and Neptune, Pluto requires detachment.

Unlike Uranus, however, Pluto is not usually sudden in its effects. Pluto represents an evolutionary power built into the nature of things. Living things develop: they grow, die, decay, and are changed into something else. At least at this point, there is no way of frustrating this cycle of development. Non-living things also develop: waves crest, break, and re-form into new waves; stars condense, shine, expand, explode, and die; rocks form, wear, and are reincorporated into new rocks. Cultures rise, fall, and become the seeds of new cultures. On the Earth, the great continental plates shift and collide, leading to earthquakes and volcanic eruptions which are Plutonian insofar as they change the face of the Earth (and Uranian in their suddenness). Nothing in a universe of change can long remain unchanged, and most of that change comes from the very nature of what is changed. It is inherent in the growth processes of the human psyche as well that there will be times when the psyche must undergo crises involving breakdown and rebirth.

People who strongly manifest the energies of Pluto are often the agents of Plutonian power in the world. They embody the forces of death and resurrection inherent in society. Uranian types may talk of revolution and the need for change, but it is the Plutonian types who will often bring it about, taking advantage of energies stirring within the culture. Plutonians, unlike Uranians, will often work quietly behind the scenes manipulating the process.

But most Plutonians are not political revolutionaries. They are usually quiet people who nevertheless strangely attract and repel others. From them comes a fascinating quality that many find charismatic and others find unsettling, disgusting, or even horrifying.

One aspect of Plutonian death and resurrection is sexuality. The purpose of sexual reproduction is to keep the species going even though its individual members die. Two individuals each shed cells containing the genetic makeup of each. The cells then merge and lose their separate identities and are eventually born as a new entity. The period of gestation in the womb can be likened to the body's period in the tomb, except that in the womb the body is built up, while in the tomb it is disintegrating. The important point is that change takes place, slowly and subtly, from one state to another, change that eventually becomes visible. Many students of symbolism have noted the connection between orgasm and death. At the simplest physiological level, orgasm is the turning point of a process that goes from excitation to release. At its most complete, it involves a momentary annihilation of the ego, followed by a feeling of renewed aliveness. So to the personal aspects of sexuality that are associated with Mars and Venus we must add the transcendental aspect of Pluto.

Plutonians are often sexually magnetic, though not always in conventional ways. Such individuals may or may not be what we commonly think of as physically attractive; their magnetism arises because they embody an aspect of the life-death force. Plutonian sexuality may or may not follow the conventional social guidelines concerning sex.

When you manifest Plutonian energies, you are intended by the universe to fulfill a cosmic purpose. When you try to bend Pluto's energies to your own ends, you find that the original intentions of the energy, those that were inherent in the energy itself as opposed to those that you had in mind, are fulfilled instead. Not only do you fail to gain your individual ends, you may destroy yourself in the process.

Often Plutonian people are found in politics. The force of history requires individuals who will manifest Pluto's power. And those who are selected, feeling that power, will usually try to bend it to their own ends. As a result, they often achieve a great deal of political power, even though in retrospect it can be seen that they themselves were not in control. Hitler, with his ability to hypnotize the masses with oratory, is an example. He rose as a manifestation of a historical process from the tensions that gripped Europe after World War I. But he believed that he was as an individual the source of that power, and his people believed it, too. The result was destruction.

It is tempting to believe that Hitler and the German people broke a moral law and were punished. But there is nothing moral or ethical about the energy of Pluto. It is a force of nature that is simply too strong to be contained by the limited capacities of the ego. Any attempt to harness its energy to the ends of the ego results in an overload, as in a circuit that carries more electricity than it was designed for. Hitler could have been a medium for the transmission of historical energies, but he chose to try to take control of them. World War II was the consequence.

Richard Nixon also attempted to use his great Plutonian power for his own purposes. Unlike Hitler, however, almost from the beginning he provoked a steady and persistent opposition, one that worked as tirelessly to bring down his power as he had worked to build it up. This is the more common response to those who abuse Plutonian power. The opposition usually builds up faster than it did with Hitler. People with strong Plutos need to be careful how they manifest their energy, and how others react to it. In Nixon's case the effects of both his natal Pluto and the Pluto in the sky at the time of Watergate were important in timing his downfall. (This is discussed at length in my book *Planets in Transit.*)

As Pluto is connected to breakdown and decay, so it is also connected to those elements of society that reflect breakdown and decay. This is the source of Pluto's association with underworld elements, organized crime, and people who are so socially disaffected that they represent a threat to society. Terrorism is a manifestation of Pluto; it comes about because the world is unwilling to deal with certain pressing problems. At this point in history the right of the Jews to a state of their own is colliding with the right of the Palestinian Arabs to the country from which they were expelled when the Jewish state was created. Terrorism has resulted because the world is unwilling to deal with this problem. The socially disaffected are only a manifestation of Pluto's power. Though criminals and terrorists seem to be what destroys society, they are merely the agents by which the destructive power already inherent in the situation manifests. They are not the source of destruction, and even if they were eliminated, something else would replace them as agents of that power.

In individual life, Plutonian periods are always periods of death, but generally not physical death. Usually an aspect of one's life passes away, making way for something new. Or an individual may experience an increase in power that causes life to be totally transformed. As we have said, the best thing one can do is surrender to the change and even assist it if possible.

Very often, Plutonian people take on the positive role of assisting others who are going through Plutonian transformations. At one level, then, Pluto is associated with healers and therapists, both psychological and physical, and those who teach techniques of self-transformation. At another level, Plutonians may appear as religious leaders who stress rebirth after death — either literal or psychological. Therapists, healers, gurus, religious leaders, and the like are the most positive Plutonians of all because they are the most in touch with the central theme of Pluto, the death and rebirth of the soul.

Helping others with their transformations is a constructive way to use Pluto, but it still has its dangers. To assist people in this way involves having a great deal of power, especially because of the knowledge such helpers gain of their clients' vulnerable spots, and the weakened condition of those undergoing crises. When Plutonians exploit this power for personal ends, they are likely to suffer the consequences. Insofar as they assist people in transforming their lives, astrologers are Plutonian and also have this responsibility.

One discipline that illustrates all of Pluto's dangers is magick (spelled this way to distinguish it from what stage magicians do). Even when pursued purely for the sake of enlightenment, magick grants a power likely to corrupt. Therefore, those who wish to study it must purify themselves of all considerations that might cause them to use the power for personal ends. If these energies are misused, they may destroy the practitioner. For those who might be unaware of the fact, magick is not supernatural in the usual sense of the word. It is a study of psychic energies in their highest form. The knowledge that one gains from its study is dangerous to the extent that the magician falls short of perfect psychological balance. And this is the way it is with Plutonian energies in general. Whether they manifest as magick or anything else, Plutonian energies cannot be used for purely personal ends.

The literature of astrology tends to dwell on the seamy side of Pluto, its association with unchecked power, decay, corruption, and death. Yet Pluto stands for something much higher. It is the purifying fire that an entity must go through in order to pass from one level of being to another. Ultimately, Pluto purifies and makes more nearly perfect; but to do this it must first completely destroy anything gross or imperfect that holds an entity back. When we confront Plutonian energies, we often see aspects of ourselves with which we cannot deal, because we have buried them in the process of creating our reality systems. So when a crisis comes in which nothing that is true can remain hidden, we have to confront our personal garbage and finally do something about it. Only then can we move on. What appears to us as the negative energy of the symbol Pluto is nothing more than a mirror image of our own negativity staring back at us.

5

Other Points in the Chart

I have already said that the planets are the primary focus of the chart. Symbolic carriers of various energies, they move through the zodiac and are related to each other by aspects and qualified and colored by the signs and houses they occupy. But planets are not the only points in the horoscope. There are other points that can make aspects, and many of these points can also be modified by sign and house position much like planets.

These other points vary in usefulness. Some have obvious effects and provide information that would otherwise be unavailable from the chart; others have effects that are hard to discern and merely duplicate symbolism already present. The Ascendant and Midheaven are absolutely indispensable; the lunar nodes, the 0° Aries Point, and various midpoints add a great deal to chart interpretation; certain asteroids, fixed stars, hypothetical planets, the Vertex, and East Point promise to add valuable insights although I have not used them a great deal; and some other points I find merely add to the confusion.

All points in the chart, including planets, fall into one of three categories. I will discuss node-type points first because they include those all-important horoscope angles, the Ascendant and Midheaven. Node-type points are formed by the intersection of two significant planes. They include not only the Ascendant and Midheaven, but also the other house cusps, newly proposed horoscope angles like the Vertex and East Point, lunar and planetary nodes, and the 0° Aries Point.

Body-type points are celestial bodies, either observed or hypothesized. Besides planets, these include asteroids, planetoids like the recently discovered Chiron, fixed stars, and the hypothetical planets proposed by various astrologers.

Planetary picture-type points arise from symmetrical arrangements of planets or other points around a single axis. Such arrangements produce sensitive points which take on importance when occupied. Arabian parts are the example most familiar to traditional astrologers, but midpoints and antiscia or solstice points are also based on this idea. The category takes its name from the Uranian school's planetary pictures, which include all the other types in this category as special cases.

Even though these other points can in many ways be treated as planets, not all carry energies in the way that planets do. Body-type points carry energies, and planetary-picture type points carry energies insofar as they represent the combined energies of planets. But node-type points represent areas in which planetary energies can manifest. Thus, an aspect involving, say, Venus and the Ascendant might mean Venusian energies (warmth, harmony, etc.) expressed in one's relations with others (signified by the Ascendant).

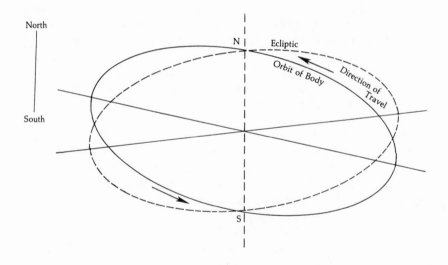

Figure 4. Nodes

Node-Type Points

All the node-type points commonly used in astrology are formed by the intersection of the ecliptic with another significant plane. To see what nodes are, imagine that everything in the sky is projected onto the inside of a sphere, much like a planetarium dome, except that it surrounds us on all sides, not just the top. This is the celestial sphere. The center of the sphere represents the center of the Earth, and all the planes we will be talking about will pass through this center. The boundaries of the planes will be at the surface of the sphere, and will thus be great circles (as opposed to small circles, which represent the boundaries of planes that do not go through the center of a sphere).

In Figure 4, one of the great circles is the ecliptic, or the apparent yearly path of the Sun through the sky. Points *N* and *S* are the nodes, where the circle of the ecliptic is intersected by the circle of another plane. Point *N* is a north, or ascending, node, where the path of the body represented by the other great circle is crossing the ecliptic headed in the general direction of the Earth's North Pole. Point *S* is a south, or descending node, where the path of the body is headed toward the South Pole.

The dashed line connecting the nodes *N* and *S* is called the nodal axis. The intersection of two planes is always a straight line, and nodes of this type are always exactly 180° apart along the ecliptic. Thus, unless we are talking about planets right at, or conjunct, one of the nodes, any angular relationship to one end of the nodal axis will be similar to its relationship to the other end. For this reason, we usually only need to consider aspects and other angular relationships to one of the pair. By convention, this is usually the north node.

The Ascendant and Midheaven   The Ascendant and Midheaven were defined in Chapter 2 and will be discussed much more fully in Chapter 12 as markers of a planet's mundane position. I mention them here only in their roles as nodes and as sensitive points that lie along the ecliptic, forming various angular relationships along the ecliptic to other points in the horoscope.

The Ascendant and Midheaven are considered the principal ends of their respective nodal axes, even though both are exceptions to the rule above about the principal end usually being the north node upon the ecliptic. The Ascendant is the north node of the ecliptic upon the horizon, meaning that in this case the horizon is the plane of reference and it is the ecliptic that is crossing the horizon in a northward direction rather than the other way around. The Midheaven changes its angle to the ecliptic so that at one time of day it could be called a north node and another time it could be called a south node. For this reason, it is defined simply as the ecliptic-meridian node that is above the horizon.

As with the other nodes, speaking of one end of the axis implies the whole axis. Thus, whatever I will say below about the Ascendant implies the Descendant also, and whatever I say about the Midheaven includes the I.C.

When the Ascendant and Midheaven are used as sensitive points, we take aspects to them quite seriously, regardless of the distance off the ecliptic of the body being aspected. Thus if, for instance, Pluto and the Ascendant have the same longitude (in other words, are conjunct) along the ecliptic, the symbols of Pluto and Ascendant-Descendant are considered to be linked, even though Pluto may be nowhere near the horizon (see page 30). The same is true when Pluto makes any other significant angular relationship along the ecliptic to the Ascendant-Descendant axis.

The Ascendant and Midheaven are special among all points in the chart, for two reasons. One reason is that, unlike the other points, the Ascendant and Midheaven, both being derived from the horizon of a specific point on Earth, depend on the place of birth. The other reason is that the Ascendant and Midheaven are the fastest-moving points in the horoscope. Whereas the planets take from about one to several hundred years to go once around the zodiac, the Sun takes one year, and the Moon takes one month, the Ascendant and Midheaven take only one day. Each moves along the ecliptic on the average of one degree for every four minutes of time. Because they indicate both the place and the time of the birth down to the minute, the Ascendant and Midheaven are what links conditions in the heavens to a particular individual on Earth.

Traveling at the speed they do, they are in a constantly changing relationship to all the other points in the horoscope, highlighting one group of planets at one time, and then another group a few minutes later. Thus the horoscope of a person born at eight o'clock can be quite different from that of another born the same day at eight-thirty.

In Chapters 12 and 15 I will describe in detail how the Ascendant and Midheaven derive their meanings from their position in the mundane cycle. Here, however, it suffices to outline their signification using a few keywords.

A key idea for the Ascendant-Descendant axis is "exchange with the environment." Planets in a significant angular relationship to this axis generally manifest in relationships and in a person's interaction with the outside world. The Midheaven-I.C. axis, on the other hand, signifies how one feels inwardly (I.C.) and expresses oneself outwardly (Midheaven), or where in life one is coming from and going to. The key idea here is "I, me, mine": this axis has less to do with relationships and more to do with one's sense of oneself. Examples of how the Ascendant and Midheaven work in combination with planetary energies can be found in the brief midpoint delineations of pairs of points in Chapter 9.

Intermediate House Cusps   As mentioned in Chapter 2, because the position of house cusps other than the horoscope angles is a matter of continuing debate, I do not consider aspects to intermediate house cusps or use them as sensitive points in any way. Only a few astrologers, such as those of the Uranian school or those who use Arabian parts extensively, use house cusps as sensitive points in the chart.

The Vertex   We have seen that the Ascendant and Midheaven axes are created by the intersection of the ecliptic plane with the horizon and meridian planes. The horizon divides the chart into up and down, whereas the meridian divides it into east and west (or, if you prefer, left and right). There is also a plane that divides the celestial sphere into front and back. It runs at right angles to the meridian, east and west directly over our heads and under our feet, and it is called the prime vertical.

Theoretically, the points where this circle crosses the ecliptic ought also to have meaning. So postulated L. Edward Johndro, a technically proficient astrologer from New York, some decades ago. His work led him to conclude that the intersection in the west is the more important, and he named that point the Vertex (and the opposite point in the east the Antivertex). He and his students, among them Charles Jayne, have found that the Vertex has to do with fateful and important encounters, either with people or circumstances. I mentioned the Vertex in *Planets in Composite*. Since then I have examined it further and still do not have a clear idea of its usefulness. What does emerge is that it is most active in situations that are dramatic and not characteristic of one's ordinary life. This would seem to accord with Johndro's and Jayne's ideas, but I do not find it useful in most cases. Other astrologers have had different experiences; clearly more work is needed.

The East Point   Another new horoscope angle that has received attention lately is the so-called East Point. In fact, it does not represent any point on the ecliptic that is due east (that point is the Antivertex). The East Point should be called the Equatorial Ascendant, because it is the degree of the zodiac that would be rising if one were born on the equator.

The East Point has been put forth as akin to the Ascendant, but its precise meaning has never been clearly stated so as to distinguish it from the Ascendant in a way that astrologers can agree upon. Because its meaning is not clearly formulated, its effectiveness cannot be tested; if you make the meaning of a symbol vague enough and use large enough orbs you can make anything work. For these reasons I am not an advocate of the East Point.

The Lunar Nodes   The lunar nodes are those degrees in the zodiac where the plane of the Moon's orbit crosses the plane of the ecliptic. As with the Ascendant-Descendant, Midheaven-I.C., and Vertex-Antivertex, the nodes are two ends of an axis 180° apart. The North Node (also called the Dragon's Head or Caput Draconis) is the point at which the Moon crosses the ecliptic heading north, and the South Node (the Dragon's Tail or Cauda Draconis), the point where the Moon crosses the ecliptic going south.

The nodes of the Moon have been obvious to astronomers since the beginning, because when the Sun is near them in its apparent orbit around the Earth, the new and full Moons tend to be eclipses. This is where the colorful terms Dragon's Head and Dragon's Tail come from: in mythology the nodes were believed to be inhabited by a dragon that swallowed the Sun or Moon whenever these bodies came too near. We now know, as did the ancient astronomers, that the nodes are simply places where the Moon and Earth become aligned with the Sun so that the Moon casts a shadow on the

Earth (solar eclipse) or the Earth casts a shadow on the Moon (lunar eclipse). The lunar nodes move backward in the zodiac at the rate of a little over 3' of arc per day, completing one turn around the zodiac every 18.6 years.

The lunar nodes are not new in astrology, but they seem to have come into general use in the West only in modern times. In India they have been widely used much longer. What they indicate is a matter of controversy. In Hindu astrology both nodes are considered malefic, but in the West the North Node is considered easier and the South Node more difficult. Some compare the North Node to Jupiter and the south node to Saturn. My own work suggests there is some truth in this. But clear distinctions can be made between the two nodes only when bodies are conjunct one of them. Otherwise, any body that aspects one aspects the other equally.

Some writers consider the nodes to indicate past incarnations. This may be true, but it is difficult to prove. Karmic astrology is too often the refuge of those who cannot bear to have their ideas tested in practice.

One widely held idea that I agree with is that the nodes relate to connections with other people: that is, they are an axis of relationship. In this context, the North Node has a joining quality, while the South has a separating quality. Since these are nodes of the Moon, it is likely that they have to do at least somewhat with connections involving the feelings. And since they come from the intersection of the orbital plane of the Moon and the plane of the Sun's apparent orbit around the Earth, they plausibly have something of the quality of the Sun/Moon midpoint. I have noticed that when the nodes are heightened in the chart there is a greater tendency to go and meet people. I also find that when two people have important connections between major factors in one chart with the North Node in another, the relationship is more constructive than if the connection is with the South Node. I have not been able to validate other ideas about what the nodes mean. The fact that astrologers disagree about them suggests that the nodes are less powerful than factors about which there is more unanimity. But I do not at this time advocate ignoring the nodes.

Until recently, astrologers used the mean lunar nodes, which travel backward in the zodiac at a uniform rate. Then in 1975 Digicomp Research Corporation published an ephemeris entitled *True Lunar Nodes 1850-2000*. This was based on the fact that while the Moon's orbital plane gradually revolves backward in the zodiac, it also wobbles so that the actual lines of intersection move back and forth over the short run. Consequently, there is disagreement about how to locate the nodes because the mean position differs from the wobbling position by up to 1°45' at any give time. The *American Ephemeris* gives positions of both the mean and wobbling nodes. The wobbling nodes are no more "true" than the mean nodes, as they are in their own way just as abstract a concept. They should not be used until research has indicated which, if either, of the two sets of nodes is more valid. The final word has yet to be said, but at this time I am more inclined to use the conventional mean nodes.

Planetary Nodes As the orbital plane of the Moon intersects the orbital plane of the Earth (or apparent orbital plane of the Sun around the Earth), so do the orbital planes of the planets intersect the Earth's orbital plane, giving rise to the planetary nodes. Viewed heliocentrically (from the viewpoint of the Sun), the nodes of each planet are exactly opposite each other in the zodiac, but shifting to the geocentric (Earth-centered) frame of reference more common in astrology causes them to appear to be not in opposition (there is, however, very little shift with the outer planets).

On the face of it, if the Moon has nodes, why not the planets? Unfortunately, because of the difference between the heliocentric and geocentric frames of reference, there are problems with the definition of the planetary nodes, and consequently, where they are located. All the other nodal points discussed here have axes that pass through the Earth. With these, the axis passes through the Sun.

In *The Node Book* Zipporah Dobyns has written the most extensive work on the planetary nodes and has included an ephemeris of their geocentric positions. There are also computer chart casting services that calculate these positions according to Dobyns's method. In his book *Astrology of Inner Space*, however, Carl Payne Tobey gives a convincing argument for using the heliocentric node positions in a geocentric chart.

But even if we decide which node positions to use, there is still a problem. According to Dr. Dobyns, the nodes of the planets have a symbolic meaning similar to those of the planets to which they are connected. This in effect gives every planet three longitudes in the chart: its actual geocentric longitude and the longitudes of the two nodes. This greatly increases the probability of chance results. To make the nodes useful, we have to come up with criteria that clearly distinguish between the nodes and their respective planets.

Again, I do not suggest ignoring planetary nodes, but using them might best be put off by beginners.

The Aries Point The first point of Aries, 0° Aries, the vernal point, or the vernal equinoctial point is, as defined in Chapter 2, where the Sun is at the astronomical beginning of spring, about March 21. It, too, is a form of node: the north node of the ecliptic with respect to the equator. Where the Sun crosses the equatorial plane going north is 0° Aries; the south node is 0° Libra.

As the beginning of the tropical zodiac, 0° Aries has been used since the ancient Greeks and the dawn of modern horoscopic astrology. Whereas in most astrological systems it has been treated only as the beginning of the sign Aries, however, it was given a new role in the 1920s and 1930s in the

Uranian system of Alfred Witte and his followers. According to Uranian usage, 0° Aries represents 0° of all the other cardinal signs (Cancer, Libra, and Capricorn) as well. The reasons for this will become clear in Chapter 8.

I have found the Aries point extremely useful. Although it is not an energy source like a true planet, the Aries point is treated like a planet in that it receives and gives aspects in the normal manner. Most important, it can be the focus of midpoint combinations (see Chapter 8).

According to the Uranian school, the Aries Point, Moon's nodes, and Ascendant represent a hierarchy of relationships. Whereas the Uranians say that the Ascendant-Descendant axis relates to general social interactions, and the lunar nodes to more intimate kinds of meetings, my own experience indicates that the Ascendant-Descendant axis signifies the more intimate contacts. I do agree, however, that the lunar nodes often signify relationships that come about because the individuals feel they have something in common, a feeling that has its roots in lunar symbolism.

Of the three nodal points of relationship, the Aries Point represents the most impersonal but also the widest social contacts: one's relationship to the larger world around one. Hence it is associated with fame and greater social significance. If one ever becomes famous or makes a significant impact on society outside one's circle of friends and associates, it is through symbols that relate to the Aries Point.

Nevertheless, a large number of aspects and/or planetary pictures or midpoint combinations to the Aries Point does not in itself ensure fame. The Aries Point and the points connected to it only tell what energies are available to one by which to make an impact should one ever wish to try. Involvements concerning the Midheaven and the tenth house are much more likely than an active Aries Point to indicate that a person will try to become famous. The reason is that an active Midheaven signifies people who have a strong ideal of significance that they must attain. In this respect, the Midheaven is strongly connected to the father complex of symbols, which includes the Sun, Saturn, Capricorn, the tenth house, and, to some extent, Jupiter. Not only should the Aries Point itself be checked, but also its midpoints with the personal points: the Midheaven, Ascendant, Sun, and Moon.

Body-Type Points

The Asteroids   Between the orbits of Mars and Jupiter lies a belt of thousands of minor bodies which represent either a planet that disintegrated or one that never coalesced. These, the asteroids, were unknown until the nineteenth century, and were not used by astrologers until Eleanor Bach published an asteroid ephemeris in 1973. Following the practice of the *American Ephemeris and Nautical Almanac*, she picked the first four asteroids to be discovered: Ceres (discovered in 1801), Pallas (1802), Juno

(1804), and Vesta (1807). Ceres is the largest asteroid known, but there are others that are larger than any of the other three.

With the asteroids we are in the midst of a potential revolution and a potential disaster. The revolution is the possibility of extending astrological symbolism using real rather than hypothetical bodies. The disaster is that there are thousands of asteroids and other minor bodies orbiting the Sun, and using present-day astrological techniques there is no way of accounting for all of them in a chart. Thus far in astrology it has been held (implicitly, at least) that the size of a body has no relation to its effectiveness. This is most dramatically illustrated in the case of Pluto, which is both small (about the size of Mercury) and extremely distant. All other bodies in the solar system that are used by astrologers are either large or much closer or both. The question with asteroids is: can we afford, practically speaking, to extend downward the size limit of bodies that we use in the chart? The asteroids are very small: all the known ones put together would be smaller than any known major planet. They would not even add up to the total mass of the Moon. If we do consider the asteroids, then logically we have to consider all orbiting bodies of any size whatsoever. Can you imagine the astrologer of the future saying to a client, "You have the Perseid meteors retrograde on your Midheaven"?

There are several ways out of this controversy. The first and easiest would be to ignore the asteroids altogether. But clinical experience with Ceres, Pallas, Juno, and Vesta already suggests that they do have observable qualities, ones that do not repeat the symbolism of the other planets, and which hence add new information to the chart. For this reason I find this the least acceptable solution.

A second route would be to figure out some way of dealing with the asteroids and other small bodies as a group or set of groups. The asteroids, the smaller ones at least, travel in families. Perhaps the resultant of the mass vectors (the average position, in a manner of speaking) could be used to represent a group of asteroids. This would require a change in the present procedure of giving asteroids the same kind of individuality as the major planets.

A third alternative is simply to continue giving the asteroids the individual kind of symbolic treatment already given the first four. In practice, what I see coming is assigning individuality to the larger ones and ignoring the smaller ones. I suspect there will be a de facto limit beyond which we will not go in using smaller bodies.

One way of defending the use of the first four to be discovered (rather than the four largest) is to say that the effect of celestial bodies is in some way related to human consciousness of them rather than to their physical properties. As the first to be discovered they no doubt made a greater impact than the thousands later to be observed.

Here are brief delineations of the four commonly used asteroids.

These descriptions are not intended to be complete; much fuller treatment is given by writers like Eleanor Bach, Zipporah Dobyns, and Emma Belle Donath. The following are a composite of my own findings and those of others. (For the relationship of these asteroids to the signs, see the discussions of Virgo and Libra in Chapter 11.)

Ceres is related to the symbol of the earth mother, as is the Moon. But it seems to relate to nurture on a material, practical level more than a psychological one. It is connected with duty, responsibility, and domestic crafts. I would also associate it with gardening and agriculture.

Pallas, like Ceres, Juno, and Vesta, is a feminine symbol, but a very independent one. It seems to relate to the critical faculty, and to a kind of sharp, incisive mentality that enjoys a good debate. It is fond of making distinctions. Of the four asteroids, its effects are the hardest to discern, possibly because its orbit is by a wide margin the farthest inclined from the ecliptic (34.8°).

Juno is associated with marriage and partnership between the sexes. I find that, especially in women's charts, it often indicates an ambivalence about whether to be associated with someone or to be free. In a man's chart, it often describes the kind of marital partner he will choose.

Vesta's orbit is the least inclined to the ecliptic of the four asteroids (by only 7.13°), and possibly for this reason its qualities show the most clearly of the four. Vesta can be thought of as the planetary equivalent of the sixth house, representing the principle of the denial of short-term gratification in favor of long-range goals. Its nature is ascetic, able to make sacrifices in the name of duty. It seems to be difficult in any matter having to do with sexual expression or other pleasurable activities. It is often connected with celibacy. Some authors feel it has to do with cultural ritual and tradition as well.

Chiron   In 1977 the astronomer Charles Kowal discovered a minor planet between the orbits of Saturn and Uranus and subsequently named it Chiron after the first of the mythical centaurs. It is believed by many to have a connection with consciousness-expanding teachings and with initiation into higher consciousness.

The Fixed Stars   Fixed stars were once used routinely by astrologers. But they have not continued in extensive use, for several reasons. First, their traditional delineations tend to be of the dramatic fortunetelling sort. They usually are malefic and designate various kinds of disasters. For example, Algol on the Midheaven is supposed, among other meanings, to denote death by decapitation. Such fatalistic delineations are not considered respectable in modern astrology, and astrologers have not yet developed alternative ideas on the symbolism of most fixed stars.

Second, most of the fixed stars are way off the ecliptic. It is therefore not clear how one should handle them with regard to aspects along the ecliptic and placement in houses.

Third, there is the same problem as with the asteroids, only more so. There are five or six thousand fixed stars visible to the naked eye, and millions more that are not visible. If we limit ourselves to visible stars, then what do we do with planets that are not visible to the naked eye?

Nevertheless, many astrologers agree that some fixed stars, mostly those near the ecliptic, have observable effects, and take note of them whenever these stars are near an important point in the chart. Usually only conjunctions with fixed stars are used, although sometimes oppositions are used too. Vivian Robson's *Fixed Stars and Constellations in Astrology* is a good summary of the existing lore on the subject, and also makes clear some of the difficulties.

Hypothetical Planets   Many astrologers use points that behave like planets, but which have not yet been observed astronomically. These hypothetical planets include the extra planets of the Uranian school, (Cupido, Hades, Zeus, and Kronos, proposed by Alfred Witte, and Apollon, Admetos, Vulkanus, and Poseidon, proposed by his follower Friedrich Sieggruen); planets advocated by Charles A. Jayne, Jr. (Rex, Sigma, Jason, Isis, Pan, Morya, Hermes, Osiris, Midas, Athena, and Lion); planets advocated by Ivy Goldstein Jacobsen (Lilith and Lulu); and others such as Transpluto, advocated by Theodor Landscheidt and the Ebertin family in Germany, and Vulcan (not to be confused with the Uranian Vulkanus). Some of these points have been derived by psychics, some by mathematical means from perturbations of existing orbits, and some by astrologers noting points of energy that seem to move along the zodiac like planets. There are dozens of these "bodies," and some, I find, especially the eight Uranian planets, seem to work.

Like the asteroids, hypothetical planets threaten to bury the horoscope in an unmanageable complexity of details. And, unlike the asteroids, these planets are only hypothetical. The positions of most of them have been found using unsafe assumptions about the accuracy of astrological techniques, and almost all appear to move in circular rather than elliptical orbits, something done by no known astronomical body. (The exceptions are the four Uranian bodies put forth by Witte.) This means that either these bodies are totally imaginary, or the early "observations" of their orbits only approximated a circle. If the early "observations" are only approximate, ephemerides based on them grow more and more inaccurate as they extend beyond the time the observations were made.

In either case, I do not recommend using hypothetical planets as a basic technical device. I would never suggest that anything in astrology not be investigated, but without further research I would not recommend basing anything seriously upon hypothetical planets.

Planetary Picture-Type Points

All the points discussed below arise from various types of "planetary pictures." That is, they are all based on symmetrical relations between planets or other points such that there are equal openings among pairs of points. Planetary-picture type points can be found either by calculation using the formulas given below or without calculation using the dial techniques given in Chapter 8.

Arabian Parts   Despite their name, Arabian parts date back at least to the Greeks, and they were also used in Renaissance Europe as well as by the Arabs. In the form that most astrologers use them today, they are similar to Uranian planetary pictures, and hence they are included here. Arabian parts have gained some articulate proponents in modern times, though most astrologers today do not use the large number of Arabian parts that have been devised. Many, however, use the Part of Fortune routinely.

The Part of Fortune is found by adding and subtracting the positions of the Sun, Moon, and Ascendant. In the usual modern method of calculating this part, the longitudes (degrees and minutes within a sign) of these points are first converted to 360° notation (see page 155) and then combined thus: Moon + Ascendant − Sun = Part of Fortune. The longitude of the Part of Fortune is then converted from 360° to sign notation and entered in the chart. All the other Arabian parts are formed using the same $A + B - C = D$ formula with other combinations of points. For example, Ascendant + Venus − Sun = Part of Love; Ascendant + Venus − seventh-house cusp = Part of Divorce. The traditional parts include the Sun, Moon, Ascendant, Midheaven, or an intermediate house cusp as at least one of the factors, but it is possible to combine any three horoscope factors in this way, and some modern astrologers have done so.

The method given above is only the simplest of several possible ways of calculating Arabian parts. Wilson's *Dictionary of Astrology* gives several older and more complicated methods for calculating the Part of Fortune using oblique ascensions and right ascensions rather than the celestial longitudes (degrees along the ecliptic) that most of us are accustomed to. At the latitude of, say, New York City, the complicated methods can yield results that differ from the results of the more familiar method by as much as 30°, and there will be an even larger discrepancy at higher terrestrial latitudes. Whether or not any of the more complicated methods of calculating the Part of Fortune and other Arabian parts is more valid than the easier method is a question that needs more research and is beyond the scope of this book.

Whatever coordinate system is used for calculating Arabian parts, using them extensively can create a bewildering array, at the rate of several new points per degree. One runs the danger of being able to devise parts that will prove anything one wishes.

Even if one only uses the Part of Fortune, I am doubtful of its meaning, at least when it is calculated using celestial longitudes. It is said to bestow grace, luck, or favor upon the individual. Being quite lucky, and having my Part of Fortune conjunct Saturn in the twelfth house (a combination that would not normally be considered fortunate), I am understandably skeptical.

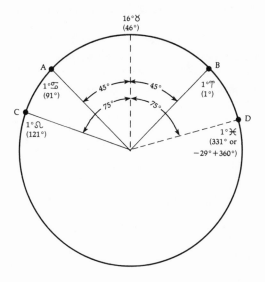

Figure 5. A four-factor planetary picture (Uranian formula A+B−C=D)

Planetary Pictures   Followers of the Uranian school will recognize A + B − C = D as the formula they use for adding and subtracting celestial longitudes to form "planetary pictures." As shown in Figure 5 Cosmobiologists would express this semi-diagrammatically as A/B=D, where the slashes stand for the common axis (16° ♉ − ♍) that these two pairs of planets share. The main difference between planetary pictures and Arabian parts calculated along the ecliptic is that the Uranians have extended the principle systematically to include all points in the chart (but intermediate house cusps are not usually used). This has the potential of producing an array of extra points as great if not greater than the array of Arabian parts. But most Uranian astrologers are aware of this danger and are trying to create a system for arranging these points into a hierarchy so that clear distinctions can be made as to what is and is not significant.

As compared with Arabian parts, Uranian planetary pictures have meanings that follow much more logically from the symbols involved. For example, the same combination that makes up the Part of Fortune,

Ascendant + Sun − Moon, is delineated by the Uranians as close connections with others (Ascendant), the body or physical well-being (Sun), and women (Moon). Put together, this spells close physical relationships with women in one's daily life.

Given ten planets, the Ascendant, Midheaven, and North Node, the number of possible three-factor combinations in a chart is immense. The way I work, I prefer to limit my use of such combinations to midpoints, which are a special case of planetary pictures in which a sensitive point is formed using two other points instead of three. I feel that all points of the form A + B − C = D (in which A, B, and C are all different) are less significant than midpoints, and that therefore they can be safely dispensed with, at least until the hierarchies of significance mentioned above are created and stabilized.

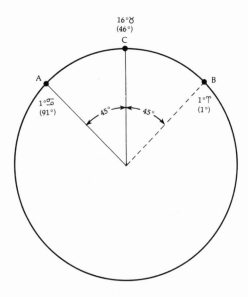

Figure 6. A three-factor planetary picture (Uranian formula C + C − A = B)

There is, however, one other type of planetary picture that may be more significant. Like the planetary pictures discussed above, it involves three factors, but, like midpoints, it has only two *different* factors. This type takes the form C + C − A = B. Using C as the axis, we look at the point on the opposite side of C from A but separated by the same angle. If A is C plus the angle, then the sensitive point, B, is C minus the angle. (See Figure 6.) I have not personally investigated planetary pictures of this type, but others consider them valuable.

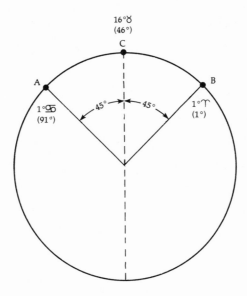

Figure 7. A midpoint (Uranian formula A + B − C = C)

Midpoints Midpoints or half-sums are like the three-factor planetary pictures just mentioned, but this time the sensitive point is in the middle rather than on one side. For midpoints, the formula would be A + B − C = C, where C is the factor in the middle. (See Figure 7.) Cosmobiologists would express this as A/B = C.

Using thirteen factors, the number of possible midpoints is less than a hundred, and there are rules for distinguishing their relative importance (see page 168) so that one is not buried in detail. I find that midpoints add new information to a chart, and I use them routinely. The rationale for them, how to use them, and how to delineate them are therefore treated at length in Chapters 8 and 9.

Antiscia or Solstice Points Used by the Arabs in the Middle Ages, antiscia have in modern times been resurrected by two independent movements: the Uranian astrologers, who call them antiscia, and more traditional astrologers, who call them solstice points, which is a good way of describing what they are.

An antiscion is another example of the type of planetary picture described above, in which two factors create a third sensitive point that is not a midpoint. But here the first of the two factors is always either 0° Cancer or 0° Capricorn, which are the summer and winter solstices. Therefore all antiscia have the form A + B − 0°Cancer = 0° (of course, 0°

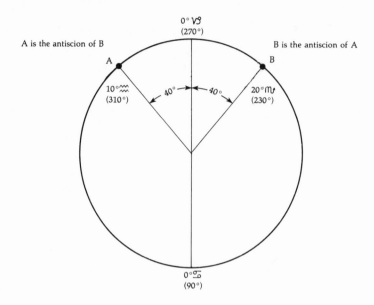

Figure 8. Antiscia

Capricorn may be substituted for 0° Cancer). In other words, 0° Cancer-Capricorn is the midpoint between any point and its antiscion. (See Figure 8, overleaf.) Like the midpoints, antiscia have the formula A+B−C =C, expressed as 270+270−A=B, 270+270−B=A, or A+B−270=270. Antiscia closer to 0° ♋ have the formulas 90+90−A=B, etc.

To calculate an antiscion, first convert all longitudes in the formula to 360° notation as explained on page 155. Thus 0° Cancer will become 90° and 0° Capricorn will become 270°. Then, given a planet or angle at $y°$ (in 360° notation), its antiscion will be at 90° + 90° − $y°$, or at 270° + 270° − $y°$. You can then convert from 360° notation back to sign notation to enter the antiscion on the chart.

According to the users of these points, the meaning of an antiscion is the same as that of the planet itself. But this is not entirely logical. As stated above, the midpoint between any point and its antiscion is 0° Cancer-Capricorn, and this, of course, is in square to the 0° Aries point mentioned above. As will be explained in Chapter 8, points that are in square or opposition aspect to each other are in Uranian astrology and Cosmobiology treated as virtually the same point. From this it follows that antiscia are in fact nothing more than part of that set of planetary pictures that includes the Aries point. Thus, antiscia include not only the symbolism of the planet or angle involved, but also the symbolism of the Aries point, and they should be delineated accordingly.

Transiting planets can make aspects to the antiscion of any body.

This may seem strange until you realize that the transiting factor on or in aspect to the antiscion is merely forming a midpoint on the Aries axis with the planet whose antiscion is involved. Although I do not use such transits, there is abundant evidence that they can be significant. I suspect, however, that such transits are less important than direct transits to natal factors.

I have not used antiscia extensively except in the form of midpoints involving the Aries axis. I do not use them because I believe it is not desirable to add more points to the chart unless they give information unavailable otherwise. If they merely duplicate, they should be dispensed with.

ANGULAR RELATIONSHIPS

6

The Aspects:
Introduction

Aspects were introduced briefly in Chapter 2 as significant angular relationships among the planets, signs, and houses. Their most important use is with respect to the planets and other points such as the Ascendant, Midheaven, and midpoints. Aspects among these symbols link energies to energies, and to areas for energies to manifest, enabling the symbols to operate in pairs or even groups. But aspects do not merely link planetary energies and other points: they link them in ways that are peculiar to the number of degrees involved in the aspect. For example, points joined by a 90° angle do not interact the same as when joined by a 120° angle.

All the angles used as aspects are derived by dividing the 360° circle by small whole numbers. Thus, $360°/1 = 360°$ (conjunction), $360°/2 = /180°$ (opposition), $360°/3 = 120°$ (trine), $360°/4 = 90°$ (square), and so forth. A progression such as this is called a harmonic series, the general form of which is as follows: $N/1, N/2, N/3, N/4, N/5, \ldots N/I$, $N/(I+1), \ldots$, where I is a series of integers or whole numbers from one to infinity. N can have any value, but in astrology it is usually 360°.

In the past, astrology has only used angles derived from division of the circle by one, two, three, four, and six. These are the aspects used by the Greeks: the conjunction, opposition, trine, square, and sextile. They are often referred to as the "classical" or "Ptolemaic" aspects, after Claudius Ptolemy (2nd century A.D.), the most influential Greek authority on astrology and astronomy.

In the Renaissance, astrologers perceived that the harmonic series is the basis of the aspects, and began experimenting with dividing the circle by five, seven, eight, and twelve. Dividing the circle by five yields the quintile $(360°/5 = 72°)$ and the biquintile $(2 \times 360°/5 = 144°)$. Seven yields the septile $(360°/7 = 51°25'42.9'')$, the biseptile $(2 \times 360°/7 = 102°51'25.7'')$, and the triseptile $(3 \times 360°/7 = 154°17'08.6'')$. Division by eight yields the semisquare or octile $(360°/8 = 45°)$ and the sesquiquadrate or trioctile $(3 \times 360°/8 = 135°)$. Division by nine, ten, and eleven were omitted, but division by twelve was introduced, because twelve is the basis of the signs of the zodiac. This gave us the semisextile ($360°/12 = 30°$) and the quincunx ($5 \times 360°/12 = 150°$).

Among the astrologers who were active in this expansion of the Greek theory of aspects were Johannes Kepler (1571–1630), known for his contributions to astronomy, and Morinus (1583–1656), the last of the great French astrologers of the Renaissanace. But division by seven never caught on well, and division by five fared little better. It is only in modern times that astrologers are beginning to look at these seriously, along with a number of other divisions.

In our own century, John Addey and his followers have been the most responsible for reintroducing the idea of aspects as harmonics and for reviving interest in dividing the circle by five, seven, and other numbers. Their research has pointed to a link between aspect symbolism and number symbolism, the idea being that aspect symbolism originates in the number by which the circle is divided. The number symbolism employed is that of the ancient Pythagoreans and the medieval Kabbalists, not of modern numerology. Table 1 summarizes number meanings derived from Addey's writings and my own work.

Table 1
Number Symbolism

One: Complete union, without the faculty of self-reflection.

Two: Polarity, complementarity, and conflict; also consciousness, which arises from self-reflection.

Three: Balance, equilibrium, stability.

Four: Resistance, matter. Two times two.

Five: The number of humanity, signifying its strengths and powers and its creative and destructive potential.

Six: Two times three. Polarity plus equilibrium; activity needed to realize a balance.

Seven: Otherworldliness, influences from beyond.

Eight: Two times four. Polarity plus resistance.

Nine: Three times three. End products, completion, the end of a cycle.

Multiplying a number by two, four, etc., produces octaves of that number, just as in music octaves are produced by multiplying sound frequencies by two, four, etc. Generally speaking, the resulting number has symbolism similar to the number that was doubled or quadrupled, but also acquires the symbolism of the number two or four. Multiplying a number by three, five, seven, etc., changes the symbolism of the original number even more than does multiplying by two. See page 154.

Interpreting aspects as harmonics suggests that astrological phenomena may be linked to the waves studied by physicists. Cycles of the planets are mathematically identical to waves of light, sound, the ocean, or a pendulum, which differ from astrological cycles mainly in that they are faster. In nature, whenever a wave effect occurs, it is accompanied by other waves that are half as long, one-third as long, one-fourth as long, and so forth. These are harmonics of the original, principal wave. If we look at the cycles of the planets, we find the cycles of position that every pair of planets goes through from conjunction to conjunction. Roughly half-way in time between conjunctions, the two planets are in opposition; one-third of the way, they are in trine; one-fourth of the way, they are in square; and so forth. This suggests that there is some kind of relation between waves and their harmonics on the one hand and planetary cycles and their aspects on the other. The results of this study may bring astrology directly in line with studies of other natural phenomena.

Families of Aspects

With the exception of the conjunction, all the commonly used aspects can be classified according to whether they are based on multiples of two or of three. This is because, as indicated in Table 1, aspects based on numbers multiplied by two have qualities that involve the symbolism of two, whereas aspects based on multiples of three have qualities that involve the symbolism of three.

The family of aspects based on division of the circle by two includes the opposition (1/2), square (1/[2 × 2] or 1/4), semisquare (1/[2 × 2 × 2] or 1/8) and sesquiquadrate (3/8), as well as all multiples of 22.5° (1/[2 × 2 × 2 × 2] or 1/16). These I call the "two-series" or "hard" aspects, because of the qualities they have in common.

The family of aspects based on division of the circle by three includes the trine (1/3), sextile (1/[3 × 2] or 1/6), semisextile (1/[3 × 2 × 2] or 1/12), and quincunx (5/12). These I call the "three-series" or "soft" aspects.

The conjunction is in a class by itself, because it could be in the two-series, three-series, or any series of aspects. That it contains the symbolism of all other aspects can be seen as follows: if the conjunction represents (1/1) × 360, it also represents (2/2) × 360, (3/3) × 360, (4/4) × 360, (5/5) × 360, and so forth.

The other aspects were rarely used until recently, apparently because astrologers were not in tune with the symbolism of numbers other than one, two, three, four, six, eight, and twelve. Classifying all aspects as "good" or "bad" makes it difficult to recognize symbolism that is neither. Also, the usual practice of writing planetary positions in terms of their sign position (for example, 23° ♊ 45′) makes it easy to recognize aspects that are divisible by 30°, and difficult to recognize all others. Most astrological analysis is still carried out with the conjunction and the two- and three-series alone, and it will be some time before astrologers are as conversant with other families of aspects as they are with these. Therefore, in the next chapter we will discuss the conjunction, two-series, and three-series in detail before moving on to the five-series, seven-series, and nine-series.

Orbs of Aspects

Planets that are in an exact aspect of any type are very strongly linked, and can be counted on to act together when one of them is triggered by transit or progression. But they do not suddenly lose their linkage the moment they go a little bit out of exactitude. The extent to which an aspect can be out of exactitude and still have an effect is called the "orb" of the aspect. An orb is measured as the number of degrees you are willing to allow both before and after the exact aspect in the zodiac. Thus, if you use an orb of 5°, you are considering a planet to be in aspect if it is within a 10° range centering on the point where the aspect would be exact.

Like many other matters in astrology, orbs have been the subject of much controversy because until recently astrologers have had no means of testing them rigorously. Now, however, with the advent of computers able to handle the vast numbers of charts that need to be analyzed in statistical testing, we are able to begin such tests. We are still in a rather primitive state with regard to this issue, because most astrologers lack the background to construct such tests correctly, but there are some preliminary results that can be reported.

First of all, some old ideas are clearly wrong. One of these is a tendency among some astrologers to treat orbs like on-off switches, such that as soon as a planet comes within orb of another planet, the aspect turns on suddenly to full strength, and turns off just as abruptly when the faster planet moves out of orb on the other side. Put in this bald-faced way, I doubt that many astrologers would take this idea seriously, but in practice this is the way many use orbs in their work. They do this whenever they use an aspect that is far out of orb to explain a strong effect in the chart that they cannot otherwise account for. At such times, astrologers simply extend the orb out to that point and then treat the aspect as if it were in full force. But other factors can usually be adduced to explain such phenomena when they occur, as I will demonstrate further on.

It is clear both from clinical experience and research that orbs do not work this way. As a planet approaches the point of aspecting another, the linking effect gradually turns on and reaches a maximum when the aspect is exact or nearly so. Some research indicates that the linking effect peaks slightly before the point of exactitude, whereas work presented by Gary Duncan of California at the 1976 AFA convention indicates that in the case of squares, at least, the point of maximum linkage sometimes occurs after the point of exactness. And work with harmonics suggests that intensity may not decline linearly, but that the linking effect rises and falls at various points as the aspect moves out of orb. I suspect the precise answer depends on the way the question is asked. Fortunately, these seem to be subtleties one can ignore in practical astrological manipulation. Nevertheless, we should stay open to the possibility that anything said here or elsewhere may be invalidated by hard astrological research.

What the question boils down to is not how far out of orb an aspect can be and still have an effect, but rather how subtle a linkage one will accept as significant. The answer depends on what techniques you use. If you put together many small factors (which is the approach taken in this book), orbs should be small, because whatever faint effect the wide-orbed aspects have will be overwhelmed by other kinds of indications, such as those from midpoints. If you use fewer symbolic elements, then each indication has to bear a greater weight in forming the overall evaluation, and the subtle effects of wide-orbed aspects will be more important. Astrology is a language of nature that may be read in different ways by different people. This kind of variability according to the inclinations of the astrologer is one of the elements of astrology that scientists find objectionable, though most psychologists would understand it.

Whether you use few or many symbolic elements determines the overall size range of the orbs you employ, but the orb of any particular aspect depends on several other considerations. Basically, there are two schools of thought about what determines the size of an orb: one emphasizes the size of the aspect, the other, what is being aspected. Most astrologers take both factors into account, but in varying proportions. Some also take into account whether the aspect is applying or separating. Further on, I will outline the rules for orbs that I find work best with my techniques, and I will close this section by discussing some exceptions to the general rules.

Determining the Orb by the Size of the Aspect   There are two approaches to considering the size of the aspect: lumping aspects together into groups, or considering each aspect separately.

Most traditional astrologers simply divide the aspects into major and minor. The major aspects, the conjunction, opposition, trine, square, and sextile, are all given the same, usually large orb, about 10°. Minor aspects, if used, are given varying orbs, commonly about 2°. The 10° orb is mainly a holdover from Renaissance astrology. Modern astrologers tend to cut orbs down to 7° or 8°, and a growing number now use even smaller orbs, 5° or less on the major aspects, 1° or less on the minors. I am basically of this last school, for reasons I will discuss further on.

Regardless of the maximum size of the orb employed, there is a problem with the above approach. Why should all the major aspects be lumped together and given the same orb? A sextile is only one-sixth of the circle. Should it not have one-sixth the orb of a conjunction? (For this discussion the conjunction should be regarded as an aspect of 360°, not 0°.)

This problem is dealt with in Addey's harmonic theory of aspects, mentioned earlier. According to Addey's ideas, the size of an orb should be directly proportional to the harmonic on which the aspect is based. Thus, if the conjunction received a 10° orb, then an opposition (second harmonic) would receive a 5° orb, a square (fourth harmonic) a 2.5° orb, a trine (third harmonic) a 3.33° orb, and so on. Both the semisextile and the quincunx, being based on one-twelfth of the circle, would receive a 0.83° orb, and the semisquare and sesquiquadrate, being based on one-eighth of the circle, an orb of 1.25°.

This is a plausible idea, but it does not seem to accord with astrologers' experiences. I am not saying it is incorrect, but some sort of compelling research would have to demonstrate it before I would be willing to accept it. In my judgment it makes the conjunction orb too large and the square, trine, semisextile, and quincunx orbs too small.

Determining the Orb by the Factors Involved   There are two basic variations on this theme. Many authors advocate what is basically an orb-according-to-aspect method but increase the orbs for aspects involving the Sun and Moon. The difficulty is that most of those who advocate this approach give the Sun and Moon orbs of up to 15° to either side, which is a whole sign! As long as the maximum orb is not too huge, I find the idea defensible, though I do not accept it personally.

A more radical approach has been suggested by Reinhold Ebertin. In his book *Applied Cosmobiology* he divides all aspectable points in the chart into three categories. Personal points (Sun, Moon, Midheaven, and Ascendent) get 5°, fast-moving factors (Mercury, Venus, and Mars) get 4°, and slow-moving factors (Jupiter, Saturn, Uranus, Neptune, Pluto, and the Moon's nodes) get 3° orbs.

Personal points are given the largest orb because of their importance in the chart, and because, with the exception of the Sun, they are the fastest moving factors. The Sun falls into this category only because of its importance (actually Mercury and Venus in the second category can go faster than the Sun). The second group consists of less powerful factors, but being rather fast moving, they move in and out of aspect quickly. The factors in the third group move slowly, staying within close orb of an aspect for a long time. Many people of the same age group will have the same aspects involving two or more of these factors. This makes such aspects less directly personal in their impact.

This manner of classifying aspects is based on the faster-moving of the two factors involved. If either of the two points is in group one, you use the 5° orb. If neither of the points is in group one, but either of them is in group two, you use the 4° orb. Otherwise, you use the 3° orb.

The orbs described refer to the hard or two-series aspects only. All the two-series aspects, including the semisquare and sesquiquadrate, are given the same orb, depending on the factors involved. In other works,

Ebertin gives consistent 5° orbs to all two-series aspects regardless of the points involved, and smaller orbs to the soft or three-series aspects. Clearly, his thinking has undergone several revolutions.

Applying versus Separating Aspects When the faster planet is moving toward the exact aspect but has not yet reached it, the aspect is said to be applying; when the faster planet has already made the exact aspect and is moving away from it, the aspect is said to be separating. Many astrologers use a larger orb for applying aspects than for separating ones.

There is possibly a difference in quality between the two. By progression, the applying aspect will increase in intensity in the years after birth as the faster-moving planet moves toward making the exact aspect. By transiting motion, these aspects usually become exact in the days after birth, which represent a critical time in one's development.* Especially if they are "hard" or two-series aspects, applying aspects will signify energies that are intensifying and moving toward a crisis. When aspects are separating, the crisis is over. I suspect, though I cannot say I have observed this clearly, that applying two-series aspects are more turbulent than separating ones. Possibly because I already use small orbs, however, I do not find that the degree of interaction of the two points is any less when the aspect is separating, and for this reason I do not give separating aspects a smaller orb.

Table 2
Suggested Orbs

Aspect	Orb	Aspect	Orb
Conjunction (0°)	5°	Semisextile (30°)	1.5°
Opposition (180°)	5°	Quincunx (5×30°)	1.5°
Trine (120°)	5°	Quintile (72°)	1.5°
Square (90°)	5°	Biquintile (2×72°)	1.5°
Sextile (60°)	3°	22.5° multiples not	
Semisquare (45°)	1.5°	covered above	0.5°
Sesquiquadrate (3×45°)	1.5°	All others	1° or less

The Orb Rules Used in This Book In general, I subscribe to the school that decreases the orb according to the size of the harmonic on which the aspect is based. I give the same orb to the conjunction, opposition, trine, and square because I cannot accept the idea that the conjunction should have four times the orb of a square, but I give a smaller orb to the sextile as

---

*Naturally, the planets go on moving after birth. When they move into aspect with the natal planets, they are said to transit them. Progressions are like transits, except that a day of transiting motion is taken to symbolize a year of life. Thus the transiting aspects on the thirtieth day after birth would if used as transits signify trends in the thirtieth day of life, and if used as progressions would signify trends in the thirtieth year of life

well as to the clearly minor aspects. The orbs in Table 2 seem to work well with the techniques outlined in this book. Using midpoints and some of the smaller aspects as I do, I find that orbs much larger than this detract from the clarity of the astrological picture that emerges from the chart.

I arrived at the 5° orb for major aspects more or less by intuition, possibly because I have always used dials to measure aspects (see Chapter 8), and orbs larger than 5° make the aspects look rather strange. But more recently, work by Geoffrey Dean of Australia has confirmed the 5° orb. Using a questionnaire in which people with various orbs were asked whether they could identify trait descriptions of aspects in themselves, he queried a fairly large sample and found that most of the effects that one would associate with a given major aspect disappeared when the aspect was more than 5° from exact. * Other authors report similar findings. Whatever orb you settle on, I think it safe to say that a very close aspect will show a stronger effect than one near the edge of orb.

The orbs suggested in Table 2 are only intended as guidelines. There are several cases in which they can be safely stretched.

Exception 1: When There Are Few Tight Orbs in the Chart. Geoffrey Dean also observes (and is reinforced by my friend and colleague, Nancy MacPhee) that the other aspects in the chart and their orbs are important in considering the orb of any one aspect. If there are a number of close-orbed aspects and several that are not close orbed, the close-orbed aspects will wipe out the effects of the wider-orbed ones. It is as if each aspect makes a noise that contributes to the overall sound of the chart. When the loud noises drown out the quiet tones, the quiet tones can be ignored. But if the chart does not have many loud noises, the quiet tones will be more important. Thus, when there are few close-orbed aspects in the chart, I recommend going beyond the 5° limit for the major aspects.

In this respect one should be careful not to overlook some of the not-so-minor minor aspects, notably the semisquare, sesquiquadrate, semisextile, and quincunx. One of these having a tight orb of less than 1° would outweigh by a considerable margin a square with a 6° orb. I also suspect that this is true of a quintile or biquintile, but I do not feel secure enough about the symbolism of these aspects to say for certain. Aside from the quintile and biquintile, then, these minor aspects are not really minor at all, but simply require smaller orbs.

Exception 2: When the Aspect Involves a Harmonic Syndrome. In the case of a grand trine, grand square, T-square, or other pattern in which several aspects are linked by the same family of aspects or harmonics, one can also allow a larger orb. Unfortunately, there are no hard-and-fast rules as to how much larger, but almost all astrologers agree on this. For

---

*Geoffrey Dean, et al., *Recent Advances in Natal Astrology* (Subiaco, W. Australia: Analogic, 1977), page 367.

example, if you usually allow a 5° orb to a square, then in a grand square, in which there are four planets, each about 90° apart in the zodiac, you can allow a larger orb.

This is particularly true if the average of all the orbs in the aspect complex is near 0°. To find the average of the orbs, you add up the number of degrees and minutes by which each aspect is out, assigning plus values to separating aspects and minus values to applying aspects. Dividing the total by the number of aspects involved gives the average of the orbs.

As I said, out-of-orb aspects do not lose all effect, they just get subtle to the point that they are not worth considering. But in the case of aspect complexes linking several planets by the same harmonic, the effect of all the aspects is cumulative, and the subtle effects of wide-orbed aspects get boosted back to the point where they become significant again. The reason for this is apparent in harmonic theory: if aspects represent waves, then several waves peaking at the same points will reinforce each other.

Exception 3: When an Aspect Is Part of a Midpoint Configuration. When two planets are in aspect and another planet exactly (within a degree or so) bisects the arc between them, the linkage between the pair of planets is intensified. If the two planets are in an angle that would ordinarily be considered out of orb of an aspect, the effect of another planet at their midpoint can be enough to make the aspect strong enough to be noticed. A planet in hard aspect to the midpoint rather than actually on the midpoint can also cause this effect. The whole question of midpoints is discussed at length in Chapter 8.

Orbs or Higher Harmonics?   Though we do not yet know quite what to do with it in practical work, recent research into harmonics has raised another consideration about orbs. The work of John Addey and others makes it appear that wide-orbed aspects differ qualitatively as well as quantitatively from close-orbed aspects. Thus a square of 96° may have a nature quite different from a square of exactly 90°, because whereas 90° is based on the fourth harmonic, 96° is based on the fifteenth harmonic ($4 \times 360°/15 = 96°$). Much research remains to be done, however, before we can use this in practical chart delineation.

Parallels and Contraparallels

Parallels are considered by most authorities to have a quality similar to a conjunction, and contraparallels a quality similar to an opposition. Unlike the aspects just discussed, however, they are not measured along the ecliptic. Instead, they are measured in terms of angles above or below the equator, the plane of the Earth's daily rotation.

For this and other reasons, they are often neglected by modern astrologers. I used to not pay much attention to them, more through inertia than through testing them and finding them lacking, but I have now begun to watch them, and they do seem to act like major aspects.

Parallels are aspects in declination. The declination is the number of degrees a body is north (+) or south (−) of the equator. The ecliptic, or Sun's apparent path through the sky, is tilted to the equator by 23°26′, and therefore the Sun can have a declination of from +23°26′ to −23°26′. Because the other bodies have orbits not quite in the plane of the ecliptic, they can have declinations of up to about plus or minus 26°.

Simply put, two bodies are in parallel if their declinations are the same, and in contraparallel if they are in opposite declinations. For example, two bodies are in parallel if they both have declinations of +10°, and they are in contraparallel when one has a declination of +10° and the other of −10°.

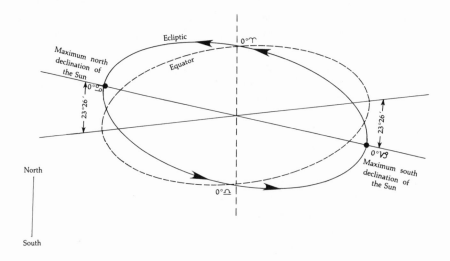

Figure 9. The Declination cycle of the Sun

Why Use Declinations?   One might well ask, if one is concerned with vertical as well as horizontal angles, why not measure them in celestial latitude, the vertical dimension that is at right angles to the ecliptic, rather than in declination, which is at right angles to the equator. Why measure horizontally with reference to one plane, and vertically with reference to another? The answer is that the parallel and contraparallel are in fact related to the signs of the zodiac, but not in an immediately obvious way.

We are used to thinking of the signs as simply divisions of longitude along the ecliptic, but their basis is actually in declination. The signs begin at 0° Aries, which, if you will remember from Chapters 2 and 5, is one of the two points where the plane of the ecliptic crosses the plane of the equator. This means that the Sun has 0° declination when it is at 0° Aries. This is the vernal equinox, when the Sun spends an equal time above the horizon as below it, or, in other words, day and night are equal in length. The other point at which the Sun has 0° declination is 0° Libra, the autumnal equinox, or second point in the Sun's yearly travel where the ecliptic crosses the equator and day equals night. But whereas in Aries the Sun was increasing in declination and the days were getting longer, in Libra the Sun is decreasing in declination and the days are getting shorter.

The Sun reaches its extremes of declination at 0° Cancer and 0° Capricorn. At 0° Cancer it is 23°26′ north of the equator, which means that in the Northern Hemisphere the Sun spends its maximum time above the horizon and the day reaches its maximum length. At 0° Capricorn the Sun is 23°26′ south of the equator, resulting in the Northern Hemisphere's shortest day of the year. See Figure 9.

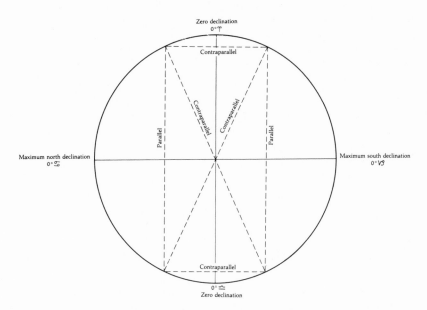

Figure 10. Parallels and contraparallels

The twelve signs can be seen as subdivisions of the angles between these means and extremes of declination. While none of the orbital planes of the other planets crosses the equator at precisely 0° Aries, all cross the equator close enough to 0° Aries to give the signs of the zodiac an approximate relation to the declinations of these bodies. Thus, if two bodies are in the same sign of the zodiac, they will also have approximately the same declination and be roughly in parallel. The "day," or time spent above the horizon by the two bodies, will be about the same length, and if two bodies are in opposite signs, they will have opposite declinations and be roughly in contraparallel. The day of one will be about the same length as the night of the other. In other words, the day-to-night ratio of the two bodies will be reversed. We can see from this that there is in fact a connection between parallels and conjunctions on the one hand and between contraparallels and oppositions on the other.

Declinations and Antiscia   But unlike bodies in conjunction or opposition, bodies in parallel or contraparallel do not have to be in the same or opposite signs. There are not one, but two places where a body can be in parallel or contraparallel to another.

For the sake of simplicity, let us again consider the plane of the ecliptic, which has 0° declination at 0° Aries, reaches its maximum declination at 0° Cancer, and has 0° declination again at 0° Libra. This means that at equal distances on either side of 0° Cancer, this plane has equal declinations. The same is true for the other solstice, 0° Capricorn. Thus two planets will be in parallel not only when they are at about the same point in the zodiac, they will also be in parallel if one of them is about the same number of degrees on the other side of 0° Cancer or 0° Capricorn. In other words, they will be in parallel if one planet is near the antiscion or solstice point of the other (see Chapter 5 for a fuller discussion of antiscia). And two planets will be in contraparallel not only when one of them is near an opposition to the other, but also when one of them is near the antiscion of the opposition. See Figure 10.

Looked at another way, two planets can be in contraparallel when they are both the same distance from the equinoxes, 0° Aries or 0° Libra. This is why the Hamburg school considers antiscia to be not only points equidistant on either side of the solstices, but also points equidistant on either side of the equinoxes. Another look at Figure 10 will make this clearer.

Antiscia are thus clearly connected to parallels and contraparallels, but the correspondence is exact only when both of the bodies involved are in the plane of the ecliptic. This, of course, is not usually the case. Most of the time, one or both bodies (unless they are the Sun) will not be exactly on the ecliptic. That is, they will have a celestial latitude other than 0°. When two bodies have latitudes of other than 0°, and are on opposite sides of the solstices or equinoxes, they will not necessarily have their midpoint at exactly 0° Cancer, Capricorn, Aries, or Libra. For this reason, we cannot assume that bodies in each other's antiscia will always (or even usually) be in an exact parallel or contraparallel.

This is not to say that antiscia and contra-antiscia are worthless.

They consist of planets forming midpoints to the solstices and equinoxes, which, as indicated in Chapters 5 and 9, seem to be important sensitive points.

Orbs in Parallels What orb to use when judging whether two bodies are in parallel or contraparallel presents a thorny question. As mentioned earlier, the range of possible declinations is only about plus or minus 26° from the equator, whereas the range of the zodiac is 360°. This implies immediately that the orb of a parallel or contraparallel should be kept relatively small, certainly no more than a degree or so.

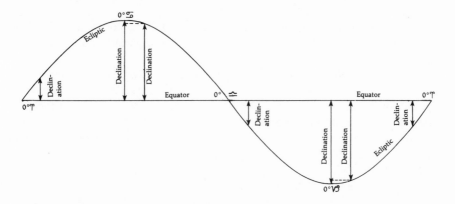

Figure 11. The Rate of Change of Declination

There is a problem, however in examining Figure 11, you will discover that as longitude changes near the solstices, declination changes slowly, whereas near the equinoxes, declination changes rapidly. This means that a body is more likely to have a high declination than a declination near 0°. If you use the same orb in all cases, bodies near the solstices will have a much greater probability of being in parallel or contraparallel than bodies near the equinoxes.

Because of this fact, one authority on parallels, Charles Jayne, recommends changing the orb of a parallel according to its longitude. I am inclined to agree, at least in principle. His method for determining what orb to give a parallel or contraparallel is as follows:

1. Decide what orb you would use for a zodiacal conjunction or opposition.

2. Take the declination of the first body that you wish to check and, using any year of an ephemeris that lists the Sun's declination as well as its longitude, find what longitude the Sun would have at that declination.

3. Do the same for the other body.

4. If the two bodies have the same longitude equivalent within your established orb (or opposite longitude equivalents in the case of a contraparallel), then you have a parallel (or contraparallel) within orb.

Remember that for any given declination the Sun will have two longitudes, one on either side of the solstice axis. For this test, use the two longitude equivalents that are on the same side of the solstice. For contraparallels, check both longitude equivalents of each body's declination to see if either member of each pair is in opposition to either of the others.

This is admittedly a time-consuming procedure. Using Table 3 instead of an ephemeris will save a good deal of page-turning. Here are some examples of how this table is used.

Example 1. Body A has a declination of +22°00′, and body B a declination of +22°42′. The orb we use for conjunctions is 5°. Are these bodies in parallel?

In the table we locate the first declination, +22°00′, in the left-hand column. Since it is a north declination, we look for its longitude equivalent in one of the columns headed "North Declinations (+)." We then look in the left-hand column for the second declination, +22°42′, and find its L.E. in the column in which we found the first L.E. It does not matter which column under "North Declinations" we use, so long as we use the same column for both L.E.'s. This is because all the longitudes in one column will be on the same side of the solstice.

For a declination of +22°00′ we find a L.E. of 10° ♊ 23′, and for a declination of +22°42′, we find a L.E. of 16° ♊ 01′. If one allows a 5° orb for a conjunction, this is not a parallel because the L.E.'s are more than 5° apart.

Example 2. Body A has a declination of +10°00′, and body B a declination of +11°00′. The L.E. of +10°00′ is 25° ♈ 53′, while that of +11°00′ is 28° ♈ 40′. These are well within the 5° orb, and therefore would be in parallel by almost any standard.

The declinations in Example 1 were only 42′ apart and yet the L.E.'s were 5°38′ apart, whereas in Example 2 the declinations were a full degree apart but the L.E.'s were only 2°47′ apart. This illustrates how the declination changes more rapidly as the longitude approaches the equinoxes.

Example 3. Body A has declination of +23°12′ and body B a declination of −22°48′. Given an orb of 5° for an opposition, are these two bodies in contraparallel?

In the columns under "North Declinations" we look up both L.E.'s of +23°12′ and get 22° ♊ 08′ and 7° ♋ 52′. Then in the columns under "South Declinations" we look up both L.E.'s of −22°48′ and get 17° ♐ 01′ and 12° ♑ 59′. As these pairs of L.E.'s are a little more than 5° of being in exact opposition to one another, bodies A and B are not in contraparallel.

Table 3
Solar Longitudes Equivalent to Given Declinations

Declination	Solar Longitudes Equivalent to:			
	North Declinations (+)		South Declinations (−)	
0°00'	0°♈00'	0°≏00'	0°≏00'	0°♈00'
1°00'	2°♈31'	27°♍29'	2°≏31'	27°♓29'
2°00'	5°♈02'	24°♍58'	5°≏02'	24°♓58'
3°00'	7°♈34'	22°♍26'	7°≏34'	22°♓26'
4°00'	10°♈06'	19°♍54'	10°≏06'	19°♓54'
5°00'	12°♈40'	17°♍20'	12°≏40'	17°♓20'
6°00'	15°♈14'	14°♍46'	15°≏14'	14°♓46'
7°00'	17°♈51'	12°♍09'	17°≏51'	12°♓09'
8°00'	20°♈29'	9°♍31'	20°≏29'	9°♓31'
9°00'	23°♈10'	6°♍50'	23°≏10'	6°♓50'
10°00'	25°♈53'	4°♍07'	25°≏53'	4°♓07'
11°00'	28°♈40'	1°♍20'	28°≏40'	1°♓20'
12°00'	1°♉31'	28°♌29'	1°♏31'	28°♒29'
13°00'	4°♉27'	25°♌33'	4°♏27'	25°♒33'
14°00'	7°♉28'	22°♌32'	7°♏28'	22°♒32'
15°00'	10°♉36'	19°♌24'	10°♏36'	19°♒24'
16°00'	13°♉53'	16°♌07'	13°♏53'	16°♒07'
17°00'	17°♉19'	12°♌41'	17°♏19'	12°♒41'
18°00'	20°♉59'	9°♌01'	20°♏59'	9°♒01'
19°00'	24°♉57'	5°♌03'	24°♏57'	5°♒03'
20°00'	29°♉19'	0°♌41'	29°♏19'	0°♒41'
21°00'	4°♓19'	25°♋41'	4°♐19'	25°♑41'
21°06'	4°♓51'	25°♋09'	4°♐51'	25°♑09'
21°12'	5°♓25'	24°♋35'	5°♐25'	24°♑35'
21°18'	5°♓59'	24°♋01'	5°♐59'	24°♑01'
21°24'	6°♓34'	23°♋26'	6°♐34'	23°♑26'
21°30'	7°♓10'	22°♋50'	7°♐10'	22°♑50'
21°36'	7°♓46'	22°♋14'	7°♐46'	22°♑14'
21°42'	8°♓24'	21°♋36'	8°♐24'	21°♑36'
21°48'	9°♓02'	20°♋58'	9°♐02'	20°♑58'
21°54'	9°♓42'	20°♋18'	9°♐42'	20°♑18'
22°00'	10°♓23'	19°♋37'	10°♐23'	19°♑37'
22°06'	11°♓06'	18°♋54'	11°♐06'	18°♑54'
22°12'	11°♓50'	18°♋10'	11°♐50'	18°♑10'
22°18'	12°♓35'	17°♋25'	12°♐35'	17°♑25'
22°24'	13°♓23'	16°♋37'	13°♐23'	16°♑37'
22°30'	14°♓13'	15°♋47'	14°♐13'	15°♑47'
22°36'	15°♓06'	14°♋54'	15°♐06'	14°♑54'
22°42'	16°♓01'	13°♋59'	16°♐01'	13°♑59'
22°48'	17°♓01'	12°♋59'	17°♐01'	12°♑59'
22°54'	18°♓06'	11°♋54'	18°♐06'	11°♑54'
23°00'	19°♓16'	10°♋44'	19°♐16'	10°♑44'
23°06'	20°♓36'	9°♋24'	20°♐36'	9°♑24'
23°12'	22°♓08'	7°♋52'	22°♐08'	7°♑52'
23°18'	24°♓04'	5°♋56'	24°♐04'	5°♑56'
23°24'	27°♓02'	2°♋58'	27°♐02'	2°♑58'
23°26'	0°♋00'	0°♋00'	0°♑00'	0°♑00'

Whether you use an ephemeris or this table, there is still a serious difficulty with solar longitude equivalents. Most bodies other than the Sun are capable of exceeding the Sun's limit of plus or minus 23°26' of declination. Using this method it is impossible to find the L.E. of a declination such as +24° because the Sun never reaches that declination.

The simplest solution is to treat such declinations as if they were in fact 23°26'. The only problem is that it is theoretically possible for both bodies to be above the upper limit (or below the lower limit) and still be over a degree apart in declination. They would pass the test, but by no means be in parallel or contraparallel.

As a cure for this, I suggest the following. Scan the ephemeris to see how many degrees of longitude either body would have to travel to reach the other's declination (or opposite declination, in the case of a contraparallel). If that change in longitude is within orb of conjunction (or opposition), consider the two bodies in parallel (or contraparallel). Fortunately, having both bodies with a declination of more than 23°26' is rare; Table 3 will usually suffice.

7

The Aspects:
Core Meanings

In the first section of this chapter, I will discuss the symbolism of three families of aspects: the conjunction, two-series, and three-series, which together include all the aspects in common use today. Then I will put forward some tentative meanings for the less-used series such as those that divide the circle by five, seven, and nine.

In the second section I take up the special properties of aspect patterns like the grand cross, T-square, and grand trine. These consist of several aspects from the same family linked together so that the aspects reinforce each other. I discuss these patterns separately here because there is a synergistic effect, such that the effect of the whole complex is not quite what you would expect from simply adding together the aspects involved.

In discussing the families of aspects, I begin with the conjunction, which is both a category by itself and an implicit part of all the other categories of aspects.

Table 4
Planetary Compatibilities

	☉	☽	☿	♀	♂	♃	♄	♅	♆	♇
☽	N	☽								
☿	E	N	☿							
♀	E	E	E	♀						
♂	N	D	N	N	♂					
♃	E	E	E	E	E	♃				
♄	D	D	N	D	D	N	♄			
♅	N	D	E	D	D	N	N	♅		
♆	N	N	D	N	D	N	D	N	♆	
♇	N	N	N	N	N	N	D	N	N	♇

E = usually easy
N = neutral; the combination may go either way
D = usually difficult

The Conjunction

The conjunction is the easiest aspect to understand, because it is simply the union of two planetary energies. The aspect itself introduces almost no coloring of its own, with one notable exception discussed below.

The main consideration when delineating a conjunction is whether or not the two planets so combined are compatible. Table 4, "Planetary Compatibilities," shows how likely a given conjunction is to work out constructively. (It is also of some use with other aspects, even though they complicate the picture by introducing qualities of their own.) Although any combination of planets can be made into a source of strength, obviously some planetary energies are more compatible than others; those that are less so are more likely to be sources of difficulty in a person's life. It is possible, however, to make positive qualities out of difficult combinations, or make the worst out of usually good ones.

The one distinctive quality of the conjunction is that it is often difficult for the person whose chart has this aspect to be clear about its effects. Usually the conjunction colors the personality so completely that it is hard for the native to get perspective on this aspect. Though the effects of a conjunction may not be apparent to the native, they are obvious to others.

The conjunction has a dynamic quality. It tends to signify patterns of action rather than passive states of being: that is, its effects usually consist of events or changes in a person's life. These are not necessarily events in the physical world; they may be psychological. The conjunction shares this eventful quality with the hard aspects of the two-series.

The Two-Series or "Hard" Aspects

Two-series aspects are dynamic like the conjunction, only more so. They usually represent an instability within the personality that must be worked on if it is to come out positively. One cannot sit still on top of hard-aspect energies: they demand action and change. Because they often manifest in events, hard aspects are easier to understand than the less eventful three-series aspects.

A particularly good metaphor for the effects of two-series versus three-series aspects has been put forth by Mario Jones, M.D., of Cleveland, Ohio. His research in medical astrology suggests that two-series aspects are no more apt to signify illness than three-series aspects, but they indicate different kinds of disorders. According to Jones, two-series aspects coincide with the onset of acute illness, which arises suddenly at a definite point in time and has a clearly defined critical phase. Three-series aspects coincide with chronic illness, which arises slowly and persists over long periods with no definite crisis. This fits with the psychological correlates of these aspects, in which two-series aspects indicate events that come at a particular point in time, have a clearly defined crisis, and then depart, while three-series aspects indicate ongoing states of being.

Traditionally, two-series aspects have been considered malefic. Even when hard aspects combined planets that we consider favorable, astrologers of the past treated them as a source of danger. To some extent, modern astrologers go to the other extreme by regarding hard aspects as sources of usually constructive tension that cause the personality to grow. This is true and is in fact a good way of looking at two-series aspects, but it does not recognize their inherently difficult nature under certain circumstances. The truth is, as is so often the case, somewhere between the extremes. Insofar as the two-series aspects represent energy patterns that are unstable and demand change, they produce difficulties whenever the individual either refuses to allow the changes to take place, or is in a situation where the changes cannot readily take place. These aspects are often relentless in their drive toward change and disruption, and it is extremely important for these energies to be given room to express themselves. It is not simply a matter of releasing the energies so that they cannot do harm; if properly released, these energies are the only real means by which any kind of creative change can come about. People whose charts consist mostly of two-series aspects have chosen in this lifetime to take a path of evolution in which the risks as well as the rewards are great. Those who do not have this emphasis, or who have primarily three-series aspects, have chosen a more secure path, one with fewer risks, but also fewer rewards.

Those who have chosen the two-series path and succeeded in it may or may not be significant in the world at large. Nevertheless, they have mastered important psychological and spiritual lessons, and in their presence one has a sense of their power and energy. We often describe such people as "wise."

Those having this kind of chart, but who do not master the energy, however, are often among the worst losers in life and appear to be victims of every conceivable misfortune. Happily, such extreme cases are rare. Interestingly, the charts of the most successful and talented are often similar to those of the most unsuccessful and unproductive: charts with many two-series aspects signify a make-or-break situation.

As with the conjunction, with two-series aspects it makes a difference what planets are linked together. Some combinations are more difficult than others, either because the planets themselves possess energies that are intrinsically in conflict, or because they indicate energy patterns whose manifestation flies in the face of social convention. Certain planetary combinations may be more difficult to handle in some eras than in others. For example, in Victorian times, aspects in a woman's chart that indicated an urgent need for sexual expression would obviously be much more malefic than the same aspects now.

Opposition (180°)   The symbolism of the opposition aspect is very much what one would expect: polarity, strife, conflict, and so on, but also partnership and cooperation, as well as consciousness itself. The opposition can be compared in its effects to the seventh house of the mundane sphere, which derives its meanings from the fact that it is in opposition to the first house.

Whatever energies are linked by the opposition, they are combined in such a way that they produce instability and change through conflict. If one examines the conflict, it is seen to arise between an aspect of oneself that has been projected outward and an aspect of oneself that is experienced inwardly. Put more concretely, the opposition signifies a conflict between an external factor and an internal one, and the external factor is the result of an inward energy that one does not as yet understand to be within the self.

For example, many who have the Sun in opposition to Uranus continually encounter others who create disruptions in their lives. It is easy for them to see themselves as victims of these other disruptive people, but on a closer look one can usually discern how the first party creates the inevitability of the confrontation with the second. The confrontation is brought about by an aspect of the self that has not been given adequate expression, and is now struggling to break free through the assistance of another person. Some people with this aspect will work in the reverse manner and try to revolutionize the lives of others by confronting them.

It should be clear, especially in the case of the individual who finds others disruptive, that the disruptive person, entity, or situation is being used by the individual's subconscious as a mirror to confront an aspect of himself which he then tries to make conscious. Thus the opposition aspect has, through such confrontation, the potential to increase the level of consciousness. This aspect usually works well only for those who are willing to grant space in their lives to the energies in the opposition that challenge them. Many people will not allow themselves to realize that they are instrumental in bringing about every confrontation in which they become involved, and that there is in every confrontation something of oneself that must be made conscious and accepted as one's own. Thus they continue to fight the battle signified by the opposition, making no progress and suffering much pain.

With an opposition, the goal is to recognize that both (or all, as the case may be) of the planetary energies are one's own, and that they must be allowed to dominate, or one will come once again to be victimized by an apparently outward force embodying the energy that one did not allow to express itself. The goal is a state of perfect equilibrium between the two energies involved in the opposition: it represents the aspect's partnership and cooperation side.

Achieving equilibrium is not equally easy with all oppositions. Some, where the energies of the planets involved are very contradictory, are harder than others to resolve. These are the oppositions traditionally considered malefic, such as Moon-Saturn, Saturn-Neptune, and Mars-Neptune. Sometimes a life will revolve entirely around balancing such energies. Nevertheless, the energy and growth in consciousness to be gained by successfully resolving an opposition is immense. The opposition aspect is an excellent example of the make-or-break quality possessed in varying degrees by the two-series. It is the most powerful aspect after the conjunction, and it is a very close second. Many astrologers consider it less powerful than the square, but this is not my experience. The square may simply claim more attention because it represents issues that are less easily resolved, possibly because the conflict itself is harder to define.

Square (90°)   The square is the *bete noire* of many astrologers. Even some who are otherwise positive in their thinking speak of this aspect with trepidation. As with the opposition, energies linked by square are tremendously dynamic, and squares are significators of change. The two energies are in conflict, but, unlike the opposition, it is not a head-on conflict. It seems as if energies linked by square get in each others' way not by going in opposite directions but by working at cross purposes. The goals of the energies are different, not opposite, such that to achieve one goal takes away from achieving the other. In many ways, the square is a test of the validity of some kind of statement that your life has made, or even of your entire life itself. It is not a test that you have to fail, however. You simply are forced through a square to prove yourself. As with the opposition, the square gives tremendous energy when it is resolved.

Resistance is an important key idea with the square. Resistance is a cosmic principle that we know in its purest form as matter. The fundamental law of matter is that two material objects cannot occupy the same space at the same time: when someone tries to make them do so, they resist each other. The entire material universe can be viewed as a collection of resistances by which a life is limited in its freedom and is forced to take on a definite form. The alert reader will no doubt notice the similarity of this idea to the idea of Saturn. The resemblance is no accident, in that Saturn is the planet of material reality, and the square is the aspect of material reality. Whereas the first step in creating the universe is to become conscious of the not-self (the opposition), the second step is to create the resistances in the universe that we call matter (the square). Thus two or more planets linked by a square represent energies that resist each other and force each other to take on a definite form of behavior. While they limit each other in some way, they also greatly increase each other's individuality.

The problem is that, whereas with the opposition there was usually one energy that seemed external while the other seemed to be coming from within the self, with the square a person may have inner-inner, inner-outer, or outer-outer conflict. It may be, for example, that there are two energies within oneself, neither of which is well understood, that are in conflict with each other; and the conflict goes on simply because one is aware only of the tension, not the sources of the tension. No matter which form the square takes, it is usually difficult to see exactly how the energies are connected and in conflict.

The most important characteristic of the square is that whatever dilemma it may pose, trying to fight the effects of the square by repressing its energies and expressing only the energies that one can accept merely results in the same problem emerging over and over again. Only by going along with the changes that the conflicts lead toward can one bring the energies into some degree of harmony. Even working at its best, however, the square creates ongoing change. This can be progress, if one allows it, but the square can never reach a point of stability. If one thinks of the square as resistance, as matter resisting pressure, then it becomes clear that the only way to deal with a square is to move in accordance with limitations imposed by the universe, not to try to go through the resistance any more than one would try to walk through a wall rather than using the door.

Semisquare (45°) and Sesquiquadrate (135°)   The semisquare and sesquiquadrate are taken together because they are both based on the division of the circle by the number eight. (In fact, some people call them the octile and trioctile.) It may very well be true that each represents a slightly different mode of linking energies, but at this point any differences between them seem too slight to be worth noting.

These are not weak aspects. An exact semisquare or sesquiquadrate is more important than a square that is several degrees out, and many traditional astrologers who have ignored these so-called minor aspects have missed out on important information.

Both the semisquare and sesquiquadrate are of the newer family of aspects discovered in the seventeenth century by Johannes Kepler. They were not recognized by Ptolemy, but then if one reads Ptolemy carefully, it is quite clear that his use of aspects in general was quite different from ours. He seems to have measured aspects simply from sign to sign: that is, for two planets to be in square, they simply had to be in signs that were 90° from each other. This could make a square of as little as 61°, if one planet were in the very beginning of a sign and the other were in the very end. Such a method, similar to that employed by modern Hindu astrologers, would obscure the semisquare and the sesquiquadrate completely. In the modern method of dividing the circle by small integers, however, the semisquare and the sesquiquadrate follow logically from the square. In fact, many astrologers, including this author, have even gone one step further and divided the 45° unit by two, using all aspects based on multiples of 22.5° as well.

The precise nature of these aspects is hard to pin down. They share all the characteristics of the other two-series aspects in that they represent a dynamic linking between two or more energies that results in instability and change. Studies of the way cycles of transiting planets affect people's lives have found that these two aspects represent times of crisis similar to the square but usually not as intense. Like the square, they are challenges to some kind of statement made or position taken by the individual, and there are resistances involved. For the present it is operationally useful to consider them to be like squares. Also as with squares, the entities that are introduced into conflict can be inner-inner, inner-outer, or outer-outer. The multiples of 22.5° are usually treated similarly.

The Three-Series or "Soft" Aspects

The three-series is established by dividing the circle by three and its multiples, usually six and twelve. Though aspects generated by dividing by nine would clearly fall into this family, astrologers are less certain about their nature. Therefore, these will be discussed under their own heading further on, and I will treat only the trine, sextile, semisextile, and quincunx here.

The three-series aspects are called "soft" because their action is less dynamic and usually less harsh than the "hard" aspects just discussed. Whereas two-series aspects are unstable and tend to force changes, three-series aspects produce energy patterns that are not only stable, but in fact resist change. The attributes of one's life that come about from three-series aspects are those that one can count on to persist throughout all life's changes.

But three-series aspects are not really static. They do result in progress and change, but they have the overall effect of producing no *net* change. They symbolize a dynamic equilibrium—a situation in which two or more processes occur simultaneously and cancel each other's effects.

The best example of dynamic equilibrium is the human body. You eat food and give off wastes in perfect balance, resulting in little net change. If you eat too much, you gain weight; if too little, you lose. Both gaining and losing weight are signs that the body's dynamic equilibrium is disturbed. The body has built-in mechanisms that resist upsets to its dynamic equilibrium.

Trines, sextiles, and the other three-series aspects have the same function in life. A chart having too few of these often signifies an individual who has difficulty in finding balance, and whose life seems in a continual state of change. But change also creates the potential for growth, so that too many of these aspects can actually interfere with the process of evolution, both spiritual and psychological. I call this "the curse of the trine." It simply serves to point out that the so-called "good" aspects, as the three-series were once called, can have negative consequences. A dominance of three-series aspects indicates one who has chosen to take a relatively safe course in evolution with few risks, but also less possibility of growth. It is neither better nor worse to choose either the hard-aspect or the soft-aspect course: it is simply a matter of style. Morality, personal integrity, and courage have nothing to do with one route of evolution as opposed to the other.

An excess of trines, sextiles, semisextiles, and quincunxes can create problems as has been indicated. When one is caught in a situation where change seems necessary, there may not be enough energy to get oneself moving. People having too many soft aspects may seem lethargic, waiting for the universe to make up their minds for them or for circumstances to force them down a path of action. Or they may simply respond over and over to the same problem in the same way.

On the plus side, a little energy goes a long way with three-series aspects. Particularly with trines, the universe and the inner self offer little resistance to activity that is appropriate to the planets involved. The activity almost seems destined to happen. And yet it usually serves to maintain a status quo, not to bring about a new order as the two-series aspects would tend to do.

Trine (120°)   The trine is the most potent aspect of the three-series, although it is subtle in its effects, especially if one is looking for events. Like the other three-series aspects, the trine indicates that the energies linked do not resist or conflict with each other in any way. They are in a state of equilibrium with respect to one another. Whenever one chooses to act according to the nature of the energies combined by a trine, there is ease of action and lack of difficulty—so long as one chooses to act within the framework of a status quo into one's life. Trinal action does not readily alter whatever circumstances may be in force at a particular time, except to restore balance after a previous state of imbalance. In mutual aspects (aspects that occur between two planets in the sky on a given day, not in the birth chart), trines often signify the end of a period of activity and the restoration of peace and quiet after a previous period of turmoil. People having many trines are often more resistant to turmoil and stress than others, seeming not to notice that anything especially untoward is happening. This is not insensitivity, however; it is the result of an inner balance that is not easily upset.

When trines do signify events, they are events in which one is passive. Things seem to fall into one's lap and work out of their own accord. For example, someone with natal Mars *square* Jupiter may have a great sense of timing and know when to make a move (assuming that the person is disciplined enough not to make rash moves, which is a negative tendency of this aspect). When someone is successful with this square, others are likely to attribute the success to good timing and skillful application of energies. With the *trine* of Mars and Jupiter, however, affairs seem to work out because of "dumb luck," or so others might see it. Actually, what is happening is that in those affairs of life that are signified by the trine, the individual has a positive intention and an optimistic expectation that does not even consider the possibility of failure. Also, the energy of this aspect is not sufficiently stormy to cause one to take risks that are unlikely to succeed. Being able to proceed in any matter without a sense of stress or resistance and without trying to push circumstances too far is an almost certain guarantee of success. An analogy might be drawn with martial arts, in which the primary tactic is to allow the energies of the aggressor to destroy themselves by not resisting them and in fact even assisting them. Thus one is able to rechannel those energies to one's own ends with a minimum of effort. Trines often work like this.

The principal flaw of trines is their passivity. Whenever the individual is challenged by the environment to make a change or adjustment, the energy is lacking. The old patterns indicated by the trine persist, and even if they are temporarily deflected, they soon return. Other astrological writers have characterized excessively trinal charts as too easy, but in fact they can be difficult. Sometimes they can assist the negative effects of a hard aspect in ways that make it almost impossible to change.

A man of my acquaintance possessed a grand trine (in which three planets form an equilateral triangle in the zodiac) of the Moon, Uranus, and Neptune. The Moon, in addition, was closely opposed by Pluto. Uranus and Neptune together relate to alternative states of consciousness (any state of consciousness—like trance, sleep, hypnotic states, meditative states, and above all, complete unconsciousness—that is other than the normal state in which we handle everyday life). The Moon signifies one's inward emotional state and, in a male chart, those energies most likely to be projected onto women. The Moon-Pluto opposition signifies intense emotional encounters and the likelihood of power struggles with women. With the Moon trine Neptune and Uranus, he was spontaneously attracted to women who were ideally beautiful (Neptune=ideal), and quite unusual (Uranus). He would then become involved in power struggles with these women as he tried to dominate them by pointing out every flaw in their beauty or personality. Eventually this would become intolerable for the woman and she would leave him. The effect of the trine here is that it created a spontaneous emotional condition that was extremely unconscious in its action. He knew he was doing this but did not understand how he went about it. The mechanics were completely unconscious. He was aware that he disliked his mother (opposition=awareness). But he couldn't see how he translated this into his relations with women in general. And, most important, he had a great deal of trouble doing anything about his problem. The trines made it easy to fall into the pattern, and also difficult to break out of it, while the opposition supplied the energy to create a conflict.

Normally, the combination of hard and soft aspects does not create this type of locked-in position. This is only a possible negative manifestation of the combination. Usually trines serve the positive purpose of giving a stable core to one's existence, a core that can resist and survive the instability threatened by hard aspects. In fact, the combination of hard and soft aspects is an ideal condition. It was unfortunate in my friend's case that it worked out negatively. Had his mother known earlier in his life that through his relationship with her he would be easily subject to negative programing with regard to women, she might have been able to treat him differently as a child.

Sextile (60°)   Since the sextile is based on the division of the circle by six, it is less intense than the trine, and there is also a slight difference in quality. The number six is the product of two times three; thus the sextile shares some qualities with the two-series aspects in that it requires more dynamism to actualize. The sextile is to the trine as the opposition is to the conjunction, and, like the opposition, the sextile often results in an increase of awareness. An even more important difference from the trine is that the sextile usually represents circumstances in which one has to exert some energy in order to take advantage of the situation that is offered. Whereas trines will often signify that matters will work themselves out, with the sextile one has to give assistance. Hence a common keyword for sextiles is "opportunity."

As the sextile requires a bit more effort than the trine to actualize, so it also is not so limiting. It is not as potent a force for maintaining the status quo and is less likely to indicate a person caught in an irrevocable balance. However, like an excess of trines, an excess of sextiles can be an indication of a lack of dynamism in the life and a tendency to adopt a passive attitude toward existence. Also like the trine, the sextile serves as a buffer against excessively rapid change and instability. The overall number of trines together with sextiles can be used as an index of the personality's ability to withstand stress and disruption without overreacting and losing perspective.

In practice, the distinction between sextiles and trines in the natal chart is not very significant. The distinction can be more important when comparing the natal chart to the positions of the planets at a given time after birth (transits). Here, sextile and trine connections may differ.

Semisextile (30°) and Quincunx (150°)   It is not generally known that Ptolemy and other Greek writers lumped the semisextile and quincunx together under the term "inconjunct." It is therefore not, strictly speaking, correct to apply "inconjunct" only to the quincunx as is so often done. The ancient use of the same word for both aspects points up the fact that they are similar. Both are based on the division of the circle by twelve. One would expect some differences between one-twelfth of the circle (the semisextile) and five-twelfths (the quincunx), but they are not great.

Only recently, astrologers have begun to get into clear touch with what these two aspects symbolize. In the past, observers merely noted that they were both based on one-half of a sextile, and they therefore drew the conclusion that both were essentially weak sextiles. This has not turned out to be the case. In fact, the weight of opinion on these aspects has changed from a judgment of weakly benefic to decidedly difficult.

The problem raised by these aspects is best symbolized by the fact that they unite points in signs that have no relationship to each other. Signs in opposition, square, trine and sextile have many similarities, but signs in semisextile and quincunx have none (see the sections on elements, crosses, and polarities in Chapter 10).

The nature of aspects does not arise out of the relationships among the signs, however. Actually, it is the other way around: the relationships among the signs arise from the numbers that divide the circle into the aspects. But the ambiguous nature of connections based on multiples of thirty degrees is still made clear by this comparison.

Looking at the semisextile and quincunx as based on the number twelve, we discover that twelve equals four times three. As the sextile acquired a little of the opposition's dynamism from the fact that six equals the product of two and three, so we would expect the semisextile and quincunx to have something of the difficulties of the square. In fact, they seem to.

Semisextiles and quincunxes combine the passive nature of the three-series with the tension and sense of unease typically associated with squares. It might be said that they represent connections between entities that have no logical connection, and there does not seem to be enough energy to change the relationship.

The nature of these aspects can be made even more clear by pointing out that the eighth and the sixth houses derive their meanings from the quincunxes that they form to the first house. Likewise, the second and twelfth houses get their qualities from the semisextiles that they form to the first house. With the exception of the second house, these houses all represent somewhat difficult and ambiguous areas of life in which many people have difficulties.

But the difficulties signified by the semisextile and the quincunx are not the cosmic kinds that make lives into tragedies. They represent tensions and difficulties that are annoying, but usually too trivial and too thoroughly bound up in the fabric of everyday life to be worth changing. The exception to this is that there does seem, according to many investigators, to be a connection between quincunxes and illnesses and death.

A typical dilemma of these two aspects is a forced choice between two conditions, which requires letting go of one entirely and going along with the other. When one tries to make a move, it turns out that one cannot let go of the alternative that has to be relinquished. A quincunx or semisextile between the Sun and Moon, for example, signifies that the emotions and the conscious will do not cooperate smoothly, and that one's emotional desires are often in conflict with what one has consciously chosen as right. There is a feeling that there are two entities within the self that are completely different, so much so that they don't even fight with each other. They simply operate as if the other did not exist.

The only resolution that can be suggested for these tensions is to become extremely conscious of the patterns of difficulty themselves and to detach oneself emotionally from them so that one can see them clearly and do whatever is necessary to alter them. The usual problem with these aspects is that their negative effects are so subtle and so bound up in the fabric of one's being that one cannot clearly see what is happening.

Other Series of Aspects

At present, for the sake of simplicity, it might be better for the reader not to be too concerned with aspects based on integers other than two and three. This is not because other aspects are of little significance, as other authors have stated; rather, it is because their principles are not as clearly formulated by astrologers as are those of the aspects we have already taken up. If you do choose to examine these aspects, do so in the spirit of research and do not take any written formulation of them as anything but hypothesis. With the aspects already in general use, the disagreements, such as they are, are not so much about the essences of the aspects as about the precise ways of formulating them into words. With these other aspects, even the essences are in question.

Having given this warning, I would like to describe for the student's guidance the formulations of these aspects that I have found thus far to be the most useful. I stress again, however, that these are hypothetical. Occasionally I will use the symbolism of planets to suggest interpretations of these aspects, but it must be kept in mind that aspects are not planets; they are ways in which planets are linked. Analogies to planets are drawn only to suggest ways of approaching the aspects.

The Five-Series   These are aspects based on the division of the circle by the number five and its multiples, such as ten, fifteen, and twenty. The basic aspect is the quintile (72°, or one-fifth of the circle). Other members of this family include the biquintile (144°, or two-fifths), the decile (36°, or one-tenth) and multiples of 36°, and the vigintile (18°, or one-twentieth) and multiples of 18°. All these aspects seem to have a quality that we usually associate with Pluto, with overtones of Venus and Mars. They seem to link planets in such a way that some kind of concrete creation or destruction is brought about. The number five has a connection with life, death, and mortality; the pentagram is the figure of humankind. John Addey, one of the leading researchers in the field of non-traditional aspects, believes that the five-series has to do with the intellectual function and all those affairs that are peculiarly human. My own observations confirm his, with the reservation that to say "intellectual quality" does not mean rarefied, dry, or detached. In my experience, the five-series aspects have a great deal of emotional tone.

Addey has suggested that intellect is the most characteristic attribute of humankind, and that therefore the number of humankind would be a number of intellect. But there is a second unique attribute of human beings, which is partly a result of their intellect, but also of something else in their nature harder to pin down. They have *transformed* their environment and the Earth in general far more than any other species. Nor have they ever been able to attain a constant balance with the environment. Some cultures have achieved more of a balance than others, but even these are usually overthrown by another, more aggressive culture eventually. Cultures rise and fall, and the only thing that we can assume is constant about human history is change. And the changes seem to come from deep within the human spirit. Most cultures cannot survive long periods without change. They atrophy and die or go through fundamental revolution. This transforming I associate with the five-series. People I have known with many such aspects seem to have their lives bound up in some way with the fundamental energies of change. This may show up in an exaggerated concern with power, or with innermost truths about the universe that enable one to know first-hand how the transforming energies work. On the negative side, we have the chart of Adolf Hitler, the only outstanding feature of which is its string of five-series aspects. On the positive side, we have the chart of Albert Einstein, a man who spent his life exploring the secrets of the universe (and, in support of Addey's position, with a great deal of intellect).

The other major characteristic of these aspects, and the one longest noted, is that they seem to grant the ability to turn creative inspiration into concrete end-products. They have long been noted as aspects of talent or even of genius, but more recent work suggests that these aspects do not in themselves grant the creative inspiration.

One last comment: the quintile and the biquintile, the two most powerful aspects in this group, appear to be extremely so, perhaps more than all the three-series aspects except for the trine. One reason this has not been noted before is that older astrologers simply logged aspects as good or evil. The quintile and biquintile do not clearly fit into either category.

The Seven-Series The division of the circle by seven produces the septile (51° 25′ 42.9″). Its multiples are 102° 51′ 25.7″ (the biseptile) and 154° 17′ 08.6″ (the triseptile). There is also the semiseptile of 25° 42′ 51.4″ and its various multiples. These are the only aspects whose angle does not evenly divide into 360° so as to produce a whole number. The decimal and sexagesimal fractions that occur in these numbers repeat to infinity. This is probably one reason why these aspects have been overlooked. They are extremely hard to see without measuring them in a chart with a protractor.

The seven-series aspects are difficult to formulate in rigorous and clear terms. Part of the reason is that they have a Uranus-Neptune flavor, which suggests that they have to do with energy linkings that are not entirely of this world. For example, these aspects are prominent in the chart of Madame Blavatsky, the founder of the Theosophical movement. They are also prominent in the charts of poets. If the five-series gives the ability to turn creative inspiration into concrete end-products, the seven-series gives the creative inspiration itself. It is as if these aspects enable one to peer outside the everyday universe into one of expanded possibilities and truths.

There are dangers here also. I have seen the seven-series indicate mental and emotional difficulties as well as creative inspiration. An excess of these aspects appears to give one a lack of connection with the physical universe as most of us know it. This is the dangerous or at least difficult side of creative inspiration.

The seven-series also shows up in connection with religion. In a study of the distribution of the birth Suns of ministers in both Britain and America, John Addey discovered that minister's Suns tend to cluster near the points of a seven-sided polygon in the zodiac.* The effect was more noticeable with British clergymen than with American. It has been suggested that perhaps this is because the British clergy are more concerned with the traditional ceremonial aspects of religion than are their American counterparts; I leave that speculation to the reader.

The Nine-Series   These are aspects based on multiples of 40°, which is the division of the circle by nine. The 40° aspect itself is called the novile or nonile. It has rarely been used in the West, but it is important in India, although it is not used there in exactly the way we use aspects. In Hindu astrology it is said to describe what the life produces in the long run, and also the individual's needs and capacities in relationships, especially marriage. As a describer of the end-products of life, the nine-series seems related to the traditional meaning of the number nine as completion and ending. The second use, for marriage, has been corroborated in Western sidereal astrology, which uses the noviens, a type of chart based on the nine-series, to describe sexual attractions.

Higher Harmonics   Little is known about aspects based on divisions of the circle by numbers larger than nine. All that can safely be said is that they may have considerable significance. Many astrologers of the old school would have us believe that nothing but the original aspects (conjunction, sextile, square, trine, and opposition) used by the Greeks

---

*John Addey, *Harmonics in Astrology* (Green Bay, Wisconsin: The Cambridge Circle, 1976), pages 62-65.

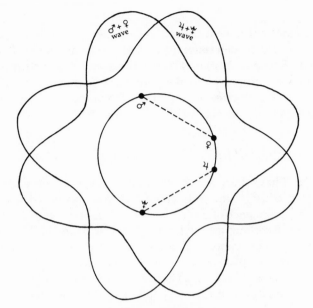

A. Unconnected aspects

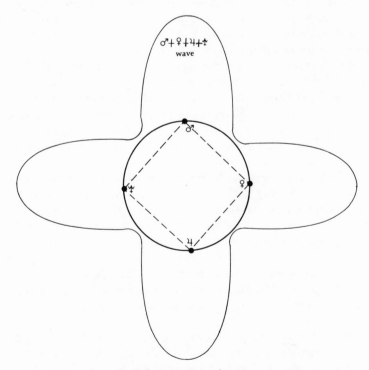

B. A harmonic syndrome

Figure 12. Unconnected aspects versus a harmonic syndrome

have any significance whatsoever. This is clearly not true, but further research is needed to determine just what the significance of the higher harmonics is. The one limiting factor in the use of higher harmonics is the accuracy of the horoscope, as the higher the harmonic, the greater the magnification of any error in a planet's longitude. In other words, the higher the harmonic, the smaller the allowable orb.

Aspect Patterns or Harmonic Syndromes

So far, I have described the meaning of single aspects and families of aspects, often adding comments about the effect produced when a chart contains a predominance of a certain aspect or aspect family. But there are two ways an aspect or aspect family can predominate. The chart may simply have a large number of aspects from the dominant family, without the pairs of aspecting planets being connected to each other. Or—and this is what will be discussed here—the chart may have a number of aspects from the dominant family, with each pair linked to the other pairs by the same type of aspect.

Figure 12 shows the difference. In chart A, there are a number of unconnected squares, whereas in chart B all the squares are connected into what astrologers call a grand square or grand cross. The planets involved are ranged around the circle at 90° intervals so that each is in either square or opposition to the other planets in the cross.

As described above in the section on the square, a chart with a simple predominance of squares means a great deal of energy, often resulting in crises. When the squares are all connected as in chart B, the energy is greatly magnified and the crises are heightened. The reason for this is easy to see when you realize that a transiting or progressed aspect to one planet in the square is at the same time an aspect to all planets in the square.

Looked at in terms of harmonic theory, it is as if two planets in square set up a wave that is 90° long. A wave of this length will repeat itself exactly four times as it travels around the 360° of the ecliptic. If there are four unconnected squares in a chart, the wave formed by one square will peak at a different set of points than the wave formed by another square (see Figure 12A). But if the waves are connected by squares or oppositions to each other, they will all be in phase, with their peaks at the same four points on the ecliptic (see Figure 12B). Thus peaks will reinforce peaks and troughs will reinforce troughs, and aspects arranged in this way will intensify one another.

As indicated above, it is only necessary that the planets be connected by the same family of aspects—not that they all be connected by the same aspect. This is because aspects in the same family are related in the same way as a fundamental and its overtones are in music. To use a classic

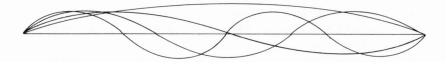

Figure 13. Harmonics or overtones in a guitar string

illustration of harmonics, a plucked guitar string vibrates not only in the fundamental tone but also, at the same time, in overtones. Figure 13 shows a string vibrating as a whole, producing the fundamental tone; in halves, producing the octave or first overtone; in thirds, producing the second overtone; in fourths, producing the double octave or third overtone; etc. We are here mostly concerned with the octave overtones, in which the fundamental wavelength is successively cut in half. Overtones besides the octave overtones are carried but are not relevant to this discussion. An opposition is one-half the wavelength of a conjunction, a square is one-fourth the wavelength of a conjunction, etc. Like the fundamental tone sounded on a vibrating guitar string, the conjunction carries within it overtones corresponding to the opposition, trine, square, sextile etc. Likewise, an opposition carries within it overtones of all octaves of the two-series higher than itself. In an aspect pattern like the grand square, the first overtones of the opposition are in exactly the same shape and position as the waves formed by the squares. In other words, the peaks and troughs of the opposition's first overtone will be in exactly the same position as the peaks and troughs of the squares, thus providing the same reinforcing effect as was provided by all the squares in phase with one another.

A grand square is one example of what I like to call a "harmonic syndrome." "Syndrome" means literally "running together," which is what the aspects in such a pattern are doing. In his heliocentric work, John Nelson has coined the phrase "simultaneous multiple harmonic" for the same sort of phenomenon, but I think "harmonic syndrome" says it more briefly and accurately.

Harmonic syndromes include the other aspect patterns long noted by astrologers: the grand trine (third-harmonic syndrome), T-square (fourth-harmonic), grand sextile or Star of David (sixth-harmonic), yod (twelfth-harmonic), and so forth. Not only does each of these patterns consist of several aspects of the same family, the aspects are also in phase with one another, so that the peaks of the waves formed by the aspects and overtones occur at the same points around the ecliptic.

The harmonic number of the syndrome comes from the highest-harmonic aspect in the syndrome. Thus a syndrome containing conjunctions, oppositions, squares, and semisquares or octiles would be called an eighth-harmonic syndrome, just as a grand square that also contains oppositions and perhaps even conjunctions would be called a fourth-harmonic syndrome. In an eighth-harmonic syndrome, there would be eight repetitions of a wave going once around the ecliptic: eight peaks, or eight points equally spaced around the zodiac in which planets involved in the syndrome could be placed.

As you may have noted, the T-square is a grand cross or fourth-harmonic syndrome with one arm empty. It is not necessary to have all the possible points in a harmonic syndrome filled, though of course the more points occupied, the stronger the effect. The higher the harmonic, the more rare it is to have all possible points filled, and in really high harmonics it is not even possible, because there are not enough planets to go around. Most astrologers have seen a number of grand trines and grand squares with all the possible points in the syndrome filled in, but they see a grand sextile, in which all six points in a sixth-harmonic syndrome are filled in, only once or twice in their careers. It is much more common to find sixth-harmonic syndromes in the form of minor grand trines, kites, and mystic rectangles, various patterns in which some of the six possible points are not filled. These patterns will be discussed below.

Here are some general rules regarding harmonic syndromes.

1. As mentioned above, the more planets involved, the stronger the syndrome. Thus, although squares are usually more powerful than septiles, if there are several planets involved in a seventh-harmonic syndrome, the septiles will collectively be stronger than a single pair of planets in square.

This is important because often horoscopes of people who have lives characteristic of a large number of squares may have no squares. Instead, you will find them to have many planets involved in an eighth-, sixteenth-or even a thirty-second-harmonic syndrome. There are also horoscopes that have a square that seems to act out of all proportion to a square's normal effect. On looking closer, you will find that the square is strengthened by having other planets attached to it by eighth-, sixteenth-, or thirty-second-harmonic aspects. For the tie-in to be meaningful, the orbs have to be small, less than 1°.

2. The syndrome unifies the chart according to the principle of the harmonic. I have already mentioned that the largest common divisor of the angles that make up a harmonic syndrome establishes the number of the harmonic syndrome. The largest common divisor also establishes the dominant symbolic quality. Thus in a syndrome containing trines, sextiles, and semisextiles, the overall symbolic quality would be of the semisextile or twelfth harmonic. But unlike a series of unconnected semisextiles, the twelfth-harmonic syndrome would also bring as an undertone the qualities of the trine and sextile, or the third and sixth harmonics.

3. As stated above, when a transiting or progressed planet conjoins one of the planets in a natal harmonic syndrome, all the planets in the syndrome are set off at approximately the same time. A transiting or progressed planet can also set off a harmonic syndrome when it is making an aspect that is a multiple of the harmonic number of the syndrome. For example, a progressed planet might make a 22.5° (sixteenth-harmonic) angle to one of the planets in an eighth-harmonic syndrome, thus setting off the first overtone of the eighth harmonic and making the entire syndrome ring like a bell. Therefore, when one is checking transits or progressions to a harmonic syndrome, one should not overlook the seemingly minor aspects that are multiples of the harmonic in question.

4. As mentioned in the previous chapter's section on orbs , you can allow a larger-than-usual orb for a harmonic syndrome because of the way a syndrome increases the strength of the aspects involved in it. But, of course, the closer the average orb of the syndrome, the more powerful the syndrome is. As I will point out below, a close-orbed syndrome also differs from a wide-orbed one in quality as well as intensity.

Meanings of Harmonic Syndromes

To a certain extent, harmonic syndromes have the same significance as a single aspect of the same type, only more so. But harmonic syndromes also add some features of their own.

First- and Second-Harmonic Syndromes: Multiple Conjunctions and Oppositions A conjunction becomes a first-harmonic syndrome when several planets are closely conjoined at the same spot in the zodiac. And a second-harmonic syndrome occurs when several planets are conjoined at one or both ends of an opposition.

Even as a single conjunction ties two planetary energies together in such a way that a person finds it hard to distinguish between them, a multiple conjunction does this for several planetary energies, with the result that the person can have a predominantly subjective viewpoint with little ability to understand positions other than his own. On the plus side, this may mean a concentration of energies that in the right circumstances can be extraordinarily effective.

A simple opposition is an unalloyed second harmonic, but in order for there to be a second-harmonic syndrome, there must be some conjunctions as well as oppositions. Thus, while the second harmonic sets the tone of the syndrome, bringing in the opposition's sense of polarity and conflict, this is modified by the conjunction's lack of perspective and its concentration of energies.

Third-Harmonic Syndromes: Grand Trines Astrologers have long debated whether the grand trine is easy or difficult to deal with. The consensus is that it is a trine in overdose. Many feel it makes energies flow

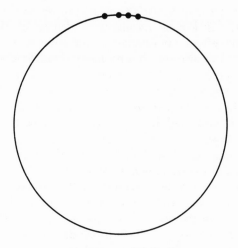

A. Multiple conjunctions

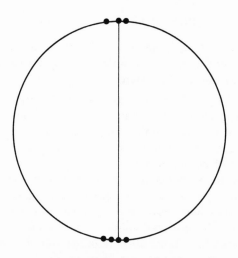

B. Multiple oppositions

Figure 14. First- and second-harmonic syndromes

so easily that the individual does not get enough of the kind of growth that can come only through confronting adversity. Being a symbol of perfect equilibrium and balance, the trine represents absolutely no power for change.

But I find the matter to be not so simple. In his heliocentric work on geomagnetic storms, John Nelson has noted that when two planets in a grand trine are inner planets (planets from Mars inward toward the Sun), the grand trine acts like a hard aspect, disrupting short-wave radio transmissions. But when two are outer planets (from Jupiter outward) and only the third is an inner planet, the effect is like a super trine in that it calms down the conditions for radio transmission to an unusual degree. The same effect may be working in the geocentric astrology of individuals, but we do not yet know for sure.

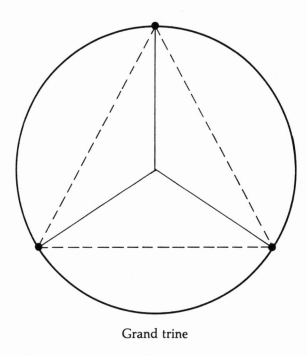

Grand trine

Figure 15. A third-harmonic syndrome

Another important effect I have noted relates to the precision of the angles involved. If none of the three trines is more than 1° from exact, the grand trine appears to have much more energy than otherwise. This seems to result from the action of midpoints (which are discussed fully in Chapters 8 and 9). In an exact grand trine, the midpoint of each pair of planets lies exactly opposite the third factor. This makes the grand trine a series of three oppositions and gives it a more dynamic character than it would otherwise have. Even when the grand trine is not exact, as long as one pair of planets has its midpoint lying opposite the third planet, there is something of this dynamic quality. This does not work unless the orb of the midpoint configuration is kept small. I do not consider midpoints beyond 1° to either side of an exact opposition, though others use orbs of 1.5° to 2°.

Grand trines that are somewhat out of orb I find to be more static and more likely to produce difficulties arising from the individual's extreme passivity or inactivity. Very close grand trines, on the other hand, will have something of the same energy as grand sextiles (see below). This means that there will be plenty of energy for any activity related to the symbolism of the planets involved, and the energy will flow smoothly. While it may seem to others that luck simply falls into a person's lap with these configurations, it is   more accurate to say that the person knows what to do with the apparent luck and has in fact done a great deal to bring it about. It is simply that not much visible effort is involved.

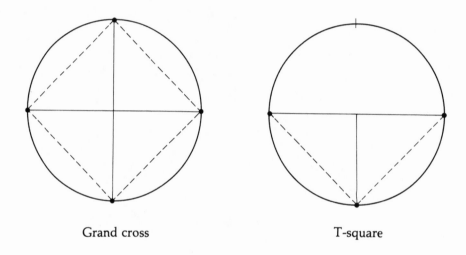

Grand cross   T-square

Figure 16. Fourth-harmonic syndromes

Fourth-Harmonic Syndromes: Grand Crosses and T-Squares   As mentioned above, a grand cross or grand square is a complete fourth-harmonic syndrome with all possible points filled by planets, whereas a T-square is a grand cross with one arm missing. Both configurations are often called very stressful. It is more accurate to say that they are high-energy aspects like all squares and oppositions, and they require some care in handling. With a grand cross or T-square, one needs to focus one's considerable energies and use them for specific purposes. If one lets the energies take control, they can result in unfortunate events, what kind depending on the nature of the symbolism. Usually they are events over which one feels one has no control. Suppressing the energies and the behavioral manifestations that arise out of them can also produce unpleasant events.

From the attitudes of many toward these two configurations, one would almost expect to see them routinely in the charts of mass murderers and the like. They occur in such charts, of course, but not that frequently. Hitler's chart, for example, has a notable lack of such aspects. (Instead, it has a tenth-harmonic syndrome, about which more below.)

Most astrologers find that the T-square with its missing arm is more unbalanced and difficult to deal with than the grand cross. Many have stated that this causes the individual to focus on the issue relating to the house where the missing arm of the cross would have fallen. I am not at all sure this kind of difference exists, though the idea is elegant.

Certainly, both the grand cross and the T-square are common and are found in the charts of many perfectly normal people. On meeting them, however, you will find an intensity lacking in others. It is as if there is tremendous energy lurking just below the surface and waiting to be released. Eventually it usually is, in ways that are constructive. Much, of course, depends on the planets involved.

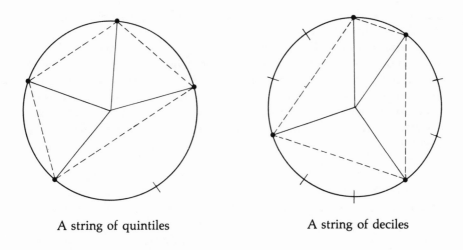

A string of quintiles   A string of deciles

Figure 17. Fifth- and tenth-harmonic syndromes

Fifth- and Tenth-Harmonic Syndromes: Grand Quintiles and Strings of Quintiles and Deciles   I have never seen a perfect grand quintile, a pattern in which five planets are ranged around the zodiac at 72° intervals. I have only seen less complete fifth-and tenth-harmonic syndromes in which several planets are involved, but they do not complete a regular polygon in the zodiac.

In these cases there seems to have been something fateful and portentous about the life. Even if there was nothing terribly significant about the person, it always seemed as if the person would use tremendous amounts of energy to achieve an objective. There is a capacity for ruthlessness with these syndromes, but also a capacity for great achievement. At opposite poles are Hitler and Einstein, both of whom have strong tenth-harmonic syndromes, and who have both been fateful figures in history.

Sixth-Harmonic Syndromes: Grand Sextiles, Kites, Mystic Rectangles, and Minor Grand Trines   Grand sextiles, like grand quintiles, are rare: I have seen only one. But other kinds of sixth-harmonic syndrome are more common. One type, called a "kite," has a close grand trine, with one of the three planets closely opposed by a fourth planet that also lies on the midpoint of the other two in the grand trine. Another type, called a "mystic rectangle" by Michael Erlewine of Michigan, is composed of two pairs of oppositions that are exactly sextile and trine each other. Yet another type, the "minor grand trine," consists of a trine bisected by a sextile.

The most important consideration with any of these is whether or not it includes an opposition to give it energy. Any sextile syndrome that includes more than two sextiles must also include an opposition, because an opposition is three sextiles.

An opposition is impossible in the minor grand trine, but here a planet is conjunct the midpoint of two other planets. This adds some energy to the configuration, but in most cases an opposition makes a sextile syndrome much more dynamic and energy-laden. The effect of the exact minor grand trine is like the effect of the exact grand trine. That is, the energy flows smoothly and at great speed, but there can be problems if one does not try to break out of the behavioral ruts that one can fall into with third and sixth harmonics.

A kite contains only one opposition. A person I knew with a kite pattern exhibited all the characteristics of someone caught in a trinal trap. That is, he had a strongly defined behavior pattern without the energy to break out of it. I suspect that the more oppositions there are in a sextile pattern, the more energy there is to prevent rigid patterns from forming, and the easier it is to break out of any existing ones.

The only grand-sextile person I have ever known is not obviously extraordinary, except that she derives no great pleasure from the good things in life falling into her lap. She feels no satisfaction unless she has earned them. This is characteristic of someone with strong hard-aspect patterns: remember that a grand sextile has six oppositions as well as six sextiles. But the sextile-trine pattern is there in that she often finds it difficult to get herself moving even when she knows intellectually that she must.

Twelfth-Harmonic Syndromes: Yods   I am skipping syndromes of

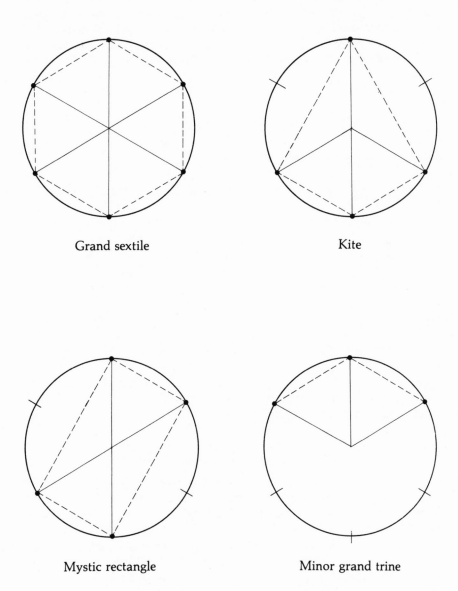

Figure 18. Sixth-harmonic syndromes

the seventh, eighth, ninth, and eleventh harmonics, as there is little to say about them that has not already been covered in the discussions of aspect families and of harmonic syndromes in general. I include the twelfth-harmonic syndrome here because one of its forms, the yod, finger of God, or finger of fate, is a commonly mentioned aspect pattern.

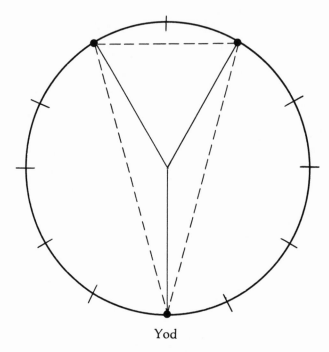

Yod

Figure 19. A twelfth-harmonic syndrome

The yod is illustrated in Figure 19. The planet at the tip of the "finger" is in clockwise and counterclockwise quincunxes to the two other planets, and these two other planets are in sextile to each other. As its other names suggest, the yod has often been considered an aspect of fatality, by which I suppose is meant that the three planets are likely to indicate an underlying theme in one's life, constant and relatively unchanging. This is consistent with what we already know about the quincunx. But what changes do introducing the sextile make in the overall symbolism? In my opinion, not many. A sextile, being two-twelfths of the circle, does not much mitigate the twelfth-harmonic nature of the combination.

Nevertheless, the two planets in sextile to each other do have their midpoint directly on the third planet. This does make a difference, assuming that the orbs are smaller than 1° to 1.5°. The direct midpoint configuration (see Chapter 8) gives the yod a dynamic quality ordinarily lacking in three-series aspects. This means that even though the yod has the static, passive quality of the three-series, it can also signify crises in which the energies have to be faced directly and specific courses of action taken in order for the energies to work out positively. Thus the yod contains the germ of its own resolution in a way that simple quincunxes do not. If the orb of a yod exceeds that of allowable midpoint combinations, however, this quality of the yod is lost.

8

Midpoints: Introduction

Midpoints are simply points in the zodiac located halfway between any other two points. Midpoints between all possible combinations of planets, the North Node, the Midheaven, the Ascendant, and the 0° Aries Point are commonly used. One can also use any other point in the chart, including the Vertex, East Point, or intermediate house cusps, but this is not as commonly done.

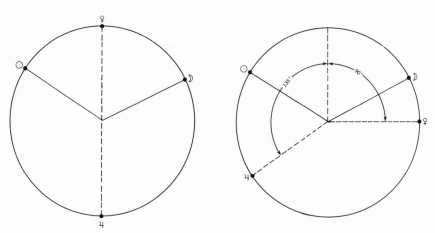

A. Direct midpoint combination   B. An indirect midpoint combination

Figure 20. Direct versus indirect midpoints

It is generally believed that a midpoint combines the qualities of the two points whose arc of separation it divides. Thus the point halfway between Mars and Jupiter would combine qualities of Mars and Jupiter. If the midpoint is occupied by another factor, we have a combination of three symbols. If the midpoints of two pairs of single factors fall at the same spot, we have a combination of four symbols. And so on.

In the way we shall be using midpoints, midpoint combinations can be either direct or indirect. In a direct midpoint combination, the factor (either a single factor or another midpoint) occupying the midpoint is conjunct or opposite the midpoint. In an indirect combination, the aspect is a square, semisquare, or sesquiquadrate. (See Figure 20.)

Midpoints are yet another way to combine symbols in the horoscope. Not only can we have a certain planet in a certain sign and house in aspect to other planets in other signs and houses; we can also have each planet involved in midpoint combinations. This enormously increases the material available to interpret.

Why Use Midpoints?

Midpoints have a plausible theoretical basis in harmonics, but in a much more complex way than aspects. The explanation is beyond the scope of this book; suffice it to say that midpoints work. I use midpoints because they often give information that would not otherwise be available in the chart. Without them, I have seen important characteristics of a person and events in a life completely overlooked.

In judging the "cosmic state" of a planet—that is, how well it can function more or less in keeping with its intrinsic nature—I look at not only the house and sign and what aspects the planet makes, but also at what midpoints the planet falls on and what midpoints it forms with other planets. If a planet is connected by midpoint to other symbols in the chart that are in tension with the planet's fundamental nature, it will make the functioning of that planet's energy ambiguous and difficult. Midpoints that are combined with a single planet in the chart become part of that planet's total expression. Whatever transit, progression, or solar arc direction sets that planet off in later life sets off the midpoints attached to it as well. Therefore, an understanding of the midpoints attached to a planet can tell a great deal about how that planet will operate in a person's life.

Midpoints give information that is more particular than aspects, signs, and houses can give. This is because there are so many midpoints: the domain of what each symbol signifies is smaller. Each symbol is thus much more clearly defined and limited. Midpoints are like planets, but with a more concentrated focus.

The result is that we can give midpoint combinations detailed, quite specific delineations. One can then tell if the horoscope is "working": whether it is really giving useful information, or whether the astrologer is simply trying to make the chart fit the client. The more precise the statement one makes from a chart, the better one learns the effectiveness of one's techniques. It is partly unavoidable with human beings, but it is also partly out of sloppiness that conventional astrology often yields delineations that are so vague as to be worthless.

Using midpoints, one can rely more on the chart itself and less on intuition. I have nothing against intuition; it can give useful information. But I think that astrologers, since they take the trouble to erect horoscopes, should be able to derive most of their data from the chart. Systematic technique can make an astrologer effective even on days when intuition is not forthcoming.

And there is one extra benefit from midpoints. A midpoint analysis of a chart for which no birthtime is known can yield more and better data than the common technique of using a solar chart (in which one uses the Sun's longitude as an Ascendant).

Midpoints As a Basic Tool

Unfortunately, midpoints have been cursed with the title of "advanced technique." For most astrologers an advanced technique is one with which the teacher is not familiar—regardless of how simple it might be to employ. In fact, in the German schools that developed modern midpoint techniques, midpoints are taught to beginners. I can attest from personal experience that using them is simpler than many of the techniques for natal analysis taught by conventional astrologers. For these reasons I feel that midpoints should be taught in beginning astrology, if only because it is easier to integrate them into one's chart-reading system early on than to make room for them later.

One reason using midpoints is actually simpler than one might suppose is that midpoint combinations involve only one kind of factor: planets and other points like the nodes, Ascendant, Midheaven, and 0°Aries. Even without mastering the symbolism of signs and houses one can derive an astonishing amount of information simply by combining planets and the like in aspects and midpoints. In fact, one of the German schools, that of Cosmobiology, manages quite well using signs very little and no houses at all.

I do consider the sign and house placement of a planet along with the midpoints in which it is involved, but this is not necessary to do at first. While one is learning synthesis, one can take a midpoint combination, make a complete judgment from it, and then later combine that judgment with what is obtained from the sign and house placement. In this way one is not overwhelmed with material.

Modern midpoint techniques were developed by schools of astrology that were set up as alternatives to conventional systems, and therefore many people think that if they adopt midpoints they must adopt the whole alternative system in which midpoints were developed. But this is largely a misconception: to benefit from what midpoints can add, one need not give up the approach one already uses.

How Not to Use Midpoints

Unfortunately, many astrologers use midpoints only to account for something in the chart when they are otherwise stumped. This is using midpoints as a "fudge factor," enabling one to get anything one wishes out of a chart. Such astrologers take midpoints out of the context of the entire chart, especially the entire midpoint structure, and exaggerate the importance of one or two midpoint combinations. If one uses midpoints at all, one should consider all of them, or at least all direct midpoints.

If we use ten planets, plus the lunar node, Ascendant, Midheaven, and 0° Aries Point, however, we have a total of ninety-one direct midpoints. And this does not count indirect midpoints, hard aspects to direct midpoints, which also are important enough to be considered. Clearly, just inserting all these midpoints in the conventional twelve-equal-wedges horoscope form that most astrologers in the English-speaking world use would result in a horrendous mess, and would get us nowhere.

The problem is, how do we handle this avalanche of detail? How do we find all these points without tedious calculations? And, once we find them, how do we pick the ones that are important?

Modern Techniques for Using Midpoints

Midpoints are found in the works of several Medieval and Renaissance astrologers, but they did not become widely popular until this century, when their use was codified into a coherent system. This system was devised by the Hamburg school (also known as the Uranian school) of Alfred Witte and later simplified by the Cosmobiologists led by Reinhold Ebertin and his son Baldur Ebertin. Both schools originated in Germany, but both have since acquired large followings elsewhere as well. I have adopted my techniques mainly from the Cosmobiologists.

In the Uranian school, midpoints are part of a much larger array of sensitive points created by adding and subtracting longitudes of planets and other points in the chart. Uranian combinations are actually all a type of midpoint, but, unlike the midpoints I and the Cosmobiologists use, the most common type of Uranian combination is based on two pairs of points that share the same midpoint, and the sensitive point is less often the midpoint itself than one of the points in the pairs. When that sensitive point becomes occupied by a planet or other factor, all four factors become tied together in a "planetary picture" which combines all four symbols. Thus this system usually deals with configurations of three planets that make a fourth point sensitive. (See Figure 5, page 97.)

In contrast, the basic midpoint pattern that I and the Cosmobiologists use is a two-planet configuration that makes a third point sensitive, and the sensitive point is the midpoint itself. (See Figure 7, page 99.) Clearly, the possible two-planet configurations are much fewer than three-planet ones.

In Uranian astrology, planetary pictures can consist of natal, directed, and transiting factors, and even factors from another horoscope, all mixed together. But in Cosmobiology and the approach I take there are no midpoint pairs consisting of one natal and one transiting or directed body, or one body from another chart. All bodies are usually from the natal chart (though the body occupying the midpoint is sometimes transiting, directed, or from another chart). Again, in Cosmobiology the number of factors one has to deal with is limited enough to be manageable.

Using methods derived from Cosmobiology, it is therefore possible to examine the whole midpoint structure of a chart. The Uranians and Cosmobiologists have left us with simple devices for finding midpoints without any calculating. These are the 360° and 90° dials. Also, in the past few years, computer chart-casting services have begun to offer midpoint lists that can be used in place of dials. I will explain these dials and lists shortly. Using either, one can pick out the important midpoint combinations according to simple rules which I shall outline in this chapter.

The Geometry of Midpoints

Before going into how to find and organize midpoints, let us examine some of their basic properties. Figure 20A (page 149) shows that any two points on a circle divide the circle into two arcs, a longer arc and a shorter one. Consequently, there are also two direct midpoints for any two bodies, one bisecting the shorter arc (which we shall call the nearer midpoint), the other the longer arc (which we shall call the farther midpoint). This is why we say direct midpoint combinations can be made by opposition as well as conjunction aspects.

The nearer and farther midpoints are always exactly opposite each other. They form an axis going from one side of the zodiac to a point exactly 180° away on the other side, much like the axes formed by the Moon's nodes, the Ascendant-Descendant, and the Midheaven-Imum Coeli. Therefore a body that is opposite the nearer midpoint will always be conjunct the farther midpoint, and vice versa. Experience shows that in natal charts there is little or no distinction between the nearer and farther midpoints. Thus we can say that for all practical purposes an opposition to a midpoint is the same as a conjunction to a midpoint. (This is not always true, however, as in the composite horoscope there does seem to be a difference in intensity, if not meaning. See my book *Planets in Composite*.) By the same token, if a body is sextile one end of a midpoint axis it is trine the other end, and vice versa. A similar relationship exists between the semisquare and sesquiquadrate.

Aspects to Midpoints

Both the Uranians and Cosmobiologists use only aspects to midpoints based on multiples of 45°. For example, trines between a midpoint and another factor would not be considered. The early writings of these schools implied that trines, sextiles, and other three-series aspects are not effective, but more recently this position has been modified. I once used aspects not of the two-series routinely in midpoint work, and they were quite effective. Despite this, my standard practice and that of both the Uranians and Cosmobiologists is now to use only hard aspects in midpoint work.

The reasons are mainly practical. Using only hard aspects simplifies things, in that there is only one quality of aspect to color all midpoint combinations. The hard aspects (see pages 122-127) differ from each other, to be sure, but even so, their similarities are greater than their differences. This is because division by two, unlike division by three or any other whole number, creates octaves. In music, the higher tone in an octave has exactly half the wavelength as the lower, but to the ear it sounds nearly the same. If two people sing the same melody at the same time an octave apart, there is not only no dissonance, there is little awareness that two sets of notes are being sung. Similarly, the two-series aspects have virtually the same quality as the conjunction, as they merely halve, quarter, etc., the arc length in the same way wavelengths are divided to produce octaves in music.

By contrast, notes related as the trine and all other three-series aspects are to the conjunction are quite different in sound from the original note. In the musical fifth, which corresponds to the trine, the higher note has one-third the wavelength of the original tone. Thus the trine (or any other aspect not of the two-series) introduces additional qualities into the combination of planets, complicating an already complicated situation.

The midpoints tied to a planet or other point by hard aspect will tell a great deal about the condition of a planet in a chart. I do not believe that soft-aspect combinations can be used in exactly this way. It has not been my experience that anything is lost by using only the hard aspects among the midpoints, as long as one gets over the traditional and not very well-founded idea that all hard aspects are "bad."

Orbs in Midpoint Combinations

Because there are more than a hundred midpoints in a chart, the acceptable orb of aspect of a midpoint combination has to be smaller than in ordinary planet-to-planet aspects. Otherwise, we get combinations overlapping with each other to the extent that we cannot distinguish among the various factor combinations in the chart. This muddies the structure of the chart and makes the chart unreadable, at least by astrological means.

Among the Uranians and the Cosmobiologists the rule of thumb has been to use no more than a 1.5° orb. This means that anything (a midpoint or a single factor) within 1.5° to either side of a midpoint is considered to be in orb (that is, the total range is 3°). I prefer to use this orb only on direct midpoints, and to restrict the orb on indirect midpoints to 1°. This makes the structure of the chart clearer and hence easier to delineate.

How to Calculate a Midpoint

1. Convert the longitudes of the two single points from the usual notation in terms of signs to notation in terms of a 360° circle. That is, count the longitudes from 0° Aries instead of from 0° of their sign. To do this, for each sign you add the number of degrees given in Table 5.

Table 5
360°-Notation Equivalents of 0° of Each Sign

Aries	0°	Libra	180°
Taurus	30°	Scorpio	210°
Gemini	60°	Sagittarius	240°
Cancer	90°	Capricorn	270°
Leo	120°	Aquarius	300°
Virgo	150°	Pisces	330°

For example, for Bob Dylan's Sun, which is at 3° ♊ 31′, we would add 60° for Gemini, giving us 63°31′ in 360° notation. For his Moon, at 21° ♉ 31′, we add 30° for Taurus, giving us 51°31′.

2. Add the two longitudes together:

$$63°31'$$
$$+51°31'$$
$$114°62' \text{ or } 115°02'$$

3. Divide the sum by 2. In our example, we are better off leaving the longitude expressed as 114°62′, because 114 is an even number. The degrees, 114 divided by 2, give us 57°, while the minutes, 62 divided by 2, give us 31. Therefore the midpoint expressed in 360° notation is 57°31′.

4. To convert this back to sign notation, go back to Table 5 and find the largest number of degrees (30°) that can be subtracted from 57°31′ without producing a negative number. We subtract 30° from 57°31′ and arrive at 27° ♉ 31′ as Bob Dylan's Sun/Moon midpoint.

In this case, where the two planets were only one sign apart, we got the nearer midpoint. If the two planets were separated by more than 180°, we would have gotten the farther midpoint.

Using Dials in Midpoint Work

Happily, most calculation can be avoided by using the 360° and 90° dials. The 360° dial chart is useful for gaining an overview and for seeing all the direct midpoints. By checking the axes in square and semisquare to the direct axis, you can also find indirect midpoints; in fact it is possible to do midpoint work using only the 360° dial.

The 90° dial, however, saves even more labor and quadruples the accuracy possible with a dial. In the 90° dial chart all conjunctions, squares, and oppositions look like conjunctions, and all semisquares and sesquiquadrates look like oppositions. Therefore all hard aspects are immediately visible along a single axis. The 90° dial is especially suited to an approach that uses only hard aspects and treats them all alike. The only disadvantage is that you cannot distinguish squares and oppositions from conjunctions, or direct midpoints from indirect ones, without writing the sign of each planet in on the 90° chart or looking back at the 360° chart.

Using a 360° dial with a perfectly centered hole and accurate degree markings, you can get accuracy up to about a quarter of a degree; with a well-made 90° dial you can get accuracy to five minutes of arc or better. In the relatively rare cases where you need better accuracy (such as in checking an orb or timing a transit) you can calculate one or a few midpoints by hand or use a computer-calculated midpoint listing.

The 360° Dial

In order to use the 360° dial you must abandon the twelve-equal-wedges horoscope form prevalent in the United States and Britain in favor of the chart form more popular in continental Europe. This form has house cusps and all other factors placed around the circle in their true, rather than approximate, zodiacal longitudes.

Not only does the 360° dial make midpoint work easy, it also provides a valuable fringe benefit as a mechanical aspectarian. While the conventional method of chart drawing using sign notation lends itself to seeing traditional aspects which are all multiples of 30°, it does not lend itself to seeing aspects like quintiles, semisquares, sesquiquadrates, or aspects based on the seven-series or nine-series. A 360° dial can be marked to show any kind of aspect you might wish to investigate and can make its presence in a chart very clear.

Drawing the 360° Chart   To draw this chart, you need a 360° protractor or mechanical aspectarian with a hole in the exact center. Some people prefer a pinhole which they use with a thumbtack; others prefer a larger hole which fits a type of set-screw available from some astrological suppliers. The center of the paper on which one draws the chart is impaledon the tack or screw, and then the dial is fitted over this with the tack or screw coming up through its center hole.

To draw the chart you also need either an ordinary ruler which you line up between the center hole and the degree marking of the planet you are drawing in, or a specially made ruler (such as the one in Figure 21) that fits over the tack or set-screw. With one of these you will be making short lines on the paper from the rim of the dial outward. These lines will indicate the position of each factor in the chart.

Begin by turning the dial so that the approximate degree of the Midheaven is at the top of the paper. Now find 0° Aries and make your first mark there. While you are drawing the chart you will want to keep the

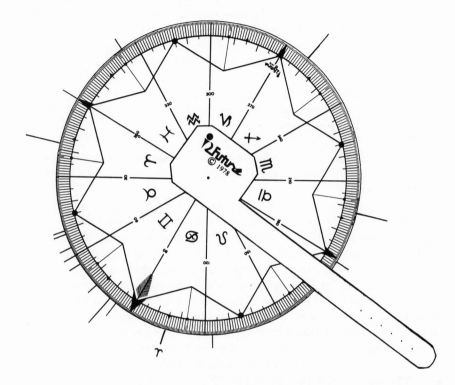

Figure 21. Drawing the 360° chart

dial's 0° Aries mark exactly on the paper's 0° Aries mark at all times. If you are using a set-screw you can tighten it to keep the dial from turning; if you are using a thumbtack hold the dial down firmly. Now, being sure that all the lines you draw point outward from the exact center of the dial, make short lines indicating as closely as possible the exact zodiacal degree and minute of each house cusp and other factor in the chart. Then you can write in the glyphs and longitudes for all the factors next to their lines at the same time as you check each line to see that you have drawn its position correctly. The ruler shown in Figure 21 is set to draw the line for Bob Dylan's Neptune.

Figure 22 shows Bob Dylan's chart drawn in this way. The dial shown is an especially good one developed by I2Future of New York made by Astro-Graphics Services for use in the Uranian system, but it is also usable for conventional astrology. The feathered arrow is at the Sun/Moon midpoint.

Using the 360° Dial to Find Midpoints   The dial originally used for placing the planets in the chart is now used as a measuring tool. To find the midpoint of any two factors in the chart, simply turn the dial so its pointer (the feathered arrow) is approximately halfway between the two factors. Now, using the degree markings on either side of the pointer as a guide, adjust the dial so the degrees on either side are exactly equal. Figure 22 shows the dial turned to indicate the location of Dylan's Sun/Moon midpoint.

As you can see, the pointer is very near Uranus. In fact, Uranus is on the Sun/Moon midpoint well within the 1.5° orb I allow for direct midpoints. We therefore write:

Sun/Moon = Uranus

To get an idea of what this might mean in the chart, you can look in the next chapter at the brief delineations given for Sun/Moon, Sun/Uranus, and Moon/Uranus.

Now you can check what other midpoints lie along the Sun/Moon axis. To do so, leave the feathered arrow on the Sun/Moon midpoint and scan to one side of the midpoint until you encounter another point. Note the arc between that point and the midpoint. Then scan in the opposite direction to see if there is another point the same number of degrees away from the midpoint. If there is one within 3° of the same arc length, the midpoint of these two points will be within 1.5° orb of the Sun/Moon midpoint. This is because a midpoint is found by splitting the arc between two points into two equal arcs. If the original arc is increased by a certain number of degrees, the midpoint will move half that number of degrees. Therefore, the difference between two arcs on opposite sides of an axis must always be within twice the orb of the midpoint configuration.

We find that the midpoint of Jupiter/Uranus is well within a degree of Sun/Moon. And so is the midpoint of Sun/Saturn. All these direct midpoints are plainly visible using the 360° dial. We now have:

Sun/Moon = Uranus = Jupiter/Uranus = Sun/Saturn

There may also be indirect midpoints in square, semisquare, or sesquiquadrate to the Sun/Moon midpoint. To check for squares, keep the feathered arrow on the Sun/Moon midpoint and find the two unfeathered arrows in square to the pointer (these will have "180" and "360" written on their lines). These two arrows are two ends of a single axis that is in square to the direct axis. Just as you looked along the direct axis for direct midpoints, look for indirect midpoints along the axis in square to the direct axis.

To check for semisquares and sesquiquadrates, find the four large dots midway between the four arrows. These dots are the ends of two more axes, each of which is semisquare/sesquiquadrate the direct axis. Look along both of these axes for midpoints or single factors that are semisquare/sesquiquadrate the direct axis.

In Bob Dylan's chart there are no midpoints within a 1° orb of

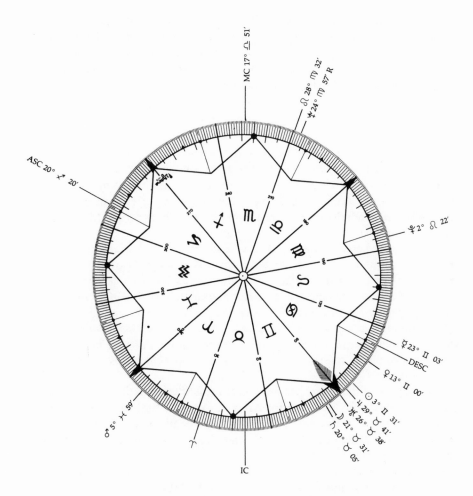

Figure 22. Finding midpoints in Bob Dylan's 360° chart

square to Sun/Moon, but Mercury/Pluto and Mars/Saturn are both semisquare/sesquiquadrate the Sun/Moon axis within the 1° orb allowable for indirect midpoints (see Figure 22). We can thus show all the midpoints connected to the Sun/Moon midpoint as follows:

Sun/Moon = Uranus = Jupiter/Uranus = Sun/Saturn =
Mercury/Pluto = Mars/Saturn

The sum total of all the midpoints and points tied to a given point or midpoint is usually called an axis. We have just been looking at the Sun/Moon axis of Bob Dylan's horoscope. Although all the above midpoints may be within the allowed 1.5° and 1° orbs of being in aspect to Sun/Moon, they are not necessarily within orb of each other. The first point in such a listing is always the center of the orb spread.

Looking at four separate axes to find all the direct and indirect midpoint combinations may seem laborious, but in actual practice we are going to be primarily concerned with direct midpoints. The indirect midpoints we reserve for detailed work. It is therefore not usually necessary to tally all midpoint aspects to a given point. Also, as we said above, the 90° dial greatly simplifies finding the indirect midpoints.

The 90° Dial

Figure 23 shows Bob Dylan's chart drawn with a 90° dial. Note that instead of being divided into 360° this dial is divided into 90°. Since there are only one-quarter as many degrees, the degrees are four times as large; hence the greater accuracy possible. There is room for each degree to be marked off in subdivisions of 5′ of arc, with longer lines for the 15′ and 30′ subdivisions.

The feathered arrow at the top represents 0° Aries, and the zodiac continues around counterclockwise from this pointer. Groups of 5° are marked off by alternating black and white areas on the inner ring. One-quarter of the way around is a large dot marking off 22.5°; one-third of the way around is a line going to the center and marking off 30°; one-half of the way around is an arrow without feathers that marks off 45°; two-thirds of the way around is another line going to the center and this time marking off 60°. And so on, to the feathered arrow at the top, which this time around represents 90°.

Note also that there are only three signs shown on the dial. The first third is marked with the glyph for Aries, the second third with Taurus, and the third third with Gemini. This is just shorthand for saying that all the cardinal signs (Aries, Cancer, Libra, and Capricorn) will fall into the first third of the 90° dial; all the fixed signs (Taurus, Leo, Scorpio, and Aquarius) will fall into the second third; and all the mutable signs (Gemini, Virgo, Sagittarius, and Pisces) will fall into the third third.

What the 90° dial does is divide the zodiac into four pieces—the first from 0° Aries to 29°59′59″ Gemini; the second from 0° Cancer to 29°59′59″ Virgo; the third from 0° Libra to 29°59′59″ Sagittarius; and the fourth from 0° Capricorn to 29°59′59″ Pisces—and then place all four pieces on top of one another. This is why two planets in square (say, from 7° Aries to 7° Cancer) or in opposition (7° Aries to 7° Libra) will in the 90° chart look as if they are in conjunction: Cancer and Libra (and Capricorn) have been placed right on top of Aries.

For similar reasons, all semisquares and sesquiquadrates look like oppositions. These are easy to see because if the feathered arrow is on a certain planet, the planet in semisquare or sesquiquadrate will always be at the unfeathered arrow opposite. Likewise (though this is not as important in midpoint work), all aspects that are 30° multiples—the trine, sextile, semisextile, and quincunx—will on the 90° dial look like trines. These can be seen fairly easily because if the feathered arrow is on one planet, the

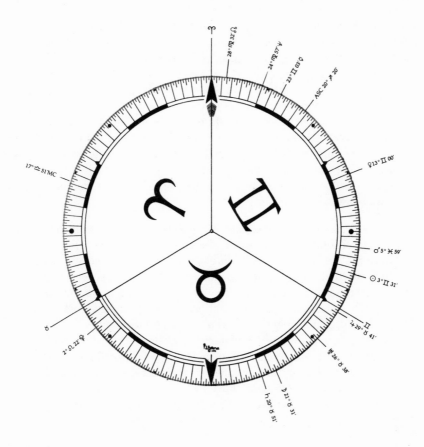

Figure 23. Bob Dylan's 90° chart

planet in a 30° multiple aspect will be at one of the two other lines extending to the center of the dial.

Drawing the 90° Chart   Impale your piece of paper and then the 90° dial on a thumbtack or set-screw, and then turn the dial so the feathered arrow points to the top of the page. Hold the dial down to keep it from turning, and with your ruler draw a longish line at the feathered arrow. Mark the line with the glyph for Aries. This will represent not only 0° Aries, but 0° of all the cardinal signs. Also go one-third of the way counterclockwise to the next line that extends to the center, and draw a line there marked with the glyph for Taurus. And go one-third of the circle further to the other line that extends to the center, and draw a line there marked with the glyph for Gemini.

You are now ready to draw in the lines indicating the positions of the planets, lunar node, Ascendant, and Midheaven (I do not usually put intermediate house cusps in on the 90° chart). It is easiest to take the positions in zodiacal order, starting with the Aries positions, then the Taurus, etc. When you get to Cancer, you are back at the 0° cardinal point and you start going around the 90° dial all over again. Then go through all the positions again beginning with Aries to check whether the lines are at the right degrees and also to draw in the glyphs for the planets. You can mark the Ascendant with "A" and Midheaven with "M." It is not necessary to enter the degree and minute of each position on the 90° chart, but if you indicate what sign each factor is in it will make it easier to distinguish conjunctions from squares and oppositions.

To see how the 360° chart translates to the 90° chart, compare Figure 23 with Figure 22.

Using the 90° Dial to Find Midpoints   Let us look again at Bob Dylan's Sun/Moon midpoint (the feathered arrow in Figure 24). Finding it is similar to finding it with the 360° dial: you merely locate the Sun and Moon and turn the dial so the feathered pointer is halfway between them. The only difference is in what information we get from doing this. We see much more clearly how exact the combinations are, and are thus better able to judge orbs. Also, not only do we see all the direct midpoints (Sun/Moon = Uranus = Jupiter/ Uranus = Sun/Saturn), with the 90° dial we also see all the indirect midpoints (Sun/Moon = Mercury/Pluto = Mars/Saturn) as well, this time by looking at only one axis (because the four axes of the 360° dial are now all on top of each other).

In order to distinguish the direct from the indirect midpoints (and to determine whether to allow a 1.5° or a 1° orb) you would need to refer back to the 360° chart. This is why it helps first to investigate the direct midpoints using the 360° dial. Then with the 90° dial you can add the indirect midpoints.

Using the 90° dial tempts one to make no distinction between direct and indirect midpoints, or between major and minor hard aspects, which is what many Cosmobiologists do. As I said, however, I like to allow a smaller orb for indirect midpoints and also to give them less weight in my judgments. Although the 90° dial is a valuable tool, not only for seeing hard aspects at a glance, but also for timing transits and directions to the fraction of a degree, I find I must rely equally on the 360° chart or on listings such as I will now describe.

Using Listings in Midpoint Work

It is possible to list midpoints in such a way that the lists can supplement or even eliminate the need for the 360° and 90° charts. Whether you use dials or listings is largely a matter of personal preference; both have their advantages. The chief bar to lists in the past was the tedious

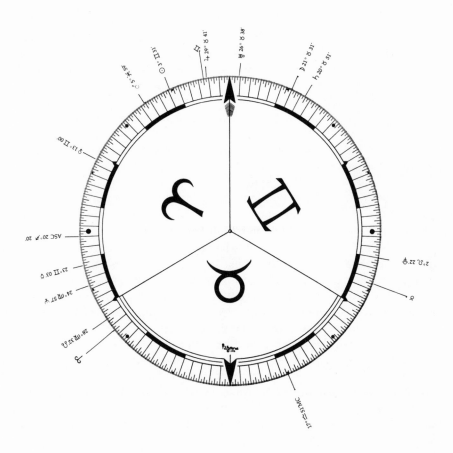

Figure 24. Finding midpoints in Bob Dylan's 90° chart

calculation they required, but this is no longer a real obstacle because many computer chart-casting services and home computer programs routinely offer midpoint listings in addition to the regular chart. Using a listing showing the actual zodiacal position of each pair of factors in the chart together with a listing known as a 45° sort, you can see all the hard aspects and all the midpoints attached to any axis just as you can with dials. The advantage of listings is that you do not have to draw dial-type charts; you can get along, at least for natal work, with a twelve-equal-wedges chart easily drawn by you or a computer. Also, you have all positions exact to the minute of arc, which helps in judging orbs accurately (particularly important in research work) and in timing transits and directions. The disadvantage of lists is mainly when you want to compare the natal chart to transits or directions for a number of different times in someone's life; ways can be devised for computers to make this easier, but using dials is generally the more convenient method in such a case.

The Zodiacal Listing   The triangular array labeled "Halfsums or Midpoints" in Figure 25 lists the degree, sign, and minute in the zodiac of all Bob Dylan's midpoints. It is arranged so that by finding where the vertical and horizontal columns cross you can immediately find any midpoint or single factor. To locate the position of Bob Dylan's Sun/Moon midpoint, you simply find the column headed "Su" for "Sun" and run down it until you find the line headed "Mo" for "Moon." Where the Sun column and the Moon line cross it says "27Tau31", which is the degree, sign, and minute of Bob Dylan's Sun/Moon midpoint.

The zodiacal listing does not reveal which midpoints are in aspect to which other midpoints. Its chief use is as an index for locating the true zodiacal position of midpoints shown in the 45° sort.

The 45° Sort   The 45° sort is based on the same principle as the 90° dial, except that in this case the zodiac is divided into eight parts instead of four before the parts are laid on top of each other. This means that the list goes from 0° Aries through 14°59′59″ Taurus, then starts at the beginning again for 15° Taurus through 29°59′59″ Gemini, then starts at the beginning again for 0° Cancer through 14°59′59″ Leo, etc.

The reason the listing is in a 45° instead of a 90° modulus is that whereas the 90° dial makes semisquares and sesquiquadrates readily apparent at the opposite end from the feathered pointer, a listing cannot do this. A listing must make the semisquares and sesquiquadrates as well as the squares and oppositions look like conjunctions.

A 45° sort mingles all the midpoints and single factors from each of the eight segments of the zodiac together into one listing in ascending degree order. Thus factors that are in any hard aspect to each other will be next to each other in the list.

Using the 45° Sort to Investigate Midpoint Axes   The bottom of Figure 25 shows a computer printout of Bob Dylan's 45° sort. To find his Sun/Moon midpoint, we can scan down the list, but it usually takes less time to refer first to the zodiacal listing at the top of Figure 25. We locate the Sun/Moon midpoint in the zodiacal listing as described above, and find it to be 27°31′ Taurus. Using the rules in Table 6 we translate the number of degrees the midpoint is in its sign into a 45° sort position. Since 27°31′ Taurus is in the second half of a fixed sign, we subtract 15° from it, getting 12°31′ in the 45° sort, and sure enough, it is the Sun/Moon midpoint.

Table 6
Translating Zodiacal Longitudes into 45° Sort Longitudes

Cardinal Signs: Degrees are the same.
Fixed Signs: First half (through 14°59′): add 30 to degrees in sign.

Second half (from 15°00′): subtract 15 from degrees in sign.

Mutable Signs: Add 15 to degrees in sign.

Now we can instantly see all the midpoints and other factors that are in some hard aspect to the Sun/Moon axis. We simply read off all the factors that are just above and below "Su/Mo" in the list, stopping when we reach the end of our 1° orb for indirect midpoints. Reading up from "Su/Mo," we find "As/Vx" (Ascendant/Vertex—this computer program includes the Vertex, which we will not use here), "Su/Sa" (Sun/Saturn), and Uranus. We continue reading up for another 30′ to find any midpoints that might be direct and therefore allowable within our 1.5° orb for direct midpoints. We find "Pl/As" (Pluto/Ascendant). To see what kind of hard aspect Pluto/Ascendant makes to Sun/Moon, we need to check the number of degrees in their signs of both midpoints in the zodiacal listing. Going back to the zodiacal listing, we find Sun/Moon at "27Tau31" and Pluto/Ascendant at "11Lib21." This is a sesquiquadrate, so we discard Pluto/Ascendant because it is too far out of orb for an indirect midpoint.

Reading down from "Su/Mo," we have "Me/Pl" (Mercury/Pluto), "Ma/Sa" (Mars/Saturn), "Ju/Ur" (Jupiter/Uranus), and "Me/Vx" (Mercury/Vertex—which we won't use) within our 1° orb for indirect midpoints. Looking as far as 30′ further down (up to 14 01) within our 1.5° orb for direct midpoints, we find "Ne/Pl" (Neptune/Pluto) and "Mo/Ma" (Moon/Mars). Again, we check the zodiacal listing to see whether these factors are tied to the Sun/Moon axis directly or indirectly. Neptune/Pluto turns out to be at "28Leo40," which is in square to Sun/Moon, and Moon/Mars is at "13Lib45," which is sesquiquadrate, so neither of these midpoints is allowable. We are now ready to write out the midpoints connected to Sun/Moon.

Sun/Moon = Sun/Saturn = Uranus = Mercury/Pluto = Mars/Saturn = Jupiter/Uranus

The principle of the 45° sort can be used to highlight aspects that are multiples of any angle. One could have 30° sorts, 22.5° sorts (sometimes used by Uranian astrologers in this country), 15° sorts, or whatever. Sorts would be especially valuable in finding multiples based on fifths or sevenths of the circle, which are very hard to examine in the conventional mode of representation.

Rules for Delineating Midpoints

When reading a chart, one uses midpoints mainly to give additional information about the cosmic state of each planet. Thus the midpoints I look for first are those attached to individual factors in the chart. Only when I am interested in finding out more about a specific issue will I look at

BOB DYLAN

Halfsums or Midpoints

	Su	Mo	Me	**Ve**	Ma	Ju	Sa	Ur	Ne
Su	3Gem31								
Mo	27Tau31	21Tau31							
Me	13Gem17	7Gem17	23Gem 3						
Ve	8Gem15	2Gem15	18Gem 2	13Gem 0					
Ma	19Lib45	13Lib45	29Lib31	24Lib29	5Pis59				
Ju	1Gem36	25Tau36	11Gem22	6Gem20	17Lib50	29Tau41			
Sa	26Tau48	20Tau48	6Gem34	1Gem33	13Lib 2	24Tau53	20Tau 5		
Ur	0Gem 4	24Tau 4	9Gem51	4Gem49	16Lib18	28Tau 9	23Tau22	26Tau38	
Ne	29Can14	23Can14	9Leo 0	3Leo58	15Sag28	27Can19	22Can31	25Can47	24Vir57
Pl	2Can57	26Can57	12Can43	7Can41	19Sco11	1Can 2	26Gem14	29Gem30	28Leo40
No	1Leo 2	25Can 2	10Leo48	5Leo46	17Sag16	29Can 7	24Can19	27Can35	26Vir45
As	11Vir55	5Vir55	21Vir41	16Vir40	28Cap 9	10Vir 0	5Vir12	8Vir29	7Sco38
MC	10Leo41	4Leo41	20Leo27	15Leo26	26Sag55	8Leo46	3Leo58	7Leo15	6Lib24
Vx	3Can29	27Gem29	13Can16	8Can14	19Sco43	1Can34	26Gem47	0Can 3	29Leo12
Ar	1Tau45	25Ari45	11Tau32	6Tau30	17Vir59	29Ari50	25Ari 3	28Ari19	27Gem28

	Pl	No	As	MC	Vx	Ar
Pl	2Leo22					
No	0Vir27	28Vir32				
As	11Lib21	9Sco26	20Sag20			
MC	10Vir 7	8Lib12	19Sco 5	17Lib51		
Vx	2Leo55	1Vir 0	11Lib54	10Vir40	3Leo28	
Ar	1Gem11	29Gem16	10Leo10	8Can56	1Gem44	0Ari 0

45 degree sorting of midpoints

*Ari	0	0	Mo/Ur	9	4	Ma/Ur	16 18	Sa/No	24 19	Me/Ma	29 31	Ne/As	37 38
Ur/Vx	0	3	Ju/Sa	9 53	Ve/Sa	16 33	Ve/Ma	24 29	Ju/Ar	29 50	*Merc	38 3
Ve/MC	0 26	Mo/Ju	10 36	Su/Ju	16 36	Me/Ur	24 51	Ma/Ne	30 28	Ju/MC	38 46
Ju/Pl	1 2	Pl/As	11 21	Vx/Ar	16 44	Ju/As	25 0	Su/No	31 2	Me/Ne	39 0
Ju/Vx	1 34	*Uran	11 38	Mo/Ve	17 15	Mo/No	25 2	Ve/As	31 40	No/As	39 26
Su/Pl	2 57	Su/Sa	11 48	Ma/Ju	17 50	Sa/Ar	25 3	Su/Ar	31 45	*Nept	39 57
Su/Vx	3 29	As/Vx	11 54	*MC	17 51	Pl/MC	25 7	Ma/No	32 16	As/Ar	40 10
As/MC	4 5	Su/Mo	12 31	*Sun	18 31	MC/Vx	25 40	*Plut	32 22	Su/MC	40 41
Ma/Pl	4 11	Me/Pl	12 43	Su/Ma	19 45	Mo/Ar	25 45	Pl/Vx	32 55	Me/No	40 48
Ma/Vx	4 43	Ma/Sa	13 2	Ve/Ur	19 49	Ur/Ne	25 47	Ma/Ar	32 59	Sa/Pl	41 14
*Sat	5 5	Ju/Ur	13 9	Sa/As	20 12	Me/Ju	26 22	Me/Ve	33 2	Me/Ar	41 32
Me/MC	5 27	Me/Vx	13 16	Sa/Ne	22 31	Su/Me	28 17	Ve/Ne	33 58	Ne/No	41 45
Mo/Sa	5 48	Ne/Pl	13 40	Mo/As	20 55	Su/As	26 55	*Vert	33 28	Sa/Vx	41 47
Ne/MC	6 24	Mo/Ma	13 45	Ve/Ju	21 20	Ur/No	27 35	Sa/MC	33 58	Ma/MC	41 55
*Moon	6 31	Ne/Vx	14 12	Me/Sa	21 34	*Ven	28 0	Mo/MC	34 41	Mo/Pl	41 57
Ve/Pl	7 41	*Jup	14 41	Mo/Me	22 17	Ma/As	28 9	*Asc	35 20	Ne/Ar	42 28
No/MC	8 12	Su/Ur	15 4	Sa/Ne	22 31	Su/Me	28 17	Ve/No	35 46	Mo/Vx	42 29
Ve/Vx	8 14	Pl/No	15 27	Mo/Ne	23 14	Ur/Ar	28 19	Ve/Ar	36 30	*Node	43 32
Sa/Ur	8 22	No/Vx	16 0	Su/Ve	23 15	Ju/No	29 7	Me/As	36 41	No/Ar	44 16
MC/Ar	8 56	Pl/Ar	16 11	Ur/As	23 29	Su/Ne	29 14	Ur/MC	37 15	Ur/Pl	44 30

Figure 25. Bob Dylan's 45° sort

midpoint axes that are not occupied by a single factor. In a few cases, such axes will be the focus of a number of midpoints and will therefore have importance. The effects of individual midpoints will be seen most clearly when they are set off by dynamic factors such as transits, solar arc directions, or progressions.

Not all midpoints are to be taken equally. Here are the criteria I use for picking out the important ones.

1. Midpoints involving the Sun, Moon, Midheaven, or Ascendant are to be taken more seriously than others. One or both factors making up the midpoint may come from this group, or the midpoint may be in a hard aspect to one of these single factors.

2. Direct midpoints—ones that are conjunct or opposite (really the same, as shown above) a single factor are more important than midpoints that aspect a single factor by square, semisquare, or sesquiquadrate. I find that direct midpoints are as important as major aspects in influencing a chart. One neglects them at one's peril; if you use no other type of midpoint, use these.

3. Midpoints of single points that also happen to be in aspect to each other are more intense and sensitive than those where the two single points are not in aspect. Even relatively minor aspects should be considered, and also those that would ordinarily seem out of orb. I think this phenomenon is responsible for the large orbs other astrologers often get away with on major aspects. In a T-square, grand cross, grand trine, or other aspect pattern that is also a midpoint configuration, one often sees orbs that are larger than 5°, and yet the aspect still seems to operate strongly. I find invariably that the midpoint of one or more of the pairs of planets involved closely aspects one or more of the other factors by a hard angle. This ties the factors together in a way that no large-orbed major aspect could. One should always check these major aspect patterns to determine whether or not the midpoints they form are in close aspect to one or more of the factors in the aspect pattern.

4. With midpoints, as with any other worthwhile technique, a theme should be repeated several times in a chart if it is to be taken seriously. Possibly the one exception to this is direct midpoint combinations, but data from these should, like any other indication, still be checked against the rest of the chart.

9

Brief Meanings of Planetary Pairs

You have now been exposed to the core meaning of each planet and each other major point in the chart. This chapter gives brief delineations of all possible pairs formed by the ten planets, the lunar nodes, Ascendant, Midheaven, and 0° Aries Point. The factors that are not planets are included here because experience has shown that their midpoints are important and can be treated the same as midpoints involving only planets.

The delineations in this chapter can be used in several ways. First, they are a short guide to how two factors in aspect will interact. Second, by scanning through them you will get an idea of what midpoint axes to look at to answer specific questions about the horoscope. Third, when you have a factor at the midpoint of two other factors, you can use this chapter to delineate a three-factor combination. For example, if you have Sun/Moon=Uranus, you can look up Sun/Moon, Sun/Uranus, and Moon/Uranus. These three delineations will give you an idea of what this three-planet combination means. You can also use this method for three-factor aspect patterns like the grand trine, T-square, minor grand trine, and yod, and can even extend it to combinations involving more than three factors.

This summary of meanings is based not only on putting together the keywords for each factor, but also on other indications that have been found by various researchers including myself—meanings that do not always follow obviously from the key ideas of the planets, at least not until one gets into them more deeply than usual.

Pairs with the Sun

Sun/Moon The balance of male and female within the psyche, which expresses itself in terms of relationships with the opposite sex. Inner psychological balance. May also at times relate to one's experience of the mother and father as a pair.

Sun/Mercury The mental and verbal expression of the will. The desire to communicate, know, and understand. Thinking about one's own self-expression. Very personal thinking. Expressing one's thoughts.

Sun/Venus   The will to have relationships, love, or create. May relate to artistic creativity, if other factors support. Personal happiness and gratification, comfort, feeling good. For both men and women this point may contribute to what they expect of the opposite sex.

Sun/Mars   The will, vitality, energy (particularly for self-expression), the masculine side of the self, personal aggressiveness and self-assertion. The ability to act and take the initiative. Particularly in a woman's chart this point may symbolize one's expectations about males. This can also be a point of conflict with males.

Sun/Jupiter   The will to grow, expand, and experience as much of the universe as possible. Physical well-being and health. Openness and liberality, but also possibly profligacy. May express itself on the spiritual as well as the material plane.

Sun/Saturn   The active expression of one's principles of right and wrong, true and false. The experience of both structure and personal limitation. The experience of the father or other guide and authority figures. The sense of personal discipline, also repression and inhibition. Limitations of the freedom of the will.

Sun/Uranus   The desire for one's unique self-expression. Rebellion and eccentricity. The desire to become free of limitation and the restrictions of the past. Originality of self-expression. The unconventional and offbeat.

Sun/Neptune   One's sensitivity to subtle forces from without. This may be experienced as weakness and lack of self-assertiveness. Inclination to mystical or spiritual inquiry. Passivity, lack of initiative, allowing another to take control. Being a medium for other's energies.

Sun/Pluto   The will to transform, to be effective, and to bring about regeneration. The will to destroy. The desire for power. Also the experience of power, destruction, or regeneration. Charismatic energies in either the self or one's world.

Sun/Nodes   The desire to reach out and make contact, to connect with others, or to meet someone (usually male). To form a group. The desire for group activity and teamwork. The experience of group desire and will.

Sun/Ascendant   Somewhat similar to Sun/Node, but more intimate relationships are involved. The desire to encounter others intimately and at close range for either partnership or competition. In the charts of either sex, may signify relationships with a male person with whom one is closely associated.

Sun/Midheaven   A part of the ego complex. One's drive to find a unique course for one's life, and the awareness of that direction. Often related to one's experience of the father. The sense of individuality.

Sun/Aries The desire to make connections in the larger world, to be known before the public, and to make an impact on the world. Can be a point of fame, if other factors in the chart give support. One's public influence, or at least influence outside of one's personal sphere.

Pairs with the Moon

Moon/Mercury Thought and communication influenced by feelings and emotions. Non-rational thought. The communication of one's feelings to others. Sensing the moods and feelings of others. Changeable thinking. A point that would be useful for public speaking and understanding the public temperament.

Moon/Venus Love, feeling happy, the emotional sense of the beautiful. Tender and nurturing love, such as a mother would have for a child. In both sexes this point relates to the experience of the mother, and in males it relates to women in general.

Moon/Mars Anger, emotional upset, emotional self-assertion. Instinctive reactions of aggression or self-defense. To act under the dictates of emotion. Childish aggressiveness.

Moon/Jupiter Feelings of protection, warmth, and nurture. Generosity. In a man's chart, positive emotional relations with women. Emotions operating on a religious or spiritual plane. Expression of emotions as a positive flow reaching out to others.

Moon/Saturn Feelings of loneliness. Feeling cut off or alienated, not caring for or being cared for by anyone. Inhibited feelings, feelings subject to discipline. Somberness, sobriety, reserve. In women's charts can be a point of self-deprecation. In charts of either sex can mean difficulties with the mother.

Moon/Uranus Emotional need for freedom. Need for unusual emotional experiences. Sudden actions dictated by feeling, outbursts of emotion. Disruptions of old patterns of living, breaks with the past, disruptions in nurture.

Moon/Neptune Extreme sensitivity and subjection to external energies and influences. Tendency to self-sacrifice or martyrdom. Passivity. Escapism, fantasies, unconscious forces influencing the imagination. Illusions created by subconscious desires or energies that have their origin in the past.

Moon/Pluto Emotional transformation, powerful feelings, intense desires, emotional fanaticism. Dominance of one's consciousness by unconscious energies. Emotional power struggles. In male charts may be a point indicating difficulty with women. Unconscious manipulation of others or by others.

Moon/Nodes   Connections with people from the past, connections based primarily on emotion, connections with women. Family groups, contacts with relations, domestic encounters, meetings with people with whom one has a strong affinity.

Moon/Ascendant   Close relationships with women, close emotional relationships, close relationships with people whom one has known for a long time. Habits in relationships. Domestic relationships. Expression of emotions to or from others in the immediate environment.

Moon/Midheaven   One's own feelings and attitudes, especially those conditioned most by early experience, family, and heredity. One's relationship with the past, and its effects on one's destiny and life direction. Probably also contributes to the experience of one's own mother.

Moon/Aries   To be known to the world for nurturing or feminine qualities or for one's emotional nature. Relations with the public. The ability to be accepted by the public as one of them.

Pairs with Mercury

Mercury/Venus   The ability to communicate love and affection. Aesthetic thoughts. The ability to be concretely creative as an artist. To use techniques to create beauty. Ability in crafts. Creative writing. Thinking influenced by considerations of beauty or harmony rather than strict logic.

Mercury/Mars   The expression of anger or conflict. Fondness for argument or debate. Energetic and vigorous thinking. Verbal self-assertion. The determination to act upon one's own ideas. Forceful intellect.

Mercury/Jupiter   The ability to make judgments based on maximum understanding. Love of negotiations and business. Judgment conditioned by ideals of fairness and justice, although sometimes lacking in precision and accuracy of thought.

Mercury/Saturn   Careful and considered thought. Caution and conservatism. One-track-mind. Depression, thoughts of sadness and separation. Preference for the concrete and practical rather than the abstract. Methodical approach to problem solving.

Mercury/Uranus   Lightning-like mind, tendency to be scattered and become nervous through haste. Sudden decisions or thoughts. Need for intellectual stimulation and excitement, need for the unusual. Often relates to ability in mathematics, science, or technology or to involvement in occult techniques such as astrology.

Mercury/Neptune   Imagination and inspiration. Possibility of confusion, muddled or irrational thinking. Nervous weakness or exhaustion. Concern with spiritual ideas and ideals. The need to transcend ordinary thought patterns.

Mercury/Pluto   The desire to influence others, to mold others' thinking. Transformations and crises in thought. The ability to be a convincing speaker or teacher. Tendency to get involved in mental power struggles. Deep thinking with great insight into motivation and human psychology. The ability to investigate or do research.

Mercury/Nodes   Mental contacts and connections. To establish connections by communication. To meet others. Correspondence, the desire to exchange ideas with others. The ability to perform mental work in groups.

Mercury/Ascendant   The verbal and mental expression of one's personality to others, and also the ability to listen to others. To speak. The reception of data from the environment by means of one's sense organs.

Mercury/Midheaven   One's own ideas, one's point of view. Planning one's own life direction, thinking about objectives. Knowing or thinking about oneself. Considering one's own individuality.

Mercury/Aries   To be known in the world for intellect or because of involvement in communications or transportation. To be involved in communications media or in the creation of public opinion. To write, especially for publication.

Pairs with Venus

Venus/Mars   Passion, sexual energy, love between the sexes. The physical aspect of sexuality. Creative energy, artistic work. To seek self-satisfaction in love. The balance between the need for relationship and individual self-expression and will.

Venus/Jupiter   Harmonious love expression, happiness. Artistic or other creative ability. To enjoy luxury and comfort, often at the price of taking initiative. Protective and nurturing love.

Venus/Saturn   Love or the desire for comfort being disciplined or restricted by practical considerations. Coldness, inability to express love, sexual repression, perversion of love. Art or creativity turned toward practical or commercial ends.

Venus/Uranus   Sudden, unusual or unstable relationships. Desire for freedom in relationships or for exciting relationships. Unusual forms of creativity.

Venus/Neptune   The abstract ideal of the beautiful, the romantic ideal. Artistic taste and creativity. Romantic ideals in relationships, illusions about or in love (often leading to disappointment). Platonic love. Love of people vastly better or worse off than oneself, including those who take care of one or need to be taken care of.

Venus/Pluto   The power of love to transform, love used as a device for creating transformation. Power struggles in love. Intensely emotional attitudes toward love, often extremely sensual and sexually intense. Love as a vehicle for transforming one's consciousness of the everyday world.

Venus/Nodes   Love connections or meetings. Connections or meetings with friends or beautiful persons. Happy meetings with others. Working with creative or artistic people or to achieve some creative objective.

Venus/Ascendant   The ability to project attractiveness, to charm others. Getting love from others. The ability to bring about close love relationships. The ability to bring about compromise and harmony in the environment.

Venus/Midheaven   One's own love and happiness in relationships. One's own creativity and love of beauty. Admiration of the self. Often a sign of creativity in the arts.

Venus/Aries   To be known as an artist or creative person, or for involvement with beauty, decoration, or the arts. To be known in some way for one's love or beauty.

Pairs with Mars

Mars/Jupiter   Fortunate action, action leading to growth. Luck arising from a good sense of timing. Physical and athletic prowess. Creative actions leading to an increase in opportunity. Often associated with births and marriages.

Mars/Saturn   Inhibited actions, inhibited anger, frustration. Disciplined or concentrated energies, hard work, energy focused on narrow objectives, the ability to perform painstaking work. In charts of both sexes, often associated with difficult father relationships. In women's charts, often signifies difficulties with males in general.

Mars/Uranus   Rebellion, non-conformity, difficulties with authority, the drive for absolute independence. Fighting for freedom. Extreme personal eccentricity. Sudden physical actions often leading to accidents. Often associated with surgery.

Mars/Neptune   Weakness, paralysis, feelings of inferiority or inability to cope. Covert actions. Connected with allergies, drug problems, and infectious diseases. Also spiritual activity and work in which spiritual rather than physical benefit is the object.

Mars/Pluto   Striving, hard work. To contend against difficult odds, often successfully. Brutality and conflict. Ambition, ruthless drive, the desire to achieve one's objectives at all costs.

Mars/Nodes   Involvement with workers in a common activity, either cooperative or conflicting. Involvement in sports.

Mars/Ascendant   Competition with others, conflicts, the ability to withstand opposition in one's environment. To stand up to others.

Mars/Midheaven   To assert oneself or one's objectives. "I act." One's own actions. To display great personal energy. The awareness of and assertion of one's own individuality with respect to others.

Mars/Aries   To be known for one's aggressive or self-assertive qualities. A person of action. To have one's intentions affect the greater world around one. People, such as athletes, known for their energy or physical prowess.

Pairs with Jupiter

Jupiter/Saturn   The balance between one's conservative and liberal sides. Optimism tempered by caution. Patient and careful growth on the material plane. Associated with business on a large scale, capitalism. Badly placed, indicates swinging between extremes of optimism and pessimism, or between complete impatience and being content with the status quo.

Jupiter/Uranus   The urge to break free of restraint, the drive for freedom. The need or desire for sudden changes of fortune, hence associated with sudden luck, either bad or good. Difficulties with restraints imposed by the law or other authorities.

Jupiter/Neptune   Optimistic dreams and speculations, the tendency to gamble or take other risks. Idealism, concern with mystical and spiritual issues. Idealistic humanitarianism, the desire to work for the greater good with little thought of personal gain.

Jupiter/Pluto   The drive to improve. The drive to grow in one's personal life, hence the drive for success and achievement. Also, the danger of conflicts with people in power or with those who might feel threatened by one's achievement.

Jupiter/Nodes   Coming together with others for mutual growth and benefit or for the study of religious or philosophical subjects. The ability to make fortunate connections with others or to meet those that can be of assistance; the ability to make a good impression.

Jupiter/Ascendant   Close relationships that help one, fortunate relationships, relationships that permit growth and expansion on many levels. Negatively, arrogance in relationships, or attracting those who are arrogant. The ability to make a favorable impression in close contact with others.

Jupiter/Midheaven Personal growth, reaching out to attain one's objectives, moving toward one's ends. Gaining personal authority or the respect of others. Personal contentment. Sometimes arrogance.

Jupiter/Aries Success in the larger sphere. People known for their involvement with religion, law, philosophy, and the like. Successful people, people in positions of respect or authority.

Pairs with Saturn

Saturn/Uranus Tension between restriction and the desire for freedom. Tension in general, often leading to sudden breaks or separations from people or circumstances that have proved restrictive. If controlled, the ability to persist under extremely tense and difficult conditions. Also, the ability to change or innovate in a disciplined manner. Associated with teaching.

Saturn/Neptune Confusion about what is and is not real. Fear, pessimism. Asceticism, extreme self-denial or denial of the physical for reasons of self-discipline. Often takes the form of chronic, non-infectious, or systemic ailments. The ability to bring dreams or ideals into concrete realization.

Saturn/Pluto Transformations that have to do with shrinking or hardening. To deal with circumstances that are increasingly rigid or restrictive. Difficult circumstances against which one may rail violently. The ability to contend with extreme difficulty and still come out ahead.

Saturn/Nodes Separations, the severing of connections. Connections that involve much restriction or discipline. Unions with older people. The desire to take control of relationships or meetings with others. Fear of matters being out of place or disorganized in connection with others.

Saturn/Ascendant To separate from another in a close relationship. Difficulty in forming close relationships. Few but deep relationships. Preference for older people. Relationships that are disciplined or restrictive. Relationships formed for reasons of necessity.

Saturn/Midheaven One's own uniqueness. To have a strong sense of who one is, to have a precisely defined sense of direction in life. Difficulty in compromising one's own ideas and ideals. Alienation and loneliness, to feel or be very different from others. To want to be alone.

Saturn/Aries People known for their discipline or rigidity, possibly teachers. To experience great difficulties in the larger world.

Success attained only by the greatest care and self-discipline. To experience separations on a grand scale.

Pairs with Uranus

Uranus/Neptune Loss of consciousness, altered or alternate states of consciousness, the mystical or occult. Revolutionary ideals. Sudden disappearances, the transition into the beyond.

Uranus/Pluto Revolutionary overthrow, complete and total transformation. Sudden changes that have long-standing causes at their root. Extreme conditions, sudden applications of power, explosive happenings.

Uranus/Nodes Unusual kinds of connections, connections with unusual people. Unstable or unreliable connections, connections that are formed and broken with equal suddenness.

Uranus/Ascendant Unusual or unstable relationships, relationships with people who are unusual or unstable. Relationships that are formed and/or broken suddenly. The need for independence in forming relationships. Relationships that have few rules or expectations.

Uranus/Midheaven One's own independence, one's sense of being unusual. To desire to go one's own way, to be free. The uniqueness of one's personal objectives or life path. Often connected with people who are in a career that is unusual or has to do with science or technology.

Uranus/Aries To be involved in large-scale movements for change or reform. To be known as unusual, eccentric, or a reformer or innovator. One's relationships to change and reform in the greater social order. Social elements that deviate from the norm.

Pairs with Neptune

Neptune/Pluto Hidden transformations, or transformations that involve the disappearance of things previously visible. Enormous creative force that takes things into and out of existence. Magic and other mysteries. One's relationships to long-range cyclical transformations.

Neptune/Nodes Confusing connections, connections whose nature is not clear, deceitful connections. Connections with others for idealistic, spiritual, or religious purposes. Connections that involve self-sacrifice.

Neptune/Ascendant Close relationships that involve self-sacrifice, or that require one person to care for another who is in difficulty. Highly idealistic relationships, platonic relationships. Relationships that are not honest or not what they appear to be.

Neptune/Midheaven   Weak or sensitive ego. The feeling of being unable to stand alone. Tendency to be easily influenced in one's life course by others. Lack of clear consciousness of objective. Spiritual or idealistic life directions, often involving self-sacrifice or self-denial. Often connected with psychic ability.

Neptune/Aries   People who are known for their involvement in spiritual or religious affairs, or for a lack of honesty. Idealists and dreamers on a grand scale. People who are frustrated or disappointed in their objectives or who feel forced to fulfill the demands of others.

Pairs with Pluto

Pluto/Nodes   Connections that transform one, or with people who are powerful and charismatic. Subversive connections or connections with subversive groups. Connections that may result in power struggles with others. Groups that aim to transform the world in some way, or that seek to understand the more hidden aspects of existence (researchers and the like).

Pluto/Ascendant   Intense relationships that have a transforming effect on one's life. Power struggles within relationships. A tendency to attract strong-minded persons. Exerting power on others or having others do so on oneself. Charisma. Ruthlessness in personal relationships.

Pluto/Midheaven   Striving toward one's goals, the desire to achieve one's objectives at any cost. The transformation of the self. Crises in one's own ego development from which a new self emerges. To be strong-willed or ambitious. To have the sense of being an agent of destiny.

Pluto/Aries   To be involved in, or the agent of, large-scale social transformations. To be known as one who brings about change, or as one with a ruthless will. People involved in subversive, hidden, or underground activities.

Pairs with the Lunar Nodes

Nodes/Ascendant   Connections of a personal nature, such as with family or relatives. Groups that one is involved with on a daily basis, in which the association is close but not quite as intimate, as, say, a husband and wife. Connections involving some group identity.

Nodes/Midheaven   To take the initiative in meeting someone, to establish a connection. Groups or meetings that affect one's life course. The ability to become part of a functioning group of people.

Nodes/Aries   To make connections with larger social groups. To become involved in a social movement. To be able to connect with many people. Facility in getting involved with groups, ease of integrating oneself.

Pairs with the Ascendant

Ascendant/Midheaven   A very important point in the horoscope, indicating one's personal attitudes concerning others. Points on this axis may exert a general influence on the chart almost as if they were conjunct the Ascendant, Descendant, Midheaven, or Imum Coeli except that the energy is not so strong. The ability to show to others what one really is or what one is really seeking in life.

Ascendant/Aries   Associated by the Uranian school with specific places, hence, one's ability to get along in a specific place on earth. The ability of one's personality to get across to the larger social world around one.

Pairs with the Midheaven

Midheaven/Aries   One's own seeking to get ahead in the larger social world. The ability to achieve one's goals in the context of the prevailing social order. Seems to relate to the ability of a person to become well known.

ZODIACAL POSITION

10

The Signs: Introduction

Of all the symbol systems in astrology, the signs of the zodiac have the most clear-cut internal structure. The first part of this chapter will outline the various traditional and not-so-traditional ways of classifying the signs: the division into four elements, three modalities or crosses, six polarities, and so forth. It will also discuss the various attempts made to conform the elements to Carl Jung's four psychological types.

At the end of the chapter, I will examine the whole idea of assigning a planet to rule a sign, or be in detriment, exaltation, or fall in a sign. I will also evaluate the use of this principle in delineating the horoscope.

Classifying the Signs

The Greeks, who gave us the zodiac in its present form, were great schematizers who enjoyed neatness and symmetry. Consequently, they organized a zodiac composed of twelve equal segments into several sequences of energies repeating several times within the signs such that every sign is related to every other sign in an orderly, geometrical way. To a considerable extent the qualities of each sign arise from its being a unique combination of the components of these sequences. Therefore a thorough comprehension of these principles will make the inner meanings of the signs more apparent.

Four sequences concern us here. The first is the four elements, or triplicities, so called because each element is given to three signs. Starting with Aries, the elemental sequence is fire, earth, air, and water, three complete times in the zodiac. Thus the fire signs are Aries, Leo, and Sagittarius; the earth signs Taurus, Virgo, and Capricorn; the air signs Gemini, Libra, and Aquarius; and the water signs Cancer, Scorpio, and Pisces.

The second sequence is the three crosses or quadruplicities, so called because each is given to four signs which form a cross in the zodiac. Starting with Aries again, the cross sequence is cardinal, fixed, and mutable. The cardinal cross is composed of Aries, Cancer, Libra, and Capricorn; the fixed cross of Taurus, Leo, Scorpio, and Aquarius; and the mutable cross of Gemini, Virgo, Sagittarius, and Pisces.

The third sequence is that of polarity. Starting with Aries again, the sequence is positive and negative, alternating six times in the twelvefold zodiac. The positive signs are the fire and air signs Aries, Gemini, Leo, Libra, Sagittarius, and Aquarius. The negative signs are the earth and water signs Taurus, Cancer, Virgo, Scorpio, Capricorn, and Pisces.

The fourth sequence is that of individual signs (the first half of the zodiac from Aries through Virgo) versus social signs (the second half of the zodiac from Libra through Pisces). This is not one of the ancient classifications of the signs but it is worth discussing in this chapter.

The Elements or Triplicities

The four elements—fire, earth, air, and water—are familiar in the popular consciousness because most people have been taught that the ancients believed all substances to be composed of them. We pride ourselves on knowing today that matter is composed not of four, but of nearly a hundred elements.*

Yet if the old doctrine of elements sounds silly, it is because modern people do not comprehend exactly what the ancients were saying. The ancients were not as concerned as we are with elements as chemical building-blocks, because they were not as occupied in establishing the objective reality of nature as distinct from human experience. Rather, reality and human experience were conceived of as one, a continuum. The same kind of symbolic analysis that today we might apply to understanding the human psyche was applied to nature as well. Thus the ancients were more interested in modalities of existence, in factors that pertain to characterisitics of the behavior of a thing, and (although they did not think of it this way) in the different modes in which people can experience the essence of a thing.

If something was experienced as hot, sharp, active, and possessing a striking individuality of its own coupled with dynamism and a kind of inherent instability, it was conceived as having the nature of the element fire. If another entity was experienced as being solid, constant, material, supportive and enduring, it was conceived as having the quality of the element earth. And so forth. If one were to ask a man of ancient times if he thought that someone with a fiery temperament actually had a greater amount of fire in him, the answer would be yes, but his conception of what it would mean to contain fire would be quite different from a modern person's. The idea of substance has changed. In the Renaissance, people in the West began to acquire a more nearly modern notion of what substances

---

*Interestingly, however, modern science has come to something very similar to fire, earth, air, and water in the four physical states of matter. Earth corresponds to solids, water to liquids, air to gases, and fire to plasmas (high-energy states of matter in which the atoms are stripped of their electrons).

are. Simply put, a modern person asking what elements something is composed of is not asking the same question as an ancient. Modern people ask what is the *objective reality* of a substance's makeup, whereas the ancients asked what is its *subjective reality*, that is, what are the components of the *experience* one has of a substance. Fire or earth describe one's experience of a substance, not its chemical nature. This way of thinking about the elements has survived unchanged in modern astrology. Thus, when we talk of a fiery temperament, we are talking of essential qualities of behavior and the way in which that behavior is experienced by others. No one in his right mind believes that a fiery personality actually contains more of the substance fire.

Fire. Fire is the most positive or yang of all the elements. It is the energy of spirit, and operates within the universe by energizing and transforming. It is not characteristic of fire to work along lines already set, or to respond to energy patterns that are imposed from without. Fire is the principle by which all entities that are self-moving acquire that ability. It is active and dominant, not willing to allow circumstances to take the initiative. It signifies will. Whether experienced through an object or a person, fire's operation within the universe is like a speedboat, which forces itself through the waves, not a sailboat, which moves through the water by taking advantage of externally supplied energies. Fire people tend to push their way through life rather than wait for times when external energies can provide them with the needed impetus.

Fire in the modern sense is not an element at all, but a process of chemical change. Even as an ancient element it is inherently unstable. Whether human or otherwise, strongly fiery entities manifest the qualities of process, change, and evolution. Fire rises: it cannot stay at one level for long. This gives fire people a dramatic, intense quality. They do not enjoy standing still. Circumstances that force a fire person to endure a static situation usually cause depression and a sense of stagnation. Often such people will try to force events before they are ripe, which may result either in things becoming fouled up because of action that is premature, or in success being attained while others wait for a better moment.

Fire is an emotional element, but it tends toward the more active and dynamic emotions—anger, joy, ebullience, and enthusiasm. It has a harder time dealing with sadness, depression, or the kind of feeling that comes from quiet contemplation of one's surroundings. Fire people are usually very demonstrative of love and affection, although they do not always express these emotions in a sensitive way that takes into account another's reactions. Fire people do not like to show sadness or grief: their typical response is to make fun of their own unhappiness. Even when they are down, they are often capable of making others feel better. But not being very sensitive to other's feelings they run the danger of inadvertently hurting those who are more sensitive.

Being an outgoing, positive energy, fire does not easily play passive roles. It may be difficult for fire people to listen, perceive quietly, or reflect. There is often too much energy pouring out to leave room for another's energy to come in. Fire connotes strength in a masculine way. Consequently fire people are apt to dislike weakness in others, especially if it reflects weakness in themselves. It must be said that the more conscious fire people do not demand more of others than they do of themselves, but they may still demand a great deal.

Earth.   The meaning of the symbolic element earth is clear from popular language. Earth signifies concern with the physical, with practical, common-sense matters. Wherever the metaphor of earthiness is involved, qualities of the element earth are implied. For example, an earthy sense of humor, which strips the world of pretension or of abstractions that obscure rather than elucidate, is a characteristic of many earth people.

Earth is a symbol for direct sense experience of the physical universe, without ideas, concepts, beliefs, or wishful thinking to cloud perception. It symbolizes the quality of being substantial and material. It is both matter and the need to deal with matter. Matter resists us; it pushes back on us as we push on it. We cannot walk through walls or occupy the same space as another material entity at the same time. Thus matter, and through it the symbol earth, signifies limits to our freedom (in which regard the element earth is related to the planet Saturn). We cannot do whatever we wish or go wherever we want because we are constrained by our own materiality and the materiality of the world around us. No matter how bound up in fantasies, ideals, or abstractions we are, we must always deal with earth and its concerns. Earth is the ultimate arena in which the acts we perform become manifest. And in the way we usually deal with the world, nothing is real unless it impinges in some way on the physical universe.

Earth must not, however, be thought of as limiting and structuring only in a negative way. It is also a support and a source of nurture. We often refer to the Earth Mother as the source of all life and being. There is a fertile aspect to earth, enabling entities to come into a form of being in which they can be perceived by all. Water is also a fertile element, but it is not so likely to manifest its fertility as something tangible.

Unlike fire, earth is stable, the most stable of all the elements. Also unlike fire, earth is passive: it needs to be acted on and formed by an external energy. For earth people to be really productive, there must be a positive, assertive energy provided by the planetary combinations in their charts. Otherwise, the earth type of personality remains passive.

Earth tends to resist change, and it can signify structures that break down under pressure because they lack the flexibility that allows adaptation. Earth often represents stubborn conservatism, in which an excessive concern for what is "real" at any moment blocks the ability for any new reality to come forth. In this way, earth can become a barrier to the very function it is supposed to assist, namely giving form and substance to what is newly created. It should be clear that fire and earth are partners, capable of acting in ways that are antagonistic but requiring each other in order to make any impact at all.

Where fire wishes to change things, earth will usually try to make the best of the status quo. Earth signifies making do with what is available. Earth people are adept at dealing with the details that must be attended to in everyday reality in order to make it work effectively. Fire may provide the motivation, but earth provides the substance.

Earth is effective for actualization, for turning dreams into reality. Sometimes the compromises that must be made with reality are more than the dreamer would wish, but at its best earth will make only those compromises that make a thing possible. Of course there are also earth types who in their efforts to actualize something will completely destroy the ideal behind it. Sometimes a lack of vision or an excessive concern with the petty aspects of reality will obscure earth's comprehension of the whole and cause it to act out of fear rather than concern with practical reality. More than any other type, earth people need a broadening education. With a broad perspective they can be very effective, whereas with a narrow one they can be very negative.

Being a relatively passive element, earth perceives better than fire. Earth people are usually close to their gut reactions to life. They are at their best when they can use their own experience and perceptions, when they do not have to rely on what others have told them. Then they have an uncanny ability to go right to the heart of the matter and perceive what to do. But because of a limited ability to handle abstractions, an earth type acting on concepts based on someone else's experience is unlikely to understand a situation well.

Earth may be very aware of the outer world that can be experienced through the senses, but it is not so aware of emotional considerations, which are more abstract, less tangible, and also more personal. Inner experience is valued less highly by the earth temperament, because earth tends to focus its perceptions externally. Virgo and Capricorn especially are inclined to sacrifice emotional needs when these come into conflict with their view of reality. Sometimes a concern for practicality actually gets in the way of practical achievement. This can happen when one neglects the emotions of those with whom one is dealing even though the emotions are as much a part of the environment which must be handled as are its purely material aspects. From this source comes the "efficiency expert" whose concern with efficiency is so great that he creates an environment in which no one can work. If carried too far, concern for what is real in a narrow, material sense may become completely irrational.

Air. While not as unstable, assertive, or willful as fire, air is a positive, yang element which shares fire's animated quality. In fact, the word animate is related to words meaning wind. The wind was a metaphor for the soul or spirit because, like them, it animates living matter causing other objects to move while it itself is invisible.

The difference between the symbols fire and air can be seen in the difference in the behavior of actual fire and wind. Fire rises, whereas wind moves horizontally. Fire strives to go higher, away from ordinary reality toward an ideal or abstraction, whereas air moves about horizontally relating everything it encounters in the physical world to everything else. Because of its association with horizontal motion, air is connected with transport, preeminently of ideas, but also of objects.

Like fire, air can become so involved in abstractions that it loses touch with physical reality and practical considerations. But unlike fire, air hovers just above the Earth's surface, so that though it is fond of abstractions, the abstractions are closer to physical reality than those of fire.

Air is associated with thinking and logic, and as such it is less personal than fire. Fire is usually connected with the vital, personal drive, or the will, and the abstractions are one's personal abstractions. But air, which has a social, external conception of truth, is more inclined to abstractions that have little to do with the individual. In this way air is similar to earth: both are primarily concerned with a reality external to the self. Fire and water are more concerned with personal, inward kinds of truth.

Air people are as willing to reform and change the world as fire people are, but they do it less as a personal expression. Air always has a strongly social quality. All three air signs have to do with relating to others—Gemini to the immediate world through mind and speech, Libra through achieving perfect balance within a one-to-one relationship, and Aquarius through group consciousness and interaction. Air lacks fire's ability to go off on its own to be itself. This may appear to contrast strongly with the popular image of Aquarius as a sign of revolution, but the fact is that insofar as Aquarius is related to revolution at all (see the section on Aquarius in the next chapter), it is related to revolutionary movements, not non-conforming individuals. Aquarian revolutionaries desire freedom to impose their ideals on society as a whole, whereas fire types simply want freedom to be themselves. Air signs are much more likely than fire signs to make accommodations to the social group, but they still need a great deal more freedom than earth signs.

Although air is very social, it is sometimes unable to handle real intimacy well. This is because air operates extensively, rather than intensively, trying to cover as much ground as possible in order to gain a comprehension of the whole. A close, highly emotional relationship may cloud one's perception and interfere with experiencing the whole. Also, getting deeply involved with one person on an intensive level interferes with the need to experience many people extensively. Libra is the only air sign in which the drive for close, personal relationships is strong, but even here there is a detached, non-intimate quality often obscured by the cleverness of the sign at being winning in social encounters.

If clear, objective vision is the great strength of air, then inability to comprehend extreme emotionalism and sensitivity is its weakness. This weakness is compounded when the typical air sign does not even see this as a problem. An air-sign personality needs to develop sensitivity to the internal, emotional aspects of other people to match its comprehension of the external, objective aspects.

Not only is the air intellect detached and objective, it is facile and quick. The air-sign mind can deal with more data faster and more efficiently than any other elemental type. It is excellent for observing, planning, and organizing. It is also excellent for creative, original thinking. It is less bound up in the status quo than earth but more concerned with effectiveness in the real world than fire. Hence it can combine the best of these other elements and signify truly effective innovative thought. Thus all fields of study involving the development of new techniques, methods, and practices are air. Air is also related to highly abstract, technical fields of study which nevertheless have some bearing on the real world—studies like science and astrology. What can be more abstract than the study of non-material ideas like the astrological elements, planets, houses, and signs? And yet when we use these to understand real human beings, what can at the same time be more practical? This combination of abstractness and practicality is an essential quality of the element air.

Water. Of the four elements, water is in some ways the most difficult to understand. This is partly because in our yang civilization, which emphasizes the patriarchal and masculine, water represents an inferior, repressed function. Water is the most yin of the four elements, and the most bound up in the maternal, feminine archetype which is so poorly expressed in our culture. Whereas in other times and cultures water was understood and given an honored place in daily life, in the modern psyche water has been relegated to a very primitive, internal level. This makes it difficult to deal with as well as difficult to understand.

Also, even strongly watery people who comprehend this element from first-hand experience cannot readily communicate what they comprehend. It is not, as is so often stated, that water people are poor at communication or unwilling to communicate. It is just that what they have to communicate is extremely difficult to put into words. This is true of all three water signs, but especially of Scorpio. Communication is difficult because water represents non-linear, non-rational, non-discriminative modes of thought—the very antithesis of air. Like fire, water's style is to grasp everything as a whole. Fire and water both represent non-rational functions, but fire has more to do with sudden, lightning-like comprehension, whereas water has a subtle, feeling-toned understanding that comes into being at no particular point, seeming rather to have existed always. Though it sees in terms of discrete factors less well then any other element, water is the best at feeling relationships and the ways every thing interacts with every other thing. Water may see and understand in a way that is hard for the other elements, especially air, to comprehend, but it sees very well.

Often the best way for water to communicate is by means of art, especially poetry and music. Water has no monopoly on artistry, but water people who happen to be artistic are fortunate because they have an appropriate medium for communication.

Another factor that sometimes places a barrier between water and other elements is that water experience is very personal. In this respect water is nearer to fire, and more distant from air and earth. Water people's personal experience can be so vivid that external reality fades into insignificance beside it. This is the origin of the apparent tendency of water people to withdraw into private fantasy worlds. Though the observations of water people are very personal, they should be taken seriously by others. Even the most personal experience has significance at some level for humankind.

Whereas fire rises, air moves horizontally, and earth stands still, water tends to sink and to penetrate. It moves down until it surrounds the roots of all things. For this reason, water is a symbol of empathy. Empathy is the ability to feel what another feels as if one were that other person (as contrasted to sympathy, in which one merely feels a kindred feeling). Water people therefore have to live in a relatively clean psychic environment. If they are surrounded by disturbed people, water types will pick up the disturbance as if the energies originated within themselves. In this way, a water person can be made to feel physically and/or psychologically ill even when actually very well.

On the positive side, a water person understands feelings and emotions better than any other elemental type, and is capable of great emotional depth and compassion for others. Water is a symbol of nurture, protection, and aid. Cancer especially has a strong maternal streak, but this trait is visible in Scorpio and Pisces as well. Although water is in some ways primitive compared to the other elements, it does not represent a lower function, except, of course, for the historical accident that our culture tends to regard the water function as inferior. Men in particular have a problem with the water parts of their nature because watery qualities are so out of accord with masculinity as defined in this culture. As a race we know both consciously and unconsciously that our ancestors came from the sea, and we regard water as a symbol for the divine matrix out of which all nature has been born. Earth may be the substance of which everyday reality is constructed, but water is the substance of the primordial universe, which preexists the formation of solid matter. More than any other element water is associated with the soul—the eternal, unchanging background that exists forever, against which the drama of individual life is played.

As water is a symbol for the matrix out of which all life has come, so water people tend to maintain a stronger tie with the matrix than do others. This is the reason for the greater emphasis on emotionalism that we have discussed, as well as for the degree of psychic ability that many water people exemplify. But it is also responsible for other characteristics. Water people often have stronger ties with the past, a stronger involvement with familiar people, places, and situations. Water tends to be conservative like earth; but whereas earth's conservativism comes from overinvolvement with the concerns of the material world, in the case of water it arises from a need for the emotional security of the familiar. The more psychologically insecure a water type may be, the worse the problem. In a strong water person, we have already mentioned the protective, maternal streak; in a weak water person, there can be emotional grasping and possessiveness.

The metaphor of water sinking has another bearing on the psychology of the water-sign type. Unless there is some kind of positive energy either from inside the person or from the environment, water types are prone to depression and moodiness. They do not try to hide it as fire and air might. Instead, they almost seem to revel in it, which can be distressing to those around them, but which may not be as serious as it looks. To a water person, depression or moodiness is preferable to emotional deadness, which indicates that the individual feels cut off in some way from the source of life. Water has a need to self-dramatize like fire; but unlike fire, water is willing to take other people's emotions seriously as well. Though fire is fond of self-dramatization, it is often impatient when other people indulge in it; consistency is not one of human nature's strong points.

Creative imagination is the positive side of what is sometimes merely fantasy. Being in touch with the primordial matrix gives the water type the ability to bring something out of that matrix into being. Although it requires some earth really to actualize something, true creativity also requires the ability to see a possible existence where there was no existence before. Water people can bring new insights into human nature and give us all the ability to understand ourselves better. When water types retreat into private fantasy, it is only creativity without the earth to actualize it, or insight without the air to communicate it.

Elemental Qualities of the Planets   As with all descriptions of types in astrology, the ones just outlined are of relatively pure elemental types, which almost never occur in the real world. Not only do most people have signs of several elements prominent in their horoscopes, there is also a factor besides the signs that must be considered before one can attempt to characterize an actual person as to elemental type. That factor is the relative strengths of the planets.

Though they represent energies which the signs only modify, planets have elemental qualities like the signs, but in more mixed form. If a planet of a certain elemental quality is strong in a chart (for example, near the horizon or meridian axis, or involved with the Sun or Moon or otherwise the focus of a complex of aspects or midpoints) this can completely alter the elemental characteristics of the chart as they would be derived from simply counting planets in the signs.

Authorities disagree on the precise amount and proportion of the elements in the planetary symbols, but what follows is a reasonably close approximation of the consensus. I find it not always safe to assume that the elemental quality of a planet is exactly the same as the sign or signs that it is thought to rule (see below, pages 201-210, for a discussion of rulership).

Fire. The fiery planets include without question the Sun and Mars, though Mars may have a touch of earth in it as well. Many consider Uranus to have a somewhat fiery quality, and I agree, though I am more inclined to assign it mainly to air. Jupiter, a hard planet to characterize as to element, is a mixture of fire and water, with some earth overtones.

Earth. The most purely earthy planet is Saturn. Much of what has been said about earth—its concern for form, structure and solidity—could have come from a description of Saturn as well. But Saturn is not totally earth, because it lacks earth's fertile quality. Perhaps Saturn could be described as sterile matter awaiting the approach of life-giving energies from water and fire. Venus has some earth, but it is mixed with water, air, and a little fire. The only safe thing to say about Venus is that the yin elements, earth and water, predominate over the yang elements, fire and air.

Mercury is often described as having an earthy side, probably because it is traditionally said to rule the earth sign Virgo. But I find this spurious: Mercury is not earthy, and it should probably not be assigned to Virgo. For my reasons, see the section on Virgo in Chapter 11.

Air. Mercury is instead the only purely air planet. The symbolism of air and Mercury are completely intertwined. Both are mobile, changeable, and strongly associated with transportation, thought, planning, and consideration. Both are involved with establishing relationships—at least the superficial but necessary first stages.

Uranus, as we have mentioned, is also strongly connected with air, though its sudden, sharp, unexpected mode of acting is more characteristic of fire. It is clearly a mixture.

Water. The Moon and Neptune are almost purely watery. Though Neptune is often more like a vapor than a liquid, it is still not at all like an air symbol. In their different ways, the Moon and Neptune connect one to the fundamental matrix of being. Both are bound up with the unconscious and the emotions, the main difference being that the Moon is not so otherworldly as Neptune. Either planet strongly placed in a chart can indicate a water personality.

Because of Pluto's rulership of Scorpio, many astrologers would call it watery; but other astrologers consider Pluto to rule the fire sign Aries. Though I do not agree with this assignment, I feel it reflects something real about Pluto. Pluto has qualities of both elements: a moody emotionalism that suggests water, and a tendency to glorify strength and power that suggest fire. I would say it is about equally both.

The Elements and Jung's Psychological Types Elements are a fourfold typology, and so are the four temperament types of the psychologist Carl G. Jung. It is thus tempting to try to connect Jung's psychological types with the four elements. Jung believed they were related, but never specified exactly how, and as a result debate has raged among psychologically oriented astrologers as to which element goes with which psychological type. Those astrologers who accept the connection at all usually agree that earth equates to sensation and air to thinking.* But they are more divided on how fire and water relate to feeling and intuition. Part of the problem is that it is hard to come to definitions of "feeling" and "intuition" on which everyone can agree. Such definitions must be the first step to understanding any relation to the elements. Therefore, before seeing whether a connection should be made between the elements and Jung's types, let us look at how Jung actually defined his terms.

To Jung, *sensation* is used in the ordinary sense: it is the function that works through perceiving via the senses. It does not make judgments, it is simply concerned with what is so in the outside world according to the senses. Because sensation by itself does not attempt to organize or judge what it perceives, Jung calls it an irrational function.

The *thinking* function is much as one might expect. It is a process of ordering and making sense out of what is perceived. It is therefore a rational function.

The *feeling* function informs the observer as to whether something is good or bad, pleasant or unpleasant. It is a judging faculty, and since, according to his criteria, it has an ordering function like thinking, Jung considered feeling a rational function. It has little to do with the usual idea of feeling as emotion.

The *intuition* function gives one a sense of understanding via a nonrational, usually subconscious, means. One suddenly realizes what it is one has perceived. Like sensation, intuition does not judge or order its understanding, and it is therefore irrational.

You can easily see the problems here. First, there is Jung's unusual use of the terms "feeling" and "rational." Jung departs from the popular use of "rational" as synonymous with "logical" or "reasonable," but he uses the word correctly in one of its senses. His use of the word "feeling," however,

---

*At least one, however, relates air to feeling. See Karen Winterburn, "Archetypally Derived Typologies: Air As Feeling," *Journal of Geocosmic Research Monograph No. 1,* 1980.

corresponds with none of the common meanings of the word. A tendency to judge the value or worth of a thing is different from a tendency to have an emotional reaction to what one encounters. The first is indeed rational, as Jung says, whereas the second is not.

Then there is another problem. The way Jung conceives of the four types, feeling is a polar opposite to thinking, and sensation to intuition. That is, the two rational functions lie opposite each other, and the same goes for the two irrational functions. In Jung's schema, one cannot be a thinking- and feeling-dominant person at the same time; neither can one be a sensation- and intuition-dominant person at once. A person has to be either a pure type or a mixture of adjacent types such as thinking-intuition, sensation-thinking, feeling-intuition, etc. In astrology, however, one can be any mixture of two or more elemental types. This should be an immediate tip-off that the two fourfold typologies cannot be equated in any simple way.

But there are more problems. First, whereas the four Jungian types are primarily concerned with perceiving, the four elemental types relate to ways of acting as well as to ways of perceiving. Second, the fit between each element and any possible corresponding psychological type varies from good to unconvincing. Let us look at each, and see what the difficulties are.

Fire suggests to many the intuition function. This is because fire tends to perceive in pictures, and to get an instantaneous grasp of a situation. Fire does not reason or think in any classical sense of the word: it either understands or it doesn't. This is why fire people can be extremely creative yet not good at logical reasoning. Both fire and intuition are nonrational in any sense of the word. But the kind of emotionally toned psychic perception that also fits Jung's use of "intuition" is not so characteristic of fire. Psychic perceptions usually relate to some hidden aspect of truth in either an external or an internal reality. The intuitive grasp of fire more often relates to something that does not yet exist—an ideal, an original concept, or simply an intention of the individual to bring something that does not yet exist into being. The psychic aspect of Jung's intuition function is more characteristic of water than fire.

For these reasons, many have assigned fire to the feeling function instead. But fire people are no more prone to making good-bad judgments than any other elemental type. This is why I think none of the four elements have anything in common with Jung's feeling type.

Earth is usually equated with sensation. The correspondence is good here, but there are still problems. It is true that earth signs are most concerned with perceiving an external, physical reality. But earth is not simply concerned with *perceiving* it, it is also concerned with ordering it in the way that is most effective in a given situation. In Jung's sense of the word, earth is extremely rational, whereas the sensation function is not. Virgo and especially Capricorn need to make judgments about good and bad, and Taurus is much concerned with pleasantness and unpleasantness. In terms of Jung's definitions, earth is almost as concerned with feeling as with sensation.

Air is usually given to thinking, and this is probably the least defective of the assignments. But here again we must realize that air connotes more than the rational analysis of perception. Like fire, air may be more concerned with things that are not yet real, that are abstract and unrelated to a given reality. Also, air connotes a restlessness of behavior, a will that goes out into the world to encounter it, rather than simply sitting back passively to make order of what it perceives.

Water presents the greatest difficulty. It most certainly relates to what is meant by the popular conception of "feeling." But even though water may feel good or bad much more quickly and sensitively than the other elements, it is no more judgmental as to whether something may be good, bad, pleasant, or unpleasant. And, unlike the feeling function, water is in no sense of the word rational, neither according to Jung's nor anyone else's interpretation of the word. As we mentioned in connection with fire, if intuition means nonrational, nonlinear perception, then water is at least as connected with intuition as fire is.

I suggest that in fact the four elements do relate to four cognitive modes as well as to other areas of life, but that these four cognitive modes are only somewhat like the four Jungian types. Here is a summary of the way I would associate cognitive modes with the four elements.

Fire perceives through pictures and sudden flashes of insight. A fire person will study something for a long time without comprehending it, and then the significance will become clear in an instant. Fire tends to be involved with abstractions and, often in an effort to bring them into being, with matters that do not yet pertain to the real world, at least the world of consensus reality. In the way that fire perceives, there is always a strong mixture of will or desire and a need to transform. Fire is often psychic, in the ordinary meaning of the word.

Earth's perception is less influenced by personal desire than fire's. It is much more concerned with objective reality. It wants to know what is really so, and it defines its criteria according to what can be collectively perceived and experienced. Not especially concerned with abstractions, it may even be impatient with them. Instead, it is greatly concerned with perceiving order in the world and with making that order more effective and apparent. Like Jung's sensation type and unlike fire, earth is quite rational in its functioning.

Air is as concerned with the relationship of things in the outer world as earth is, but air is more interested in abstractions. It is less taken up with the order that may be inherent in observed matter, and more with the order that mind may impose on matter. Much more than earth, air will take simple sense data and build on it elaborate intellectual structures that will often lead away from the sense data. Air is quite rational in both Jung's and the popular sense of the word.

Water gets information from emotionally toned perceptions that may not come via the senses. Whereas fire tends to think in pictures, water perceives by means of feelings. Water is feeling in the conventional rather than the Jungian sense of the word. Like fire, water perceives in a very personal way, and it is concerned less with consensus reality than it is with personal experience. Water is even more psychic than fire, but it is far more difficult for water to translate its perceptions into words. Water is definitely irrational in every sense of the term.

What we have in this section is one example among many of astrologers attempting to make a one-for-one translation from one symbol system (Jungian psychology) to another (astrology). Often this is done in order to legitimize astrology, but this is unfortunate, because astrology understood as a system of psychology in its own right has a symbolic framework much more powerful than any in orthodox psychology. It would be unrealistic to expect that one man in one lifetime could develop an understanding of symbols as profound as that of astrology, which has been developing for thousands of years.

The Crosses or Quadruplicities

We have just shown how the elements or triplicities refer to a broad range of characteristics, both psychological and philosophical—kinds of behavior and action, and especially modes of perception. The symbolism of the crosses or quadruplicities is not as deep and rich, nor does it cover as many facets of the individual. Yet the crosses are important, partly because they represent three different modes of creativity. These three modes are: *cardinal,* which symbolizes initial creation, the impetus to create, and the making of beginnings; *fixed,* which symbolizes the sustaining of what has already been created, and the creation of stability; and *mutable,* which symbolizes the alteration, transformation, and adaptation of what has already been created.

When events have been initiated from outside, the three quadruplicity types also relate to modes of reaction. *Cardinal* reaction is counteraction, the making of a second initiative to counter the first. *Fixed* reaction is resistance, the effort to endure in the face of external initiative, and to avoid change. Again, the emphasis is on stability. *Mutable* reaction does not actively resist what is happening, but tries to alter it indirectly by bending the course of events onto a desired path.

The crosses are also important because when combined with the elements they distinguish each of the twelve signs from every other. Thus each sign is a unique combination of element and cross: there is only one cardinal water sign (Cancer), one mutable fire sign (Sagittarius), and so forth.

This means that in each elemental triangle, there is one cardinal, one fixed, and one mutable sign. Looking at the element earth, for example, earth action and life receive their impetus from Capricorn (the cardinal earth sign), are sustained in Taurus (the fixed earth sign), and are transformed, altered, and sometimes made transcendent by the symbolism of Virgo (the mutable earth sign). More specifically, Capricorn desires to build and to achieve on the material plane; Taurus desires to have, to hold, and also to enjoy the material stability resulting from Capricorn's action; and Virgo wishes to change and make more effective the products of the material world created by Capricorn and sustained by Taurus.

In the water element, the cardinal sign, Cancer, symbolizes the reaching out of feeling and emotion, the desire to encounter the world on a feeling level. Cancer also reaches out to create and nourish new life. The fixed sign, Scorpio, prefers to dwell deep within the inner world of emotion to experience and understand this realm as thoroughly as possible. The mutable sign, Pisces, uses that understanding to bring about a transformation of the self through losing the ego and surrendering the soul.

In the air element, Libra, the cardinal sign, brings about an understanding of the simplest kind of relationship, the one-to-one, and symbolizes the beginning of awareness through the creation of a relationship between the self and the other. The fixed sign, Aquarius, symbolizes the effort to understand the relation of everything and everyone to everything else without centering that understanding on the self or limiting the experience to one-to-one relationships. (This view of Aquarius leads logically to some conflicts with popular view of the sign.) The mutable sign, Gemini, takes the understanding of the relation of everything in the universe and attempts to build systems of understanding on the foundations laid by Libra and Aquarius.

In the fire element, Aries, the cardinal sign, represents the first out-thrusting of Will into the universe. In many ways it is the ultimate cardinal sign. The fixed sign, Leo, represents the will now established within the universe, regarding itself and being regarded by others. In the mutable sign, Sagittarius, that same will tries to re-create and transform the world based on its inner desires and understanding.

These portrayals of the signs only by element and cross are limited, because there are additional factors that give the signs their individual meanings. Some of these factors, like the polarities and the individual versus the social signs, are known and will be discussed in this chapter. Others are not known, and their presence can only be inferred from the way the actual manifestations of the signs depart from the formulas outlined here.

The Crosses and the Seasons   What follows is neither proof nor justification of the qualities of the quadruplicities. It is merely an illustration of their relationship to a natural phenomenon, the changing of the seasons in the temperate zones of the world.

The first third of each season is a cardinal sign: in this period the qualities of that season are asserted strongly. It is a period of dynamic change as the new season takes hold upon the Earth. The new season is often in conflict with the one that preceded it, but eventually it triumphs.

The second third of each season is a fixed sign. Here we have the qualities of that season stabilized and most perfectly represented. The weather has settled down and is reasonably predictable.

The last third of each season is the mutable sign. Here the qualities of the season are giving way to those of the next. Again, we have dynamism, but it is the dynamism of something giving way to something else, rather than that of something asserting itself.

Psychological Qualities of the Crosses   Like the elements, the crosses or quadruplicities each suggest a type of personality.

Cardinal.   As we have already pointed out, the essential nature of the cardinal signs is to initiate action. This does not mean cardinal signs are especially aggressive or assertive. Aries may be quite aggressive, but Cancer is not at all so. It is simply that each cardinal sign represents in its own way the first manifestation of its elemental quality.

The chief psychological quality in cardinal signs is a fondness for starting things, often without regard to sustaining them in the future or planning for future growth. The pure cardinal type is extremely active but not very persistent. Cardinal types often start projects without finishing them. As soon as a project is able, at least to some extent, to continue of its own accord, the pure cardinal type loses interest. On the plus side, cardinal types are not daunted by a lack of precedent for whatever they do. This quality applies mainly to issues related to the element involved. For example, Cancer is often conservative in areas not relating to water, though in the area of human feelings it is quite willing to go out and initiate an emotional contact (unless, of course, other factors in the chart indicate that the individual is insecure about encountering people). Likewise, Capricorn may be conservative in thought, but eager to take the initiative in action on the physical plane.

In evaluating the cardinality of an individual as a whole, the planets must be taken into consideration. Planets themselves are not especially cardinal, fixed, or mutable, but certain planets are so strongly aggressive about taking the initiative that they will do so routinely regardless of the quadruplicity. Mars, Uranus, and the Sun have this tendency. Pluto also does in a subtler way.

Fixed.   As we have said, the fixed signs have the function of preserving and sustaining. But fixity is not conservatism; rather, it fulfills the need for activity to be carried on daily in a predictable and reliable manner. Aquarius, though definitely fixed, is not in the least conservative. Aquarian types may come to radical conclusions about the world, but, once formed, their ideas are not changed. (See the article in the next chapter on Aquarius.) Taurus, on the other hand, is genuinely conservative, while Scorpio and Leo may be anywhere on the spectrum.

The most obvious characteristic of the fixed signs is stubbornness and persistence. What cardinal starts, fixed continues. The fixed signs give existence some degree of stability. The difficulty is that the fixed type may not allow change when it becomes absolutely necessary. At this point fixity can be a barrier to progress.

Mutable. Exactly as their name implies, the mutable signs are involved with change, transformation, and adaptation. They symbolize the flexibility needed to allow structures to survive amid changing realities. As a consequence, people in whom mutable signs are prominent are more adaptable and less resistant to change. They may not always initiate change, but they coexist with it well. And on one level, they do initiate change: they are able to take whatever has been created and sustained by the other two quadruplicities and transmute it so it can operate on a higher level.

Interestingly, all four mutable signs have to do with some aspect of knowledge or consciousness. Gemini is ordinary consciousness and thought; Virgo is the knowledge of the physical world that can enable one to use it more effectively; Sagittarius is the broad overview that enables one to fit every part into a whole; and Pisces is the knowledge that comes only when the intellect is surrendered to the experience of the One.

The Polarities

The third basic sequence of energies in the zodiac is the alternation of positive and negative (or, in Ptolemy, masculine and feminine) signs, starting with Aries as positive. Polarity is partly the result of the changing of the elements (fire and air are positive, earth and water negative). But I believe that polarity also has an independent signification in its own right.

Not all signs are equally positive or equally negative: some are more so than others. In general, fire signs are the most yang, and water signs the most yin, with air and earth signs in between.

It is safe to say on the basis of astrological experience that the positive signs are usually more objectively oriented and more outgoing, assertive, and interested in what is going on around them. The negative signs are more likely to be inwardly directed and concerned with subjective experience. The main issue is not passivity: some positive signs are actually more passive than some negative signs. For example, the negative signs Capricorn and Scorpio are not especially passive, while Libra, a positive sign, is often so. The key to being positive or negative is whether one's attention and energies are focused primarily on external or on internal affairs and experience.

Clearly, sign polarity is one of the factors that must be checked when determining whether an individual is primarily introverted or extraverted.

Individual Versus Social Signs

Though it has no roots in ancient astrology, dividing the zodiac into a first and a second half is not only strongly implicit in the symbolism of the signs, it is also one of the strongest connections between the signs and the houses. According to this scheme, the signs Aries through Virgo are more concerned with the development of the individual, whereas Libra through Pisces are more concerned with the relationship between the individual and society or higher and more spiritual forms of the collective. Thus a sign in the second half of the zodiac will represent an issue similar to its opposite sign in the first half, but the emphasis will be social rather than individual. Here are some of the clearer examples.

Aries-Libra: Aries represents the first assertion of individuality, while Libra represents the first encounter of that individuality with other. More inclusively, Libra symbolizes the dialectic between the individual and external entities in general. Whatever may be the case in Aries, in Libra there is an equal emphasis on the self and the unself, and an effort to reach a balance between them.

Leo-Aquarius: Whereas Leo is the individual alone and centered on the self, Aquarius has to do with integrating into the collective while at the same time realizing one's individuality. Both signs are tremendously concerned with ego, but one is in an isolated context, and the other is in a social context.

Virgo-Pisces: Both signs represent the individual's having to make an accommodation to external necessity. Virgo represents that need on a more immediate level for reasons of personal necessity. In Pisces, the necessity is that of the race, or humankind as a whole with respect to the universe. The necessity to which one must surrender is more abstract, and the surrender is more complete.

One can make similar comparisons using the other signs. I have not done so, because if it is done simplistically it does violence to the basic symbolism of the individual signs. The pattern exists, but it is clearer in some sign pairs than others.

Dignities: The Relationship of Signs to Planets

One of the most ancient, persistent, potentially useful, and, at the same time, potentially troublesome parts of the lore about the signs of the zodiac is the teaching concerning the "dignities" of the planets, or their relation to the signs.

According to tradition, every sign has a planet that rules it. A planet in the sign it rules is said to be "in dignity," or "in honor," meaning favorably placed; modern astrologers often say that such a planet works well because it is in a sign with which it has some qualities in common. When a planet is in the sign opposite the one it rules, it is in its "detriment," where it is said to work badly.

A planet is also in dignity in another sign, its "exaltation," where it is supposed to work especially well. In the sign opposite, the planet is in its "fall" and is reputed to work particularly badly. Table 7 shows the planets that are dignified or debilitated in the various signs. While almost all astrologers agree on the rulerships that have been assigned to the more newly discovered planets, Uranus, Neptune, and Pluto, there is less agreement on the exaltations and falls of these planets.

Table 7
Planetary Dignities and Debilities

	♈	♉	♊	♋	♌	♍	♎	♏	♐	♑	♒	♓
Rulership	♂ ♇	♀	☿	☽	☉	☿	♀	♇ ♂	♃	♄	♅ ♄	♆ ♃
Detriment	♀	♇ ♂	♃	♄	♅ ♄	♆ ♃	♂ ♇	♀	☿	☽	☉	☿
Exaltation	☉	☽		♃ ♆* ♇*		☿	♄	♅*		♂		♀
Fall	♄	♅*		♂		♀	☉	☽		♃ ♆* ♇*		☿

*Modern exaltations and falls.

Rulerships and Detriments   The true origin of rulerships and detriments is probably lost forever, but we do have a simple and elegant explanation of them from Ptolemy. Unfortunately, the perfect symmetry of his schema was upset by the discovery of the planets beyond Saturn.

Ptolemy started out with the two signs Cancer and Leo, because these are where the Sun is in its northernmost passage, in the Northern Hemisphere's summer, when there is the greatest heat. He assigned the Moon to Cancer because Cancer is feminine, and the Sun to Leo because Leo is masculine. Then he took the opposite signs, Capricorn and Aquarius, and assigned them to Saturn, because the Sun's passage through these signs marks the coldest time of the year, and Saturn, the farthest visible planet from the Sun, is to astrologers cold in nature. Then he assigned Sagittarius and Pisces, the next signs on either side of Capricorn and Aquarius, to Jupiter, the next planet in toward the Sun. The next pair of signs, Scorpio and Aries, were given to Mars; the next pair, Libra and Taurus, to Venus; and the last pair, Gemini and Virgo, to Mercury, which has the closest orbit to the Sun.

In effect, Ptolemy was putting the planets in the order of the distance of their orbits from the Sun, though he, of course, believed the planets orbit the Earth. He was merely observing the length of time it takes the planets to go once around the zodiac (the farther out from the Sun they are, the longer it takes). In the case of Venus and Mercury, which from Earth both appear to take about a year, he was observing that Venus never appears farther than 46° from the Sun, and Mercury never appears farther from the Sun than 28°.

Although Ptolemy discussed the similarities of the signs and their ruling planets to some extent, it is clear from his discussion that similarity of symbolism was not the main concern. The main concern was the neat schema.

All went well for about 1,700 years, until Uranus was discovered in the late eighteenth century. This completely upset the schema of rulerships as described by Ptolemy, and beginning at that time there was a change in the principle governing rulerships. Whereas before, the schema was the basis for assigning planets to signs, now the basis became the similarity between the signs and their respective ruling planets. For reasons that are not entirely clear to me (see the article on Aquarius in the next chapter), Uranus was assigned to Aquarius, sometimes as a joint ruler with Saturn, and sometimes displacing Saturn altogether. Then when Neptune was discovered, it was assigned to Pisces. When Pluto was found, those more interested in a schema thought that the progression should continue and wanted to give Pluto to Aries. But a greater number have felt that the symbolism of Pluto is more Scorpionic than Arian. I am inclined to agree.

There is also another reason for assigning Pluto to Scorpio—a reason I have not seen discussed elsewhere. The outer planets have more to do with transpersonal, collective energies, much in the way of the second six signs from Libra to Pisces. Thus I find it hard to relate Pluto to a sign that represents such a basic, primitive, individual function as Aries. Scorpio, on the other hand, is in the collective half of the zodiac and makes a better candidate on those grounds as well as on the grounds of symbolism.

The schema of rulerships has been further complicated by additional bodies, particularly the asteroids Ceres, Pallas, Juno, and Vesta. These have been either all assigned to Virgo, or Ceres and Vesta have been given to Virgo and Pallas and Juno to Libra. I believe that assigning the asteroids to this part of the zodiac is consistent, since the location of the orbits of these bodies between Mars and Jupiter would logically place them on the boundary of the first and second halves of the zodiac.

Clearly, the Ptolemaic criteria for establishing sign rulership are in chaos and cannot be maintained. And with the addition of the asteroids and planetoids such as the recently discovered Chiron it is likely that we will eventually have more bodies than signs. This creates a serious problem for the traditional idea of sign rulership, although not for every part of it.

Exaltations and Falls   The lore of exaltations and falls emerges full-blown in Ptolemy, and beyond this, their origin is obscure. There seems little logic to support exaltations and falls. Sometimes there is clearly an affinity between a planet's symbolism and that of the sign in which it is exalted. For instance, the Moon, with its need for emotional security and support, obviously has strength in its exaltation sign, Taurus, which symbolizes the need for roots in the earth and for physical security. And Venus's creative and artistic sides are reinforced by the mystical-spiritual qualities of its exaltation sign, Pisces.

But other connections are less obvious. For example, Saturn is exalted in Libra, the sign ruled by Venus, even though Saturn is usually considered to inhibit Venus. And while Mars is exalted in Capricorn, Saturn's sign, Saturn is said to be in its fall in Aries, Mars's sign. Why should one combination of Mars-Saturn symbolism be beneficial while the other is not? Of course part of the answer is that planets are not identical with the signs they rule: Mars is not Aries and Saturn is not Capricorn. But one would logically expect Mars in Capricorn to be just as conflicting as Saturn in Aries. Clearly, whatever logic there is in the assignment of planets to rulerships is lacking in the assignment of planets to exaltations.

In his *Encyclopedia of Astrology* Nicholas DeVore attempts to find a pattern. He points out that using traditional rulerships (giving Scorpio to Mars, Aquarius to Saturn, and Pisces to Jupiter) the sign in which a planet is exalted is always in a three-series (traditionally favorable) aspect to one of the signs the planet rules. Thus Libra, Saturn's exaltation, trines Aquarius, which Saturn rules; and Capricorn, Mars's exaltation, sextiles Scorpio, which Mars co-rules. But Libra also squares Capricorn, Saturn's other sign, and Capricorn squares Aries, so DeVore's observation is not a convincing rationale.

Ptolemy's rationale is not much better. Reasonably enough, he assigns the Sun to Aries because in Aries day first becomes longer than night. But then he gives Saturn to Libra because Libra is opposite Aries, just as Saturn rules Aquarius, which is opposite the Sun's rulership in Leo. This is pure schematicism, the assignment of relationships only because they seem elegant. Ptolemy assigns the other planets to their exaltations based on the seasonal changes and climate of ancient Greece, characteristics which would be quite different anywhere else. His reasoning looks suspiciously like after-the-fact observation, as if he had inherited a completed scheme and was trying to make sense of it, exactly as modern astrologers have attempted to do.

There is another tradition in Western astrology that the exaltations and falls of planets are not just signs, but specific degrees, as shown in Table 8, and herein may lie a clue to their origin. These degrees at first suggest that the exaltations are some kind of horoscope. But this is not possible because the exaltation of Mercury is more than 28° from that of the Sun. Pursuing a similar line of reasoning, however, the Irish siderealist Cyril Fagan has derived an interesting theory.

Table 8
Exaltation and Fall Degrees

Planet	Exaltation	Fall
Sun	19° Aries	19° Libra
Moon	3° Taurus	3° Scorpio
Mercury	15° Virgo	15° Pisces
Venus	27° Pisces	27° Virgo
Mars	28° Capricorn	28° Cancer
Jupiter	15° Cancer	15° Capricorn
Saturn	21° Libra	21° Aries

In 786 BC the Assyrians built a new temple to Nabu, their god of astrology. In that year, according to Fagan's calculations, all the traditional planets heliacally rose at or very near the degree of their exaltation in a sidereal zodiac. A heliacal rising is the first appearance of a planet after conjunction with the Sun—the date of the planet's first rising at dawn after it has been hidden by the Sun's rays while conjoined with the Sun.

Fagan's work has not been checked using more accurate computer-generated positions for the planets, but the tables he used are probably accurate enough for his purposes. His work has been challenged, but I think it likely that something of what he suggests is true. If the exaltations are nothing more than the degrees of heliacal risings in the dedication year of a temple, it is likely that we can ignore them in any zodiac. See Fagan's works for more information on this subject.*

The Use of Planetary Dignities

Traditional Western astrology uses dignities in two ways: first, to evaluate whether a planet's energy will flow smoothly or not; and second, to link planets to houses. Let us take these one at a time.

To Judge the Ease or Difficulty with Which a Planet Will Work Using dignities to evaluate a planet's strength or weakness is often referred to as determining a planet's "cosmic state." A planet is deemed more apt to work well if it is in good cosmic state, and less apt to if it is not. Malefics (traditionally Mars and Saturn) in bad cosmic state were considered especially disastrous, but even benefics (Venus and Jupiter) were only supposed to be really useful when in good cosmic state. Older books like Wilson's *Dictionary of Astrology* give elaborate tables for evaluating a planet's cosmic state, based not only on signs of rulership and exaltation, but also on house placement, aspects, and even on subdivisions of signs such as decanates, terms and faces. (Though decanates still have a wide

---

*In particular, *Zodiacs Old and New* (London: Anscombe, 1951).

following, terms and faces have been almost completely dropped by modern astrologers. I do not use any of these subdivisions. If you are interested, they are discussed in Wilson and in DeVore.)

Although he gives these tables, Wilson is skeptical about their use. I am inclined to concur, and pay little attention to most of these ideas. I find that the most powerful factors affecting "cosmic state" are the aspects and midpoint combinations in which a planet is involved. I feel that sign placement can affect the smoothness of a planet's expression, but prefer to consider the logical relation of the symbolism of a planet to the sign in which it is placed. I acknowledge that a planet placed in the sign it rules does seem to function more smoothly than elsewhere, but planets are not uniformly debilitated by placement in the sign opposite their rulership. As regards exaltations, some express real affinities between signs and planets, but others do not. The next chapter shows how the signs affect planets placed in them, giving special attention to the planets that are most strengthened or interfered with by the sign. This is based solely on symbolic affinity and not on ancient horoscopes that may have nothing to do with modern people.

To Connect Planets to Houses The second major use of dignities employs the signs as intermediaries to connect planets to houses. According to tradition, there are six principles by which a planet can affect a house. Of these, only the last three employ dignities, but in order to evaluate the use of dignities in this manner, we need to examine all six principles.

Principle 1: The planet may be in the house. No planet-sign affinities are involved here, and dignities play no part in establishing the connection. Astrologers who use houses are unanimous in agreeing that a planet in a house indicates a strong connection between the planet and the house.

Principle 2: The planet may aspect a planet in another house, and thereby affect that house. This principle also does not depend on dignities. Most astrologers agree that, just as two planets in aspect will affect each other, they will affect each other's houses. And if a planet aspects more than one other planet, as many do, it will affect more than one house aside from its own.

Principle 3: The planet may aspect the house cusp. This, too, has nothing to do with dignities. Many astrologers believe that a planet's being within orb of an aspect to a house cusp gives the planet an important influence over that house. Certainly this is true of planets that aspect the Midheaven, Ascendant, I.C., or Descendant, which are also the tenth-, first-, fourth-, and seventh-house cusps in most house systems and which fall in the same place for a given horoscope regardless of the house system. It is less certain that this works with the other house cusps, which vary in position according to the house system used.

Principle 4: The planet may rule the sign on the cusp or a sign that lies within the house. This is the major type of planet-house linkage based on dignities or planet-sign affinities. To give an example, if any part of Leo lies within the third house, then the aspects, house, and sign position of Leo's ruler, the Sun, would be considered to affect third-house affairs. Or, an astrologer determining the parents' effect on an individual would not only check the planets in the fourth and tenth (houses that signify one's experience of one's parents), but also the planets that rule the signs within the fourth and tenth houses. These planets are said to rule the houses, just as they are said to rule the signs.

Things are usually made more complex by there being more than one sign in each house. Because in all but equal-house systems houses can be larger or smaller than 30°, there can be part or all of two or three (and in high latitudes, where the size of houses becomes very irregular, even more) signs within a single house. (Signs that are wholly contained within a house are said to be "intercepted." Many astrologers—myself not included—consider interception to indicate some degree of trouble for the ruler of that sign and for any planets in the sign.)

In cases where there is more than one sign in a house, the rulers of all signs in the house need to be checked. Normally, however, the ruler of the sign on the cusp is considered the most important. But the ruler of the second sign in the house becomes the most important (1) if the house cusp is at the very end of a sign so that the largest part of the house is in the next sign, or (2) if there are no planets in the house within the sign on the cusp, but there are planets in the second sign of the house.

Astrologers who use rulerships in this way also use Principles 1, 2, and often 3. They generally concur that planets actually located in a house influence the house more strongly than planets that rule the house. But when there is no planet in a house, they grant greater importance to the rulers of the signs in the house.

Principle 5: The planet may be exalted in the sign on the cusp or a sign within the house. This is not used as widely as Principle 4, but many astrologers hold it to be important. The mechanism here is the same as for a planet ruling a house cusp or a sign within a house.

Principle 6: The house may be connected to a sign and therefore to its ruling planet by means of the "natural zodiac." In the natural zodiac the signs are considered to be a universal house system, such that Aries is the first house, Taurus the second, Gemini the third, and so forth. This means that the planets ruling these signs will have a permanent relationship to the issues associated with the houses that correspond to their signs. For example, many astrologers consider Venus, which rules Taurus, the second sign, to be connected to second-house matters like money and possessions. Or they think that Mercury, which rules Gemini, the third sign, has to do with third-house matters like short journeys, brothers, sisters, neighbors, and relatives. Undeniably there are some affinities. Jupiter, which rules Sagittarius, the ninth sign, does indeed have many ninth-house connotations. It is therefore tempting to go along with this principle.

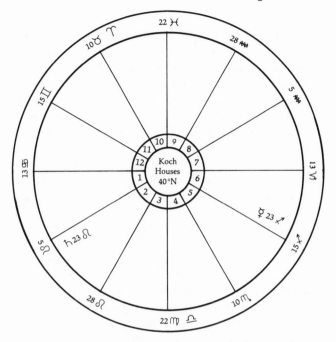

Figure 26. Connecting planets to houses by rulerships

Figure 26 illustrates how, using the above principles, a single aspect, Saturn in Leo in the second house trine Mercury in Sagittarius in the sixth, can involve almost all the houses. Obviously, by Principles 1 and 2, the second and sixth houses are involved, as they contain the two planets in question. And if we admit Saturn to be within orb of a quincunx to the tenth-house cusp, Principle 3 brings in the tenth house.

Principle 4 brings in six more houses. Mercury rules Gemini, the sign on the cusp of the twelfth, and Virgo, the sign on the cusp of the fourth. Virgo is also extensively present within the boundaries of the third. Saturn rules Capricorn, the sign on the cusp of the seventh, and many would say it co-rules Aquarius on the cusps of the eighth and ninth (the cusps are rather close together in that part of the zodiac when Cancer rises, as it does in this chart). We have just added houses three, four, seven, eight, nine, and twelve.

Principle 5, bringing in the exaltation of Mercury in Virgo and Saturn in Libra, merely repeats the involvement of houses three and four, but if we used Placidus houses instead of Koch, we would have Libra, the exaltation of Saturn, on the cusp of the fifth, thus involving one more house.

And, as if we needed more house involvements to confuse us further,

Principle 6, the natural zodiac, not only repeats the involvement of the third, sixth, and tenth (Mercury rules the third and sixth signs, Gemini and Virgo, and Saturn rules the tenth sign, Capricorn) but also drags in the eleventh (Saturn co-rules the eleventh sign, Aquarius). We now have a single aspect involving all the houses except the first.

Reasoning like this gives us so much information it really gives us none. Using it in retrospect, we can get almost anything we want out of a horoscope, but using it in advance, it is impossible to pick out the valid information from a sea of possibilities. Obviously, we cannot use all of these principles without hopelessly confusing ourselves: we need to pick out which are the most reliable ways of relating planets to houses and establish some guidelines for their use.

Principle 1. If you use houses at all, there is no question that planets in houses are linked to those houses. Nevertheless, I have often seen a planet indicate circumstances that have nothing whatsoever to do with the house in which it is placed (or with the houses it rules). Rather, the signification has come from the planet's own symbolism. For instance, a Venus-Saturn contact may indicate inhibitions in the individual's ability to relate to others, even when neither of these planets is in (or rules) a house of relationship. But if Venus and Saturn are involved in houses of relationship, it increases the effect. I would say that though the principle of planets in houses probably takes precedence over all the other principles mentioned above, a planet's own intrinsic symbolism coupled with the intrinsic symbolism of other planets in aspect or midpoint combination with it takes precedence over the symbolism of their house positions. You must consider the planet's own signification independently of the house involved, even when you take a planet's house position as significant.

Principle 2. I definitely feel that planets aspecting planets in other houses link those planets to the houses in which the other planets are located. I consider this a particularly reliable technique (with the cautions advised under Principle 1).

Principle 3. Treating house cusps as sensitive points having the same signification as the house itself would be a useful idea—if astrologers could agree on house systems. I use the Koch system partly because its cusps do seem to work as sensitive points. But this idea needs much research. With the exception of planets aspecting the Midheaven, Ascendant, I.C., and Descendant (which are more definite boundaries than are the other house cusps), at present I must classify this as an unreliable technique for linking planets to houses.

Principle 4. I find that using rulerships to connect planets to houses not only can grotesquely increase the number of houses you have to deal with, it is also much less reliable than Principles 1 and 2. My biggest errors have come from using planets ruling houses they are not in, and I have noted that when other astrologers use this principle their readings increase in vagueness rather than in reliable information.

If you must use this principle, you can gain some clarity by differentiating between planets in a house and planets connected to a house by rulership. According to the great Renaissance astrologer Morinus, the house ruled by a planet indicates conditions *causing* or *preceding in time* the conditions signified by the house in which a planet is placed. For example (to use some old-time house significations that I prefer not to use), if Saturn (hindrance) is in the tenth (social advancement) and rules the twelfth (hidden conditions that work against one), it suggests that one's social advancement is hindered by hidden conditions or individuals—not that Saturn hinders both social advancement and hidden conditions. The twelfth-house symbols produce the tenth-house effect. Most modern astrologers do not distinguish between planets in houses and planets ruling houses, so that the picture becomes hopelessly muddied.

Principle 5. Given the shakiness of the whole doctrine of exaltations, everything I have said about the unreliability of planets ruling signs in houses applies doubly to planets that have exaltation signs on cusps or within houses.

Principle 6. I believe the natural zodiac principle to be completely unreliable. Astrologers seem to use it mostly in retrospect to explain a character trait or event when all else fails. It is based on giving identical meanings to planets, signs, and houses—an idea to which I am opposed.

To summarize, of the six ways of connecting planets to houses, the least reliable are the three that connect planets to houses through their dignities or their relationship to signs. Principle 3, which can connect a house to a planet through the planet's aspect to the house cusp, is also at least partly suspect. This leaves us with only Principles 1 and 2 to rely on.

Many astrologers will object that the four principles we have just thrown out are the only principles that enable us to delineate houses that are devoid of planets. But, as said above, planets have their own intrinsic symbolism and are related to each other by aspects and midpoint combinations. Even though there is no one-to-one correspondence between planetary symbolism and house symbolism, the two do overlap enough so that planet combinations alone can give indications about the areas of life that would be covered by an empty house. Another clue to the meaning of empty houses lies in the mundane (non-ecliptic) aspects that houses make to each other. This is further explained on pages 311-315.

Conclusions concerning Dignities

Clearly, my approach to astrology differs from the classical approach in several respects. I do not feel that dignities have any special value apart from the logical affinities and conflicts that exist between signs and planets. If a planet is said to be dignified in a sign with which it has no obvious affinity, I am not inclined to take the dignity seriously. By the same token, I am not inclined to take the debility of a planet in a sign seriously unless there is some clear conflict between the symbolism of the sign and the planet. I feel that signs are a far less reliable indication of a planet's cosmic state than are aspects and midpoint combinations.

Moreover, I take the greatest exception to using sign rulerships and planetary exaltations for assigning planetary rulers to houses. Added to what I have already pointed out, there is another telling argument against this technique.

In India, which has the greatest number of astrologers of any country in the world, a sidereal zodiac is most commonly used. Their "Aries" differs from our "Aries" by around 24° to 25°. Where we might have Virgo on a house cusp, for example, the Hindu astrologer would at least five-sixths of the time have Leo. Therefore the rulers of the signs on the cusps would usually be different. Hindu astrologers use planets ruling signs on house cusps exactly as most Western astrologers do, and, if anything, they rely on them even more extensively. Yet a Hindu astrologer reading a chart with sidereal-zodiac rulerships will usually get the same results as a Western astrologer using the tropical zodiac. This means one of two things: either house rulerships play only a small part in one or both of the delineation schemes (which is patently untrue at least with the Hindu), or the astrologers involved only think that planets ruling houses are important in their scheme, while they are actually deriving their results intuitively. If either explanation is true, then planetary rulership of house-cusp signs is not a reliable technique without the use of intuition. In both systems, planetary rulership of house-cusp signs seems to be most useful in after-the-fact explanations. If a technique is only useful after the fact, this is a good sign it is not useful at all.

11

The Signs: Core Meanings

Each of the following descriptions begins with a general essay on the symbolism of a sign, showing the personality traits the sign suggests and how the sign relates to the rest of the zodiacal cycle. Then I discuss how nearly or remotely the sign's symbolism resembles that of its planetary ruler. I close each description by showing the specific ways the sign colors the various planets.

Aries

Element: Fire
Quadruplicity: Cardinal
Polarity: Positive
Ruler: Mars

Aries is the beginning of the Sun's cycle through the zodiac. By extension it is considered the beginning of all planetary cycles. Thus more than any other sign Aries symbolizes beginnings.

Aries is primitive more in the sense of "being first" than "crude." But it is crude insofar as it is a sign of raw, unharnessed energy with no direction as yet and no clear application. It is an energy of ego drive, saying "I want to become what I am," but it is not yet what it could be. It is willful, but the will is not stabilized. Its intention can change rapidly: whatever it may want is important now, but tomorrow it may want something else.

Aries is a strong yang energy looking for something to fertilize, something that will manifest its strength on a concrete level. To find this, Aries must learn to adjust to the presence, pressures, and needs of another. This is its fundamental challenge, one it does not often fulfill. It is easier for Aries to preserve its individuality in isolation, backing away from confrontation and mutual accommodation with another. Thus Aries can be asocial or even antisocial.

When Aries does relate to others it likes to lead them. But Aries is not especially interested in power over others: it merely wants power to do what it wants without others making demands.

Its desire to be itself on its own terms also means that Aries needs far less social reinforcement than other signs. This enables Aries to do the unprecedented, to pioneer. As long as others are willing to let it do what it wishes, Aries does not much care if others approve.

In fact, the fiery nature of Aries enables it to act with little concern for whether the action is reasonable, prudent, timely, practical, or even effective, as long as self-expression is achieved. Because it does not have to be practical, Aries can live and work at a high level of abstraction, but the abstraction must reflect personal needs and desires.

As a fire sign, Aries puts out energy more easily than it takes it in: often Aries is a better talker than listener. As a "dry sign" with little water in its makeup, Aries does not handle displays of emotion well, except for enthusiasm, assertiveness, and sometimes anger. Its anger is short lived: once the energy has been expressed, the matter is concluded. Long-term resentment is not in the nature of the sign.

Aries is often impatient, lacking in persistence and stamina. Its style is to strike frequently and lightly rather than make a strong, sustained attack. Yet its energy level can be high enough to have the same impact as a more sustained approach.

One of the finer side effects of Aries's need to be itself is that it is unwilling to become compromised by acting falsely or deceitfully. It is not so much that Aries has a moral objection to deceit as that its need to be itself does not square with misrepresentation.

The Relationship of Aries to Mars   Mars as the traditional ruler of Aries is one of the closer sign-ruler correspondences. Both symbols relate to the raw assertion of ego energy, the self proclaiming to the universe that it will be what it is and that it will resist others' attempts to change its nature. Neither is especially cognizant of social contexts, and both work best alone. Both are fiery and willful. The primary difference between them is the difference between a planet and a sign. And there is also a difference of degree. Mars, as a symbol of self-assertion, is much more powerful. But this is true in every case where a planet is similar to a sign.

The assignment of Pluto to Aries by some is not as strange as it might sound. Pluto as the significator of major transformation and as an index of a concern with power is more allied with Scorpio. But Pluto as it is connected with rebirth does logically have an affinity with Aries, the sign of spring and the rebirth of nature. Otherwise, however, Pluto and Aries are too different in their symbolism for Pluto to be considered a ruler of this sign.

The Effect of Aries on Planets   Any planet in Aries operates more decisively, quickly, and in a more ego-oriented way than usual. This can be a problem for planets that are not especially ego-oriented such as Venus, the Moon, or Neptune. Such planets will express themselves somewhat tensely because they cannot easily resolve the conflict between their natural inclinations and those of the sign. In particular, Venus, a planetary energy signifying interpersonal contact, is in conflict between its desire to get along with others and the desire of Aries to do things its own way.

Planets in Aries lose some of the stamina they may otherwise possess. They may act assertively, but if challenged may not be able to sustain a long conflict.

Taurus

Element: Earth
Quadruplicity: Fixed
Polarity: Negative
Ruler: Venus

Taurus is the next phase in the cycle. Its function is to provide a vessel for the energies of Aries so that they can be made manifest. Aries, the solar energy of early spring, warms Taurus, the soil, so that living things may grow.

Taurus, like the Moon, symbolizes a container or matrix for the manifestation of energy. And like the Moon it has suffered from our culture's reverence for the active and denigration of the passive without truly understanding the role of the passive (see page 54). The passive matrix is, however, consummately valuable, because without it the energy of Aries would never come to anything at all. The container represented by Taurus provides the medium whereby the energy symbolized by Aries can become manifest on the physical plane. And because the container is necessary for the manifestation of the contained, the container is as valuable as what it contains. No value distinction can be made.

Any medium in which energy is manifest affects the nature of the energy and thereby acquires a creative potential of its own. The energy for creation may be from another source, but the style and nature of the creativity arise from that which receives the energy.

Taurus is the remedy for almost all of Aries's deficiencies. To the erratic energies of Aries it grants stability, constancy, and persistence. Where Aries energies are scattered, Taurus can limit and concentrate them. Concerned with the reality of the physical universe, Taurus can bring Aries's abstract energies into the realm of real, experienceable effects.

Also, whereas Aries is fiery and harsh, Taurus is cooling and soft (although among earth signs Taurus is by far the warmest; again, think of the soil warming in the springtime). Fiery Aries is somewhat sterile, whereas Taurus, the fecundated earth, brings fertility.

Taurus is earthy in the popular meaning of the word: it enjoys the physical world. It sees the physical universe as neither an arena in which to perform nor as a tool. Rather it wants to be a part of, involved in, and especially to experience the wonder of the physical world.

Like Aries, Taurus is not especially social. Though it lacks Aries's rampant individualism, Taurus is content to be by itself, relating to the world in its own way. It does not especially need applause.

It does, however, enjoy the opposite sex, as through it Taurus can experience physical sexuality. Although Scorpio is popularly represented as the most sexually oriented sign, Taurus, the sensualist, is more likely to fit that role.

Aries and Taurus form the first positive-negative pair of signs in the zodiac, and even though they contrast, when put together they represent a whole. Together, they are the living body, animated by the fire of Aries and given form by the earth of Taurus. Nevertheless, it is a body as yet unaware of its relationship to others: its consciousness needs to be developed. This will be carried out in the remaining signs of the zodiac.

The Relationship of Taurus to Venus and the Earth   I do not consider Venus the best ruler for Taurus. It is easy to see how the rulership came about, but I believe it is time to change our views.

In ancient mythologies, the goddesses of sexual love were Earth goddesses who also presided over the fertility of nature. The symbolism of sexual goddesses was mixed with that of mother goddesses, and no clear distinction was made between the different aspects of the feminine. In modern astrology, however, Venus has taken on the symbolism of love, creativity, and art; and while it is clearly an energy favorable to fertility and agriculture, this does not seem to be its principal concern.

It seems at first as if we have no planet with a clearly Taurean symbolism, and yet we do: the one planet whose symbolism on a planetary level fits perfectly with that of Taurus on the sign level is the Earth. Taurus is the most perfectly earthy of earth signs. Everything we think of as pertaining to Earth goddesses, everything that relates to adjectives like "earthy," pertains to Taurus. The Earth has much in common with Venus, but it could never be the significator of romantic love, which is too unreal, not sufficiently sensible, and too removed from the affairs of the daily world to be relevant to an Earth person.

Since the horoscope is centered upon the Earth, how do we locate the Earth in the chart as a point with a definite longitude and latitude? Here is a suggestion. Although for astronomical reasons we treat the horoscope as if it were geocentric (centered on the center of the Earth), it is actually topocentric (centered on a point on the Earth's surface). The line that connects us on the surface to the center of the Earth goes straight down. If we project that line onto the ecliptic so that we can express its position in terms of the zodiac, the longitude of the topocenter-to-geocenter line is the Imum Coeli of the horoscope, the fourth-house cusp.

In fact, the Earth has never been absent from the horoscope, because houses reflect our relationship to the planet Earth. The Earth occupies half the chart from the Ascendant in the east through the Imum Coeli to the Descendant in the west. Its apparent orb extends a full 180°—how could it fail to affect us tremendously?

The Imum Coeli or fourth-house cusp is the focus of this relationship, and the symbolic fit between it and the Earth is not bad. According to tradition, the fourth house signifies real estate, actual physical land (that is, earth), one's home, and that which gave one birth. I do not know if this is the answer to the Taurus rulership problem, but it is an idea worth considering.

The fourth-house cusp symbolizes both earthy and lunar matters, and the similarity between these areas of experience may account for the tradition that the Moon is exalted in Taurus. Clearly there is an affinity between Earth symbolism and Moon symbolism, but there is a major difference as well. The Moon relates to emotional security and the feeling of belonging, whereas the Earth relates to practical, physical security, to actually possessing what one needs to survive in comfort. Taurus is like the Earth rather than the Moon in this respect.

The Effect of Taurus on Planets   As the earthiest of earth signs and the most fixed of the fixed signs, Taurus is the slowest sign in the zodiac. But slowness should not be equated with dullness. The end-result of the activity of planets in Taurus can be as intelligent, precise, clear, and insightful as that of any other sign, but the result is arrived at carefully, methodically, and with great attention to making sure that the work has practical relevance. All planetary action in Taurus is slowed down and bent toward practical objectives.

The only planets that may really suffer from this are those in which high-speed action is intrinsic.

Among the most affected are Mercury and Uranus. Mercury in Taurus can be experienced as a liability, because most people expect Mercurial energies to be fast, and Mercury in Taurus is not. If given a chance to operate at its own pace, however, Mercury is just as effective here as in any other sign.

Uranus in Taurus is difficult because the revolutionary, rebellious and instantaneous quality of Uranus is not suited to the slow and gradual nature of Taurus. Signs such as Gemini allow Uranus to release its energies in a series of small discharges, preventing it from blowing up. But the nature of earth resists the electricity of Uranus such that when the energy is released, it is released in a tremendous explosion.

Mars in Taurus is also supposed to be difficult, because the naturally slow pace of Taurus tends to cause the energy of Mars to be held in rather than released. This enables the energy to build so that when it does blow off it can be destructive. But if the individual is not repeatedly provoked the energy may never have to blow off. On the positive side, Mars in Taurus can have great steadiness and persistence once it gets going.

Gemini

Element: Air
Quadruplicity: Mutable
Polarity: Positive
Ruler: Mercury

Gemini begins the second positive-negative pair of signs. In Aries and Taurus we had the building and animating of the physical body; in Gemini and Cancer we have the development of the mental and emotional aspects of the individual. Gemini represents the mental part.

Gemini is probably the most perfectly mutable of all mutable signs, because there is something inherently mutable about air. Like the wind, the nature of Gemini is to move rapidly from place to place, covering everything it encounters, but perhaps too rapidly to get a deep impression of anything. Preceding Cancer, the first water sign, Gemini is not yet aware that there are deeper aspects of reality that are not immediately amenable to logic and rational analysis. It understands quickly but does not empathize. It learns quickly but does not develop that deep, feeling understanding of the world that enables some people to live skillfully without really having to think.

Gemini's compensation for this is its speed and curiosity. It is the first sign to concern itself with the relationships of various elements in the environment. It does not evaluate these relationships, nor does it particularly concern itself with its own relationship to them. It merely wants to know what is going on out there. In this respect, Gemini, the third sign, is often related to the third house. And the relationship *is* quite close. I seriously question the idea that Gemini has anything to do with brothers and sisters, however, even though the constellation Gemini represents twins (of course, that constellation now occupies the sign Cancer).

Gemini is usually quite sociable, and enjoys meeting people. The sign has a fairly high energy level which other people find refreshing, yet the level is not so high as to be exhausting to those of a slower temperament. Gemini makes even the casual social contact interesting, but when it comes to deeper, more profound connections, the sign is somewhat resistant. It regards strong attachments as confining and feels that they get in the way of its need to range about widely in search of experience.

Being mutable, Gemini tends, like the wind, to go around obstacles rather than confront them directly. If subjected to really strong pressure, Gemini will simply change. Consistency and constancy may be difficult for Gemini, which loses interest quickly.

One aspect of Gemini that has not been stressed in the literature is that it is a sign of game-playing and trickery. It loves card games and mentally oriented board games, and it also enjoys games in the sense of complicated social maneuvers. Gemini's tricks are not intended so much to deceive or misrepresent as they are mental activities that Gemini enjoys. Unfortunately, Gemini's lack of empathy and any real understanding of feelings may cause it to hurt others where no hurt was intended.

The Relationship of Gemini to Mercury There are those who maintain that Mercury rules Virgo, and that something else rules Gemini, but I cannot accept that argument. In my opinion the fit between Mercury and Gemini is about as close as possible for a planet-ruler pair. Both the sign and the planet represent the same questing intellectual drive to establish connections between the self and the environment. Such connections are needed to establish common bonds with other people and a relationship to the environment in general. Both sign and planet are predominantly mental and extremely changeable. Both are more concerned with discovering an idea than with making practical use of it. People in whom Mercury is strong often appear similar to those with the Sun in Gemini. I have the Sun closely conjunct Mercury, and, although I do not look like one, people have thought that I am a Gemini more often than they have thought I am a Sagittarius (my Sun sign) or a Cancer (my rising sign). Just as Gemini is the consummate air sign, Mercury is the consummate air planet. The game-playing trickster side of Gemini discussed above is also characteristic of Mercury.

The Effect of Gemini on Planets In most respects Gemini is the opposite of Taurus. It tends to quicken the energy of planets, and to make them work at a more abstract level. Planets concerned with feeling, emotion, and sensitivity are the ones most negatively affected by Gemini. Among these are the Moon and Neptune. Venus is often fickle in Gemini, but otherwise it is not seriously affected. Slow-acting planets such as Saturn do not seem to be seriously affected by the sign, but they do operate at a higher energy level.

A person with many planets in Gemini is likely to be freedom-loving and possibly lacking in persistence. To make up for the sign's frequent lack of depth of knowledge, Geminians can cover great amounts of ground very quickly.

Cancer

Element: Water
Quadruplicity: Cardinal
Polarity: Negative
Ruler: the Moon

Cancer completes the development of the individual as an individual, with the unfolding of the emotional faculties. It does so by putting one back in contact with one's source, one's roots, the groundspring of all being.

Cancer is not merely feeling; it is feeling *part* of something. Where Gemini is an intellectual awareness of relationship, Cancer is an emotional awareness, one that can be inchoate, unformulated, and too deep for simple, rational expression. Particularly, Cancer is awareness of relationship to the past: one's childhood, family (especially mother), community, and even homeland. Cancer is not so much an awareness of one's relationship to other individuals in general; that is the function of the air signs.

Because Cancerian needs are so fundamental, interference with their fulfillment can have particularly bad effects. Cancer symbolizes the need for emotional security, for feeling that one's environment will support one's existence, and for feeling nurtured by those around one. If these aspects of the energy work properly, Cancer also symbolizes the need to support and nurture others, giving to others what one oneself has already received. But if the needs of Cancer are not fulfilled, one often becomes caught in infantile patterns of behavior: behavior that is grasping and emotionally possessive from fear of losing those that are loved. The love one gives may be smothering. Also, material possessions may become symbols of emotional security; those with Cancerian problems may surround themselves with things in an effort to get from physical objects the emotional support they really need. The traits that have sometimes given Cancer a bad reputation are not intrinsic to the sign; they result from vital needs not being gratified.

On the plus side, Cancer symbolizes patterns that are essential to the social good. In every group there must be those who support others, nurture them, take care of the needy, and reassure the insecure. If Cancer did not manifest, everything would be purely functional, rational, cold, and dead. In fact, today's breakup of the family and increasing reliance on the state for the care of the young, the old, and the infirm represents a trend toward the destruction of those Cancerian elements necessary for social cohesion. Cancer's needs for roots and community conflict with Gemini's needs for getting around, having experience, and being free—needs that are dominant in our culture now. It should be noted that, astrologically speaking, Gemini is a more primitive function in the development of the individual than is Cancer.

The Relationship of Cancer to the Moon   This is another close sign-ruler relationship. Along with the Moon and the fourth house, Cancer is part of the mother complex of symbols. Both the sign and the planet relate to nurture, to the feeling of belonging, to the idea of coming from somewhere and from something. Cancer and the Moon are strongly concerned with emotional security, and both can be infantile in the way they express their needs when thwarted, especially if emotional security is lacking early in life.

The principal difference is that the Moon is a planet and Cancer is a sign. Also, the Moon is one of the bodies that affects the individual chart most strongly, whereas Cancer is part of a set of general relationships that may or may not strongly affect an individual. For example, having Saturn in Cancer indicates one is born in a period of general weakness of the nurturing principle, but having Saturn conjunct the Moon is a strong, personal statement concerning an individual's experience of nurture.

The Effect of Cancer on Planets   Cancer is at its best with strongly emotional planets like the Moon, Venus, and possibly Neptune and Pluto (although Pluto in combination with the maternal group of symbols can be so intense as to signify difficulties). Jupiter is favored in Cancer not so much because of its emotional quality as because it shares with Cancer a protective feeling and the desire to support those who are still growing.

Airy planets such as Mercury and Uranus have a harder time in Cancer: water, which is personal and subjective, interferes with the clear mental observation and detached judgment of air.

The strong ego energies of Mars often have difficulty in Cancerian areas of experience (such as one's relationship to home, mother, and family) that ought to be relatively free of ego tension. Similarly, Saturn is difficult in Cancer because it creates barriers in these same areas, areas that ought to be among the few in which emotional energies can flow freely without obstacles. One should not have to feel the need to perform to a high standard in order to be accepted by one's family. In one's family one should not have to feel that one is constantly being judged and required by others to be what one is not. Saturn in Cancer may accompany this kind of problem, but the lengthy time Saturn stays in a sign usually makes its effects general rather than personal.

Leo

Element: Fire
Quadruplicity: Fixed
Polarity: Positive
Ruler: the Sun

With Leo, the basic structure of the individual entity is complete. This is clear in that Leo is a sign of developed ego and self-confidence, with strong needs for self-expression, admiration, and uncompromising personal integrity.

Many issues that Aries confronted reemerge in Leo, but with important differences. Whereas Aries was a sign of potential vigorously trying to actualize itself, Leo is a sign in which that potential *is* actualized. For Aries we said, "I want to become what I am;" for Leo we say simply, "I am."

While Leo represents the entity complete in its basic structure, however, the individual is still socially incomplete. One has yet to deal with one's relationship to others. One is like the child who has just accomplished something new, and who is not happy until every adult within reach knows about it. Even though every human being in history may have achieved the same thing, for the child, the accomplishment is new and fascinating. This is the basic psychology of the Leo principle (although, of course, most adult Leos are far from being that primitive about it).

Nevertheless, there is a genuine fascination with the self, and a desire that others be similarly fascinated. But only in defective strongly Leonine personalities does this pattern emerge as egotism or show-off behavior. In most adult Leos it comes out as a need for personal recognition, a desire to be impressive, and a need to control one's destiny. The desire to be impressive is usually a desire to be genuinely so—that is, to be an individual of real significance, not merely to appear significant. Leo, like Aries and for the same reasons, is an honest sign.

The metaphor for the mature Leo is that of the king or the Sun. Leo desires to be an energy source, one that provides not only for its own accomplishments but also for those of others. Just as the Sun by its own reflected light enables the planets to shine, the Leo personality desires to be a center of light in which others may bask and shine back.

All the above has a potential for arrogance, and this is the most common Leonine flaw. Yet Leo is a relatively simple personality type with clearly defined needs. If these needs are fulfilled, Leo can be counted on to perform energetically and with honor.

There are other important differences between Aries and Leo. First, Leo is a fixed sign, while Aries is cardinal. Thus, unlike Aries, Leo has persistence and can be stubborn.

Second, there is a difference in the social awareness of the two signs. Aries likes to be left alone, free to do what it wishes. When it is aware of interactions with others, it is aware largely in a competitive way. Leo, on the other hand, is beginning to be aware of others as a regular part of its environment. Yet it is only ready to deal with others insofar as they allow it to be the center of the stage. We are still in the first third of the zodiac; the individual is still finding itself with respect to itself. Only when we get to Virgo will the individual find that external necessity must be taken into consideration, and only when we get to Libra will the individual fully realize the need to get along with others. Self-expression is still Leo's major goal, and the more perfectly this sign can be itself and accepted as such, the better off it is.

Leo's only real dependency upon others is that it badly needs their acknowledgment. Therefore, unlike Aries, Leo cannot thrive in a vacuum and, despite its drive toward self-expression, Leo can be coerced by others. All they need do is withhold approval. But being coerced is damaging to Leo, because it knows that only by truly being itself can it be effective.

However childlike certain aspects of the sign may seem, Leo is fundamentally correct about what it needs, and when it gets what it needs—that is, when it is allowed to be totally, completely, and authentically itself—it is one of the most admirable types of human being.

The Relationship of Leo to the Sun   Although this is another fairly good correspondence between a sign and its ruler, there is an important difference between Leo and the Sun. Leo, because of its position in the zodiac, represents an early stage in the development of the individual. The Sun is an energy—one that is neither primitive nor advanced.

Also, much more fundamentally than Leo, the Sun is the drive of an individual to be what it is, a drive for personal self-expression and authenticity. As the Sun moves through the signs it takes on each one's style of being in turn.

Many astrologers equate Leo, the Sun, and the fifth house. Even though a sign and a house are not the same thing, there are affinities between Leo and the fifth. But a total equation is impossible. Children, and especially childbearing, are among the things symbolized by the fifth house; yet, according to tradition, Leo is a barren sign, that is, unfavorable for childbearing. Leo on the fifth-house cusp was supposed to be a particularly bad sign for a woman who desires children. This old idea may or may not have merit, but it does indicate that equating Leo with the fifth house in all regards is a relatively new idea, one with little basis in tradition.

The Effect of Leo on Planets   Like all fixed signs, Leo has a stabilizing influence. It tends to make the energies of planets located within it operate in a steady, relentless manner: one would not expect a strong Leo type to give up easily. Leo, a fixed fire sign, however, does not have the slowing effect of Taurus, which is fixed earth.

Because of the strong ego-orientation of Leo, planets in this sign are more likely to be directed toward the service of self (assuming that they are not, like Neptune, incapable of being bent to that end). Issues surrounding planets in Leo are likely to be areas in which one's pride or sense of self-esteem is involved. For example, Mercury in Leo would indicate that one speaks one's own mind forcefully, or that one takes pride in one's mental capabilities, or (at worst) that one can see only one's own point of view. Saturn in Leo might give one a strong sense of pride in being disciplined, careful, and righteous. And so on.

Virgo

Element: Earth
Quadruplicity: Mutable
Polarity: Negative
Ruler: Mercury and various asteroids

There are few adjacent signs that are as different as Leo and Virgo.

And yet, as in all positive-negative pairs, the later sign is a fulfillment and completion of the earlier. Virgo represents the completed individual, not as in Leo standing alone and glorying in itself, but rather confronting both the physical and social universes and trying to come to terms with them. Virgo approaches the physical universe as an obstacle to which one must adapt, a framework through which one can learn to be effective, and a reality that must be served. It approaches the social universe in the same way. From the arrogance of the negative Leo we move to the submissiveness of the negative Virgo. From trying to be self-sufficient in Leo we try to be totally efficient in Virgo. Virgo justifies its existence by how effective it is in getting along in the world and making the best of it. The emphasis on total individuality is gone.

The Virgo type needs little social recognition for the quality of its workmanship: its sense of achievement is based on knowing it has done the job well. In confronting the reality of the external physical and social universes, Virgo has at least to some extent become cautious and maybe a little fearful in the face of that with which it has to deal. It is almost as if Virgo is the result of the childishly exuberant egotism of Leo encountering its first severe defeat. It is chastened and careful. And even though the Virgo type does not need others to affirm the quality of whatever work it does, it is not quite sure of itself as an individual and it is therefore not very resistant to external pressure. With respect to behavior, Virgo under social pressure can be one of the most conformist signs of the zodiac. It does not need to be treated like royalty, but it does need to be accepted by others for itself.

I do not mean that all Virgos are timid, lacking in confidence, or conformist. I am merely trying to place Virgo in the scheme of the developing personality that the zodiac describes. Virgo is the individualism of Leo sobered by the encounter with external necessities and duties. Any actual Virgo personality is as capable as any other sign of being strong and successful. Virgo affects the *manner* in which one becomes successful, not the fact of success.

Virgo does not depend on abundant self-confidence to get ahead, nor would it ever try to bluff others into making them think it is more than it is. Virgo attempts to be realistic about self-evaluation. If anything, it will err on the side of humility. It is as honest as Leo and as unwilling to compromise itself by misrepresentation. Virgo attempts to achieve by mastering the tools that the world offers it, by creating an orderly, dependable relationship with the world around it.

Virgo may be chastened by its confrontation with the physical universe, but it is not crushed. In fact, it strives to achieve what some Leos think they already possess: perfection. Self-criticism and self-analysis are the keys to perfection, and Virgo may be merciless in judging itself when it fails (and also sometimes merciless when others fail).

Here we have the key to Virgo as a mutable sign. Unlike Taurus, which for the most part deals with the world as it is, Virgo attempts to change itself, and eventually the world. Virgos may not enjoy being out in the open in what they do, but success in effecting changes is important to them.

While it does not insist on being boss, Virgo needs to feel effective. Yet the physical world is not an entirely reliable place: things go wrong even with the best of plans. This bothers Virgo more than most signs. Thus in an effort to achieve control by letting nothing escape its notice it tends to concentrate on details. This makes the sign good at analysis but less good at getting the grand overview. The details may overwhelm the large viewpoint.

The concern for order may also cause Virgo to become extremely neat in personal habits, but if Virgo cannot achieve perfect order, it may give up completely. In fact, the extremely high standards that Virgo holds in many areas of its life may cause it to give up completely when it fails to live up to them. Otherwise, the sign is moderate in most regards.

Virgo has high aesthetic standards. It is the sign of crafts, in which function is united with form, such that each completes the other and neither takes from the other. But Virgo is not especially patient with beauty that has no function; always a practical sign, it believes that some purpose should be served by everything.

The Relationship of Virgo to Mercury and the Asteroids Mercury is the traditional ruler of Virgo, but modern astrologers are feeling increasingly uneasy about this assignment. In my opinion, Virgo and Mercury make one of the worst sign-ruler fits of all. Mercury is airy while Virgo is earthy. Mercury loves abstraction while Virgo is practical. It is true that both have a mutable quality, and that Virgo does have strong intellectual concerns, but Virgo's are largely for the sake of being effective, while Mercury's are for their own sake. The game-playing aspect of Mercury is missing in Virgo; Virgo is very serious. Mercury has no special concern with duty, while Virgo does.

The astrologer Eleanor Bach has suggested that the four major asteroids rule Virgo. This is a tempting idea because the woman holding the sheaf of wheat who is pictured in the constellation Virgo is in fact the goddess Ceres, which is also the name of one of the four major asteroids. And the astrological effects of Vesta, which are the most clearly observable of the four asteroids, are extremely Virgoan. Both Vesta and Virgo are strongly concerned with duty and responsibility, especially the duties of home and hearth. Both have strong connections with work and with being efficient. Neither symbol has an easy time with play: Vesta is much like Saturn in its reserved and serious attitudes. And of course, Vesta is a virgin goddess.

Assigning the other two major asteroids, Pallas and Juno, to Virgo is less obvious. Zipporah Dobyns, who has done extensive work with asteroids, gives these to Libra along with Venus for reasons mentioned in the section on Libra. But Pallas has a quality of critical, fighting intellectualism that seems more Virgoan than Libran to me. And Juno, at least in her capacity as goddess of domestic crafts and household responsibilities, also seems Virgoan.

I am inclined to give all four major asteroids to Virgo, although a case can be made for assigning Ceres to Taurus or Cancer insofar as the goddess is an earth-mother symbol as both Bach and Dobyns seem to feel. Clearly, with all the new planets and asteroids discovered since ancient times, the once-neat order of rulerships has been badly disturbed.

The Effect of Virgo on Planets   The principal effect of Virgo on planets is to make them work with extra precision and care. Planets with exuberant and explosive energies (like Mars and Uranus) do not get along as well in Virgo as those (like Saturn) whose nature is steady and cautious. Whether or not Mercury rules Virgo, it is favorably placed there. Venus does not seem to do well in Virgo from a sexual point of view, because Virgo, as its name suggests, tends to be sexually modest. But Venus in Virgo is more successful with regard to creativity, especially of the craftsmanly kind.

Because it is interested in dealing efficiently with the physical universe, Virgo can be changeable when it perceives new contingencies that have to be met. Also, its lack of self-confidence can cause it to change according to the pressures to which it is subjected. Therefore a large number of planets in Virgo will tend to increase the mutability of the horoscope as well as its level of earthiness.

Libra

Element: Air
Quadruplicity: Cardinal
Polarity: Positive
Ruler: Venus and various asteroids

With Libra we enter the second half of the zodiac. In the first half, the signs traced the formation of the individual from the first assertion of individuality in Aries to the complete individual in Leo, and concluded in Virgo with the first realization of an external necessity to which rampant individuality must be somewhat subject.

In the second half of the zodiac the individual learns to relate to and integrate itself into the reality and social order beyond itself. This half of the cycle extends from Libra (signifying the first and simplest interpersonal relationship, the one-to-one intimate confrontation) to Pisces (in which the socially integrated individual encounters something beyond society and reality as normally conceived: the mystical oneness of the universe).

To some extent, each sign in the second half in some way parallels its opposite sign in the first half, carrying out on a social level what was begun in the opposite sign on a personal level. But we should not get carried away with this idea. Each of these signs also possesses an individuality of its own which in many cases does not seem to follow from its being the social counterpart of its opposite sign.

So it is with Libra. Though it is the sign in which the individual first makes an accommodation to another individual in a one-to-one relationship, it is also a sign of aesthetic development, with a strong love of beauty and harmony. Also, it is not as immature with respect to the social integration of the individual as Aries is with respect to the formation of the individual. We have to remember that Aries is the first fire sign, whereas Libra is the second air sign. Thus Libra is farther along in the air cycle of development than Aries is in the fire cycle. Libra is deft in dealing with others, has a highly developed knowledge of the art of getting along, and can often get what it wants from another by apparently giving in. That Libra is the sign of the sweet and beautiful goddess Venus is often noted; that it is also a cardinal, positive sign is noted less often. Libra excels at taking the initiative in such a way that others do not realize the initiative has been taken.

Being the sign of the simplest of all relationships, the one-to-one, Libra has difficulty in thinking of other modes of relationship. It sees in terms of polarities: I versus you, this person versus that person, we versus they. And very often for "versus" one may substitute "together with." The key idea is that Libra cannot conceive of self in a vacuum. Self is developed only in connection with another self. Libra needs another with whom to have a dialogue. But Libra does not need to be subservient to another; in fact, it may well be dominant.

Because Libra needs the juxtaposition of itself to another in order to develop self-understanding and self-realization, Libra people tend always to be involved in an intimate relationship. As soon as one ends, another begins. Libra persons may also be good at professions that involve one-to-one counseling such as the law, psychology, and any other field in which one acts as a consultant. However, these professions also require strong indications from other parts of the chart.

Libra completes a process begun in Virgo. In Virgo, one becomes aware of external necessity and tries to accommodate oneself to it by serving it, being useful to it, and learning to function as efficiently as possible with respect to it. In Libra, the individual encounters the other as an equal. Interdependence is the key rather than one-way service; partnership rather than subservience.

The most Venusian aspect of Libra is its concern with beauty and art. Libra does not necessarily indicate artistic ability, but Libra persons seem to need art more than others. Libra likes beauty, and it may not appreciate art that is stormy, intensely personal, dramatic, and emotional if those qualities of self-declaration take precedence over beauty. Libra may have a taste merely for the pretty if the individual has not learned to handle the emotional content of art. Libra is an air sign, and in all its encounters with the world, both in art and relationship, it has the usual air-sign difficulty in dealing with intense feeling.

The Relationship of Libra to Venus and the Asteroids   We have already discussed the problems of relating Venus to Taurus. While I prefer Venus as the ruler of Libra rather than of Taurus, I must acknowledge at least one difficulty. Venus is clearly a negative, yin planet, while Libra is a positive, yang sign. In this respect, Venus would clearly seem to be more suited to negative, yin Taurus. But it is by no means unprecedented to have a sign with a ruler of different polarity: few would be reluctant to assign Saturn to Capricorn, yet here is a clearly masculine planet (although the most yin of the yang planets) assigned to a yin sign (although probably the most yang of the yin signs). All this means is that one cannot completely identify signs with their ruling planets.

As Capricorn is an extremely yang negative sign, so is Libra an extremely yin positive sign. In fact these two signs are so much at variance with their alleged polarities that they call the whole polarity idea into question. Nevertheless, I believe that the idea of polarity is sound. It is just that the polarity of a sign refers to a fairly specific attribute of the sign, not to the sum of all its attributes.

As mentioned above, Zipporah Dobyns assigns the asteroids Pallas and Juno to Libra. The goddess Pallas Athena is a fighter and could represent the type of Libra whose one-to-one intimate confrontation takes the form of a fight. But I have not seen many Librans who operate this way, except for those with strong Mars or Pluto indications, and in these I suspect that the Libra indication has been overridden.

Juno is a better case, since among other things the goddess Juno was the patroness of marriage and wives. Marriage is definitely a Libran relationship. But the goddess Juno does not embody Libran traits such as the love of beauty, art, and harmony. Traditionally a sign of peace, Libra does not go well with the shrewish nature of Juno (or, for that matter, with the aggressive Pallas Athena). But arguments from mythology, unsupported by experience, are dangerous. Their resolution must be allowed to develop from observation of astrological effects.

The Effect of Libra on Planets   Obviously, planets in Libra increase the airy and cardinal qualities in a chart. Also, Libra is more favorable to planets that are relationship-oriented and generally peaceable in nature. Libra is at its worst with individualistic planets such as Mars. Mars in Libra does not know whether to go it alone and live its way, or try to get along in a Libran manner. It indicates someone likely to create intimate one-to-one relationships of the combative type.

Oddly enough, Libra is the traditional sign of Saturn's exaltation. There is a certain appropriateness here. Saturn is not a relationship-prone planet, of course, but it is not an individualistic one, either. Its role is to remind one of one's connection to the greater social world. Saturn relates to Libra in that it stands for the obligations and duties of a relationship. It takes away the frivolous aspects of Libra and leaves the serious.

The recent transits of Neptune (1941-1956), Uranus (1968-1975), and Pluto (1970-1984) through Libra seem to symbolize the changes that have been occurring in our concepts of marriage. Neptune created an almost unrealizable idealization of one-to-one relationships while eliminating many of the social restrictions concerning them. The Neptune-in-Libra generation has been responsible for the widespread social acceptance of unmarried people living together, as well as the increasing respectability of homosexual relationships. Uranus and Pluto have been in Libra during the adulthood of those born with Neptune in Libra, and this well describes the actualization of what was portended by Neptune's transit of this sign. Uranus symbolizing revolution and Pluto symbolizing breakdown suggest the increasing divorce rate and tendency toward multiple marriages. Clearly, a new view of human relationships is emerging from these transits.

In general, planets in Libra will bend the issues concerned with each planet more toward relationships and getting along with others. At the same time, planets in Libra will tend to operate in a lighter, less serious manner than in other signs (especially the next sign, Scorpio).

Scorpio

Element: Water
Quadruplicity: Fixed
Polarity: Negative
Ruler: Pluto (traditionally, Mars)

Scorpio is one of the most misunderstood signs in the zodiac, and one of those with the worst reputation. While it does deal with serious issues, it does not deserve most of the negative things that have been said about it. In fact, it can be very positive.

As for polarity with the opposite sign, Scorpio seems to have little to do with Taurus. In a way, Scorpio is more a prefiguration of Pisces. Scorpio is the first encounter with ego death. It completes the process begun in Libra, where the individual entered into a dialogue with another while both individuals remained separate entities. In Scorpio the two merge into one on an emotional level, and this is the first kind of ego death.

While the above places Scorpio into the scheme of the signs, however, it is not the essence of the sign. The essence is transformation, and it is inherently mystical. This is not the mysticism of Christianity, which is primarily otherworldly, ascetic, and self-denying. It is a mysticism that sees the power of transformation at work in ordinary reality. Rather than deny the physical universe in order to transcend it, Scorpio will immerse itself in physicality and even drown in it in order to go beyond it.

Scorpio is the first sign to be aware of the heights and depths of the universe. Feeling the relative nature of all things, it will freely declare there is no difference between good and evil, and be misunderstood as a result. Scorpio sees living as a series of deaths and resurrections, and instead of trying to avoid these experiences it will plunge into them headlong in order to experience the revivification that results.

On an ordinary level, this manifests as Scorpio's fondness for living intensely. Nothing is to be done superficially. It is better completely to experience little than superficially to experience much. Obviously, Scorpio is a dramatic sign, one that loves emotion even while it appears pained by its own experiences. It is better for Scorpio to feel bad than to feel nothing.

Concomitantly, Scorpio loves mysteries. It enjoys digging into the depths of any issue or person to find out what is going on inside. As a consequence, Scorpio is associated with investigation, research, and psychotherapy—the last for two reasons, the probing of the psyche and the opportunity to assist in an individual's self-transformation.

Whether in criticism or in envy, Scorpio is often called an extremely sexy sign. But if one is referring to the simple enjoyment of sex, Scorpio is not necessarily sexy. In fact, the sign is capable of denying itself sex altogether. Yet there is a relationship between Scorpio and sexuality. It is not the search for pleasure that brings a Scorpio to sex, it is the search for transcendence. The orgasm offers one of the few experiences of ego death and self-transcendence that is accessible to the ordinary human being. And it is characteristic of Scorpio that this is also one of the few such experiences in which ego death and supreme ego gratification are experienced at the same time. Scorpio does not feel the need to separate the two as much as other signs do. To a Scorpio, no matter how attractive and sexy the partner is in other respects, love that does not contain drama and emotional intensity will not endure.

Although the above portrait is fundamentally true to the nature of the sign, it is not an especially accurate portrait of the typical Scorpio. The typical Scorpio often does not appear especially preposessing or dramatic. More than most signs, Scorpios have a tendency to look ordinary, and they can be easily overlooked—that is until a confrontation. Then it is discovered that running close after Taurus, Scorpio is the second most fixed sign in the zodiac, and it is the only water sign that will fight. In fact, it will even enjoy fighting, for fighting is another way for the individual to enjoy a peak experience. War continues partly because it allows people to live at the height of their abilities. The Scorpio, especially, enjoys this. Like the other water signs, Scorpio is sensitive and easily hurt by others, but unlike Cancer and Pisces, Scorpio will fight, often fiercely, when hurt.

Scorpio's outstanding difficulty with others is the height and depth of its understanding. Much of the emotion Scorpio feels is extremely primitive and does not lend itself to verbal communication and intellectual analysis. Also, much of its knowledge is not easily communicated because it is beyond most people's understanding. When Scorpios try to communicate what they see, understand, or feel, they are often badly misunderstood. They then tend to keep silent because the misunderstanding that results from silence is better than the misunderstanding that comes from failed communication. Less secure Scorpios may react to the misunderstanding by blaming themselves and concluding that they are rotten inside. Burdened with a sense of inward decay and corruption, they do not realize that the "evil" thoughts they harbor are quite often felt, if a bit less intensely, by others as well. From all this comes Scorpio's reputation for secrecy.

All the above may result in Scorpio seeming self-involved and brooding. Because of the fixed nature of the sign, neither negative nor positive feelings die away rapidly. This is why many writers have described Scorpio as a sign that seeks revenge, one that will harbor long-term grudges. But Scorpio is also slow to anger. If others do not repeat hurts or add insult upon insult, Scorpio is no more vengeful or grudging than any other sign.

The Relationship of Scorpio to Pluto and Mars   Scorpio and Pluto fit each other well. Both are symbols of death and resurrection, and of major transformation in general. And both have to do with the kinds of transformation that come about because of processes inherent in whatever is transformed. Both are introverted symbols, being found in persons who are concerned with their inward state and who feel internal experiences intensely.

The main difference between the two symbols is one of degree. Pluto, a planetary symbol, is much more intense, and from its intensity it gains a greater connection with power. The Plutonian is much more likely to desire power than is the Scorpio. But in both cases, whatever power one may gain endangers one unless one only uses it for the benefit of something larger than the self.

Mars was the traditional ruler of Scorpio before the discovery of Pluto, but this seems to be one of the worst sign-ruler affinities. Mars is fiery, outgoing, and overt; Scorpio is reserved and subtle. Both symbols can indicate aggression, but Mars is direct and confronting, whereas Scorpio is likely to be devious. Mars releases its energy quickly, Scorpio slowly.

But then there seems to have been some change in the meaning of Scorpio since ancient times. In ancient texts, particularly Manilius's *Astronomicon*, Scorpio is described as more Martian than it is now. One does not have to accept the sidereal zodiac to realize that the tropical signs may change meanings slowly over the ages. One need only recognize that different cultures see symbols differently. Scorpio is now much more Plutonian than Martian.

The Effect of Scorpio on Planets   Any planet in Scorpio is likely to become an agent for the individual's transformation. Planets in Scorpio operate with intensity, usually emotional intensity. Airy planets like Mercury do not operate well in Scorpio because the emotionalism of the sign interferes with the detachment necessary for their functioning. Also, Scorpio's tendency to personalize everything it experiences works badly with social planets. Thus Venus in Scorpio, while not a severe problem, is less able to maintain detachment or objectivity about relationships in which it may become involved.

The Moon is often said to be severely debilitated in Scorpio, but I am not inclined to agree. A Scorpio Moon may be difficult for others to understand, but it is at least in touch with its own feelings. It is certainly not a Moon inclined to repress emotion.

A large number of planets in Scorpio will increase both the emotionalism and the stubborness of the chart. Issues associated with these planets may not be communicated as clearly as others might wish, but they are not usually misunderstood by those who experience them.

Sagittarius

Element: Fire
Quadruplicity: Mutable
Polarity: Positive
Ruler: Jupiter

With Sagittarius we enter a stage of development symbolized in the final four signs. As you will recall, Aries through Cancer related to the development of the individual as an individual, and Leo through Scorpio related to the development of the individual vis-a-vis other people, where these others were personally related to the individual in question.

The last four signs describe the individual's integration into society as a whole. Society is understood on a much more abstract level than with the second group of four signs. The individual relates not only to those who are known, but also to the fabric of the social order itself, which cannot always be experienced personally.

The key idea of Sagittarius is the individual encountering a social context and learning to understand it and to express his or her will in it. Sagittarius is the most advanced of the fire signs, in that the expression of will must now transcend purely personal self-expression. Yet being the first of the four social signs, Sagittarius is the most ambivalent in its relationship to the social order. It values personal freedom and self-expression as highly as any other fire sign, and therefore it may have trouble adjusting to the restrictions of the larger social order. Yet the sign is unable to escape the knowledge of its relationship to society, and so it seeks a social role that allows it maximum self-expression while it is doing something socially useful. This sign is associated with idealism, with those who cannot accept the status quo and who would thus reform society. Yet, ambivalent as this sign is, it also symbolizes those who act as spokesmen for the social order and keep it whole.

In either case, the relationship of the individual to society is rather abstract. This sign is more concerned about principles and general patterns than it is about the details of implementation. Recall the relationship of Aries to Taurus, in which Aries operates as the abstract, unembodied will which receives its physical body in Taurus, the earth sign. Only by encountering the principle of earth can the will of Aries be made manifest. Similarly, Sagittarius states the principles of social cohesion even while being ambivalent about its relationship to society, and then Capricorn looks for ways to implement those principles.

Like two other mutable signs, Sagittarius was often called a dual sign in the older literature. Whereas duality is not an especially fruitful notion for explaining Gemini or Pisces, it is more so with Sagittarius. Sagittarius feels ambivalent about its placement in the zodiacal scheme, and thus there are two distinct types of Sagittarian. (Old books associated these types with the first and second halves of the sign, but I have not found this to be reliable.)

The first type is a classic freedom-loving fire-sign personality. It craves room in which to move and freedom with which to express itself. It is usually exuberant and likable but is not entirely reliable in keeping agreements. Nor is it especially consistent: it is extremely mutable. Even though this sign is well beyond Libra, it is reluctant to tie itself down in relationships, not because it prefers being alone, but because it wishes to be free to relate to whomever, wherever, without limits being imposed by social convention. This type is happy to encounter new experiences and is not especially tradition-bound.

The second type of Sagittarian has achieved a successful integration into the social order and is concerned with the fabric of that order. This type has a need to study everything about the world in order to relate each part to every other part. Thus it is likely to be attracted to the sciences, philosophy, religion, or any other discipline that reveals the interconnectedness of all things. This type is concerned about wisdom, which it prefers to mere knowledge: an idea is good only insofar as it aids in understanding the world so that one can live in it more effectively. But (and this is true of both kinds of Sagittarian) such ideas may still be abstract. Neither type enjoys grappling with the details of implementing what it understands, but the latter type is more willing to do so. Although this type is also very mutable in that it will adapt to adversity or challenge rather than fight it, it is much more consistent than the other.

Both types enjoy travel, which they see as both consciousness-enlarging and liberating from the constraints of everyday life. Both types are also idealists, but the second is more easily able to separate the real from the ideal.

There is no way of telling from the horoscope which type one is dealing with, because the two types are actually phases in the development of a single type. The first kind of Sagittarian is likely to evolve into the second if environmental influences permit. A strong Saturn may cause the first type to change into the second earlier in life.

The Relationship of Sagittarius to Jupiter   What is true of Jupiter is often true of Sagittarius. Both are concerned with social integration, with the holistic viewpoint, with law, philosophy, and religion. Both symbolize the reaching-out of the individual to encounter the larger world.

But there are differences: Sagittarius is much more changeable than Jupiter, more freedom-loving and irresponsible. Sagittarius is less likely to symbolize the acquisition of material goods. Also, being a sign and therefore a less powerful symbol than a planet, it is less likely than Jupiter to operate at an excessive level. Sagittarius is less likely to signify waste, excess, or arrogance.

One other important difference is that Jupiter has a much stronger nurturing and protecting aspect than Sagittarius. Sagittarius, a fire sign, is too concerned with individual freedom and self-expression to be really happy taking on the responsibility of caring for and protecting another individual.

The Effect of Sagittarius on Planets   Planets in Sagittarius increase the general quantity of mutability and fire in a chart, and indicate a desire for freedom. Sagittarius gets along best with planets like Mars, Uranus, and the Sun, which are fast-moving, energetic, and not resistant to change. Mercury, which is traditionally in detriment in Sagittarius, does not seem to be all that bad there, its main difficulty being that it loses the ability to operate with precision and to deal with detail.

Obviously Sagittarius is somewhat incompatible with Saturn. The effect is to make Saturn try to concern itself with broad, sweeping ideas while still coming from Saturn's extremely detailed approach. But this is not a serious problem unless Saturn is very prominent in the chart.

Planets that have a strong emotional component may not be difficult in Sagittarius, but they do not operate entirely true to their nature. Venus, for example, is reluctant to form binding relationships. It is not uninterested in sex, but it tends to prefer friendship to a more conventional sexual tie. The Moon operates well enough, but not much like a Moon: for example, there is not as much liking for tradition and being in touch with one's roots.

Neptune, which is in Sagittarius as of this writing (1980), has stimulated the idealistic side of the sign beyond all bounds. Almost exactly coincident with its arrival in Sagittarius in 1970 there began the flowering of gurus and cults that has characterized the decade.

Capricorn

Element: Earth
Quadruplicity: Cardinal
Polarity: Negative
Ruler: Saturn

Capricorn has little of Sagittarius's ambivalence. It is very socially oriented, feeling completely at home in a context defined by its social milieu. Though negative in polarity, Capricorn is far from passive. Capricorn may allow the external world to define its criteria about what is and is not real, important, and acceptable, but having once accepted these definitions and even gloried in accepting them, it turns with gusto to play the game according to these rules.

To truly understand Capricorn, it is necessary to understand the horoscope's symbolism of the father-complex, of which Capricorn is a manifestation on the sign level. Capricorn is unusually subject to the influence of authority figures and of those who claim knowledge that is universally applicable (that is, objectively real). It tends to place relatively little emphasis on its own subjective viewpoint. Yet, and here is an apparent contradiction of the type, Capricorn eschews abstractions that cannot be reduced to experience. Capricorn is concerned with an objective idea of truth that is at the same time experienceable. Thus Capricorn arrives at an idea of truth that it grants absolute reality.

And the truth must work for oneself. This means not only that Capricorn accepts what society considers real, but also that Capricorn sets out to be effective in practical terms. Efficacy is something Capricorns desire above all else. The idea of being dependent on others and not in control of oneself terrifies a Capricorn. The sign would rather control others, although it usually has too much of a sense of responsibility to be power-mad.

Capricorn desires to take the rules it has been taught about the external world and use them as well as possible to build a monument to its own existence. It wants to be able to say to the world, "I did it, I built that." Whatever it builds must be important not only to the Capricorn but also to the world whose rules the Capricorn has tried to master.

Not only is Capricorn in early life particularly subject to authority in determining its views of reality; later on, it itself becomes the embodiment of that authority. Again we have the association between Capricorn and the father archetype: the energy that tells the child that it must not only be wrapped up in its own life, it must also come to terms with what exists outside the self. As Cancer is the sign manifestation of the infant's support system, so Capricorn is the sign manifestation of the energy that thrusts the child out of the home into the world.

Both Sagittarius and Capricorn may pose as representatives of the social order, but they differ in how they do it. Sagittarius is concerned with the principles that unify society, and with theories of social integration. Often it desires understanding purely for the sake of its own consciousness expansion (even though it is not, like Gemini, entranced by ideas purely as ideas).

Capricorn, on the other hand, is not concerned about principles so much as their practical implementation. It wants to know what is "really real," not what is theoretically true. Capricorn is more concerned with the social order's details than its generality.

We might consider Sagittarius the academic philosopher of the social order and Capricorn the businessman. Again the principles of the fire sign are enabled to manifest on the physical plane by the earth sign that follows it.

Clearly, Sagittarius and Capricorn should be a team. Yet their psychology is so different that it is hard for them to get along. Sagittarius is unhappy about what it conceives as Capricorn's grubby materialism and inordinate social ambition, and Capricorn is unhappy about Sagittarius's tendency to take flight into airy abstractions and avoid the responsiblity of handling the "real" world. Yet when the two do get together, the understanding of Sagittarius is truly impressive when combined with the practical effectiveness of Capricorn.

Capricorn's only serious problem is that it is so bound up in being effective in the "real" world it does not play easily. An activity is only justifiable to a Capricorn if it is significant. This causes Capricorns both to be overly serious and to rationalize. There may be something a Capricorn really enjoys doing, but to be enjoyable is not enough. Capricorn must convince itself that what it enjoys is also socially important. Therefore, Capricorn reasons, it has more of a right to what it enjoys than do others to their less "important" amusements. Capricorn likes to pat itself on the back for "doing its duty" when it is in fact only doing something it enjoys. The Capricorn often identifies play with work.

Despite the serious nature of the sign, Capricorn has produced more than its share of humorists. The humor is usually of the wry, self-deprecating, rather than playful kind, and is probably Capricorn's way of maintaining a sane balance in the face of its tendency toward seeking importance.

The Relationship of Capricorn to Saturn   Capricorn and Saturn are very similar. Both strive for material achievement, and both are strongly concerned with social recognition. Both are symbols of self-denial and the deferral of immediate gratification in favor of long-range necessity. Both are strongly connected to the father and to all symbols of authority and guidance, and in both discipline is strong. But Capricorn is usually more like a positive Saturn: it is not quite as strongly repressive as the planet.

Indeed, the main differences between Capricorn and Saturn are ones of strength and degree. That is, Saturn aspecting a planet has a much more powerful effect than that planet's simply being in Capricorn. Being in Capricorn almost never signifies a serious denial of a planet's energy in the way that being aspected by Saturn may. Only in a heavily earthy and watery chart with inactive fire signs and planets can Capricorn become as difficult an influence as Saturn.

The Effect of Capricorn on Planets   Planets in Capricorn tend to increase one's reality orientation and may limit one's ability to get outside the social viewpoint in which one was reared. For this reason, the sign is best with those planets that are not especially concerned with freedom and innovation. Uranus is probably not at its best in Capricorn. Neither is Jupiter, though I have observed that Jupiter in Capricorn is not as tense a combination as Saturn in Sagittarius. Jupiter is often quite happy to turn its attention to the achievement of social status and importance.

Some authorities feel that Jupiter in Capricorn may signify problems with the father. But Jupiter, which remains in a sign for one year, cannot, I think, simply by being in Capricorn foul up an entire year's worth of children's relationships with their fathers. Of course, the father-child relationship may be strained if the Jupiter in Capricorn is otherwise prominent. My own feeling is that this is one of those debates that is too subtle to be settled.

Mars is said to be exalted in Capricorn. This does not entirely make sense, since one would not expect the combination of Mars energies and Saturn-like Capricorn energies to be easy. Yet it does seem that Mars energy in Capricorn is disciplined rather than blocked. In Capricorn, Mars energy is turned away from its narrow ego-orientation and given a larger social basis so that others are more likely to respect one's intentions.

Strongly emotional planets do not do well in Capricorn because the sign tends to repress emotion in favor of discipline. The Moon is particularly difficult here, because Capricorn will not allow the Moon to enjoy being dependent on others, a mode of relationship that is absolutely essential to the Moon's functioning at some point in life.

Venus is also not at its best, because its emotional criteria for choice are likely to be subordinated to practical criteria. Venus in Capricorn can also indicate an attraction to older persons who can serve as authority figures as well as lovers.

Whatever a planet's normal inclinations may be, in Capricorn they are subjected to practical considerations and must be made to serve the sign's need for effectiveness. If this is not done they operate ambiguously and therefore tensely. One wonders what Neptune in Capricorn will be like.

Aquarius

Element: Air
Quadruplicity: Fixed
Polarity: Positive
Ruler: Uranus (traditionally, Saturn)

With Aquarius we enter the last pair of signs, which completes the evolution of the archetypal individual. In Aries we started with the most purely individualistic assertion of the self. After building up the various aspects of the self and then socializing those aspects, we arrive at Aquarius, where socialization is completed.

Aquarius is the sign of the individual as a cooperative unit of the group. It is a sign in which, theoretically at least, the individual ego and its needs are subordinated to those of the larger social unit of which the individual is a part. I say theoretically, because what actually happens is often quite different.

It is true that Aquarius is at its best as part of some kind of social grouping, just as Libra is at its best as part of a couple. Aquarians are gregarious and enjoy social interactions. They value friendships, and respect what group effort can do. It is as if no activity has meaning to an Aquarian unless it has a social dimension. But just as the Libran tends to be the dominant person in a relationship, the Aquarian tends to be the dominant member of a group. Like Librans, Aquarians need social interaction in order to define themselves, but having done so they are strong individuals who tend to dominate.

In order to understand Aquarius, one has to recall that it is opposite Leo. Leo is the sign of the completed individual, strong and self-confident on her or his own. The ego is fully or even overly developed. Aquarius is the sign of the completely socialized ego. Its ego is just as strong as Leo's, but whereas Leo takes its sense of self from awareness of self alone, Aquarius takes its awareness of self from the group and identifies the interests of the group as its own. If Leo says, "I am grand and magnificent in myself," Aquarius says, "I am nothing except that I am the embodiment of what society wants." Putting it another way, Leo when egotistical is overtly so; Aquarius is more likely to be covertly egotistical. This does not mean that all Aquarians are covert egotists, it means simply that Aquarians derive their sense of ego from an identification with something external to themselves.

Paradoxically, this socially oriented sign can produce radical or innovative thinkers who seem highly individualistic and self-sufficient and do not seem to need the approval of society at all. But actually, even if the Aquarian radical or reformer does not need to be tied to society as a whole, he or she always needs some kind of group with which to identify. Usually that group thinks it is a truer embodiment of society than is the prevailing social order. Also, most of the radical ideals that an Aquarian might hold have social consequences. Aquarius is not content merely to perfect itself; it desires to perfect all of society. Though it is an intensely freedom-loving sign, the freedom it loves is the freedom to change all of society to what it thinks society should be. It is not happy letting others have their freedom if their view of freedom differs from its own. It is, after all, a fixed sign, and no matter how radical (or conventional, for that matter) its ideas are, once they are arrived at, they do not change easily.

A real problem for Aquarius comes from both its social orientation and its being an air sign. Aquarians tend to have strong social ideals about how people ought to be, but they do not relate easily to individual people except perhaps insofar as they embody social issues. Aquarius is the sign of the humanitarian who loves all mankind but no individual human being. Being an air sign, it is not especially at home in the emotional give-and-take of a close personal relationship: Aquarians are more at home with friendship than with love.

I have dwelt on the problematical aspects of Aquarius to counteract the propaganda in recent literature about the coming (or already-here, depending on whom one reads) Aquarian age, in which all the social ills of the Piscean Age are to be miraculously redressed. If the coming age is really Aquarian, it may be an era in which individual considerations, emotional ties of love, and bonds of tradition are ruthlessly rooted out in favor of various utopian orders that are conceived entirely in the head and not at all in the heart.

Nevertheless, Aquarius does have many strengths. Being an air sign, it has a detached and fair-minded view of things. It genuinely concerns itself with the good of all, not merely its own good. It is an idealistic sign, with a strong commitment to what it believes. It is also unusually free of restraints imposed by the past and tradition (an attribute that has both good and bad sides).

Aquarius's main flaw is that it commits itself to society, something that is actually no more real than the individual. In fact, it is less real: society is nothing more than an organized collection of individuals. And the level of organization that exists in society is not yet complex enough for any society to have an organic existence of its own. That is, a society is not a living entity in the same way that an individual is. Insofar as society is a valid entity necessary for the maintenance of human life, the identification of the Aquarian with some form of social order is valid. But insofar as society is an abstract entity with no real organic existence, this identification is damaging. It remains for Pisces to make the real and universally valid identification with something beyond the self.

The Relationship of Aquarius to Uranus and Saturn   In my opinion, Aquarius and Uranus make one of the worst sign-ruler parallels. Uranus is trans-social and trans-egoic. Highly individualistic, it is even anti-social much of the time. More truly freedom-loving than Aquarius, Uranus is more willing than Aquarius to grant freedom to others' different ideas. And whereas Aquarius is fixed, Uranus is unstable and mutable, needing constant change.

There are some similarities, however. Both Aquarius and Uranus are airy, though I believe Uranus has some fire in it as well. Both are inclined to radical, innovative ideas. Both tend to be ruthless and unfeeling in their pursuit of right. Neither is an especially warm or emotional symbol.

There is also a Saturnine side to Aquarius. Saturn, the traditional ruler of Aquarius, is much more fixed than Uranus. In a way that Uranus is not, Saturn is oriented to society as opposed to the individual. Like both Aquarius and Uranus, Saturn does not handle emotion well. But Saturn is otherwise very earthy and is not fond of abstractions to the extent that Aquarius and Uranus are. Aquarius's symbolism seems to reflect a mix of Saturn and Uranus, rather than one or the other.

The Effect of Aquarius on Planets   Aquarius is most beneficial to planetary energies that are airy and/or socially oriented. Airy Mercury and socially oriented Jupiter are well placed in Aquarius. So is Saturn, for the reasons discussed above.

Although the Sun is traditionally in its detriment in Aquarius, there does not seem to be any serious problem for the Sun here, though of course its expression is not allowed to be so self-centered. The same is true of Mars, which, while not especially badly placed in Aquarius, does have a more social expression here than it does elsewhere.

Emotional planets such as Venus and the Moon have more difficulty in Aquarius. Venus here tends toward pal-ship rather than love, and the Moon is caught in a struggle between its natural emotionalism, its attachment to the past and what is familiar, and the emotional dryness of the sign. A Moon in Aquarius may or may not be troubled, but it is almost never a typical Moon.

Pisces

Element: Water
Quadruplicity: Mutable
Polarity: Negative
Ruler: Neptune (traditionally, Jupiter)

With Pisces the cycle is complete: the archetypal individual has reached the final stage of evolution. This, however, is not at all clear from traditional descriptions of the sign. Just as we stressed some of the more negative aspects of Aquarius to balance the excessively uncritical material that has been written about it, with Pisces we must do the opposite. It is my observation that of all the types in the zodiac except possibly Virgo, Pisceans have the worst image of their sign. This is due to astrological writings, not to the intrinsic flaws of Pisces.

The problem with Pisces is not that it is weak or colorless or without energy. The problem is that the sign symbolizes the most difficult stage in human evolution, the transcendence of the self. In this, Pisces continues the process begun in Aquarius, but with a difference.

In Aquarius the self is submerged in or, more precisely, identified with the social group, often resulting in an inflated ego in a humble disguise. And as we pointed out in the discussion of Aquarius, it is questionable whether the social group to which one belongs is an entity superior to oneself.

In Pisces the subordination is not to a social group, but to the universe itself, and that which propels it. Whatever one may feel about a God, there is something that makes the universe (the "one-turning" in Latin) One. The ego—born, developed, completed, and socialized through the other signs—is now surrendered in Pisces to something higher. Personal systems of reality, personal ideas of right and wrong, are now to be subordinated to What Is. In the language of mysticism, Pisces symbolizes the surrender of the soul to God. Yet few individuals ever do this. It is something difficult to do half-way, and incomplete self-surrender can bring disaster.

Another aspect of Pisces must be understood: it is both an end and a beginning. The zodiac is not a circle, but a helix, so that each time one goes around one has also moved up. Pisces is the last phase of each turn of the helix, but it is also the phase just prior to Aries. As such, it stands for the stage just prior to the birth of a new self. Indeed, Pisces at the end of a cycle indicating surrender of the mature self is a prelude to rebirth at a higher level in the next encounter with Aries. Thus Pisces can be looked at as either the pre-egoic or the post-egoic state of consciousness.

The structure of one's ego gives rise to the nature of one's reality system. Thus we can see that Pisces is a sign that has either not yet developed a reality system or has just transcended one (it is this that leads to Pisces' highly imaginative quality).

The Pisces symbol is two fishes swimming in opposite directions, and like Sagittarius and Gemini, Pisces is traditionally referred to as a dual sign. There are two types of Piscean: the advanced (Pisces as the last stage in the evolution of the archetypal ego or self) and the primitive (Pisces as the stage just prior to a new beginning in Aries).

In both types the ego is less strongly defined than in other signs.

Consequently the desire to assert oneself, to be something in particular, is less. Both Piscean types are extremely receptive. In the primitive type this leads to passivity and inaction and to being a victim because one is unwilling to take responsibility. In the advanced type it leads to a desire to know the truth at a deep spiritual level, and even to sacrifice oneself for the truth. This is a manifestation of the martyr, in the true sense of the word, as opposed to the victim.

As we have said, the reality system is either not strongly developed in the primitive type, or one is detached from it in the advanced type. This gives the advanced type the ability to deal with alternate realities, to see aspects of being that others would consider impossible. The primitive type may merely be confused.

Both types may glimpse things that are invisible to most people. Pisces is connected to psychic ability (though much more than a strong Pisces indication is necessary for one to be psychic, and one need not be strongly Piscean if other indications are strong). In most Pisceans the psychic tendency comes over as sensitivity to people around them such that energies and impressions are easily picked up. Because Pisces tends to experience these energies as its own, when the energies are sufficiently negative, both types can become weakened.

To both types things are not as clearly distinct from one another as they might be to another sign. Categories are weakened. The advanced type sees much more unity in the universe than is immediately apparent to others, while the primitive type is again merely confused.

Caught in a world it is not yet quite ready to enter, the primitive type is likely to take refuge in fantasy. Even the advanced type often takes refuge in a private world to which few others are admitted. The remote quality of many Pisceans is actually the consequence of their hypersensitivity.

Because of its lack of ego emphasis, the Pisces type is often attracted to social service: taking care of the physically or mentally ill or of others who need to be looked after. This may seem similar to Aquarius's social idealism, but Pisces is without the identification of self with the group that can result in covert ego-inflation. In Pisces the self is more truly subordinated.

But there is one danger in the Piscean kind of service. Primitive Pisceans may try to shore up their shaky egos by taking care of those they deem less fortunate. The problem is that in order to maintain their one-up position, these Pisceans must make sure that those they are "helping" never get better. This pernicious type of covert egotism is also a danger with Neptune.

Most Pisceans are neither primitive nor advanced types, but mixtures in varying degrees. An individual may be sensitive and compassionate yet at the same time the victim of surrounding negative energies, or be aware of the infinite possibilities in the universe yet at the same time be confused by them. Whether Pisces is viewed as coming into or going out of the world, in neither case is it completely here. Coming to grips with conventional reality systems when it may in fact have something superior—this is the central dilemma of the sign.

The Relationship of Pisces to Neptune and Jupiter The connection between Pisces and Neptune is strong. Both are symbols of ego-transcendence and union with the infinite. Both also confer a great deal of sensitivity and imagination. And in both, imagination may go to excess and become illusion and deception. Even the conflicts associated with Neptune are found with Pisces. Both are connected to sacrifice and victimhood; both often signify a lack of strong ego; both are very watery with all that that implies.

Jupiter as the traditional ruler of Pisces is not as easy to see. Where both Neptune and Pisces place strong emphasis on faith, Jupiter wants knowledge. Where Neptune and Pisces tend to be retiring and passive, Jupiter can be arrogant and assertive. Perhaps the main connection is that Jupiter, like both Pisces and Neptune, has a religious dimension. This arises directly out of Jupiter's association with integration, the relationship between parts and wholes. But Jupiter is much more associated with theology than with direct mystical experience: it is the priest rather than the mystic. Therefore, although Jupiter is rather well-placed in Pisces, we have to give Pisces to Neptune.

The Effect of Pisces on Planets A large number of planets in Pisces tends to reduce the forcefulness of the personality while increasing its level of empathy and its receptivity to others. Planets that are strongly yin tend in Pisces to take on a dreamy, fantasy-prone quality. This can be very creative and imaginative, but may also weaken the individual's hold on reality. The Moon is especially vulnerable to this. Venus may become excessively romantic under Pisces's influence, but it is also capable of the most selfless kind of loving.

It is planets associated with the will and with energy that suffer most in Pisces. Mars in Pisces lacks energy, and Pisces does not give it much scope for its willfulness. People with either the Sun or Mars in Pisces can successfully dedicate themselves to a purpose that transcends their own narrow individuality. This will release the energy that might otherwise be caught up in Piscean conflicts such as those described above.

Saturn, because of its strong and rather narrow reality orientation, is also not at its best in Pisces. Jupiter, on the other hand, whether or not it rules Pisces, is at its best in this sign, which gives infinite scope to the Jupiterian need for consciousness expansion.

MUNDANE POSITION

12

The Horoscope Angles

We have seen how aspects and midpoints indicate the interaction of planetary energies, and how zodiacal position indicates whether the cosmic environment of the planetary energies is favorable or not to their easy functioning. In this final section of the book, I will explore how the mundane position of planetary energies symbolizes their orientation within the life and psychological structure of the individual.

The horoscope's most fundamental indicators of mundane position are the so-called "'angles"—the Ascendant, Midheaven, Descendant, and I.C. As you will remember, Chapter 5 discussed the horoscope angles as sensitive points along the ecliptic. As such, they can form aspects and planetary pictures with planets and in this way combine their symbolism with planetary symbolism.

In the present chapter I will treat the horoscope angles in a slightly different light: as ecliptic-based indicators of the most important stages in the day cycle. First I will take a closer look at how being near the angles makes planetary energies strong. Then I will show how the four angles form a basic symbolic framework for understanding how the planetary energies are structured in a person's life. This will lead into a discussion of the houses, further subdivisions of the day cycle, in the remaining chapters of this book. As the essential technical details about the horoscope angles have been covered in Chapters 2 and 5, I will concentrate on the symbolism here.

The Importance of Angularity

Astrologers have long noted that a planet near one of the horoscope angles manifests with great strength, but only recently has this observation been supported by systematic research.

The French statistician Michel Gauquelin set out to disprove astrology. After many tests with negative results, he encountered the report of a test performed many years earlier that seemed to show that the planets nearest the angles have a strong determining effect on profession. Especially as there were procedural errors in the earlier test, Gauquelin expected the same negative results he had found in his other experiments with astrology. Therefore he was surprised when, even with the procedural errors removed, the correlation held. Using large samples of people prominent in various professions, he found that, indeed, Mars did tend to be near an angle significantly above chance for sports champions, Jupiter near an angle for actors, Saturn for scientists, etc.—much as astrologers would expect.

Later tests indicated it was not profession that the angular planets seemed to be determining, but dominant psychological traits, which would in turn predispose people to success in certain professions. Thus famous people with an angular Mars had biographies containing a high frequency of words like "active," "eager," "reckless," "courageous," etc.; those with an angular Jupiter were characterized as "good-humored," "likable," etc.; those with an angular Saturn were "reserved," "conscientious," "organized," etc. These correlations, which have held up under much retesting, are among the strongest confirmations of astrology.

One detail of the Gauquelin results ran counter to astrological tradition, however. In traditional astrology, the so-called angular houses—houses one, four, seven, and ten, which come just after each angle going counterclockwise—have been considered the strongest placements for any planet. Very often when an astrology text refers to an "angular planet," it means a planet in one of these houses whether or not it is very near the angle. But Gauquelin's work showed the points of greatest strength to be a few degrees to the *other* side of the angles, in houses twelve, three, six, and nine, the so-called cadent houses, which come just before the angles. Partly this could be explained by assuming a systematic bias in reporting the time of birth late, which is indeed plausible in view of the experience of those connected with hospitals. But even if the births tended to take place a few minutes earlier than reported, so that the peaks would be closer to the "angular" houses, the cadent houses would still be quite strong, not weak as they were traditionally thought to be.

Gauquelin's work plus the work of John Addey and others indicates that a planet becomes particularly strong four times a day, when or just after it rises, culminates, sets, and anticulminates. The peaks at rising and culmination, or near the Ascendant and Midheaven, seem stronger than those at setting and anticulmination. And just as there are four peaks of planetary strength, there appear to be four weak areas, each about halfway between the horoscope angles in the four quadrants. I will mention this again when discussing house quadruplicities in the next chapter. Then, in the second half of Chapter 15, I will discuss how these findings fit in with the symbolism of the houses. For the present, however, I will just indicate what these findings mean for planetary intensity at the horoscope angles.

For most purposes, at least until further research demonstrates otherwise, I think you can assume a planet to be angular, and hence particularly strong, if it is within about 7.5° to either side of a horoscope angle. Of course, as mentioned in Chapter 2, if a planet has considerable celestial latitude (that is, if it is not close to the ecliptic), it may not be as near the horizon or meridian as its degree on the ecliptic might lead you to believe. But usually for all planets except Pluto and the asteroid Pallas, the horoscope angles will give an adequate approximation of whether or not a planet is crossing the horizon or meridian, which is what seems to give it strength.

Thus, planets within 7.5° of a horoscope angle should usually be considered the most important planets in the chart, and the closer they are, the more important. Though lack of such planets does not seem to indicate the lack of anything in the chart, when they are present they color people's entire personality and may be found in just about every form of behavior or activity that is important to them. Often these planets will indicate the choice of profession, but only insofar as people are adjusted to their world and are able to be themselves. Maladjusted people and those who feel compelled by early childhood training or experience to hide much of their true personalities from the world usually will not follow a profession appropriate to an angular planet but will instead try to manifest its function in other ways. Often the results are less than satisfactory.

The Angles as a Symbolic Framework

The circle has been from the beginning of human symbolism the symbol for a perfect whole. It has always meant completion, fullness, and totality. In ancient times the circle was used to symbolize the universe when all of being lay in a state of potentiality and nothing was as yet manifest. The circle is also a symbol of the complete self.

Now existence as we know it must consist of the interplay between action and experience. There must be something for one to perceive and to act upon, even if it is only an arbitrary division within the self. Therefore at the very base of existence there must be a duality between subject and object, an actor and an acted upon, an experience and an experiencer. No consciousness as we know it is capable of operating without this distinction. Even when we think about ourselves, *we* think about *ourselves*. That is, we divide ourselves into an imaginary subject and object for the purpose of self-reflection: I and myself, or we and ourselves. But somewhere in our consciousness we know that I and myself are in fact one, and that our division is nothing more than a convenience for the purpose of conceptualizing. I think this is also true of the universe as a whole, that the division of the universe into subject and object is nothing more than an illusion created for the purpose of dealing with the universe consciously.

This is the basis of my belief stated in Chapter 1 that we are one with what we experience. For the moment, however, all we have to do is agree that this division of the world into subject and object is a fundamental aspect of our experience of life. Every sentence has a subject and an object or predicate. Most of our language is aimed at defining our relation to something outside of ourselves. "I am here." "I did this." "I saw that." These are all statements normal to human consciousness.

In astrology, the subject-object split is symbolized in a number of ways. In Chapters 3 and 4, I mentioned the Moon-Sun, yin-yang dichotomy. This split is echoed in the basic divisions of the celestial sphere.

To get a feeling for what I am talking about, imagine you are lying in a field, face-up with your feet pointed to where the Sun would be at noon. In the Northern Hemisphere, this would be toward the south. Planets will rise to the left of you in the east, and set to the right of you in the west. When the Sun is exactly due south of you, it will be exactly half-way between its rising and setting, and therefore on the upper part of the meridian circle. At midnight, if you could see through the Earth, you would realize that the Sun is behind you, below the horizon exactly due north, halfway between its setting and rising, and therefore on the lower part of the meridian circle. The horoscope is a schematic diagram of this view of the celestial sphere.*

The horizon divides the celestial sphere into an upper and a lower hemisphere. This boundary is represented in the horoscope by a horizontal line, the Ascendant-Descendant axis, which cuts the circle of the ecliptic into two equal parts. In terms of mundane position, this is the fundamental division between subject and object. But there is also a secondary subject-object division: the meridian divides the celestial sphere into an eastern and a western hemisphere. This boundary is represented in the horoscope by the Midheaven-I.C. axis.

The Division at the Horizon

The horizon is an interface between two realms. Above it, the planets are visible; below it, they are blocked from view by the mass of the Earth. This symbolizes the split we feel between inner and outer, subjective and objective. If you will again visualize yourself lying in the field, the horizon represents your eyes or your skin. Everything above the horizon is in front of your eyes or outside your skin. You can see what is "out there"

---

*In the Southern Hemisphere the situation would be reversed. The Sun would be to the north of an observer. If you were facing north, the Sun would still rise in the east, but this would be to your right. It would appear to move counterclockwise to culimination, and would set in the west to your left. The horoscope as usually drawn for the Southern Hemisphere is a mirror image of the correct representation. This is so that astrologers, educated in the Northern Hemispheric viewpoint, do not have to think in terms of planets rising and setting counterclockwise and transiting the zodiac clockwise.

objectively; you perceive it as other than yourself. But what is below the horizon is behind your eyes or inside your skin. You cannot see it; you can only deduce its presence. Except when you make an effort, you are unaware of it, because it is so much a part of you.

The horizon can be the boundary between what we perceive as inner and outer, but, as I will show with the houses at the end of the next chapter, the horizon can also be interpreted as the boundary between many other sorts of realm. It depends on what level of reality you are talking about. The horizon can act as a boundary between I and thou, we and they, mine and yours, or even personal and nonpersonal aspects of the world. Or, entirely within one's psyche, the horizon can be the boundary between the conscious and the unconscious mind.

The Upper Hemisphere   In general, the part of the horoscope that is above the horizon is associated with those aspects of life that are less personal and more social. It represents the not-self, the outer self, other people, the social world, the more conscious mind, one's role in the social world, thou, they, and the future.

The Lower Hemisphere   The part below the horizon is more personal and less social. It symbolizes the self, the inner self, one's closest family and associates, the less conscious mind, the basis of one's conception of self, I, we, and the past. I use comparative rather than absolute adjectives to make it clear that the upper-lower split is relative rather than fixed.

The Ascendant   When planets rise or cross the horizon in the east, they are passing from the inner realm to the outer. This is the point where energies from the self are made manifest to the not-self. In other words, this is a point of self-manifestation. One would expect this point to govern the effect or impression one has on the outer world, or the kind of action one takes upon the world. Here energies emerge from the individual (lower hemisphere) and begin to affect others (upper hemisphere). This is why the Ascendant is often related to the personality, personality being defined as the outermost aspect of one's inner being. It has also been related along with the whole first house to the form, health, and general state of the physical body.

The Descendant   The Descendant is where planets set, or cross the horizon in the west, passing from the outer realm to the inner. The logical as well as the spatial opposite of the Ascendant, it relates to the kind of impression the not-self makes upon the self, the effect of the immediate environment upon one, or the kind of action the world makes upon the self. To put it more precisely, since we have seen that the horoscope indicates one's experience of things, not their objective reality, the Descendant relates to one's experience of energies from others and the outside world. Even more precisely, the Descendant describes those aspects of oneself that one experiences through relationships with others. Therefore, it also describes what one looks for in others, whether consciously or not. In this respect the Descendant is much like the seventh house.

The Horizon Axis   From the above meanings, you can see why in Chapter 5 the horizon axis, consisting of the Ascendant on one end and the Descendant on the other, was said to relate to self-other interactions. The general situation of this axis by aspects, midpoints, and sign placement is important in determining how well an individual will get along with others at close range. The relationships signified are of an intimate kind; I do not find this axis a good index of how well one gets along with groups, where both one's own individuality and that of others is less clearly defined than in a one-to-one situation.

The Division at the Meridian

With the division of the horoscope into an eastern and a western half by the meridian, our original circle now has a cross inside it. The horoscope thus becomes a mandala, an ancient symbol for wholeness that yet is able to deal with the illusion of division.

The Eastern Hemisphere   On the eastern side, planets are rising. This means that the planetary energies are moving away from the lower, more personal pole of the chart toward the upper, more social pole. This half thus symbolizes that which is acted on by the inner self (though not always successfully, as we shall see with the twelfth house). Energies situated in this half have to do with the world's perception of the self, and they are considered to be more active and under personal control.

According to many authors, the chart's eastern hemisphere is associated with being self-determining, that is, with being the source of most of the initiatives in one's life. Someone who has many planets in this half would be one who takes action, and therefore I call such a person an actor as opposed to an experiencer.

Actors are often said to be in control of their destinies, people who are seldom afflicted with self-doubt. They are supposed to take the initiative and never wait for others, always to act and never to react. But I find that the only thing that can be said about actor types is that they tend to act first and observe later. This does not necessarily make them more effective or more in control of their lives, as is often alleged. In order to be effective, one must not only take action; one must also act consciously, with a clear idea of the consequences and of how others might react. In other words, to be in control one must not only take action but also observe others. Actors who do not do this are as out of control of their destinies as anyone else.

Though a large gathering of planets in this hemisphere, especially in the first house, seems to denote this type of personality, some caution is needed in identifying an actor. The planets in the east should not be ones that, like Saturn, tend to frustrate action, or, like Neptune, weaken the basis on which one would act. Saturn tends to make one very cautious and too concerned with the feelings, needs, and opinions of others to act precipitously. Neptune is a weakening planet in all matters that require self-assertion and self-confidence. The closer these planets are to the Ascendant, the greater will be their tendency to cancel out the effects of an eastern-hemisphere emphasis.

Planets that tend to strengthen the actor temperament are the Sun, Mars, Jupiter, Uranus, and Pluto. Yin planets such as the Moon and Venus tend to weaken the actor temperament, though they are not as debilitating as Saturn or Neptune.

Planets in the twelfth house may also weaken the actor temperament. For the reasons, see the section on the twelfth house in Chapter 14. Though people can overcome planets in the twelfth, most do not do so completely, at least as regards using planetary energies for taking the initiative. For most people, twelfth-house energies require caution and consideration before being allowed to manifest.

The Western Hemisphere Planets in the western half of the chart are moving away from the upper, social pole of the chart toward the lower, personal pole. This half thus symbolizes one's experience of and perception of the world. It represents the part of the self that is acted upon, that is passive and not under one's personal control.

Corresponding to the eastern-hemisphere actor type is the western-hemisphere experiencer. According to widespread tradition, those with an emphasis in the western hemisphere are supposed to be passive and out of control: that is, victims. But it does not take much observation of actual horoscopes to show that this is not the case.

What actually happens with experiencer types is that they observe before acting. They are more a considering type than actors are. All they need do to gain control over their lives is to take control of their reactions to any given situation. By controlling their response and making it appropriate to the situation, experiencers can become as powerful an influence over the course of events as actors are. They will certainly be more in control than actors who do not observe others' responses to their actions, or actors who never bother to look before acting.

The real difference between eastern- and western-hemisphere types is that one type tends to think in terms of direct action first, while the other thinks in terms of getting maximum understanding first. Of course, just as one can have the negative actor type who invariably goes off half-cocked, one can also have the truly passive, overcautious experiencer who is so concerned about observing that he or she never acts. Both these types are out of control.

As with determining the actor type, there is more to evaluating the experiencer than counting planets in the western hemisphere. When in the west and especially when near the Descendant, the very yang planets such as Mars and the Sun and sometimes Pluto and Uranus may indicate the way people act with respect to others rather than the energies that they experience from others. This may cause such people to behave more like actors. The Moon, Neptune, and Venus here heighten the tendency to be an experiencer. Saturn does not seem to have much effect one way or the other. A prominent Saturn will always heighten caution and slow down one's taking action, but Saturn in the west is not more extreme in this respect than Saturn in the east.

Just as the twelfth house seems anomalous with respect to the eastern hemisphere, the fifth house is anomalous in the west. As we shall see in Chapters 13 and 14, the fifth is primarily a house of energy release and self-expression. There is little about the fifth to suggest that it is predominantly oriented toward experience rather than action. Yet something about the fifth does show its western orientation: fifth-house activities usually involve being with other people, and, while the primary emphasis is on the self, there must be an awareness of others that is not usually to be found with a first-house emphasis. Nevertheless, a strong planetary emphasis in the fifth house does not usually indicate a classic experiencer type.

The Midheaven Within the upper and lower hemispheres, described above, there are obviously points that represent the highest and lowest a planet can go before changing direction. These are the upper and lower poles already referred to. Symbolically, let us call these the poles of the outer and inner. In the circle they are up and down, but in the psyche they are out and in. In the horoscope these poles are represented by the Midheaven above the horizon and the I.C. below it. Just as the Ascendant and Descendant most perfectly embodied all the attributes that were assigned to the eastern and western hemispheres, the Midheaven and I.C. are the quintessence of all that the upper and lower hemispheres represent.

The Midheaven is a point of the maximum externalization of the self. It represents the social world, farthest removed from personal and intimate life. Thus it is considered to refer to one's social position, role, status, and life direction as expressed in external terms. Traditionally it has been associated with one's career, and this is true to the extent that one defines oneself by what one does. But there are other points that relate to career as well.

The Midheaven is not especially informative about personality characteristics, but it is nevertheless extremely important in one's life, as it helps to define what one does rather than merely how one does it. Perhaps the most important attribute of the Midheaven is that it helps to identify what people need to do with their lives in order to grow.

The I.C. As the center of energy in the lower or nothern hemisphere, the I.C. is the most intimate, personal point in the mundane circle. It represents one's innermost feelings, roots, and sense of being, and it relates to the internal definition of the self. Also, being opposite the Midheaven, it represents the base laid down in one's past and private life for the roles that one will play according to the symbolism of the M.C.

The Meridian Axis   The meridian axis, consisting of the Midheaven on one end and the I.C. on the other, describes one's orientation in the world, both social and personal. The axis has to do with one's sense of identity, but rather than telling much about the way one expresses oneself, the Midheaven-I.C. axis indicates the objective toward which one is working and the experiences from which one is coming. Whereas the horizon had more to do with how one reaches out to one's surroundings in space, the meridian has more to do with how one travels forward and back in time. Whereas the horizon axis describes how one interacts with others, the meridian axis relates to the individual more purely as an individual. Various German schools of astrology have gone so far as to consider the meridian axis as being the "I" or ego. There is merit to this, but it is an oversimplification.

How the four quadrants formed by the horoscope angles are subdivided into houses will be the topic of the remaining chapters in this book.

13

The Houses: Introduction

Houses are one of the basic symbol systems used in horoscope delineation, yet at the same time they are one of astrology's greatest sources of difficulty. Their central idea is simple: it is that planets affect different areas of life, action, and experience according to where they are located with respect to the horizon of the birthplace. There is little controversy about this formulation of the house effect, and in fact there is even good statistical evidence for some of it in the work of Michel Gauquelin.

The problems arise in implementing the house principle. Controversy rages over what geometry to use in dividing up the mundane sphere, over where the houses begin, and over whether in fact they have any sharply defined boundaries at all.

In this chapter I will first try to throw some light on these points. Then I will outline the traditional ways of classifying the houses, and close by considering the various levels of house interpretation.

The Problem of House Division

There are dozens of ways of dividing the diurnal cycle into twelve parts, and no one seems to have discovered the ideal method. It is easy to divide the zodiac into equal sections, but when we are working in several obliquely inclined planes, just what do we divide? The ecliptic (as in the Equal House and Porphyry systems)? The equator (as in the Meridian and Regiomontanus systems)? The horizon (Horizontal system)? Or something else (Placidus, Campanus, Koch)?

Even the number of houses is not cut-and-dried. At least one modern writer has proposed a twenty-four-house system. And the Irish sidereal astrologer Cyril Fagan has unearthed ancient references to the *oktotopos*, an eightfold division numbered clockwise from the Ascendant instead of counterclockwise as we are used to. To make matters worse, the first eight houses of our twelvefold systems have meanings similar to the eight houses (usually called "watches") of the *oktotopos,* even though only part of the fifth house of the two types of system coincides in space.

Once we do decide on the number of houses and how to divide them, there is still the problem of how to regard these divisions. Is house symbolism uniformly intense throughout a house, only to change abruptly to the next house's symbolism at the cusp? Or do house meanings shade gradually into one another? If houses had clear-cut boundaries, it seems to me that by now astrologers would have agreed on the most effective system of house division. But a multiplicity of house systems remains in use, indicating that astrologers are still in disagreement as to where the boundaries are. This leads me to believe that there are in fact no firm boundaries between houses.

Granted that a house's symbolism does not stay at the same intensity throughout the house, the next question is, where is the strongest manifestation of the house? This is a different issue from the one of simple planetary strength in relation to the angles. Many modern astrologers assume that the cusp of a house both begins the house and is where the house manifests most strongly. But ancient Greek tradition and modern Hindu astrology both hold that while the cusps are peaks of a house's intensity, they are not located at the beginning of the house. The Greeks placed the cusps slightly after the beginning, and the Hindus place them squarely in the middle. Thus the Hindu first house would extend from the middle of our twelfth to the middle of our first house. We are left with the question, is the peak of a house's intensity at the boundary, in the middle, or somewhere in between?

Why Use Houses at All?

There are yet other difficulties with houses, in addition to the controversies about the location of their boundaries and their peaks of intensity. In Chapter 12 and again later in this chapter I mention how Gauquelin's studies have called into question the traditional ideas about angular houses. There is also the fact that, of all the symbol systems in astrology, the houses have the most simple-minded, fortunetelling-oriented meanings, meanings that are an embarrassment to any psychological- or philosophical-minded astrologer.

In the face of all these difficulties, some astrologers have jettisoned houses altogether. The sidereal astrologer Arthur H. Blackwell refers to house division as "heavenly surreal-estate" and, like many other siderealists, uses only the horoscope angles. The Ebertins in Germany have also devised a system that does without houses and works quite well.

Although I do not yet reject houses, if the way should become clear I am prepared to reinterpret what they are in a way that would amount to a rejection of house doctrine as it is now. I am particularly willing to accept the idea that there are not twelve houses or any other number of discrete houses. What seems more likely is a continuum, in which signification changes gradually from area to area.

For the time being, however, I do use houses, for the following reasons. First, the position of the planets with respect to the horizon is clearly very important. At present, other than houses, there is no existing tradition of meaning for dealing with this. Although houses may not give a completely accurate picture of planetary relationships to the horizon, they are a helpful approximation.

Second, as I hope to show in the next two chapters, it is possible to make enough sense out of traditional house meanings to attain a fairly profound understanding of human beings.

How Houses Are Used in This Book

If one is going to talk about houses, one is more or less forced to choose a house system. My present choice is the Koch or Birthplace system of houses.

At the outset, I did not use houses, but when I first started to investigate them, I used the Placidus system, simply because Placidus tables were the most available. Then, when for a time I followed the sidereal school of Cyril Fagan and Garth Allen, as an experimental alternative to Placidus I used the Campanus system, which is fashionable among siderealists. Campanus houses are neither tropical nor sidereal inherently, any more than are Placidus houses, but one tends to follow all of a school when one follows any part of it.

Later I was exposed to Edith Wangemann's use of the Koch system. While I was not totally convinced of the validity of its geometry, in her hands it delivered results that I have seen in no other system. Also, and this was a decisive factor, it made something clear about my chart that was not clear from Placidus. Whereas in Placidus I have a sixth-house Sun, in Koch I have a Sun that is a mixture of the sixth and fifth houses. This tallies better with my experience.

Since adopting Koch, I have changed my use of house cusps. I now follow the ancient Greek idea that a cusp is the peak of a house's energy, though not the beginning of the house. Such a cusp is not in the middle of a house, either; it seems to be 3° to 7° after the beginning, the actual number of degrees being dependent on the length of the previous house. The longer the previous house, the further into the next house the cusp is. Determining the actual beginning of the house is not important, however, because it is also apparent to me that the transition is not sudden, but gradual. Thus my Sun, which is about 4° back from the sixth-house cusp, is in the border area and is a mixture of fifth and sixth.

It is important to apply this principle consistently. I do not advocate moving the effective beginning of a house back a few degrees whenever you feel like it, or in order to save a precious theory. Such changing of the rules in midstream is the bane of astrological technique.

Classifying the Houses

As with the signs and all the other symbol systems, there are some general patterns that can help one understand the individual houses. First, there is the division of the horoscope into hemispheres, which has already been mentioned in Chapter 12 and will be developed further in the second part of Chapter 15. There are also traditional groupings of houses that correspond to the groupings of the signs into elements and crosses.

House Triplicities The triplicities or triangles of houses correspond roughly to the division of the signs into the four elements. In fact, authors such as Zipporah Dobyns consider the element of a house as significant as the element of a sign. To them, the first, fifth, and ninth are fire houses; the second, sixth, and tenth, earth houses; the third, seventh, and eleventh, air houses; and the fourth, eighth, and twelfth, water houses. This idea has some merit, but for the following reasons I do not accept it quite as formulated.

As said before, houses are not energies like planets, nor do they modify the manifestation of energies the way signs do. Elemental indications that come from planets and signs tell us about the style in which an individual behaves, whereas houses represent issues confronted in life. Houses describe where in one's life one may act out or experience planetary energies. A planet in a so-called water house may or may not act in a watery manner, but it will confront watery issues. Therefore, to disregard the sign on the cusp of a house or the planets in it, using instead whatever elemental quality the house may have as a house, is to change the purpose for which elements are intended in delineation.

It is also misleading. For example, judging from the number of important planets in my second and sixth houses, I have, from the house standpoint, a fairly strong emphasis in earth. But otherwise my earth credentials are slight: no planets in earth signs. Whatever earth qualities I have come from a Sun-Saturn opposition. Now, is the style of my behavior earthy? Those who point to my earth qualities say I am a reasonably orderly thinker and a careful worker. But these are air, not earth, qualities. A heavily earth person is impatient with excessive cerebration, something I am prone to, with Mercury conjunct the Sun. I am very involved in abstractions, which is not at all characteristic of earth. What my planets in "earth houses" do is deny me the luxury of ignoring practical affairs, though I would much prefer to ignore them.

While house and sign triplicities are not the same, the pattern of house triplicities is quite strong. For example, the fact that the fifth house is related to the first by house triplicity seems more influential than the fact that the fifth is on the experiencer side of the chart. Likewise, the twelfth house's being related to the fourth is more important than its location on the actor side of the chart. Nevertheless, despite the obvious influence of the house triplicities, I have not found them as significant as the sign triplicities in getting an overview of the chart. In seeing the house cycle as a whole it is useful to organize the houses into triplicities, but in delineating I prefer to deal with the houses as individual entities rather than as members of groups.

Whatever elemental qualities the houses may have, they do not have the same significance as the elements of signs and planets. Therefore, though there are elemental qualities in the descriptions that follow, I do not give elemental names to the triplicities of houses.

The *personal houses* are one, five, and nine. The first house, signifying personal energy release into the world, sets the keynote for this triplicity. Whereas the first is oriented toward being effective in the world, the fifth house continues the theme of personal energy release, but is more oriented toward recreation and amusement. The ninth signifies one's ability to perceive what is so about the external world and to make the resulting understanding part of one's life and a tool to increase one's effectiveness in the world. This triplicity corresponds to the fire signs.

The *practical houses* are two, six, and ten. Perhaps this is not the best term for them, but it is more accurate than calling them earth houses. It is better, perhaps, to consider them houses of what appears to be practicality. The issues of these houses may cause one to sacrifice short-term gratification or the expression of one's will in order to get along in social reality, not physical reality. This is the chief reason why the term "earth" is not appropriate. The tenth house sets the tone here. It is a house of social status, role, and prestige. All these are socially defined. It is difficult to have social prestige in a vacuum. Money, usually associated with the second, is merely paper. Its value comes entirely from the social contract. The sixth in its aspect of signifying work that one does for others or that is done for oneself is also social. The health signification of the sixth is not, however, as clearly associated with the general nature of this triplicity.

The *social houses* are three, seven, and eleven. Whereas the practical houses are socially defined, the social houses signify relationships in the conventional sense. The third signifies the everyday, casual relationships (as with relatives and neighbors) that are so routine they do not usually surface as issues to be faced in life. The seventh deals with one-to-one relationships in which the individual must, at least to some degree, be aware of the other and be conscious of what is needed to make the relationship work. The eleventh relates to one's interaction with groups (as well as to what one hopes for in life). Inasmuch as air is associated with the social function, these can be thought of as air houses, but inasmuch as air is associated with cerebration, only the third house has much to do with mind.

The *unconscious houses* are four, eight, and twelve. All three have to do with either unconscious mental processes or the emotions. The fourth and twelfth are both houses of the unconscious mind, the fourth being the deepest level that ties one to one's roots and origins, and the twelfth being the personal unconscious. The eighth has no obvious ties to the unconscious, but the issues associated with it seem to be heavily emotional. It has a sense of fate and brooding, and its association with death connects it to the most intense of all transitions into unconsciousness. At least, so it seems to others around the dying. These houses could be called water houses, except that the eighth is often associated with joint or shared finances, which is more of an earth than a water issue. All three houses appear to operate in hidden or mysterious ways.

House Quadruplicities   The quadruplicities of the houses are much more explicitly stated in traditional astrology than are triplicities of any kind. They are the angular, succedent, and cadent houses. And yet this is the division that has been most upset by the Gauquelin data mentioned at the beginning of Chapter 12.

Traditionally, the angular houses (one, four, seven, and ten) have been considered the houses in which planets have their greatest effect. The succedent houses (two, five, eight, and eleven), so called because going counterclockwise they succeed the angular houses, have been considered next in strength. The cadent houses (three, six, nine, and twelve), which take their name from the Latin *cadere*, "to fall," were considered the weakest. Houses six and twelve are considered much weaker than three and nine.

But the Gauquelin studies have clearly invalidated these traditional teachings. Figure 27 (adapted from page 52 of *Cosmic Influences on Human Behavior*) shows the typical pattern of planetary strength Gauquelin found. When studying the mundane position of various planets at the births of those who express those planetary energies strongly, he found a much greater than chance frequency of the appropriate planet in the twelfth and ninth houses, with smaller peaks in the third and sixth houses. In direct contradiction to the traditional teachings, the strongest areas were in the middle of the cadent houses, with the twelfth house being extremely strong.

The Gauquelin data also show that planetary strength is not uniform within a house. And while there seems to be a fourfold rhythm of strong and weak in the daily cycle of a planet, there is no special tendency toward a twelvefold division. I retain the twelvefold division in this book as a convenient approximation rather than as a scheme of twelve clearly defined spaces.

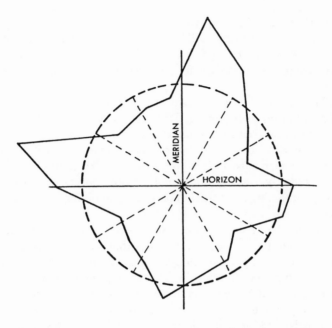

Figure 27. Mundane position and planetary strength

Actually, not all tradition runs counter to the Gauquelin findings. The third and ninth houses have throughout most of Western tradition been considered much less weak than the other cadent houses. Also, as mentioned earlier in this chapter, in Hindu astrology the angular houses surround the horoscope angles, running from the middle of our cadent houses to the middle of our angular houses. Thus they include about half of each Gauquelin peak area.

So far, I have only been talking about planetary strength in the houses, which is all Gauquelin talks about. But the traditional lore considers the angular houses not only strong but fortunate, and the cadent houses, at least six and twelve, not only weak but difficult. While I do not accept the cadent houses as weak, they do very often signal problems in a person's life for reasons that I will detail below and at the end of Chapter 15.

Following is a summary of some of the ideas that have been advanced about the qualities of the house quadruplicities.

The *cadent houses*—three, six, nine, and twelve—have traditionally been called mental houses. There is some merit to this, but it is hard to apply to the sixth house. The third house signifies the mind's routine, daily processes, the ninth, its straining outward to comprehend the world, and the twelfth, the fears and phobias (among other things) that may condition its responses. Houses six and twelve seem to be critical, in that planets in these houses represent issues in life that must be handled well if they are not to become major sources of difficulty. The reasons for this are not at all clear from traditional views on houses; they will, however, become clearer in Chapter 15.

The *succedent houses*—two, five, eight, and eleven—are often described as houses of resources. This is clear enough for the second and eighth, and can be seen to a lesser extent with the eleventh, but it makes little sense for the fifth. One traditional idea that definitely holds up is that planetary placement in succedent houses is a stabilizing influence. Planetary energies in these houses are not usually major sources of crisis (though a sufficiently conflicting combination of planets involving these houses can be difficult).

The *angular houses* are one, four, seven, and ten. Though they do not occupy quite the preeminent position that tradition assigns, they are still quite strong. Zipporah Dobyns has suggested that these houses represent four types of relationship. The first represents independence or no relationship; the fourth, dependence, or the relationship of one needing care to those who provide it; the seventh, interdependence, or the relationship between equals; and the tenth, dominance, or the relationship between one in authority and those who are subordinate. These are not, however, the same as the houses of relationship mentioned under triplicities. The relationships signified by the angular houses are not necessarily social relationships, as they signify the four main orientations between oneself and anything.

In view of the Gauquelin data, it is hard to recognize the correspondence that is usually drawn between the angular houses and the cardinal signs, and between the cadent houses and the mutable signs. This is yet another instance of the need to keep houses and signs somewhat distinct. This correspondence will be examined further in Chapter 15. The terms "angular," "succedent," and "cadent" relate to a view of the houses that no longer seems valid, but we will continue to use them for the sake of their familiarity.

House Polarities An alternating positive and negative polarity is not as evident in the houses as in the signs, but there is probably some sort of similar effect. There is little about this issue in the literature. The problem is that one would expect negative houses to be passive with respect to the positive houses adjacent to them. But the active-passive polarity in houses seems more clearly related to the east-west polarity as described in Chapter 12 than to alternating houses. Therefore, little use will be made of house polarity in this book.

Levels of House Delineation

Traditional house meanings come in a strange mixture of levels. For example, the fourth house relates to one's most personal life, family, home, and real estate. Many consider it also to relate to one's unconscious mind. Some of these meanings deal with the individual psyche, some with interpersonal relationships, and some with conditions in the environment. Looking at these, one gets the impression that the houses are grab-bags of different meanings assigned by no regular system. This is one reason why the more radical astrologers have chosen to disregard houses altogether.

Yet there is a concept that will assist us in finding underlying order in house meanings. This, the concept of the relativity of house meanings, will be discussed below.

The Moving Boundary of Polarity In Chapter 12, I mentioned that houses below the horizon tend to indicate the more personal parts of life and those above the horizon the less personal parts. And yet we cannot make this the basis of a typology, certainly not an introverted-extraverted typology, because actual people with emphasis above or below the horizon fail to fit the descriptions one would expect.

As we move through the house descriptions in the next chapter, we will see that houses both below and above the horizon may refer to inward experiences, personal experiences, relationships, and even entities completely external to the self. Yet at the same time, with respect to any particular matter that has an inward-outward polarity, if we take any pair of opposite houses, one below and the other above the horizon, we find that the lower house relates to issues that are more inward and personal. For example, using traditional fortunetelling meanings, the second house relates to one's personal finances, while the eighth relates to finances held by others or by the individual in connection with others. Similarly, the third house relates to one's immediate environment, while the ninth relates to environments far removed from ordinary experience. On a more internal level, the third house represents the day-to-day semiconscious functioning of the mind, while the ninth describes the mind's more conscious functioning. This shows us that each house can relate to both external and internal matters, but that the lower house always relates to the more inward end of any given polarity.

It seems, then, that the horizon does not act as a fixed boundary between two spheres of action and experience. Sometimes the line between personal and social should be drawn at one point, sometimes at another. The horizon represents the boundary between the two ends of the inner-outer polarity on any level. What determines the point of division between two issues is not an absolutely fixed criterion that separates inner from outer, but rather a moving criterion that is determined by the relationship of the poles to each other. Taking the third and ninth houses again, the third may signify one's daydreaming and internal musings, while the ninth signifies looking out toward the external world. Or the third may signify looking out at one's immediate world, while the ninth signifies looking at the world further removed from one's experience. Similar cases can be shown for the other pairs of opposite houses. Houses can work at several levels, and the horizon is the dividing line for whatever level is operative.

The Three Levels Any division of the levels at which houses operate must be somewhat arbitrary, but for clarifying the idea of levels, I have found it convenient to use a threefold scheme. The most fundamental level operates purely within the individual; I call it the internal level. The middle level covers self-other interactions; I call it the relational level. The outermost level covers things that seem to be completely outside the self; I call this the external level.

The *internal*, intrapersonal, or intrapsychic level of manifestation is the primary level at which all house energies operate. That is, all horoscope energies actually operate by creating effects within the self that in turn may be reflected at the other two levels. Expanding one's awareness means becoming conscious of the internal origin of the other levels. By knowing who and what one is on this level, one understands one's relationships and environment at the source and is better able to control them.

On the internal level, the horizon signifies the boundary between that which is more unconscious and hard to understand, and that which is more often and more easily made conscious. Energies that are nearest the I.C. are the most unconscious, and those nearest the M.C., the most conscious. But as the horizon is a moving boundary, there will be times when all the houses, even on the internal level, operate consciously, and times when all, especially the twelfth house, operate unconsciously.

What house energies do at the internal level establishes the basic style of their manifestation at all levels. Manifestations on the other two levels are a projection, literally a "throwing out," of the energies within the self. This includes even environmental circumstances over which one apparently has no control.

On the *relational*, interpersonal, or self-other level, one is aware of dealing with either an external circumstance or another individual. There is a sense of energies playing back and forth between the self and the other, such that one is aware of one's own involvement in acting upon and experiencing the circumstances or the other individual.

At this level the horizon signifies the boundary between that which is more personal and that which is more associated with the other. Energies that are nearest the I.C. are the most personal, and those nearest the M.C., the least personal. But here again the horizon is not a fixed boundary, so that the location of each house in the self-other continuum is relative, not fixed. Any house can pertain primarily to one's own point of view in a self-other interaction, and any house can symbolize primarily the experience of the other. Traditionally, only houses three, five, seven, and eleven have been regarded as houses of relationship.

At the external, societal, or environmental level, houses are also statements about relationships, but in the broadest sense of the term. One cannot be aware of something without being in some relation to it. Yet at this level one is not so aware of one's own position in the relationship. This is the level at which entities in the external world appear to have an objective reality, a reality apart from one's relationship to them. This is the level at which houses symbolize specific things, like money in the second house, friends in the eleventh, or one's spouse in the seventh. This is also the level of house manifestation at which astrologers become the most confused about the realities of astrology. They seduce themselves into thinking that the energies of the house describe objective realities about the circumstances or people surrounding the individual whose chart is being examined. But actually a house only states the individual's relationship to the issues represented by that house. This is the level at which astrology most often becomes fortunetelling.

The external level is the one most removed from the source of the energy patterns, one's inner self. Here the basic energies are the most disguised and hard to discern. Consequently, trying to manipulate the externals of one's life without getting at their psychic underpinnings is usually unsuccessful. Changing the circumstances of one's life without changing oneself merely brings the old circumstances back in new forms.

At the external level, the energies nearest the I.C. symbolize those outward circumstances that are most closely related to oneself. Those nearest the M.C. symbolize those circumstances and persons that are either farthest away from oneself or are related to one's least intimate social roles. Again, the exact relationship of the houses to each other is not fixed but relative.

The Importance of the Levels   All houses operate on all three levels at once. It is only our changing awareness that makes it appear that a house energy is operating at any one level alone. The importance of this idea is that it forces us to look for the inner dimension of all events in life. In doing this, we can become aware of how an energy operates in our life, what it does for us, what it does to us, and why it acts as it does. Then, in turn, we can take responsibility for our lives, which is the first step in taking control of them.

Traditional astrology was implicitly fatalistic in that it treated the horoscope as a description of factors beyond our control influencing, if not totally determining, our lives. Thus the houses, even to this day the most fortunetelling-oriented part of astrology, have mostly projected meanings, meanings that do not relate to the total consciousness of the events in question. But, as we have shown, every facet of the chart comes from the inward structure of the psyche. Astrology has not paid enough attention to this, and that is why houses have always had a missing dimension. For this reason, in the next chapter the internal delineations of the houses will in many cases appear strange and new. But with a little reflection you will see that the operation of the energies on this level easily gives rise to the more familiar manifestations I have characterized as either relational or external.

14

The Houses: Core Meanings

For each house below I first summarize the traditional significations, and then try to derive its core meanings by probing the seemingly unrelated traditional meanings for their deeper psychological significance. Then comes a modern interpretation of the house's significations divided into the internal, relational, and external levels outlined at the end of Chapter 13. Each discussion ends with an indication of how planets tend to behave in that house.

The First House

One's personality, the way one appears to others, physical appearance. Physical body, health, vitality. Traditionally associated with life expectancy through planets placed in the house and through the ruler of the rising sign.

The above traditional meanings all seem to work in chart interpretation, though as usual it is not readily apparent why this should be so.

The first house is the area of the heavens occupied by the Sun during the two hours or so before sunrise. In terms of human biological cycles this period is the day's low point. From this it should be obvious that the first house, although potent, cannot be quite so potent as tradition has made it.

The first house is the last house occupied by each body before it rises. Thus it represents energies that, while they still operate primarily in the personal hemisphere of the horoscope, also determine the relation of the personal area of life to the social. The first house is an interface: a boundary between two areas of existence that mediates how energies flow between the two. Therefore it corresponds to all interfaces that have to do with the transmission of energy from within the self to without.

On the psychological level the interface is the personality, that is, the complex of psychological patterns that regulate the flow of energy from within oneself to the outer world. "Personality" is derived from *persona*, a Latin-Etruscan word for "mask." The personality is the face we present to the world.

The first house has much to do with individual self-expression, but it is also a house of relationship. The expression of self signified by the first house is always with respect to others. In first-house matters, one does not operate in a vacuum: one is the active person in relation to others. Serious planetary stresses in the first house will affect one's intimate relationships just as severely as stresses in so-called "relationship" houses like the seventh and eleventh.

On the physiological level, the interface represented by the first house is the body, especially the skin and physical appearance. Of course, according to tradition, many factors affect one's appearance: not only planets in the first house, but also planets aspecting planets in the first, planets aspecting the Ascendant, and so forth. Simplistic correlations cannot be made between rising signs or rising planets and physical appearance, and one must also consider racial characteristics. The planet and sign symbolism of the first house is more likely to affect the *impression* one's body makes on others, rather than just the way one looks.

Health is also a first-house issue, in that the physical body is the medium through which we transmit our intentions, will, and desires into the world. Disease is not just discomfort, but also the inability to affect the world around one as vigorously as one would like. In sickness one is to varying degrees helpless and dependent on others.

The body is also a receiver of energies from the world, and disease can be the result of not adapting to the outside world successfully. But this intake of energies belongs to the sixth house more than the first, which has to do with putting energies outward.

Internal Level   On the psychological level the first house symbolizes the part of the self one chooses to mediate between oneself and the world. We create a face and then come to regard it as what we are. Thus the first house represents a self-image as much as an image presented to others. This is not so much a misrepresentation of ourselves as an incomplete expression.

Relational Level   Most traditional first-house significations are at the level of inner-outer interactions: personality, the physical appearance, oneself as opposed to someone else. The first house represents our sense of being polarized with respect to someone or something in the environment.

The first house is oneself as an active agent with regard to other people: at this level the house has no meaning apart from one's relationship to others.

External Level On the level of things outside oneself this house signifies one's own group as opposed to another group: We versus They. I am not referring to the overall ability of the individual to relate to groups; that is the domain of the eleventh. The first house signifies one's own group only in relation to an external group. This facet of the first house is seen clearly in horary astrology, where in the matter of sports competitions the first house signifies "our team" as opposed to "their team."

Planets in the First House Planets in the first signify energies that become part of the individual's expression of self with regard to others. A concentration of planets here is likely to increase an individual's tendency toward subjectivity. Such people are likely to take the initiative in situations and may have difficulty in cooperating because so many of their planets are involved with putting energy out into the world rather than experiencing the energies of others. Being able to react to others as well as act is essential in cooperative relationships.

Some planets in the first tend to lessen the degree of emphasis on the self. Neptune, for example, tends to cloud one's awareness of how one projects energies toward others. Such an individual may gain the ability to project multiple personalities such that others never really know who the individual is. I do not mean split personalities, where the individual is not in control of the process, but rather people who invariably seem to be playing a part.

With Saturn in the first, one can be so concerned with responsibility and external demands that it is difficult to place oneself ahead of others. A strong notion of propriety or right and wrong tends to dominate one's energy projections into the world.

The Second House

Money and movable property (as opposed to real estate). Values, attitudes toward wealth and property.

The older interpretation of this house as money and movable property works well enough in practical horoscope delineation, but it is clearly oriented toward fortunetelling and leaves us in the dark as to an inner meaning that clarifies the psychology of the individual. More recent writers come closer to a psychological interpretation of the second house by expanding it to mean one's values and attitudes toward possessions. But as it stands, this interpretation has two flaws.

First, for all too many astrologers it has resulted in corrupting the symbolism of Venus and Taurus, both commonly identified with the second house, so that they, too, are held to rule values and attitudes toward wealth. This seems part of the general trend of forgetting that Venus is primarily the symbol of love, affection, and art.

Second, "values" as a kernel idea of the second house is ill-defined. Are one's moral values signified? Is the second a house of anything one might value: one's reputation, social status, loved ones? If so, the meaning of the house is expanded way beyond what was implicit in the older and simpler, albeit fortunetelling, meaning. Such broad notions make the second house overlap grotesquely with other houses. It is necessary to keep astrological symbols as distinct as possible; otherwise there is an amorphous mess to interpret. One can pull anything out of a house to explain something one already knows about, but there is no way of sifting through the myriad possibilities to find out something new.

Given some adjustment and clarification, however, associating "value" with the second house is not completely worthless. Instead of looking at values as something we have, let us look at valuing as something we do. What is the function of valuing? Why do we do it? Why does many people's concern with money go far beyond their need for material security?

Valuing is a process of identification. When we value something, we extend our ego over it and regard it as part of ourselves. Imagine you have a new automobile, and someone is coming at it with a sledge hammer. How do you feel? You probably feel much as if you yourself were being attacked. When people's homes are burglarized, they report feeling personally violated. The more we identify something as part of ourselves, the more we value it, and the more we respond in this way. If you do not respond strongly to having a possession stolen or destroyed, you have not made it part of yourself. In other words, you do not value it.

Identifying something external to yourself as part of yourself, at least on an unconscious, psychological level, is a process of attachment. Buddhists call this the cause of human suffering, what keeps us on the wheel of life, incarnating and reincarnating. In this idea, I think, is the real meaning of the second house. The planets and signs in the second symbolize those energies through which we attach ourselves to the universe of our choice.

Unlike some Eastern and Western mystics, I do not believe we incarnate as the result of a cosmic error, tragedy, or accident. Though we are usually out of touch with the part of our being that makes these decisions, I believe we incarnate intentionally, out of a need to encounter certain experiences. That we incarnate is neither fortunate nor unfortunate: we simply choose to do so for our own reasons.

In choosing to incarnate, and in agreeing to play according to the rules of whatever universe we choose, we must attach ourselves to that universe. By making part of it part of ourselves, we gain a stake in it. This is the process symbolized by the second house. Being unattached eliminates a great deal of sorrow, to be sure, but the less attached we are, the less stake we feel in whatever happens in our universe. The trick is to be involved, but to realize that the involvement is merely a choice we have made, one that can be changed. In other words, we should be the master of our involvements, rather than having them master us. The tragedy of the overpossessive is that they become their attachments: most of their individuality is tied up in what they value.

There are some entities to which we become attached that do not properly belong to the second house. Loved ones are an example. Though it is possible to treat loved ones as possessions and thus make them second-house matters, doing this deprives them of their individuality and makes them mere extensions of one's own identity. While we may value loved ones, if they are truly loved we do not try to take away their independence and separate identity. Love is the mutual valuing of two individuals by each other without extending the ego of one over the other. In love two people may identify with each other without destroying each other's identity. Unlike the second-house process, this process is mutual. The second house is normally limited to physical objects because most people agree that these have no identity of their own.

Social prestige, honor, and status are also things we value that are not second-house matters. These are not *things* over which our egos extend, they are part of our ego. They are aspects of our self-worth as experienced in our social interactions. One's self is never in the second house: by definition, one cannot be the object of one's own possessiveness.

Moral values I also reject as being a second-house matter. These, too, are aspects of one's ego, not external entities over which one projects one's ego. There is no one symbol for moral values: Jupiter signifies honor, integrity, and honesty; the Sun, self-worth and integrity; Saturn, responsibility and keeping commitments; the ninth house, one's religious and philosophical values; and the tenth, one's social honor and prestige as a function of one's morality. Morals concerning relationships are symbolized by the planets, signs, and houses that affect one's relationships. And so forth.

Internal Level On the level entirely within the psyche, the second house signifies the part of the ego that is willing to flow beyond the boundaries of the body and attach itself to external entities, making them part of one's being. Seldom conscious, this process of attachment is usually accepted by the individual as given. We thus unconsciously make ourselves one with our automobiles and our bank accounts, and when what we have attached ourselves to is not upset or endangered, we feel secure. That what we possess may also in fact be useful and enable us to be more effective is a consideration, but one that is secondary to the extension of ego.

Relational Level On the level of interaction with the outside world, the second house signifies attitudes toward possessions and other things to which one is attached. It shows how one acts upon and experiences them. It symbolizes one's relationships to attachments and the actual expression of one's valuing as it manifests in one's behavior. Also it may symbolize one's awareness of what one is attached to as opposed to what is attached to others. An example is one's own money versus someone else's. And it may represent one's awareness and experience of attachment as opposed to energies that detach one from attachments.

External Level On the level outside the self, we have the traditional meaning of the second house as the objects or entities themselves: one's wealth, physical possessions, and resources. The second house may be fundamentally the process of valuing on an inward level, but on the external level it is the things that are involved.

Planets in the Second House A large number of planets in the second house tends to increase one's possessiveness, that is, the number and kinds of things to which one is likely to become attached. But certain planets in this house lessen the degree of attachment. People with Uranus here tend to want to be free of physical-plane attachments, which limit their freedom of movement. Of course, a second-house Uranus can also indicate one who has Uranian possessions, things that enable one to have an offbeat lifestyle.

Jupiter, if aspected in ways that emphasize its freedom-loving side, may also have this effect. But if it is associated with other possessive energies it can greatly increase one's possessiveness.

Mars may cause one to act recklessly with resources. It looks as if one did not care about them, but this is only an appearance. What one is actually doing is demonstrating one's control over resources by disposing of them in any manner one chooses.

The Third House

The lower mind, that is, the mind operating on its normal, day-to-day level. Routine interactions with others. Communication. Short journeys and moving about. Brothers, sisters, neighbors, and all other relations except parents.

The third symbolizes a greater number of seemingly unrelated ideas than any other house except the fifth. The thread by which most modern astrologers have attempted to connect these ideas is "interactions with one's immediate environment." The only difficulty with this is that it is a purely external delineation of a house that, being below the horizon, should have a particularly strong internal dimension.

The traditional signification of the third house as "lower mind" does, however, suggest an inner, personal, and psychological level of symbolism. But what exactly is "lower mind"? At no time in astrology has it meant the mind primarily dominated by emotions and irrationality. Nor is this "lower mind" anything like the Freudian id, an animal consciousness that motivates one to do only what one wants at the most primitive level. Lower mind usually results in actions that are more or less reasonable, although it is not a reflecting and judging level of consciousness. Its function is to deal with everyday existence.

The third-house mind can be conscious. You can reflect upon it at will. If you choose, you can look at your attitudes and mindset in any given situation and see what is happening. As you speak, exercising a third-house function, you can pick and choose your words carefully if you desire. More likely, however, you will look at the world and not be conscious of your attitudes and mindset. Your speech will follow patterns you have used routinely all your life and which seem to suffice for most purposes. The third house is a level of mind that most of the time operates unconsciously, but it can be made conscious whenever you choose. It is unconscious not because you cannot look at it, but because you normally do not choose to. I call lower mind the level of unacknowledged consciousness.

Lower mind is an important capability. It is like an automatic pilot. Normal interaction with the world does not require any special attention; you can deal with it in a routine manner. In fact, you must: you cannot afford to consume your conscious energy examining everything you do and say in the course of a day. Occasionally you may find yourself in a situation where you cannot function on this level. You may be in unfamiliar surroundings, have your every move judged, or be in some other stressful situation in which you must be aware of everything. Whenever this occurs, you realize that a tremendous amount of concentration is needed. Few have the energy to operate at this level of consciousness for very long. We all need to spend time in which we can relax and operate automatically without self-consciousness.

Some activities are hindered by conscious thought. Muscular skills like walking or riding a bicycle are mastered only when one has learned them so well that the processes involved become unconscious (at this point they become part of the lunar mind). One can choose to be aware of these processes, but if one tries to govern them at the fundamental level by conscious intent, they are likely to be disrupted. Some processes must become part of the unconscious patterning of the body in order to work, even though they may have started out in the conscious mind.

Communication is a major part of the third house's semiconscious functioning. Like muscular skills, using language becomes largely unconscious. When you are telephoning an order to a store it is not the time to reflect on the mechanics of speech. Also, communication normally is the act of establishing connections with one's immediate surroundings for the purpose of routine interactions. When communication involves an expansion or leap of consciousness, it belongs to the ninth house more than the third.

Short journeys are a projection of the third-house function onto the physical plane. They are simply getting about in your everyday world. The key idea is that the journey does not take you out of the world with which you are familiar on a daily basis. If a journey takes you into a new and unfamiliar world that requires much conscious reflection and consideration in order to deal with it, it is not a third-house experience no matter how short the physical distance. Astrologers have long tried to distinguish between third-house and ninth-house journeys by length of time or distance traveled. I think the criterion is how far out of the realm of everyday experience the journey takes one. LSD experimenters in the 1960s experienced ninth-house journeys without even getting out of a chair; not for nothing did they call the experience a "trip."

Brothers, sisters, and relatives are harder to fit into the "lower mind" scheme. Here we are involved with a common problem in astrology. Although houses often seem to symbolize other people and entities, we have already pointed out that they really only symbolize our *experience* of these things. In other words, houses symbolize on the interpersonal and environmental level our orientations and relationships to these entities. The third house does not indicate our actual brothers, sisters, and relatives, but rather our relationship to something they have in common, namely, that they are all people in our environment with whom we deal more or less automatically. Relationships with them are not especially conscious, nor are they consciously chosen, like seventh-house partners or eleventh-house friends. They are simply there as part of our world. Also these relationships do not involve any of the kinds of interactions that would place them in the fourth or tenth houses.

The above paragraph implies that if we had brothers, sisters, or relatives who were not part of our early environment or with whom we did not develop the particular kind of close, unconscious relationship we usually have with relatives, these people would not be symbolized by the third house. And yet even when we have never met them before, when we do meet a sibling or a relative, we often fall into a particular style of relating. I remember meeting some cousins for the first time. It took only an hour before we were relating like relatives, not unrelated people who had just met. A close common tie, like that of genes, can enable one to relax and act automatically.

Neighbors, like relatives, are part of the day-to-day human interactions we have been discussing. The important thing is not physical proximity, but the fact that the relationship is sufficiently familiar that it can take place with a minimum of conscious consideration.

Internal Level   At its deepest level of manifestation the third house symbolizes those aspects of the mind that take over consciously learned mental and physical functions and make them operate automatically. As the unconscious basis of the individual's fundamental mindset, the third house also symbolizes the aspect of the subconscious mind that most influences the experience of everyday reality. The third house is thus, along with the fourth, one of the areas determining habits. The third-house part of habit is the patterning of the psychic energy that makes up the habit, that is, what psychological processes actually occur when the habit is operating. It is much like the structure of a computer program as opposed to the purpose. The fourth house represents habit as a response to conditions or conditioning in earliest life.

Relational Level At the level of dealing with the outside world, the mind works on "automatic pilot" in everyday interactions. This level manifests as speech and routine communications, and serves to maintain one's relationship with the everyday world. It represents not only the expression of one's attitudes and basic behavioral programs but also one's experience of the attitudes and behavioral programs of others in the immediate environment.

External Level Most of the traditional third-house delineations are at the level of entities outside oneself. Brothers, sisters, other relatives, and neighbors are all closely involved in one's intimate, personal world. The third house also represents all situations and places that are part of that world: the neighborhood supermarket as opposed to Calcutta, India. Short journeys are simply one example of going about in one's personal world and making routine connections with others.

To summarize, the third house symbolizes any aspect of life that does not require the mind to expand its awareness by encountering the unfamiliar. It indicates matters that can be handled adequately by one's unconscious, habitual patterns of thought and communication.

Planets in the Third House A concentration of planets in the third indicates involvement in many small interactions with one's personal surroundings. One does not usually withdraw into a corner and meditate the day away. There is too much mental energy not to allow it to spill over into the immediate external world. Often there is little sense that anything important is being communicated: it is as if the individual simply wants to vent excess mental energy. People gossiping or prattling away in endless small talk are an example. Others are physically restless. They are not happy staying in one place within their personal world, although they may not often need to leave the world that is familiar and comfortable.

Most planets simply manifest their energies in third-house matters. But a few seem to alter the nature of the third house or be ill at ease when situated there. Among these is the Moon, whose emotional quality can interfere with third-house functions by clouding and confusing communication. What is said can be so emotional and personal that not even those close to the individual can relate to its content.

Neptune presents similar problems. Here it is not the personal quality of the communication that makes it difficult for others to relate to, but rather its obscure quality. Third-house energies usually operate in a linear manner; that is, one thought, action, or perception follows another in sequence. With Neptune, the sequence may be unclear or difficult to follow. Often this is because Neptune opens the mind to perceptions that cannot easily be communicated in linear terms.

The Fourth House

The home. One's most personal and intimate life. One's family, both childhood and adult, one's mother or father, one's forebears, one's native land. One's past and relationship to tradition. Real estate, lands. The end of life.

The core meaning of the fourth house is somewhat clear from the traditional interpretations. It is a house of inward and personal life, as opposed to outward and social concerns.

It is also a house of matters that support one's existence on both the physical and emotional levels. This support is different from second-house support. Money and material resources support one's existence, but attachment to resources as extensions of the self, not support, is the crux of the second house. The primary house of support is the fourth.

Yet the core symbolism of the fourth house lies deeper than this. To find it, we have to look at the meaning of the fourth-house cusp or I.C. As mentioned in the section on Taurus, the I.C. is the direction of the Earth from one's place of birth, insofar as that direction can be shown in the zodiac. And the Earth is the basis of all support for life upon it. In the most literal sense, it is the support under our feet. In a broader sense, it is the ultimate support of our physical existence. It is the Great Mother: from its substance come our bodies, and later our food, clothing, and shelter. All fourth-house symbolism can be shown to spring from such images of the Earth.

Our home, both physical and emotional, is our piece of Earth, where we settle down and put out roots. It is the place of intimate, personal life to which we retire after a day of confronting the outer, social world. Our family is, or at least should be, those people who not only share our roots, but also provide emotional support for us as we do for them. Our community is an extension of family, as is our native land. This is not a government or political order, it is one's land as a physical place to which one belongs.

The idea of *belonging* is one of the most important ways of distinguishing between the fourth house and the second. Second-house matters belong to oneself, whereas one belongs to fourth-house matters.

Real estate is our private piece of Earth, land on which we build our home. But I doubt that the fourth has anything to do with land bought for speculation; that seems to fall more into the fifth house, which is connected with speculation, or into the second, which has to do with possessions.

The most controversial aspect of the fourth house is its connection with one of the parents. Which parent should be placed in the fourth, the father or the mother? For reasons that are not clear to me on either theoretical or empirical grounds, most astrologers place the father in the fourth and the mother in the tenth. But there is an almost equally strong tradition that reverses this, putting the mother in the fourth.

I find that either parent may be symbolized by the fourth, depending on what role the parent is playing in the eyes of the child. The fourth house symbolizes the parent as provider of the support system in early life, whereas the tenth symbolizes the parent as authority figure and disciplinarian. Both parents play a fourth-house role at various times. According to the sex roles still prevalent in our culture, the father usually provides the physical support, while the mother usually provides the emotional support and does more actual taking care of the children. Insofar as both parents discipline their children, they are tenth-house figures.

Nurturing, caring for, and providing a support system I call the maternal aspect of parenting, while teaching and disciplining I regard as the paternal aspect. But these two sides of parenting are not necessarily tied to the biological sex of the parents. This, I think, is why there is confusion about which parents are symbolized in the fourth and the tenth.

Locked within the Earth are the traces of our past: rock strata from earliest ages, traces of ancient civilizations. Likewise, the fourth house signifies our past and our relationship to tradition. It symbolizes the physical structures, psychological patterns, attitudes, and memories that we inherit from the human race, from our immediate ancestors, and from life in and just beyond the womb.

Most important, the fourth house represents what is buried in the psychological sense: the unconscious mind. We are referring not to Freud's notion of a personal unconscious so much as to Jung's notion of a collective unconscious. The collective unconscious is common to all humanity simply by the fact of our all being biologically similar. It is not a function of individual experience but comes through either heredity or experiences that are absolutely, inevitably common to us all regardless of cultural or individual variations. It is made up of brain processes that take place beneath our awareness, such that we cannot make them conscious even if we choose. Some of these are the functions of the autonomic nervous system; others are simply aspects of the brain's functioning that we never become aware of except through symbolic patterns in our dreams, fantasies, and myths. The symbols of astrology operate at this level: each planet represents a complex of symbols in the collective unconscious.

The collective unconscious serves, among other things, to connect us all to each other, and this is where its relationship to the fourth house comes in. It is not clear in Jung, but it is implicit in astrology and occult systems that at some level of the unconscious mind we are all in fact a single entity and that there are no boundaries separating individuals and possibly even species. Our connection with the oneness of life is obscured only by our reliance on the conscious mind. On a certain level we are always connected with everything, always at home everywhere. The collective unconscious, symbolized by the fourth house, is the umbilical cord connecting us to all life.

The fourth house as the end of life is also clearly symbolized by the Earth. We are not only born from the Earth; in death we return our physical substance to it. The earth is both womb and tomb. As will be mentioned in the next chapter, the fourth house can be seen as both the beginning and the end of the cycle of houses.

Internal Level   At the innermost level, the fourth house symbolizes the psychic functions that connect us to the rest of life. It governs feelings of belonging, being at home in, and being connected. It is our link to the collective unconscious, to the psychological patterns we share with all human beings. It also symbolizes psychological structures that are genetically inbuilt or formed in earliest life. These are acquired preverbally and are so bound up with what we are that it is impossible to see them directly: we only deduce them through their products, such as dreams or odd bits of behavior. These aspects of the psyche are like the Earth, of which we as astrologers are largely unconscious. Probably because the Earth is so much a part of us, probably *because* it is the closest planet, we neglect to put it in the chart.

Relational Level   At the level of our conscious relationship to other entities, the fourth house symbolizes our most intimate ties, those involving our family and others who support and nurture us, and later in life those whom we support and nurture. The fourth house thus shows the most personal and inward aspects of our social existence, those usually unseen by people outside our most intimate circle.

Because the fourth house also symbolizes this kind of intimate relationship, it relates to infant and even prenatal experiences, the consequences of which are unconscious and become part of the internal level of the house. Such experiences may or may not be sources of difficulty when they surface in adulthood as habits and behavior patterns whose function is not clear. Whereas third-house habits are once-conscious patterns that become deeply ingrained and forgotten, the origin of fourth-house habits is never conscious at all.

External Level   The outermost level of the fourth house includes individuals like the nurturing parent and others with whom we have fourth-house relationships. It also includes our experience of our house, home, childhood and adult family, community, home town, nation, and so forth.

Planets in the Fourth House   A larger-than-average concentration of planets in the fourth house indicates the likelihood of a strongly personal, subjective manner of dealing with the world. Such people tend to be very private, and while not exactly withdrawn, they value being alone in their own space, or with those close to them. This is often an indication of introversion in every sense of the word.

If not nurtured in early life, later on such people can become withdrawn, emotionally insecure, and possessive. If well nurtured in childhood, later they can become nurturing and caring figures for others. There is often a strong maternal impulse, regardless of the individual's sex.

People with strong, well-functioning fourth-house planets have a feeling of belonging. To feel good, they do not need to prove themselves or go out and conquer the world. They accept life's circumstances and are not easily upset by unexpected changes. They have an equilibrium and a psychological stability that most others lack.

But Saturn, Uranus, Neptune, or Pluto in the fourth, particularly if they are badly aspected, may indicate disturbances in giving and receiving nurture. Saturn in the fourth tends to restrict the flow of fourth-house energy so that one feels that nurture is limited or curtailed. Uranus signifies that the flow is erratic, unpredictable, or occurs in unusual ways. Neptune often gives the feeling that the nurturing flow is weak, without vitality, or occurs on an abstract, nonphysical level. Pluto in the fourth does not particularly restrict the flow of energy; in fact it may increase it to the point where one becomes trapped or bound by its effects, resulting in the persistence of infantile issues or behavior into adult life.

The Fifth House

Play and amusements. Self-expression and creativity. Love affairs. Childbearing and children. Gambling, speculation, and investments.

The above hodgepodge of ideas makes it hard to discern a single core meaning for the fifth house, and yet there is one arising from the traditional meanings "play" and "self-expression." The idea of play and amusements is the oldest interpretation given the fifth house; self-expression is a modern way of phrasing essentially the same thing except that it sounds more dignified. It also adds an idea to "play" that is in fact intrinsic to the word but which has been lost in our modern attitudes. Play to many people today is trivial: an activity we all enjoy, but do not take seriously. In the late twentieth century, however, self-expression is taken almost as seriously as work. In fact many of us work hard at it, which is absurd when you stop to think about it. As play and self-expression lie at the core of the fifth house, let us look at them more closely.

To survive, one ordinarily needs to perform certain functions: earn one's bread, find shelter, and so forth. There are also many things we do either to get ahead or simply to survive in society. What all these activities have in common is that none is carried out for its own sake. They are only done out of necessity (real or imagined) or to serve some other purpose than the activity itself.

But some activities we do carry out for their own sake. It is simply in us to do these things: we want to, like to, and choose to do them. Doing them not only releases our own energies, it also makes a statement about who we are and what we are about. Making the statement is not the purpose of these activities, however; the important thing is that the activities are their own ends sufficient unto themselves.

One may explore the depths of the universe simply because one wants to know what is there; one may develop athletic skills out of the exuberance of a body doing what it does well; or one may create works of beauty or deep meaning: art for art's sake. There are even those who live their lives as a work of art.

Clearly, these activities are self-expressive and also playful. Both self-expression and play are pursued for their own sake. Even though they may in a subsidiary way do so, they do not *primarily* serve another purpose.

Science—that is, pure science as opposed to technology—is essentially play. While we hear rhetoric about the usefulness of expanding our knowledge (and it often is useful), at the root science is the activity of people who enjoy asking questions about the universe. Many astrologers, including myself, have the same motivation. Science and astrology both require work, but the work only serves the ultimate activity, which is play.

In fact, the role of work in general is to assist in play. Choosing to live is itself a decision to play the game of life. Even if, as Christianity teaches, life is for the purpose of glorifying God, it serves what is in fact God playing.

Play is neither trivial nor unimportant. It is in fact what being is. Work, though necessary, is secondary: it serves the play. All activity must either be its own motivation, or must eventually serve the purpose of another activity that is its own motivation.

The fifth house is closely related to the first, which is also in the personal triplicity of houses. But unlike the first, the fifth does not imply an outer reality into which the energy is released. It is simply the domain of those energies within the self that want to be released for their own sake. The strength of these energies may help an individual to put energy out into the world via the first house, but the energies of the fifth are not in themselves social.

This brings us to love affairs, which you would expect to belong to a relationship-oriented house. How, then, can the house of love affairs be a house of personal self-expression with little social dimension? The answer is that this house relates to only one aspect of love relationships: that of simple enjoyment, fun, an activity that is pursued for its own sake regardless of what it leads to. In its pure form, unmixed with other considerations, romantic love is glorying in a state of being for no other purpose than that it feels good.

And ideally, love enhances self-expression. Through the eyes of a lover one finds new aspects of one's being, and, being appreciated by another, these aspects flourish. An enormous proportion of our art has arisen from the self-expression of lovers.

The fifth house signifies dating and courtship, with their attendant fun. This is the stage for two people simply to enjoy being themselves with each other, with little thought of making a serious effort to operate as partners in a unit. The latter is the domain of the seventh house. A fifth-house relationship is less serious, less committed, and less of a close, one-to-one encounter.

To the older generation, the legal act of marrying established the transition from a primarily fifth-house to a primarily seventh-house relationship. But among many younger people there is no single act that does this. Moving in together may be like a legal marriage, but it can also be done so casually that the relationship is still not truly seventh-house.

Obviously, a love relationship is not either fifth-house *or* seventh-house in nature: all love relationships are a mixture. The most committed marriage can have its aspect of two people simply enjoying each other, and the most casual relationship has some kind of dialectic going on between the two people.

Another signification perhaps difficult to relate to the self-expression and play motif is having children. Children are a major source of responsibility. How can having a child be "play"? Clearly this is not play in the trivialized sense. But it *is* play as an activity that is an end in itself and as the release of an energy from within that expresses who and what one is.

Having a child serves no practical purpose for most people, a fact that has been brought out in much anti-childbearing literature of late. Yet people choose to have children. Even teenage girls who ought not to have children because of their age and level of maturity often have them because of something it means to them, something that cannot easily be expressed in practical terms. It can be argued that having children is a form of self-expression, in which people create variations on themselves and also transmit something of who they are. Also, through one's children one re-establishes touch with the tendency to play and exuberant self-expression of one's own childhood.

Having children is clearly play in the expanded sense: it isn't all fun. As with other play there is work attendant to it (think of an athlete's training, which is also work subsidiary to play). There is also often pain, beginning with the pangs of childbirth. These are the pangs of creation, shared by mothers and artists alike. Getting what is to be expressed out of the self is not always easy. And what is expressed is not always pretty:

children don't always turn out well, and tragedies like *Hamlet* are also a form of play.

The fifth house was not the only or even the primary house of children in natal astrology until the twentieth century. In older books children were signified by the tenth, eleventh, fourth, and fifth houses in that order. The fourth and tenth both signify kinds of parenting, and as such also relate to those toward whom one plays a parenting role. The eleventh signifies relationships to groups of all kinds, one's own family being the primary instance of such a relationship. The fifth house signifies the actual creative act of bringing children into the world. This older way of looking at children through the horoscope of a parent covers parenting as a multi-aspected process, and seems to me much more complete than merely looking at the fifth house alone.

The remaining meanings of the fifth house are gambling, speculation, and investments. All are essentially gambling (I would limit fifth-house investments to speculative ones). As gambling, they fit into the fifth house as a form of amusement.

Does gambling's chance element relate to the core meaning of the fifth? Perhaps. There is certainly a chance element in the creation of a child: which sperm gets to the egg is not unlike a horserace or a game of roulette. And in art as well as childbearing, one can never be sure of how the product of one's creative self-expression will turn out. Like a gambler one throws one's energies out into the world with a certain recklessness and never can be quite sure of the return.

Internal Level   The fifth house symbolizes those parts of the psyche that wish to express the nature of the self. As a symbol of being, the fifth is "being myself." It represents a drive to play out the role one has chosen.

In another sense it represents a drive to create. The fifth house is a place of energies within the individual trying to get out; as they come out, they give the individual a feeling of being alive and unique. These energies may or may not require another individual for their complete expression.

Relational Level   On the self-other level, the fifth is the house of all relationships that are formed mainly for pleasure or self-expression. This includes love affairs and also just the enjoyment of being with another person of whom one is fond.

The fifth house also signifies one's relationship to the product of one's spontaneous creative activity. This is one way the fifth relates to childbearing. This is the primary house to consult about how childbearing, as opposed to child-rearing, will work out. (For child-rearing, see houses ten and four.)

External Level   At this level is our experience of external-world fifth-house entities like places of amusement, gambling, and speculation. Also at this level is the fifth-house component of one's experience of one's children.

Planets in the Fifth House   A preponderance of planets in the fifth house signifies an individual who has a strong need to release abundant energies. Often the individual has much to give out—ideas, creativity, and exuberant energies—but is not so good at receiving the same things from others. Usually these are people one would describe as fun-loving, but this depends on the planets involved.

Whereas most planets simply signify what kind of energy will enter into one's creative self-expression, Saturn is notoriously contrary to the nature of the fifth house. People with this placement may have difficulty releasing the energies of the fifth. They may be more serious than most, or find it hard to have a good time unless they can find a "significant" reason for doing what they want to do.

The Sixth House

Service, servitude, servants. Work, employees. Sickness. Hygiene, nutrition. Small animals.

Servitude and work are matters that deny the individual immediate gratification in favor of an immediate necessity. Even as the fifth was a house of self-expression, the sixth can be thought of as a house of self-denial, insofar as the ego wishes something for itself right now. The sixth pertains to all activities pursued not for their own sake (as in the fifth), but for the sake of something else. This something else may be another purpose one chooses, external necessity one does not consciously choose, or circumstances that limit one's freedom of choice.

The signification of the sixth house is not always pleasant, but like Saturn energy it is necessary for human happiness. Any activity done for its own sake must be supported by other activities that assist it in its functioning. In the section on the fifth house we mentioned the athlete who undergoes rigorous training in order to enjoy playing a sport. Keeping in mind the pleasurable activity that the work supports, most individuals can put up with short-term denial of gratification in favor of a greater return later on.

People have problems with the sixth house when the supportive activity, the work, becomes too far removed from the pleasurable activity it is supporting. Then the work becomes oppressive, a denial of play rather than a supporter of it. This is a common problem in a culture that respects work more than self-expressive activity. We tend to think of work as an end in itself, losing track of the fact that all work eventually, directly or indirectly, serves the free self-expression of the individual. Self-expression is the ultimate end of work. When the relationship of an activity to its point or purpose becomes unclear, there is pointless activity. Play or self-expressive activity is never pointless; the only pointless activity is work that ultimately serves no self-expressive purpose.

An objection could be raised here. What about self-sacrifice, altruism, people who work for the benefit of others? Willing self-sacrifice is a free choice an individual makes as an act of self-expression. If I give of myself to you for your benefit, even when for me there is no clear benefit and perhaps even harm, that is my statement of who I am and what my life is about. The purpose served by the action is that I am making a statement purely for its own sake, perhaps for something in which I believe. And that in which I believe is, after all, an aspect of what I am.

The same can be said for some people who seem to work constantly. For them it is not truly work. Some of the hardest-working people I know are strongly fifth-house, not sixth-house people, because what others may consider work is their form of play. But people with a strong Saturn or sixth-house emphasis as well may often feel compelled to give others the impression they are working, because working seems nobler; we all have our little ego games.

The ancients called the sixth the house of slavery. In doing so, they pointed up the chief pathology of this house: that its activities can become divorced from supporting the self and self-expression. Slavery by definition is forcing people to work ceaselessly for ends that do not serve them at all but always something or someone else.

That the sixth is supposed to relate to employees and servants reveals something else about this house. It is the house not only of one's own work activities, but also of receiving the benefits of other people's labor. Put another way, this is the house of one's relationship to work and service in general.

Sickness is another major sixth-house concern. Whereas the first house was more involved with the strength and physical characteristics of the body, the sixth is more taken up with factors that interfere with the body's functioning. Some commentators relate illness to the other functions of the sixth by calling this the house of efficiency—health, they reason, being simply the efficiency of the body. I think this misses the essence of the sixth house, which is factors in the inner or outer life of the individual that deny self-expression. Sickness not only inhibits physical self-expression, it can arise when self-expression on any level is thwarted.

To understand this idea further, remember that sixth-house activities do not always have a clear purpose or point. What is not generally recognized in modern literature is that the sixth house may describe factors that seem to interfere gratuitiously with self-expression. Of course, even illness may have a purpose in the context of one's entire life (or even past lives, if you will). But to normal ego consciousness, illness usually seems unnecessary. Taking this admittedly narrow view, sixth-house affairs may seem to interfere pointlessly with one's life.

The relationship of a sixth-house activity to its purpose is important here. If there is a purpose, you must always try to understand its relationship to the sixth-house activity. If there is no purpose, you need to create one. If this is not done, illness can result. Illness usually develops in a body weakened by an inappropriate style of activity or a debilitating psychological state. For example, illness can result from work (also a sixth-house matter) that does not serve the individual's interests or that demands too much of the individual's energies for the benefit obtained. When one understands the reasons for illness, it is often possible to improve one's life tremendously.

Some who do medical astrology have concluded that the sixth house's connection with illness is at best limited when compared with the eighth. Certainly the eighth, traditionally the house of death, is more concerned with life-threatening illnesses. Though I find that the sixth does indeed have something to do with illnesses, I believe that the eighth and first are implicated as well.

Nutrition and hygiene seem related to the health and sickness issue, and in a way of course they are, in that they maintain health. But fundamentally these are subsidiary activities needed to maintain the body and mind so that the individual can function and the self can be expressed. As such, these are related to the work rather than the health aspect of the sixth.

"Small animals," the last remaining signification of this house, probably comes from the days when small animals like cats and dogs were kept mainly for catching vermin or guarding property. Insofar as such animals are like servants they belong to the sixth, but insofar as they are pets (that is, kept just for fun), they are better symbolized by the fifth.

Internal Level   The sixth house symbolizes the psychological factors enabling one to defer self-gratification. This is probably the nearest equivalent on the house level to Saturn.

Like the first house, the sixth is just below the horizon. It is in the lower hemisphere, which corresponds on the internal level to the inner part of the psyche, but it is right next to the upper hemisphere. As such, it is influenced by awareness of external situations. It represents the part of the unconscious mind that absorbs energies and influences coming down into the inner self from conscious experience. It is the house where experience is incorporated into the psyche.

This is undoubtedly one of the bases for this being a house of illness. Illness can be a symptom of energies coming into the inner self that are difficult for the mind or body to handle.

Relational Level   The sixth house's being just below the horizon is also significant at the relational level. If we think of energies coming down into the personal sphere through the western horizon, we can see that this is the house that also has to absorb experience on a conscious level. This is undoubtedly why this house is concerned with necessities that originate in external circumstances. It is at this level that the sixth is the house of work and other activities not pursued for the sake of individual self-expression.

In regard to relationships, the sixth symbolizes all those in which one is subservient to others or others are subservient to oneself. It also indicates relationships formed out of necessity, duty, or responsibility rather than out of self-expression or pleasure.

External Level   At the objective level the sixth house represents one's experience of employers and employees. One's attitudes toward necessity and service affect how one reacts to such people. If one has difficulty relating to one's own work in the broad sense of the word, one will have difficulty in relating to those who serve one and to those whom one must serve.

The sixth house also signifies the day-to-day activities of one's profession: the actual tasks one has to perform. One's work as an expression of who one is in society, however, belongs to the tenth house. The sixth house is the chief area determining one's profession only if one's profession is primarily a means of supporting oneself and does not fulfill one's life purpose. For example, the job of grocery clerk, unless a person is unusually dedicated to and identified with such work, is more likely to be signified by the sixth house than the tenth. In such cases the tenth house will signify whatever activity one uses to make one's life meaningful regardless of whether it brings an income.

Planets in the Sixth House   An abundance of planets in the sixth indicates that the issue of work may take up a large part of one's consciousness. But it does not necessarily mean one loves work or is hard-working. To the contrary, one may often feel that the world demands too much, that too little room is left for whatever one really wants to do. But if there are indications that the individual finds self-expression in work, a strong sixth-house type will enjoy working.

A sixth-house emphasis may also mean a great concern about health. This is certainly consistent with the symbolism and in accord with my experience. One often observes sixth-house types who work so hard to remain healthy that they never get in touch with what health is for—the enjoyment of life. The dictum "Eat to live, not live to eat" can be carried too far. This is a classic instance of sixth-house functions that are out of touch with the purpose they serve.

Contrary to the older literature, I do not find that sixth-house types tend to be more sickly. Because of their concern with taking care of themselves, they may in fact be very healthy indeed.

Of all planets, Saturn is the most at home in the sixth, except that it may signify one who forgets what the work is for. The other planets in the sixth usually signify what areas work may come from or with what areas in life it is associated.

While the Sun may not be as exuberant and self-expressive in the sixth as in other houses, it does get one strongly involved in whatever one may have to work at. None of the planets really interferes with the basic symbolism of the sixth house. Even Uranus usually only signifies that the work is performed under Uranian conditions or with Uranian entities.

The Seventh House

Marriage, partnership. Open enemies, open conflicts, lawsuits. Counseling relationships.

That both marriage and open enemies are symbolized by the seventh is a clue to understanding this house. The seventh represents a certain kind of relationship common to both marriage and two persons locked in combat.

To truly understand the seventh we have to contrast it to its opposite, the first house. Both are houses of the self-other relationship, but whereas the first emphasizes the self, the seventh emphasizes the other. In particular, this is the intimate other, with whom the individual forms the kind of close bond that makes two people, insofar as they can be, one.

In the first house the self puts energy out into the world; in the seventh the self experiences, as intimately as possible, the world putting energy back into the self. The seventh house is both above the horizon and in the western hemisphere, which makes it a house of experiencing others. This brings us to an important point, already implicit in what we have said, but let us make it explicit.

Traditional literature gives the impression that the seventh house describes one's partner or opponent. But all houses that seem to describe other people are really describing the energies one tends to experience through them, not the objective reality of the people themselves. In fact, the planets in the seventh may describe the energies one puts into as well as receives from intimate relationships. The difference between the seventh and the first is that first-house energies are generally broadcast to the world at large as the individual encounters it, whereas seventh-house energies are put out only into close relationships.

It is not possible to say from a natal chart alone whether a person will manifest the energies in the seventh house in terms of *action* or *experience*. Most people seem to experience seventh-house energies as other people, but an astrologer cannot safely assume this. This is a situation where the astrologer is better off asking than trying to figure it out.

Something not made clear in many older texts is that not all sides of marriage are signified by the seventh house. Marriage is a complex of energies related to the seventh, coupled with energies that relate to an individual's sexuality both psychologically and physically. Partnership is closer than marriage to the essential signification of the seventh.

In a seventh-house relationship, two people establish a close dialectic, an interchange in which the two either use each other as reference points against which to define themselves to themselves, or use the relationship to create oneness. The first type includes conflict and counseling, the second, partnership and marriage. In both cases the two people feel squared off face-to-face with each other in all their mutual dealings. From this it should be clear that two people engaged in direct competition with each other are also in a seventh-house relationship; hence the significations "open enemies, open conflicts," and "lawsuits."

The seventh house is distinguished from the eleventh in that the eleventh is principally a house of one-to-many relationships. When it does indicate a friendship, there is no sense of two being one, or two standing face-to-face. If there is this sense, the friendship has become a seventh-house relationship.

In counseling relationships, as with a psychologist or astrologer, one uses another person to help define one's own position. By means of the counselor's insight, by seeing oneself through the counselor's eyes, one gets a clearer idea of where one is. Objective self-awareness through intimate encounter with another is an important seventh-house idea. This is symbolized by the seventh and first houses being in an opposition, which is the aspect of confrontation and awareness.

The most important facet of the seventh house comes from the nature of relationships themselves. Relationships are opportunities to experience parts of ourselves that we choose not to experience internally. There are two reasons why we might not choose to do this.

Sometimes we fear a certain side of ourselves. Believing it evil or undesirable, we choose to bury it and so it surfaces in our relationships. (More about this in connection with the twelfth house.)

The other reason is that the game of life requires that we experience the object as well as the subject. Consciousness requires a dialectic between our inner selves and outer experiences: without something to be conscious of, there can be no consciousness. At the same time, we populate the realm of possible experiences with our own energies, because seeing our own energies external to ourselves as well as being them is a powerful way of getting in touch with what we are. Only when we deny our contribution to so-called "objective" reality do we become victims of what are in fact aspects of ourselves. The seventh house is the most intimate encounter between subject and object. At the highest level, this house is the symbol of the subject-object dichotomy in which the subject and object are actually one.

Internal Level On the psychological level, the seventh house symbolizes those aspects of ourselves that manifest whenever the outer world comes in really close to us. As we have shown, the energies of the seventh may either color our experience of what appears to be external reality, or determine how we react when confronted with real closeness from the apparent other. Using the relationships we set up between ourselves and others, we define ourselves to ourselves. An example is pitting ourselves against another to measure what we can do in comparison with that individual. Even though one usually experiences its energies as coming from other people, the seventh house is almost as important as the first in indicating the nature of one's own personality.

Relational Level On this level the seventh signifies the way we reach out to others to form close interpersonal relationships that link "I" and "thou" into a pair. This is the primary level of the seventh house as a one-to-one encounter. At this level we feel seventh-house energies within the relationship rather than being completely aware that they are ours or experiencing them as if they come from the other person.

External Level At the external level we confuse our experience of the other with the objective reality of the other so that the seventh house seems to describe the nature of one's marital partner, business partner, enemies, or those against whom one chooses to compete.

Once one gets involved in any kind of seventh-house relationship, one tends to look to the other person as the cause of one's experience. Many who have had one bad marriage after another blame the whole opposite sex, overlooking the fact that their peers may get along very well in such relationships. The thing to remember is that whatever patterns you experience in intimate relationships over and over again are really telling you about yourself.

In a we-they relationship, just as the first house was "we," the seventh house is "they." This is only applicable when there is a sense of "we" facing off against "they" directly; that is, "they" must be "you" in the plural sense. Instead of signifying one's personal opponents, the seventh house in this case signifies the opponents of a group with which one identifies.

Planets in the Seventh House A large number of planets in the seventh indicates someone who feels incomplete alone and strives to fill the void with close partnerships or intimate confrontations. Such people function better in interaction with another. Not necessarily passive or dependent, they can be assertive and take the initiative in forming relationships. They may even encourage others to become dependent on them, thereby maintaining the relationship they need.

To fill the void in their lives, some heavily seventh-house people pick partners with whom they constantly fight. To them, having a good battle is better than being alone. If other factors in the chart support it, a strong seventh-house individual can be contentious. The seventh is not really a Venusian house, contrary to what is implied by those who equate the seventh, Libra, and Venus. Venus does refer to relationships, but only ones that are loving and warm. The seventh house has no such inherent connection with love.

Most planets in the seventh merely signify the kinds of energies experienced through relationships, but Neptune and Saturn can alter the normal style of the seventh house. Neptune may cloud awareness such that one does not get a clearer image of oneself through relationships. The nature of the self-other interaction may be completely unclear. Neptune can also upset the balance between the self and the other. Usually a seventh-house relationship is between equals, but with Neptune here one may feel far above or far below the partner. One may also choose Neptunian people.

Saturn here can symbolize infrequent relationships. This is either because one feels a tremendous gulf between oneself and others, or because one feels overwhelmed by a sense of responsibility toward others in relationships. It is easier not to get involved. Alternatively, the person related to may be Saturnine or one of the partners may be much older than the other.

The Eighth House

Death. Inheritance. Other people's money.

The primary traditional meaning of the eighth house survives from the fortunetelling era of astrology, when astrologers were much concerned with their clients' time and manner of death. Predicting anyone's death is now rightly considered taboo, for several reasons. First, it assumes that one's fate is fixed, something few astrologers today are willing to concede. Second, because many face death with fear, the astrologer runs the risk of literally scaring someone to death at the appropriate time by the mere fact of forecasting it. Modern researchers on death and dying have found that the expectation of death by those around one can be a major factor in bringing it about.

Clearly, with only its traditional meanings, the eighth house has limited usefulness to modern astrologers. But in the light of its core meaning the eighth assumes a vital importance.

In essence, the eighth is a house of transformation of which death is only one kind, and not the kind most often encountered. To be sure, eighth-house energy may be strong when someone dies, but most of the time strong eighth-house energy means other types of powerful transformation. Something but not usually someone dies at these times.

The eighth is not only a house of death, but of resurrection. An old order passes away and a new one begins; there is renewal as well as destruction. There is reason to be hopeful when confronted with strong eighth-house symbolism, for it often indicates that something that has outgrown its usefulness is being removed from the life, thereby granting the individual new freedom.

Being above the horizon, the eighth house is likely to be experienced in connection with other people. It is also opposite the second house, which implies that the eighth house is for the other what the second is for the self. From this comes the notion of the eighth as other people's money. More important, it tells us that eighth-house transformations of the individual come about through the dialectic of the self with not-self. As with the seventh house, one encounters energies reflecting inner aspects of the self that one has chosen not to experience internally. If the second is the house of one's attachments, then the eighth signifies factors that tend to cut one loose from whatever one is attached to. Let us look at this idea in connection with death and transformation.

The physical world is by nature inflexible: matter resists change. We call something in the physical world material when we cannot pass a hand through it without resistance. Even air offers some resistance to motion. Therefore, when we attach ourselves to anything in the material world, and, by extension, anything that is not material, it encumbers us to some extent and limits our ability to change.

We need some attachments to anchor us, and some, like money, to operate effectively in the physical universe. But eventually our attachments begin to limit more than support us, especially when they resist the changes that come with growth. It is like a crab which, outgrowing its shell, must shed it in order to grow further. This is the action of the eighth house. It may be our own power that forces us to shed what is no longer necessary in our lives, but more commonly it is external circumstances, especially relationships. Authors like Zipporah Dobyns have noted the connection between this house and intimate relationships. But whereas the self-other encounter in seventh-house relationships enables us to define what we are, the self-other encounter in eighth-house relationships causes us to undergo transformation.

Many authors have related the eighth house to sexuality, but it is not the only house so related. Sex as a pleasurable activity pursued for its own sake is fifth-house, and as it helps bind an interpersonal relationship it is related to the seventh. But in the orgasm itself there is a momentary loss of ego-consciousness and a feeling much like death that truly belongs to the eighth.

Eighth-house energies are strongly emotional. They seem mysterious, weird, and, above all, fated. This is because however much they may affect material considerations, they ultimately operate on a deep, inner level which is usually experienced emotionally.

The eighth house is also associated with psychic and occult matters. The power that enables one totally to transform one's life can also enable one to transform the world around one, as if by magic. But as a house that undoes the attachments the ego makes, the eighth is ego-denying. Eighth-house energies usually seem uncontrollable by conscious will, and it is difficult to use these "magical" energies of transformation for the intentions of one's ego. They can only be used if one becomes a vehicle for ego-transcending energies within the self. In this respect the eighth house is much like the twelfth.

Let us return to the eighth house as other people's money, or, in terms of our delineation of the second house, other people's attachments. This comes partly from the idea of the eighth as factors that force us to shed our attachments, in that these factors are often ones in the external world. But that does not quite complete the association. The main reason for this idea being associated with the eighth house comes from its being a derived as opposed to an intrinsic signification of the house. Transformation and rebirth is the intrinsic signification; the derived signification comes from the eighth's being the second house (money) from the seventh (the partner, the other). In traditional astrology all houses have derived as well as intrinsic significations, but only in the eighth is a derived signification considered as prominently as an intrinsic one. This is probably because death, the traditional intrinsic signification of the eighth, is not applicable in most cases. The idea of the eighth as transformation and rebirth is, however, commonly encountered in life, and I believe that this signification is preferable in most cases to the derived one. Chapter 15 discusses derived house interpretations in more detail.

Derived and intrinsic significances combine in the eighth-house meaning, "inheritances," which are someone else's money coming to us through death. Inheritances may be shown by the eighth, but one cannot assume this house will refer to an inheritance. It is necessary first to establish that an inheritance is possible.

Internal Level The eighth house relates to all inner energies that force the individual ahead toward growth and change. Within the person are the psychological forces that want to reach out and experience the world. These inner forces cause one to shed whatever one has taken on that limits the experience and the resulting growth. This pertains especially to physical attachments when they begin to restrict us.

These energies are irresistible because they result from the individual's own inner dynamic. They come not from an external fate, but from one's own growth plan: they result from one's life choices. If eighth-house energies appear fated, it is partly because one's most inevitable experiences are the result of one's firmest choices. It is also because these are seldom conscious choices, and we often experience both the subconscious and transcendental aspects of ourselves as other than our own.

Relational Level At the relational level the eighth house signifies our encounter with outer circumstances that reflect our inner dynamic toward change. Many astrologers have observed the eighth on this level as a house of relationships, because intimate relationships can bring about inward change, often of the most radical kind. The death-and-rebirth experience of the orgasm belongs to this level. So does our ability to use experience as a guide for change.

External Level   At the external level the eighth house symbolizes our experience of all outer-world events and circumstances that bring or represent transformation: the death of others, and situations involving breakdown, decay, and rebirth. It also symbolizes circumstances that force us to become detached from our attachments or to deal with the attachments of others. It is this aspect of the eighth that causes it to mean other people's money.

Planets in the Eighth House   A large number of planets in the eighth signifies someone whose life to a great extent revolves around change: that is, a person who finds any continuous state of affairs tedious and consciously or unconsciously engineers circumstances that periodically totally transform the life. The resulting crises may appear difficult to others and even to the individual, but such people often feel truly alive only when they are undergoing such catastrophes.

Particular planets in the eighth signify the manner in which one approaches change and transformation. For example, Saturn in the eighth resists transformations, which is why the older astrologers associated this placement with a difficult death. It is not so much a sign of a difficult death as of resistence to the idea of any kind of change.

The Ninth House

The higher mind. Philosophy, religion, the law. Long journeys.

The ninth house is best understood as being opposite the third. As we saw, the third house symbolizes the part of the mind that deals with routine, day-to-day affairs. Though capable of being conscious, these mental functions usually go on at an unconscious level.

In contrast, the ninth house symbolizes those mental functions that reach out to deal with whatever is not routine or day-to-day. It is the house through which come new ideas, perceptions, and modes of thinking: a house of consciousness expansion. In order to be effective, these processes must function on a conscious level. Whenever one is consciously aware of thinking about something, this belongs to the ninth house.

The ninth-house style of perception is not only conscious, it is synthetic rather than analytic. It strives to perceive what relates parts to a whole and what pattern organizes any group of entities. It is not satisfied with simply perceiving a fact: it is equally concerned with meaning. It is very much concerned with what is "out there," but it is concerned with the relationship of the self to what is "out there" as well.

The ninth house symbolizes religion, philosophy, and the law because all these are concerned not only with the patterns that relate things in the external universe, but also with how the individual fits in with these patterns. Religion deals with what binds humankind in a relationship to the universe. Philosophies, at least older ones, describe the organization of the universe on moral and ethical as well as natural grounds. The law is a study of the social contract by which human beings govern their relations with each other.

The ninth house has a strong social element, in that external factors or other people are often the source of new ideas. But it is not a house of relationships in the conventional sense of the word: one does not look there to find out how someone relates to others except in the most indirect manner. Rather it is a house that deals with the understanding of how things are integrated into systems. It is the house-level counterpart of Jupiter. Although it lacks the freedom-loving aspect of Jupiter, it shares Jupiter's concern with truth.

The ninth house is traditionally associated with long journeys, as opposed to the short journeys of the third. Long journeys place one in an unfamiliar situation and hence expand one's consciousness. As stated in the discussion of the third house, the essential difference between third- and ninth-house journeys is not the length of the trip, but the degree to which the journey carries one out of the normal, everyday environment. It is probable that the original distinction between third- and ninth-house journeys arose in an era when traveling any distance at all inevitably meant entering an unfamiliar world. Even adjacent counties were often very different. But today it is possible to travel thousands of miles without leaving a homogeneous world-wide industrial culture.

At their best, ninth-house energies bring foresight. Reaching out to see into the distance far beyond the ordinary concerns of the individual, these energies can detect in advance what may be coming in from the outer world. This enables one to avoid being caught by surprise when events come near enough to concern one's intimate, everyday life.

Even though the ninth is an outward-directed, above-the-horizon house, these same energies may sometimes go within in an attempt to understand the self. From the viewpoint of normal consciousness, one's inner being may be as alien as the outer world far away from ordinary experience. Unless ninth-house planet and sign energies permit otherwise, however, the understanding gained by the inward questioning of this house may be purely intellectual. Various planetary functions need to translate ninth-house insights into the gut-level understanding necessary to make such information useful.

The ninth is commonly considered the house of higher education, and the third the house of elementary and high school. This is not necessarily true. Insofar as it operates to expand the awareness of an individual, all education is ninth-house in nature. Insofar as education serves only to impose discipline on an individual and inculcate the mores of the society without expanding the individual's awareness of truth, it is not ninth-house. It is then a mixture of tenth-house (disciplining), sixth-house (work), fourth-house (babysitting), and third-house (programing) functions. This illustrates the principle that houses do not signify anything in the actual world at all: they only signify functions that the individual may experience, and relationships to the individual of things perceived in the outer world.

Though it may be plausible to look at the ninth as the house of intelligence in the sense of I.Q., it is not safe to do so. I.Q. is a measure of ability to perform on I.Q. tests. Although it may correlate with academic success, it does not necessarily show ability to succeed in the world. Real intelligence probably has more to do with creating, innovating, and fathoming one's own life. Because we do not really understand "intelligence," I suggest not assigning this term to the ninth house. I prefer instead to call it *a* house, not *the* house, of wisdom. Wisdom I see as knowing what is true for oneself and the world and operating so as to give everything its due and no more. The wise are not constantly overwhelmed by inner signals urging them to actions that are inappropriate as judged by the results.

Internal Level The ninth and tenth are the two houses most connected with the conscious mind. But whereas the tenth has to do with the conscious mind acting upon the world, the ninth symbolizes the conscious mind experiencing, perceiving, and understanding what it perceives. While not primarily concerned with action, the ninth is not entirely passive, either: its energies make one want to *reach out* to perceive the greater world around one. Assuming that the planets and signs connected to this house do not oppose such a reaching-out, there is a desire to experience as much as possible.

As a house of active experiencing, the ninth is the home of those psychological patterns that modify and influence one's perceptions. People do not passively observe the world; the structure of their consciousness influences how and what they perceive. Through ninth-house energies one builds a framework by which to organize experience: a philosophy, a world-view, even a reality system.

Relational Level On the inner-outer level we have the individual actually looking out into the world. Here the ninth house symbolizes the kinds of experiences one uses to shape one's views of reality. Among such experiences might be consciousness-expanding travel as we have characterized it above.

External Level At the outermost level the ninth house signifies all entities that seem remote from everyday experience: foreign countries, philosophies, religions, and ways of life; or people with a foreign background or a lifestyle and viewpoints that are very different from one's own. At this level the ninth also symbolizes teachers, in the sense of gurus more than disciplinarians. Here is an excellent example of the external level of a house manifestation being always a projection of internal-level energies: ultimately, one's guru is nothing more or less than the external experiencing of an energy within.

Planets in the Ninth House   Having many planets in the ninth is a strong sign of being unwilling to accept the limits of the everyday world in which one was brought up. Such people will always reach out to experience the new and unfamiliar, to find out more about the world and what is true. They are often interested in consciousness-expanding disciplines like religion, philosophy, and the law, or in traveling widely on the physical rather than the mental plane.

Ninth-house planets affect one's philosophy of life and how one deals with ideas. For example, a ninth-house Uranus indicates someone who is comfortable with new and radical ideas and who tends to reject the traditional. Neptune in the ninth can indicate someone attracted to religious and spiritual concepts and perceptions, as well as possibly someone whose philosophy of life is unclear. Saturn in the ninth might indicate an individual whose ideas are definite, fixed, and of a practical nature. Venus might indicate someone whose ideas are influenced by aesthetics more than logic. Each planet in turn can stamp its own energy on the individual's style of thinking about the world.

The Tenth House

One's career or profession. One's social status, honor or reputation. One's father or mother. People in power over one, such as bosses, employers, or government officials.

It is plain from the above list that the tenth is an external house, a house of the individual being very much out in the world. This is one side of the tenth; the other is that, like all the houses from seven through twelve, the tenth is best understood in terms of its opposite house. The tenth symbolizes those energies that counterbalance the fourth house and draw one away from its concerns.

As we saw, the fourth symbolizes one's most personal world, the background from which one comes, the place to which one withdraws, and one's early experience of nurture. Throughout life, the fourth symbolizes all in the individual that is most inward and farthest from the outer world. This includes the unconscious mind.

The tenth, on the other hand, symbolizes the individual going out into the world, those persons who guide the individual in doing so, and those aspects of the mind that most deal with the external world.

In order for one to develop from an infant into an adult who plays a role in the social universe, there have to be energies that draw the individual out of the womb and the childhood home, bringing about an increasing interaction in the outer world. These are tenth-house energies.

In childhood these energies are experienced through the parents as they discipline the child, support its efforts to grow, and teach it how to get along in the outer world. While both parents do this to some extent, the tenth house usually symbolizes the person (parent or otherwise) who most played this role. In my experience the tenth is a house of fathering, but this is not always related to one's biological father.

Those whom one experiences as tenth-house figures in early life are, of course, authority figures, and one's experience of them sets the pattern for all experience of authority figures later on. This is the basis for the tenth house signifying people in authority over one and even one's relationship to the government as a whole.

Tenth-house figures also help one find goals in life: something to become, a role to play. Whereas the fourth signifies a state of being that is fundamentally satisfied with itself, the tenth often signifies a state to which one aspires but has not yet attained. Thus the theme of dissatisfaction with wherever one may be in life is inherent in tenth-house symbolism. Similarly, whereas the fourth is a house in which one merely exists without having to prove oneself, the tenth is strongly associated with the idea of performance, of doing, and of playing a role by which one may be identified.

People usually reply to "What are you?" by describing what they do for a living. Out of this comes the association of the tenth house with one's career or profession. This is not sixth-house work, which one does simply to earn a living, but work that provides a social role, work that one can identify with and by which one is identified.

If one's job does not provide this sense of identity, some other area of life may. For example, one might be a post-office clerk for a living and a nationally known stamp collector for a hobby. If stamp collecting provides a sense of identity and one is primarily known for it, then it, not post-office work, is the tenth-house activity.

From the above it should be evident why the tenth signifies one's social status, honor, and reputation. In fact, older astrology put more emphasis on the tenth as an index of social status than as a determiner of career.

Implicit in this, but not covered in extant literature concerning the tenth, is something I have found extremely important. The tenth house can be the key to understanding one's self-transcendence: that is, in what direction one must evolve until one is living out the symbolism of one's horoscope at the highest, most conscious level, with all the various energies within the self integrated with each other to the highest possible degree.

Why should this be so? It is in the nature of one's evolutionary pattern to grow into an interaction with the world outside oneself. This is the game of being incarnate in the physical universe. From the womb one moves out into the home and family, the school, the world, and then into a social role of one's own, and it does not need to stop there. Why should not these same tenth-house energies, given reinforcement from one's surroundings, lead one to worlds beyond the social universe? If the Earth is the womb of physical existence, and the tenth house symbolizes energies that draw us out of the womb, then the tenth would logically symbolize energies that guide us into transcendental understanding as well. Whereas the ninth symbolizes the guru within who leads us to reach out and understand more, the tenth symbolizes our reaching for a role to play in the world to which the guru leads us. The tenth can be a calling beyond the mere calling of how we make a living.

In practical terms, of course, the tenth house is usually limited to roles in the social universe. But I find that, looking at the symbolism of the tenth house from a metaphysical viewpoint, one can get valid data about how an individual can grow on the spiritual as well as the mental plane. At the very least, the tenth can guide one toward making one's life work more effective and rewarding.

Like other houses that signify one's experience of another individual playing a role, the tenth house also signifies how one plays tenth-house roles for others: how one will serve as a guide, authority, or disciplinary figure. As mentioned in connection with the fifth house, the tenth used to be one of the four houses signifying children. Even as the tenth signifies one's own experience of whoever played the father role, so it can also indicate one's own ability to play the role of father in relation to one's children. (Again, keep in mind that either parent can play the father role at various times.)

Internal Level   Even at the internal level, the tenth house does not operate in a vacuum totally apart from other people. In its concern with answering the questions "Who am I?," "What am I?," "What am I doing?," and "Where am I going?" it normally requires a social setting in order to arrive at its definitions of the self.

Whereas the ninth house symbolizes the greatest possible consciousness of the not-self, the tenth represents the greatest possible consciousness of the self. And while the ninth symbolizes the conscious mind reaching out to *experience* the external world, the tenth represents the conscious mind reaching out to *act* in the external world, to be an agent and play a role.

The tenth house at this level can also indicate the internalization of energies that were originally external. For example, we mentioned above that the tenth can indicate one's ability to play the father or guide-figure role toward another, especially a child. This results from one's internalizing one's own experience of fathering: the father figure, whoever it may have been, becomes an aspect of one's own mind. From this level comes the Freudian superego, which roughly corresponds to the conscience, the internal arbiter that decides between right and wrong.

Relational Level   The tenth house signifies all relationships between oneself and another in which there is inequality: where one person plays a dominant role to the other, who explicitly or implicitly takes the role of a child or dependent. The essence of such a relationship is that the person taking the dominant role teaches or guides the other. The inequality inherent in these relationships is usually normal and proper rather than pathological. The superior knowledge of the guide figure and the guidance being given are useful and necessary to the one receiving them.

External Level   At the external level is one's experience of those who act as guide figures, disciplinarians, authority figures, or people in power over one like bosses, employers, and government officials. The way one experiences these people is related to the way one experienced fathering in early life. Certain planetary indications can suggest that one may react strongly to kinds of fathering that embody that planet's energy, or that one may tend to attract authority figures with whom one has difficulty. This suggests that the difficulties one has with one's father or father figures (including, very likely, one's mother) are the source, or perhaps more accurately the first manifestation, of one's pattern of dealing with such people in later life. If no effort is made to become conscious and overcome this, one may spend one's whole life fighting the battles one fought with one's parents.

Planets in the Tenth House   A large number of planets in the tenth signifies a strong father orientation in the personality. This comes out as a need to achieve, to be and to be recognized as a person of importance in the world, to have others dependent upon one, and to justify one's self by the degree and quality of one's performance. An active tenth house does not guarantee fame, but it does usually indicate that one is or tries to be in charge of one's destiny.

Saturn in the tenth tries to act as a professional father-figure to others. This often comes out as schoolteachers who emphasize discipline and playing a proper role in society rather than stress the expansion of consciousness (which is a ninth-house style of teaching).

Neptune in the tenth can indicate one who has difficulty finding a role or life direction. Often the best resolution for this is to become involved in something that transcends one's individual importance. This may be a cause, a spiritual quest, or simply helping others. Pisces in the tenth house has a similar effect.

Uranus in the tenth can indicate someone who is uncomfortable with the whole idea of this house. It often expresses itself as an unusual calling or life direction.

The Eleventh House

One's friends and social circle. One's hopes, wishes, and ambitions.

There are two distinct themes in the traditional meanings of the eleventh house, and they are not obviously related. "Friends and social circle" can be understood in terms of the house's being above the horizon in opposition to the fifth house. But the origin of "hopes, wishes, and ambitions" is obscure. Hopes, wishes, and ambitions (or, collectively, aspirations) are in an above-the-horizon house, but it is not immediately clear how they relate to social contact or what sense they make in terms of the eleventh being in opposition to the house of play. I suspect that part of the mystery results from using "aspirations" in too broad a sense. The eleventh house probably does not indicate aspirations in general, but rather a particular kind of aspiration that does fit in with its other core meaning. After looking at the other core meaning it may become plainer how aspirations have to do with social relationships.

The eleventh house being in opposition to the fifth suggests that the two houses stand in some kind of polarity: that the eleventh house is in some way polarized to personal self-expression and play or activity pursued for its own sake. But we do not usually think of friends as opposed to play; in fact, they often go together.

The polarity exists in the idea of personal self-expression. The fifth house is almost completely self-centered. Even when it relates to love affairs, it relates to the personal enjoyment of love affairs and to one's ability to be oneself with another. Like the fifth, the eleventh is a highly self-expressive house, but the expression is socialized; that is, it occurs in a social context, and the self-expression is modified by the demands of relating to others. The eleventh house does not usually demand that one repress one's identity; rather, the identity is integrated with, and often expressed as part of, a group identity.

As the seventh house symbolizes one-to-one relationships, the eleventh can be thought of as one-to-many relationships. This includes friendships, for whereas people only have one mate, they usually have a number of friends. While the seventh house signifies an intense, face-to-face confrontation, the eleventh is more casual and oblique.

In addition to friendships, the eleventh house signifies relationships such as membership in societies, organizations, and other social groupings. For example, one's relationship to a corporation of which one is a member will be signified by the eleventh house.

The thing to remember is that the eleventh house describes one's ability to get along in any situation in which one has to relate to several people at once and in which one has to modify one's behavior in order to get along. At the same time, the friends or group must in return support the individual.

The eleventh house is above the horizon, indicating its social nature, and is also a succedent house, indicating it has something to do with resources. It is useful to think of it as a house of social attachments, in contrast to the second, which is a house of personal, often physical, attachments. As the second anchors one in the physical universe, the eleventh anchors one in the social universe. The idea of the eleventh as social attachments has roots in Hindu astrology, which uses basically the same house meanings as we do, but with some additions and deletions. The Hindu version of the eleventh signifies how one gets money. The second then becomes the house of what money one has rather than how it was gotten. Gaining money and resources is a direct function of one's social integration, and social interaction is necessary to do it.

Now let us turn back to the eleventh house as hopes, wishes, and ambitions, or, as we have summarized them, aspirations. First, I think that most interpretations of "ambition" do not properly belong to the eleventh house. As the need to be effective in general, ambition belongs to the first house, the house through which one makes an impact on one's immediate environment. Professional ambition is usually signified by the tenth. Social ambition, or the desire to be someone important, also belongs to the tenth, traditionally the house of one's social status and honor. Ambition probably should not be used at all as a keyword for the eleventh house.

"Hopes and wishes" implies ideals, and therefore this house is often called a house of ideals. I agree that there are ideals associated with the eleventh, but I do not call it primarily a house of ideals. I prefer to assign intellectual and philosophical ideals to the ninth house and moral and spiritual ideals to the twelfth.

But ideals and aspirations are influenced by one's group relationships, one's social class, one's friends, and one's associates in any field of activity. In fact, really to be part of a group means to share that group's ideals and aspirations. At the very least it means having ideals and aspirations that are compatible with the group's. One belongs to groups in order to work together for what all believe in. Thus the eleventh house becomes not a house of ideals and aspirations in general, but of shared ideals and aspirations, that are influenced and modified by the groups to which one belongs. This does not change the usual understanding of the eleventh house as much as one might think, because one's ideals and aspirations are seldom held in a vacuum; they are usually conditioned by group relationships to a much greater extent than one realizes.

Internal Level   On the inner level the eleventh house signifies one's need to reach out and establish contacts with others and become integrated into a group. Although the eleventh is one of the most social houses, it still has an internal dimension, that is, a level of energy that exists within the individual prior to any external manifestation. This can be seen when some planetary energies in this house (Saturn, for instance) indicate a reluctance to connect with groups, and the reasons for this reluctance can be seen only in terms of inward, personal criteria.

Also at this level is the eleventh as shared ideals and aspirations. Such ideals may seem at least partly to originate in external experience, yet the eleventh, as an eastern house, is a house in which acting upon one's world takes precedence over experiencing it. In other words, one has the ideals and aspirations to share with others before one finds the others with whom to share them. Then ideals may be modified by the resulting interaction.

Looking at the eleventh on the internal level as a house of group or social attachments, it can be seen as signifying one's ability to identify with other people, and to make the identity of the group as a whole part of one's personal identity. This relates the eleventh to the second house, which signifies one's tendency to make objects in the outer world part of one's identity.

Relational Level   At the self-other level, the eleventh house signifies lighter relationships like friendships as well as relationships in which one is part of a group. Such relationships are most of the time more superficial than partnerships, but occasionally they can become close, one-to-one seventh-house confrontations, as when two friends sit down for a heart-to-heart talk.

External Level   The eleventh house on the external level signifies the people and groups to whom we relate. As in all houses operating at the external level, these people embody energies from within ourselves.

Planets in the Eleventh House   A large number of planets in the eleventh usually signifies people who act out and experience a large part of their lives in connection with friends or social groups. They are not usually rugged individualists, because they need group support to feel right about their position in life. But they will not usually be followers, either. They will be active parts of the groups, which they will support and which will in turn support them. They will also share most of their ideals and aspirations with the group. In connection with the common idea of the eleventh house as hopes and wishes, I have seen little evidence that people with strong eleventh houses are any more hopeful or wishful than average.

By and large, the planets in the eleventh indicate the kind of friends one attracts, or the planetary energies one experiences in group contacts. Most planets do not greatly modify the effects of this house or inhibit the formation of group contacts, except for the following.

Saturn in the eleventh may indicate loners who are reluctant to form friendships. Such people may feel that friends or social groups demand too much of their energy and deny them opportunities for self-expression. They find it easier to be alone, where they at least have the freedom to do what they wish. When they do find a friend or group that does not inhibit them too much, friendships or group relationships can last a long time. Alternatively, Saturn in the eleventh may simply indicate a preference for Saturnine friends.

Uranus in the eleventh may also indicate difficulty in forming group contacts. The Uranian is often too independent to settle down and follow the ideals of any one group. But more commonly, Uranus in the eleventh indicates someone who forms contacts with Uranian groups or individuals.

If Pluto is in the eleventh and aspected so as to indicate the danger of power struggles, then it, too, can signify disruptions in one's group contacts.

On the other hand, the Sun or Moon in the eleventh indicates a particularly strong need for group interaction or for having friends. All other things being equal, these individuals will only really thrive when they live in the context of shared ideals and aspirations, which support them in their pursuit of life.

The Twelfth House

Self-undoing, sacrifice, karma. Secrets, secret enemies. Hospitals, institutions of confinement or imprisonment.

There are few traditional interpretations of the twelfth house that one could really look forward to experiencing. Not only does this house have a malefic reputation, it is also traditionally the weakest house, such that any planet placed in it is supposed to be of little or no use to the individual. Yet it is clear from the difficulties that people have with twelfth-house planets that it is not a weak house. Planets in this house often signify one's most serious difficulties in a way they could not do if they were weak.

In more recent times Gauquelin's work has demonstrated that as an indicator of profession and temperament, at least, the twelfth house is one of the strongest areas of the chart. Clearly, some sort of reevaluation is in order; I attempt one here and elsewhere in this book.

As I shall show in the next chapter, we can look at houses as a sequence of evolutionary stages not only in the traditional counterclockwise order starting with the first house, but also clockwise, starting at the I.C. and moving up into the third, second, first, twelfth, and back around to the fourth.

I raise this point now because, of all houses, the twelfth is made clearest by this scheme. Planets rise into the twelfth from the first after crossing the horizon in the east. The twelfth is where the Sun is just after dawn. This fact does not square with the traditional view of the twelfth as a dark, hidden, secret house. Dawn is not dark! But dawn *is* the first, tentative manifestation of the energy that has just come forth from the personal, inward hemisphere below the horizon. The twelfth is the house in which we first put energies out into the world. Such energies are immature, inexperienced, vulnerable, and easily defeated, but they do not have a weak effect on the personality. On the contrary, they are at a critical point and consequently have a strong, though sometimes hidden effect. If these energies become the focus of a crisis early in life, the negative consequences of such a crisis can be especially severe. We can look at such a situation in the following manner.

Consider the newly risen energies in the twelfth house to be the individual's first tentative attempts to put something out into the world. Vulnerable and inexperienced efforts, they are easily countered by more established energies and are often defeated. If so, the individual either consciously or unconsciously pulls these fledgling energies back into the inner self.

When a person consciously decides not to express one of these energies, it becomes one of the individual's secrets. More commonly, the individual cannot accept the energy as part of the self and so represses it into the unconscious mind.

But unacceptable energies must still manifest. If the conscious mind is unwilling or unable to accept them, they have only two places left to surface: the body, in which case the twelfth house becomes a house of sickness similar to the sixth, or the environment, in which case the energies manifest as other individuals who embody what one oneself fears. In other words, those aspects of the world that work against one—one's secret enemies, both individual and circumstantial—are nothing but embodiments of rejected aspects of oneself. They are rendered evil not by their intrinsic nature, but by one's rejection of them. This phenomenon has been noticed by depth psychologists. Any aspect of one's psychic energy that is not integrated into the whole system of psychic energy that makes up one's being becomes autonomous and alien. It is experienced either as something within that feels external, like possession by a spirit, or as something that appears totally external, such as a circumstance or person.

The twelfth house, insofar as it is a house of repressed and therefore unintegrated energies, is a house of the unconscious mind, of the personal unconscious, of one's private garbage heap. This is opposed to the fourth-house idea of the collective unconscious, the aspect of the psyche that is inherently unconscious rather than unconscious because of repression.

Energies that have been subjected to the twelfth-house process of repression are part of the self but not of the conscious identity. They confine one by working against one's expression. They undermine one's ego because they are denied by it. To the extent that one is attached to one's ego (or, more accurately, to the extent that one *is* rather than *has* an ego) and to the extent that one considers one's social identity to be what one truly is, the repressed energies of the twelfth house will work against one. Only insofar as one is able to detach oneself from the ego can these energies be made to work in one's favor. From the ego's point of view this is sacrifice.

Practically speaking, this means that in order to deal with twelfth-house energies that have been a source of difficulty, it may be necessary to do work with them in a way in which one's credit and reward is not an issue. This means altruistic work, done for another's sake or for a cause that goes beyond any individual. Working at a level higher than ordinary consciousness can understand, this activity will integrate twelfth-house energies into one's life and will enlarge and strengthen one's being. It is for this reason that many astrologers associate the twelfth house with sacrifice, spiritual work, and even enlightenment.

Karma as a meaning of the twelfth house comes from this same source. I believe that whatever energies may hang over from previous lives, the patterns associated with them are restated very early in this life. If it is difficult karma, these patterns are likely to be associated with some kind of twelfth-house difficulty.

I would like to take this opportunity to condemn what is called "karmic astrology." Many of its practitioners have taken to reading the twelfth house in terms of negative karma, that is, conditions that limit and structure this life without the individual being able to do anything but endure the consequences. Most often a limitation in this life is viewed as a punishment for sins of a past life.

This practice has several pernicious consequences. First, it is usually a projection onto the cosmos of the practitioner's own, usually primitive, Judeo-Christian morality. The astrologer speaks as a righteous prophet laying down the "word of God" to the client. This makes the client feel wrong and inadequate, and actually worsens the problems associated with the twelfth house, which is, to begin with, a house of rejected aspects of the self.

Second, because there is no reliable way of validating a previous incarnation, clients are put in the position of having to believe or disbelieve what they have been told. If they disbelieve, there may still be a lingering doubt that will weaken their ability to cope with the problem. If they believe, they are deprived of the opportunity to do anything about the problem. After all, what can one do about divine punishment? Also, being preoccupied with karmic causes, one is less likely to be in touch with experiences in this life that later on may throw light on the problem and enable one to do something about it. Astrologers exist to help those who want to understand and do something about their lives. They do not exist to dispense divine judgments.

Most of the above assumes that the energies of the twelfth house have been defeated in crises, resulting in repression and alienation of the self from the self. This is not always the case. In many people twelfth-house energies are not defeated in early life. For such people, twelfth-house planets become a source of strength, not difficulty, and come to signify dominant energies in their personalities and lives. This explains why the twelfth house can determine profession, and, what is even more important, dominant psychological characteristics, as shown in the research of Gauquelin.

Internal Level   Whereas in the first house we have the potential for putting energy out into the world, in the twelfth we have the energies that are actually put out. These energies can become sources of early-life defeats or victories, either of which may come to dominate the life. When defeated, these energies become part of our repressed or unacknowledged self, and their lack of integration with the conscious self may cause them to work against us and thereby to surface as our fears. When seen, these aspects of the self are seen as evil, or at best weaknesses. Often they are not seen at all, but can only be deduced from one's behavior or from the circumstances one draws to oneself.

In working out twelfth-house problems, it often helps for the ego to sacrifice itself in a way that is symbolically appropriate to the energies involved. Thus the individual can integrate these energies into the self at a level higher than the ego. In this way the twelfth house may tell as much about self-transcendence as the tenth. The tenth can signify the direction of self-transcendence, while the twelfth can tell what we have to do in order to go in that direction.

Relational Level   The twelfth house is very important at the self-other level because we often project the hidden aspects of ourselves onto our intimate relationships. In fact, the twelfth often tells as much as the seventh about intimate relationships, in that we are often driven into dealings with people who embody what we fear in ourselves. It is as if our non-integrated parts are seeking reunion with the rest of ourselves by coming back into life through another individual. Needless to say, such relationships are often difficult, because, being estranged from the twelfth-house aspects of oneself, one will have difficulty with anyone who embodies them. The people to whom we relate in this way are often like mirrors, able to tell us much about ourselves once we accept their relationship to us. Unless we accept their being a manifestation of ourselves, however, we will see ourselves as victims of their activity.

There are also positive twelfth-house relationships in which one serves another—not out of victimhood or martyrdom, but out of devotion. In such relationships, the negative energies of the twelfth house are transcended as they become symbols of something beyond the individual.

External Level   At the outer level of the twelfth house are all social circumstances and situations that are difficult because we find them undermining. These, too, are projections of our inner fears and sense of inadequacy.

The twelfth house can also represent social entities and circumstances that assist us in overcoming the consequences of our twelfth-house energies. These include hospitals and other institutions that care for us when we are in trouble with ourselves. They also include teachers and spiritual institutions. Through these, we can overcome our twelfth-house difficulties by learning to transcend our egos, recover the lost parts of ourselves, and expand those parts so they are capable of digesting and integrating the once-unacceptable energies.

Planets in the Twelfth House A large number of planets in the twelfth house means that a number of planets are in a critical stage. Since most people have difficulty handling several crises at once, it is likely that a person with many twelfth-house planets will fail to resolve some of the crises, and the planets that represent them will then become part of the negative twelfth-house energies discussed above.

One cannot usually deduce solely from the chart whether a twelfth-house energy will be a positive or a negative force. Contrary to what many astrologers believe, a twelfth-house energy is not necessarily difficult, and when it works positively, it is not limited to spiritual, self-denying, or ascetic activities. Take, for example, the Sun in the twelfth, the usual description of which indicates a retiring, withdrawn individual who prefers to be alone and who shuns the limelight. According to the birth data generally accepted, however, Jimmy Carter, Rosalynn Carter, and Henry Kissinger all have twelfth-house Suns. Of course, Kissinger has worked in a secretive manner, and the Carters have strong religious concerns and a greater than usual sense of privacy than have most people in politics. But none of these people can be called a shunner of the limelight (especially Kissinger, who seems to have greatly enjoyed being a public figure). These three cases as well as the Gauquelin data clearly indicate that not only can twelfth-house planetary energies be very evident in a personality, they can also work for, not against, an individual's ego expression so long as they have not been the subject of a major ego defeat early in life.

It must be acknowledged, however, that twelfth-house energies are often difficult for people to handle, and that many never do learn to use them effectively except possibly altruistically with little concern for personal gain. Each planet in the twelfth can indicate an energy from which one is alienated.

This is especially true if cultural or social conditions tend to work against the expression of that planetary energy in the individual. For example, for those who believe in traditional sex roles, Mars is too masculine an energy for women to express. Mars in the twelfth on top of the prevalent sexual stereotyping makes it doubly likely that a woman will be alienated from her own Mars energy, and will experience it through the men she attracts. Such men may be strong, aggressive, and independent, or, more likely, harsh, domineering, and arrogant. Usually Mars characteristics experienced in this way are negative, because the repression that the twelfth house symbolizes makes an energy negative. For men, the Moon or Venus in the twelfth may be difficult, at least in relationships with women, because, again, the repressive tendencies of the negative twelfth house reinforce the social training that puts men out of touch with their femininity.

15

The Houses: Two Alternative Views

Having covered the more common ways of looking at the houses, I would, before closing, like to take a more radical look at why houses have the meanings they do.

I believe that, basically, houses derive their meanings from two sources. One is the aspect relation the houses have to each other. I have already touched on the way a house can derive at least a part of its meaning from its position in relation to other houses. In the first half of this chapter I will discuss both what I feel is an abuse of deriving house meanings in this way and what I feel is its proper use.

The more important source of house meanings is probably the relation of the houses to the horizon and meridian circles. I will close this chapter with a demonstration of how house meanings become clearer when we see them growing out of a clockwise progress between these fundamental divisions.

Derived House Meanings: Their Use and Abuse

As you saw in the previous chapter, each house has several significations, most of which can be deduced from a single core meaning. But in discussing the eighth house I mentioned that at least some of its meanings come from the relationship of the eighth to other houses. For example, its meaning "other people's money" can be derived from the eighth house being the seventh house (other people) from the second (money). Or its being "the partner's money" can be derived from the eighth being the second house (money) from the seventh (the partner). These meanings do not follow directly from the core meaning of the eighth. They are derived, as opposed to intrinsic, meanings.

Although derived meanings do not follow directly from core meanings, I feel that in a certain way the core meanings are ultimately derived from the relationship of the houses to each other. After all, houses are stages in the day cycle, and the nature of any stage in a cycle comes from its unique relationship to every other stage. I have touched on the relation of the houses to each other in the section "Classifying the Houses" in Chapter 13 and in the house delineations themselves in Chapter 14. In the section to come I would like to show more explicitly how the meaning of a house can arise from its being in opposition, square, trine, sextile, semisextile, or quincunx to one of the other eleven houses. I will not only show how deriving house meanings from aspect relationships can give new insights into houses, but also how it can help you to interpret empty houses. Before getting to this, however, I find it necessary to dispose of a common and, I think, totally misguided, way of deriving house meanings.

Deriving House Meanings from House Relationships Derived meanings are often used so that every house is read as if it were the first house for the issue with which that house is associated. For example, taking the third house as the house of one's brothers and sisters, you can look at the fourth house as the second house from the third. This would make the fourth the house of the money or possessions of one's brothers and sisters. The horoscope's ninth house would be read as the seventh from the third, signifying the marriages and partnerships formed by one's brothers and sisters. The horoscope's seventh house would be the fifth from the third (the house in question is always counted as the first) and would indicate the children of one's brothers and sisters. And so forth.

According to the best evidence I have seen, this way of using derived house meanings was not originally applied to natal horoscopes at all, but was brought over to natal work from horary astrology. Horary astrology is a technique for answering specific questions, like "When will my lawsuit be settled?" or "Which team will win the World Series?". It seldom uses the natal horoscope, but instead uses a chart drawn up for the moment the question is asked. Suppose the question is "What will happen to my brother?". The horary astrologer would read all the houses as if the third house (brothers and sisters) were the first, just as I outlined above, looking at the fourth as the brother's finances, the fifth as the brother's neighbors and other siblings, the sixth as the brother's home, and so on around the circle.

It is easy to see how a natal astrology primarily interested in fortunetelling would adopt horary's method of using derived house meanings, because this method can cover specific questions about almost any conceivable issue. But just as I question a fortunetelling approach in natal astrology, I also question reading the houses in this way. Derived house meanings like this work best in an astrology that is trying to be definite about future events, which implies that such events cannot be changed. Yet neither I nor most other modern astrologers believe the future is immutable.

These meanings work well *only* with simple-minded, concrete house interpretations. With the core psychological meanings from which these more superficial meanings originate, they work ungracefully at best. Even if it is not philosophically profound, the derived fifth-house meaning "a parent's money" is at least clear. But when the fifth house is reinterpreted as the second house from the fourth in terms of the basic psychological significance, it becomes "the attachments to the physical world of the energies associated with one's experience of nurture." Even if one could make sense out of this, its relation to the core idea of the fifth, "activities pursued for their own sake," remains obscure.

Basing derived house interpretations on core meanings may produce nonsense, but basing them on fortunetelling meanings implies that the superficial meanings are more fundamental than the psychological and philosophical ones. This cannot be so. If it were, it would mean that your tenth house is not the experience of fathering energies, but is literally your father as an objectively real person, and that every other house describes not your experience of reality but the reality itself. If that is so, what do you do with two brothers, one with Saturn conjunct Neptune in the tenth, and the other with Jupiter in the tenth trining the Sun? They had the same father, yet their experience of fathering differed. Obviously the symbolism does not describe the reality of the father or father figures, but the experience of being fathered. Any other system of core meanings would have the same problem with derived house significations, as long as it was based on the idea that houses describe not objective realities, but energies that modify experience.

My other objection to using horary-type derived house meanings in natal astrology is similar to my objection to using planetary dignities to connect planets to houses (see Chapter 10). It increases the possibilities for interpretation to the point where a single house can mean almost anything. To give an example, does an indication in the fifth house pertain to one's having children (intrinsic meaning), to one's parent's finances (second from the fourth), to the death of the other parent (eighth from the tenth), or to one of nine other possible meanings? How are we to judge which meaning is the important one? In horary, the possibilities are narrowed down by the question asked, but in natal astrology the things one could say about a person are almost infinite. Such a wide set of possibilities with no guidelines for judging which is the strongest can only create confusion when you are trying to make sense out of a situation. As with other suspect techniques, this one is useful chiefly when an astrologer is either (a) psychic or (b) trying to explain an event after it has happened.

Deriving House Meanings from Aspect Relationships   The above idea of house interpretations implies that houses are more fundamental than aspects. Indeed, many astrologers think that the aspects derive their meanings from house relationships. Therefore, their reasoning runs, all squares have the nature of the relationship between the fourth or tenth house to the first, so that all squares affect relations with one parent or the other. Similarly, all trines have a fifth- or a ninth-house quality; all oppositions, a seventh-house quality; and so on. But modern evidence indicates that things are in fact the other way around: houses derive their meanings—in part, at least—from the aspects.

Houses make mundane aspects to each other, as opposed to the zodiacal aspects we are more used to dealing with. Houses aspect each other in the plane on which the particular house system is based. Only in equal house systems is this plane the ecliptic. Rather than being whole-number subdivisions of a planet's progress around the zodiac, aspects between houses are usually whole-number subdivisions of the various ways astrologers measure the daily rotation of the Earth. Thus the fourth house is in a non-ecliptic square to the first, the fifth in a trine, the sixth in a quincunx, and so forth.

The idea that house relationships are determined by the aspects that each house forms with every other house can be extended to all house relationships. And when one approaches derived house meanings in this way, the meanings that emerge are compatible with, and clearly related to, the intrinsic meanings described in Chapter 14. We do not have to resort to superficial interpretations, and neither do we acquire a tremendous array of additional meanings for each house that makes delineation hopelessly complicated. I believe that the traditional derived interpretations of houses that work do so because they are compatible with the principle of deriving house meanings from aspects.

Below are some specific examples of how each aspect can relate a pair of houses. These meanings are derived from the aspect meanings presented in Chapter 7.

Opposition. Opposite houses create consciousness and understanding concerning each other's issues. Each tends to counteract or balance the excesses of the other, identifying what needs to be done whenever an issue associated with the other house threatens to dominate. The opposition has the quality of polarization, which can sometimes bring about conflict.

Examples: If one is self-centered (overdeveloped first house), a close relationship (seventh house) will help to correct this. A seventh-house relationship can also help bring out aspects of the personality (first house) that might otherwise stay hidden.

Similarly, an extreme fifth-house manifestation like doing whatever one wishes without considering others may be corrected by eleventh-house activities with friends and groups of people.

If one becomes too enslaved to one's possessions (second house), one often encounters circumstances that force one to give them up (eighth house). This can take the form of house cleaning, taxes, or even death (the giving up of one's goods and physical body). Except (as far as we know) for death, one often increases in awareness as a result.

Becoming too preoccupied with everyday reality (third house) is corrected by ninth-house matters that pull one's awareness out of that world into broader perceptions.

Likewise, becoming overly wrapped up in one's intimate, personal circle (fourth house) is offset by tenth-house matters that draw one out into the greater world where one functions as an adult. But if one's calling or career (tenth house) becomes too strong an issue, one can retire to one's home and family environment (fourth house) to recoup one's energies.

Trine. Houses in trine indicate areas of life that are related in ways that are outlined in the "House Triplicities" section of Chapter 13. Such houses reinforce each other, creating energy systems that interlock easily and which normally work together in a harmonious, or at least a consistent, way.

Examples: The so-called "personal houses" one, five, and nine are all areas where one releases one's energy into the world. One's general impact on one's surroundings (first house) is aided and abetted by one's self-expression (fifth house) and by roaming far and wide (ninth house). Or, one's effectiveness in the world (first house) is enhanced by one's ability to enjoy oneself (fifth house) and one's ability to see the overall picture (ninth house).

Among the "practical houses," the work activities and vocation signified by houses six and ten make possible the possessions signified by house two. Conversely, possessions such as tools make sixth-house work easier. Ideally, one's daily job (sixth house) furthers one's life purpose (tenth house). And the possessions one owns (second house) often determine or are determined by one's social status (tenth house).

Among the "social houses," the kind of relationship one has with one's partner (seventh house) often blends into the kind of relationship one has with people in one's everyday world (third house) and with friends (eleventh house). Although one's actual friends may be in conflict with one's partner or siblings, each house's type of relating supplements that of the others.

The hidden parts of the psyche symbolized by the "unconscious houses" also feed into and reinforce each other. One's earliest home life and sense of being nurtured (fourth house) have much to do with the repressed energies that tend to be our undoing (twelfth house). Feelings about sex and death and giving our possessions up to others (eighth house) are another source of twelfth-house repression. And repression is often overcome in the course of psychological "death and resurrection." Also, our sense of being nurtured and protected in early life (fourth house) has much to do with our feeling free to let go (eighth house) of possessions, ego, body, or whatever else makes us feel secure in adult life.

Square. Houses in square indicate areas of life that test each other, forcing the issues associated with each to become more clearly defined and take on more definite meaning. Often a symbolic statement in the individual's life will take on concrete form. There may be conflict between the two areas, but the conflict is necessary.

Examples: An infantile personality, reluctant to venture away from the nurturing atmosphere of home (fourth house), cannot make an effective impact (first house) on the world. One must grow up in order to deal with the world as a personality in one's own right.

The tenth house, indicating fathering, tests one's ability to deal with the world, as for instance when the parent tells the child how to behave. Or, one's effective interaction with the outside world (first house) demands knowing what one's goals are (tenth house). Or there may be a conflict between one's personal expression (first) and one's sense of duty to society (tenth).

A second-fifth square may signify a conflict between one's attachments in the world and the pure self-expression of energy. For example, earning money may take up so much time that one has no time for pleasure; or one may spend so much time playing there is no time for earning a living.

An eighth-eleventh square may signify the conflict between an eighth-house transformation of the self and eleventh-house social involvements.

Sextile. Houses related by sextile represent activities that support each other, even though they are not as closely related as those signified by houses in trine. It takes slightly more effort and awareness to bring such activitites into a cooperative relationship.

Examples: Social involvements (eleventh house) are often useful to an individual in making an impact on the surrounding world (first house). Likewise, friends can usually count on one for help when necessary.

The first-third sextile works in a similar manner: for the eleventh house's friends, substitute the third's relatives and neighbors. Also, the third's semiautomatic consciousness that deals with everyday surroundings liberates one's mind to be more effective in dealing with others and putting energies out into the world.

Physical security (second house) is one of the things that makes emotional security (fourth house) more likely to happen. Or, one's financial resources determine the quality of the place in which one lives. Or, one's possessions are usually stored in one's home.

Semisextile. This is a sometimes ambiguous relationship, in that the affairs of adjacent houses often seem totally unrelated and even antithetical. And yet each house is in some way completed by the house that follows it. This is especially true taking the odd-numbered houses as the first of each pair.

Examples: An activity pursued for its own sake (fifth house) must be supported by other activities that are pursued for the sake of something else (sixth house). One keeps the body in good shape for sports and other enjoyments (fifth house) by eating sensibly and doing exercises (sixth house), bathes and dresses (sixth) before going out on a date (fifth), or gains the money for a vaction (fifth) by working at a job (sixth).

The ninth and the tenth illustrate the way adjacent houses lead into one another and also the strain that occurs between them. Using the greater awareness of the external world gained in the ninth house, one can know how to make one's way in the world more effectively in the tenth. But the ninth's philosophical and idealistic tendencies can be difficult to reconcile with the tenth's practical concerns.

Quincunx. The quincunx relationship is similar to the semisextile, except that the ambiguity is greater and the extent to which the two houses make up a whole is less. Houses in quincunx often seem to restrict each other and to create a kind of negative equilibrium in which neither can operate effectively. Unlike the square, which forces a perhaps unpleasant but very useful testing and concretization of the affairs of the houses involved, the quincunx may reach a point of stasis in which neither house is able to operate effectively and no progress is made. Only a tremendous increase in self-awareness can reveal the thread that unites the two houses. In order to render the relationship useful, this thread must be found.

Examples: The classic cases are the first-sixth and first-eighth quincunxes. If the first house is seen as one's ability to make an impact on one's surroundings, the sixth is the limitations necessity imposes on one's freedom to do so, and the eighth is the letting-go of ego that threatens to disrupt one's usual manner of confronting the world. It is easy to see how relations between these houses can reach an impasse. Limitations can constantly hinder without really stopping one, and the fear of letting go can actually lock one into ineffective ways of dealing with the world.

Similarly, if the first house is the physical body, then the sixth, as illness, limits the activities of the physical body while at the same time illness is an attempt to restore the body's equilibrium. Unless insight is achieved, it is all too easy to become stuck in having chronic minor complaints, with the body somewhat limited and constantly trying to right itself. The body can also balk at a major transformation (eighth house) that would free it but at the same time destroy its established way of interacting with the environment.

Using Aspect-Derived House Meanings in Delineation   What I have been discussing here is not just abstract speculation: it also has a practical application, particularly in delineating empty houses.

Suppose we are examining someone's one-to-one relationships, and the seventh house is empty, but there are several planets in the tenth. The seventh and the tenth are in mundane square. The horary approach would be to say that the tenth house, being the fourth from the seventh, refers to the home or family roots of the relationship. The loaded tenth house implies that from the viewpoint of the relationship there is a strong concern with finding a home or location where the relationship can take place. But experience has shown that a strong tenth house coupled with a weak seventh does not indicate a relationship looking for a home. Rather, it indicates a person whose relationships run afoul of a much more highly developed need to get out into the world, achieve something of importance in social terms, and find a rewarding career or life direction. These goals will be more important than finding a relationship that works. Or, if you look at the seventh house as non-marital partnerships (such as business partnerships), you will find that the heavy tenth indicates a person too concerned with his or her own achievements to be very good at the give-and-take of an equal partnership. You don't need to use horary-type derived house meanings to deduce from a loaded tenth house something about every other house's issues as well. This method works even when there are no planets in aspect between the houses in question.

To take another example, suppose you have a heavily populated eleventh house and an empty seventh. The eleventh and seventh houses are in mundane trine. This indicates that the issues of the two houses support each other, or at least interact in a regular, ongoing way that never causes crises in either of the houses. This suggests an easier time with one-to-one relationships. But instead of having a truly intimate quality, these relationships will always be more like friendships—less intense, and having less of the dialectical quality associated with the seventh. This is because the individual's style of relating is set by the loaded eleventh house rather than the empty seventh.

Now suppose a pair of planets is in a trine that goes from the seventh to the tenth. In other words, there is a zodiacal trine involving houses that are in mundane square. This suggests that the person has a relatively easy time connecting intimate one-to-one relationships with career. At least the two areas are not experienced as unrelated or tensely related. Marriage or other partnerships may further the career, or the marriage may be made closer by common career interests with the partner. The trine is a smooth-flowing link, but its results are not necessarily constructive. The trine involving the seventh and tenth houses can also indicate someone who cannot keep a clear distinction between personal relationships and career.

Let us reverse the pattern and look at houses that are in mundane trine containing planets that are in zodiacal square. Looking at the eleventh and seventh, we get an indication of a possible tension between group relationships and intimate, one-to-one relationships. This can take the negative form of friendships that disrupt marriage or partnerships, or it can force one to make clear distinctions between the demands and obligations of friends and those of one's intimate partner. Unlike the trine, the square does require one to give concrete form to the energies that are in aspect. No looseness or vagueness is allowed; the issues of the two houses test each other. In this example, one is forced or at least obliged to put the two modes of relationship into separate compartments so that they do not overlap and therefore conflict.

Mundane aspects between houses are the most useful when you are considering empty houses. When houses are occupied, I find that the zodiacal aspects between the planets tell more about the interaction of the houses involved. Whereas mundane aspects between houses show the inherent relation between the issues of those houses, the zodiacal aspects of planets show how the inherent relation of the house issues is changed by the perspective of the individual.

The Case for Clockwise Houses

You may have noticed that, while the houses mark the clockwise daily motion of the planets, they are numbered in counterclockwise order like the signs. Deferring to convention, in Chapter 14 I discussed the houses in the usual counterclockwise order. Here, however, I will take a fresh look at them in the order that the planets actually move through them in the course of a day. This, I believe, will shed further light on the core meanings of the houses, helping to solve the mystery of where these meanings originated.

When you think about the direction the planets move in during the course of a day, rising in the east and setting in the west, counting the houses in a clockwise order seems quite plausible. If you will recall, at least one house system, the *oktotopos*, was in fact numbered in clockwise order. But the idea of looking at houses in this way does not often occcur to people, probably because the houses have become identified with the signs, which the planets transit in a mainly counterclockwise fashion.

It is not clear whether the twelve houses were originally intended to be related to the twelve signs, but at least in Ptolemy and other Greek writers no strong relationship exists between the meanings of the signs and the houses. Neither does there seem to be any strong connection in the Renaissance. Yet in modern times there has been an increasing identification of the houses with the signs, such, for example, that Aries and the first house are considered by many writers to be essentially the same, albeit on different levels. Some have extended this and considered the first house, the sign Aries, and the planet Mars (Aries's ruler) to parallel each other in meaning.

But there are problems with this. Not only does the primary motion of the planets go in the opposite direction from the secondary motion, the high points of the two cycles are different. The Midheaven derives its meaning from the fact that the Sun is on the Midheaven at noon. This is the peak of the day cycle, when people are most active and involved with each other. The Midheaven's association with fame, honor, and social standing comes from its association with the elevated position of the Sun.

When we associate the signs with the houses, however, the Midheaven corresponds to the beginning of Capricorn. This is the winter solstice, the time when, in the Northern Hemisphere, the Sun reaches its lowest declination. This is the low point of the year, the time when all life is at an ebb. By the same token, the I.C., which is the location of the Sun at midnight, the bottom of the day cycle, would be connected to the summer solstice, the peak of the seasonal cycle in the Northern Hemisphere.

The symbolism is no better in the Southern Hemisphere. True enough, the beginning of Capricorn is the high point of the Southern Hemisphere's seasonal cycle, making it analogous to noon, the high point of the day cycle. But spring in the Southern Hemisphere begins with Libra, which we associate with the seventh, not the first, house. Spring means that the Sun is crossing the equator and increasing in declination, whereas at the seventh-house cusp the Sun or other planets are crossing the horizon and decreasing in altitude.

Some astrologers, such as those of the Uranian school, have tried to change this by making the Midheaven correspond to the beginning of Cancer, and the I.C. to the beginning of Capricorn. But then this makes the first house associated with Libra, not Aries. Again, as with the Southern Hemisphere example, an increase in altitude is linked to a decrease in declination.

Despite these differences, real similarities do of course exist between the signs and the houses. It is natural that two twelvefold divisions of cycles into phases would exhibit parallelisms. And in fact, day-for-a-year progressions are based on the idea of the parallelism of the day cycle and the year cycle. But we must not be blinded by thinking that the cycles are identical. By concentrating too much on their similarities, we tend to overlook the obvious astronomical fact that planetary motion within the houses is clockwise.

In order to see how well house symbolism works in a clockwise order, let us first take one more look at the symbolism of the horoscope angles and hemispheres.

The Two Poles of Being   There appear to be two sources of energies that we experience as separate from our conscious being. The energies of both seem to cause events in our lives that appear to be beyond our control. The first and most obvious source is the outer world, the circumstances of which seem to shape our lives without any help from us. The other source is our inner depths. Likewise, the urges welling up from the unconscious seem to the conscious mind as if they come from an external source. In fact, in many cultures these urges have been attributed to gods or demons.

Ultimately it is likely that, unawares, we are the source of both energies. But at the level at which we play the game of life, it seems as though we are standing midway between the two poles, neither of which we feel is really a part of us. Our free will seems limited to an area in between, where the two sources of energy are nearly in equilibrium.

This middle zone is represented in the horoscope by the horizon. The Earth is what we are standing on, and the horizon is the level at which we live. Hidden deep beneath us is the I.C., representing the inner pole of energies, and high overhead is the Midheaven, representing the outer pole.

During the course of a day, every day, all the planets rise upward in a clockwise fashion from the I.C., past the Ascendant, to the Midheaven. And then they descend from the Midheaven, past the Descendant, back to the I.C.

Therefore, in the eastern hemisphere of the chart planetary energies are proceeding from the inner pole toward the outer. This hemisphere is primarily under the influence of the inner energies. It stands for action that is either our own or the product of our inner life, such as impulses and emotional drives.

In the chart's western hemisphere, the energies are on their way from the outer pole toward the inner. Therefore the western hemisphere is under the influence of the outer energies. It stands for actions of others, our experience of the outer world, and the manner in which we incorporate this experience of the outer world into our inner being.

The Four Quadrants We now have an inner and an outer pole of being, with the horizon marking the boundary between the inner and outer realms. The I.C.-Midheaven axis and the Ascendant-Descendant axis divide the horoscope into four quadrants, which we number clockwise from the I.C. Starting from the I.C. (instead of the Ascendant) is much like starting our day at midnight. This way we will see the upward sweep of energies from their most secret and private to their most public manifestation, and back down again. And the old symbolism of the fourth house suggests that the I.C. is a proper starting place. The fourth house is the womb, just prior to birth. It is also the tomb, and the end of the matter. Although I am starting at the I.C. rather than the Ascendant and proceeding clockwise, I will keep the usual house numbering to minimize confusion.

Quadrant I (houses three, two, and one) is a quadrant in the inward hemisphere dominated by energy flowing from the inner pole. It suggests one's experience of the inward and personal dimensions of life as they are influenced by inner impulses.

Quadrant II (houses twelve, eleven, and ten) is an outer quadrant dominated by energy flowing from the inner pole. It indicates our personal action on, and incorporation into, the outer world.

Quadrant III (houses nine, eight, and seven) is an outer quadrant dominated by energy flowing from the outer pole. It indicates external energies coming toward us from outside, our experience of those energies, and those external aspects of our lives that seem not to be under our personal control or influence.

Quadrant IV (houses six, five, and four) is an inner quadrant dominated by a flow from the outer pole. It suggests those aspects of our personal world that are most affected by external energies, and our incorporation of those energies into our inner being.

Subdividing the Quadrants   Since the progress from one angle to the next is a continuum with no sharp boundaries, it is possible to divide the quadrants into any number of parts. So that an alien scheme does not become more alien, however, I will retain the subdivision of each quadrant into three parts. In this way you will have an indication of how the twelve conventional houses would derive their meanings from the clockwise movement of energies.

From analyzing the houses, it appears that the logical threefold subdivision of each quadrant would be into the following phases:

1. *Entry*, corresponding to the cadent houses. Crossing into a new quadrant, a planetary energy enters as an alien force which meets with resistance in the new realm. Its initial difficulties in adjusting produce a crisis.

This view of the cadent houses accounts for both their traditionally evil reputation and the fact that the Gauquelin research finds them to be strong. Having just emerged from the angle, the planetary energies are fresh and at the beginning of a cycle. But the resistance they meet often produces difficulties. It is also possible that the challenge of a crisis calls forth the full strength of a planetary energy.

Traditionally, houses twelve and six are considered much more difficult than houses three and nine, and I have observed this to be true. The reason for this becomes clear from the model I have proposed. While we are likely to experience the I.C. and Midheaven areas as being separate from our consciousness and will, the areas about the horizon are "where we live," so to speak. Thus the shifts and discontinuities that occur here are more difficult for us to deal with. Looked at another way, the Ascendant and Descendant are those critical points where our inner being must confront the outer world. The change from one realm to another is a more difficult shift than the simple change of direction that happens at the Midheaven and I.C. Yet another explanation is that houses three and nine are in mundane sextile and trine to the Ascendant-Descendant axis, whereas houses six and twelve are in quincunx and semisextile to this vital axis of confronting the world.

2. *Incorporation and fixation*, corresponding to the succedent houses. This is a phase of settling in. Planetary energies adjust and reach their point of maximum integration into the new quadrant. As they approach this point, they become stable and cease being the subject of major tensions. Being at a point of fixity, they have little impact, at least from the standpoint of the dynamic development of the personality. This may explain the Gauquelin findings that planets seem to manifest least strongly when in this part of the quadrants.

3. *Preparation*, corresponding to the angular houses. Planetary

energies now prepare to enter a new quadrant and a new crisis stage, and are busy laying foundations for the changeover. Following the stillness of the incorporation phase, planetary energies are beginning to become active again. But they have not yet reached the pitch of activity that they will reach in the crisis phase. This seems to correlate with the sharp upward swing planetary strength seems to take in the Gauquelin findings as the planets approach the angles from the angular houses.

The signs and other planets encountered in the preparation phase determine whether the energy will enter the next quadrant with ease or difficulty.

The Dynamics of the Quadrants   We are now ready to look at the succession of the houses in the quadrants. As you will see, though the conventional counterclockwise scheme was presented first for the sake of familiarity, the clockwise scheme has in fact been the origin of many of the observations made in this book. The meanings we come up with when looking at the houses clockwise will be much like the meanings already stated, but now their origin should be clearer. Even with the houses viewed clockwise, we still have the operation of each on an internal, relational, and external level.

Quadrant I. In the first quadrant, the flow from the inner pole begins to impinge on consciousness. In general, we experience this flow as impulses, compulsions, and desires that we do or do not wish to have.

In the third house, the flow from the inner pole programs and structures the awareness with which we deal with everyday reality. The third house is our experience of and reaction to psychic energy as it flows from our innermost patterns of thinking. At the external level, this affects our speech, communications, and everyday dealings with the world. We do not normally experience this energy as critical except that we are usually somewhat out of control of what we are doing, and this can cause difficulties when the patterns are inappropriate. How many of us are really aware of our innermost mental programing and the ways it affects our innermost mental processes? We can become aware of it, but we are not usually so.

In the second house, the flow from the inner is stabilized. As in all the middle trisections or succedent houses, this stabilization, fixation, and incorporation process consists of becoming attached to something. In the second house the issue is attachment itself. To feel secure, we build structures within ourselves to prepare for launching ourselves into the outer world. On the external level, this manifests as attaching ourselves to possessions, which make us feel more secure, effective, independent, and capable of dealing with what we will encounter.

In the first house, we gather our inner energies in order to make an impact on the outer world at the Ascendant. Consequently, this is the house that most affects how others see our energies. Thus the first house describes our personality, in the sense of the face that we present to the outside world.

It seems to me that the meaning of the first house becomes much clearer when viewed in a clockwise framework. Going counterclockwise from the first, we are moving toward the inward pole, but going clockwise we are moving toward the outer, more public area of life. It is toward the public area of life that the personality is directed.

Quadrant II. The energy now crosses the Ascendant. The flow from the inner that seemed slightly alien in the third house is now completely ours as it crosses into the upper hemisphere. This quadrant represents inner energy with which we attempt to act upon the world.

The twelfth house is one of the most important houses in the chart. It is here that our inner energies meet their first challenge as they encounter the outer world. Because these energies are raw and untried, the encounter is often unsuccessful.

The eleventh house is another area of stabilization, fixation, and incorporation. As in every other middle trisection, a feeling of separateness disappears. In the twelfth we felt that the outer world resisted us, but this feeling vanishes in the eleventh. Here our inner energy establishes itself and becomes integrated into the outer world. The eleventh is thus the area in which we integrate ourselves into groups. Whereas the second house represented attachment to possessions, the eleventh represents attachment to our niche in society.

In some schools of Hindu astrology, the eleventh house relates to the way one gets money, whereas the second only relates to the way one deals with the money one already has. This fits well into our scheme because getting money involves the way we present ourselves to and act upon the outside world. The second house does not at its deepest level mean having money; it symbolizes the way we attach ourselves to entities in our personal lives. The eleventh is the process of making the attachment to something external or social. Money always comes from outside sources.

In both the clockwise and counterclockwise schemes, the second house (having money) precedes the eleventh (getting it in the first place), so that the effect appears to precede the cause. This is not a problem, however, when you remember that though we can speak of energy beginning at one or the other poles, we are actually talking about motion around a wheel, which has no beginning or end. Energy does not merely move from pole to pole, it is carried around the wheel completely, again and again. Our experiences (the western half of the chart) are the consequence of our actions (eastern half), and vice versa. Our inner lives arise from our outer circumstances, and our outer circumstances arise from our inner lives.

The tenth house is the phase when planetary energy reaches its outermost projection. This can manifest as career, calling, or the way we transcend ourselves. Here we can show the way to others who follow us, which is why this house represents the fatherly aspect of parenting.

As with the other houses, the tenth does not always work at the external level. Contrary to what many astrologers believe, a populated tenth house does not necessarily mean an individual concerned with social status or being in the public eye. People with a strong tenth house may instead choose to manifest its internal or relational level. They may be retiring in a social sense but choose to be guide figures to those in their personal world. Such people may be teachers either professionally or informally.

Quadrant III. Crossing the Midheaven, we shift from an area primarily concerned with the action of the inner upon the outer to an area where the outer is the primary source of energy. But, as mentioned above, energy also comes over from the other side, manifesting as our experience of things in the outer world that arise as a consequence of our own actions.

Just as in the third house energy from the inner pole imprinted our inner consciousness, in the ninth energy from the outer pole imprints our outer consciousness. Being above the horizon here, we are dealing with a much more conscious type of thought. So the ninth house symbolizes our ability to see energies coming into our lives from far off, long before these energies can affect us intimately. In the ninth we have the perspective for seeing the big picture and the patterns that integrate things.

These energies often seem strange and alien because they originate so far from our intimate lives. We need to strain to adjust our consciousness to comprehend what we see. This may require an expansion of consciousness, or leaving familiar environments for ones distant from our own. This is why the ninth is associated with long-distance travel and whatever is foreign.

The eighth house is another area of fixation, stabilization, and incorporation. The energies of the outer were in the ninth house in many ways too distant and too newly entered into our lives to affect us except at the level of expanding consciousness. In the eighth house these energies consolidate and begin to attach themselves in our world so that they can become effective with respect to ourselves. Here we have the eighth house as the opposite of the second. On the external level, eighth-house attachments are property and physical resources, but those of other people, not our own. On the internal level, the eighth house signifies the way the outer world attaches itself to us, pulling us away from those personal concerns and attachments that limit us. Thus it allows, if not forces, us to grow. This leads to the ideas of transformation and death. In terms of the clockwise scheme, the eighth house pulls us away from our own attachment structure toward something external and sometimes higher than our own personal, intimate levels of being.

The seventh house signifies the energy of the outer preparing to enter the personal, inner world. The outer energy becomes as intimate as it can be while not yet within us. Thus the seventh house represents our experience of the intimate other, our polar complement in the outer world. This can mean a personal enemy as well as a lover.

Seen in this light, the seventh house also signifies what we perceive as the "personality" of the outer world, what we expect from other people, especially those close to us. This is the obvious polar counterpart to the first house as personality. But just as the first house is our expression of the self on an intimate level with respect to others, so the seventh house is usually our experience of others on an intimate level.

Quadrant IV. As the energy crosses the horizon, there is another crisis.

The sixth house has always been considered difficult because as the energies of the outer come into the inner hemisphere, the inner resists them. We strive to take in and assimilate the energy of the outer in this house, but just as the inner energy was a stranger in the twelfth, the outer energy is a stranger in the sixth.

The sixth is a house of health because our health depends so much on how we react to what we take in. Psychosomatic illness often results from taking in at the psychological level energies that we cannot handle. We then experience on the physical level a symbol of our rejection of that energy.

On the psychological level, in the sixth house we experience our personal lives shaped by externally imposed energies. Our wills can feel constrained by the externally imposed limitations of work, duty, and responsibility. Yet as with the twelfth, if we overcome the limitations we experience in the sixth, we can make the energies work to our own ends. This is why the area relates not only to our work for others, but also to others who work for us.

In the sixth house, the external energies are experienced as alien and intrusive. There is still an awareness of separation between our inner lives and the externally derived energies.

The fifth house, however, completes the assimilation. The energy of the outer is integrated into the inner, just as in the eleventh the inner energies are integrated into the outer. In the fifth house we are no longer aware of resistance to the outer energy. What we have experienced is now our own. We can stop fighting it and use it. This and the fact that the fifth house is in mundane trine to the first makes us experience the fifth as a house of self-release. Our working with the energies of the outer is no longer work, that is, activity directed by an externally imposed necessity. Now it is the expression, within the inner part of the self, of energies that were originally derived from the outer part of the self. (Keep in mind that we are never really talking about energies that are truly external, but rather about energies that are experienced as external.) This is why, while the fifth symbolizes play in both the highest and most trivial aspects of the word, the games played here are usually played with, and invented with the aid of, others.

I mentioned in the previous chapter's discussion of the fifth that having children is an activity pursued for its own sake, that there is often no special purpose served by having children. Yet looking at the reasons most people have children, it seems as if a deeply internal drive to procreate originates in social necessity. Fifth-house activities are often spontaneous personal expressions of drives that began in the outer pole.

The fourth house is where the energy of the outer makes its deepest intrusion into the inner and becomes part of the most private famework of the individual. The fourth house symbolizes one's experience of the womb, nurture, and one's infantile support system, but all these come ultimately from the outer pole. To complete the idea of the dialectic between outer and inner, what we are inwardly is to a great extent what we were given by those who preceded us in the outer world. And what we experience is the result of what we put out into the world. The cycle of energy is continuous. There is no real distinction between the energies of the inner and the outer, except what comes from the splitting of our experience. The end of the matter is the beginning.

Starting at the I.C. and going clockwise around the chart, the fourth house is the last. Even as we were born out of the Earth, our ultimate mother, in death we return to her. In the course of life, we go from dust to dust, or from the Earth (the I.C.) to the Earth—only, presumably, to begin the cycle again.

The Relationship between the Two Views of the Houses I feel that the clockwise model is the better one from which to derive the significations of the houses. Yet I am aware that there are years of tradition and practice working against its general acceptance. I am also not convinced that the counterclockwise model is totally invalid, as the planets do go through the houses both clockwise in their primary motion and mostly counterclockwise in their secondary or zodiacal motion. It is thus inevitable that coherent patterns of cyclical change would emerge looking at the cycles in either direction.

I think we will get the best results if we suspend our prejudices and look at the houses both ways. This will help us better to understand the core meanings of the houses, and will liberate us from the superifical understanding of them that we may have had in the past.

For those who are completely closed to this bi-directional approach, I would like to point out that the signs are also bi-directional. The Moon's nodes, at least, transit the signs in reverse order, clockwise. We could easily derive a clockwise model for the sign cycle that would give us new insights into the signs and their symbolism. In fact, Carl Payne Tobey has already done so in his book *Astrology of Inner Space*. But a clockwise discussion of the signs is not so essential. I have treated the clockwise interpretation of the houses here because, contrary to the general perception, the more significant motion of the planets through the houses happens to be clockwise.

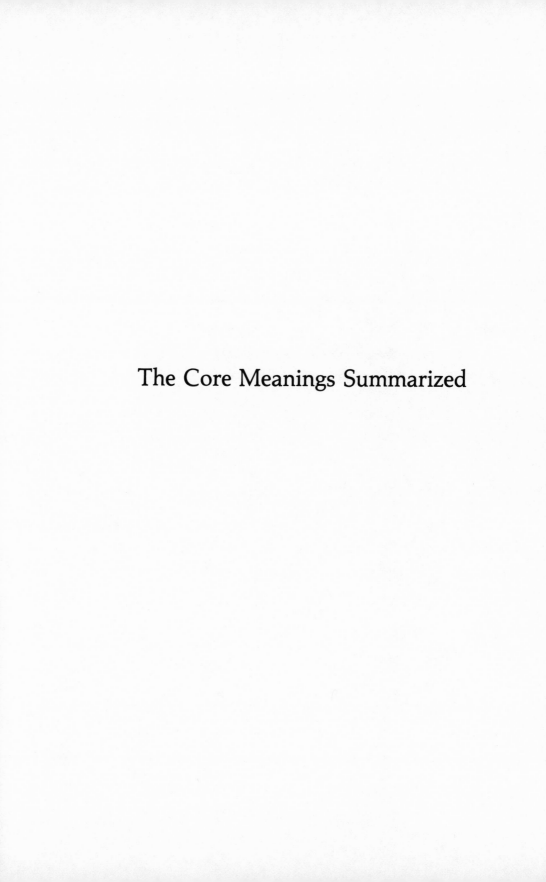

The Core Meanings Summarized

Planets

The Sun

Yang: the basic energy of being; light, consciousness, will, power, desire ('wanting to'), integrity, individuation; libido (Jungian sense); physical energy; the Hero, masculinity, initiative, independence; fathering, the experience of having one's autonomous will fostered; fatherhood; rulers of a country as opposed to their subjects.

The Moon

Yin: Container, medium, environment, matrix, womb, mothering, home; subjects as opposed to their rulers. One's Ultimate Source; the Great Mother; personal past, childhood, heritage, family, heredity, homeland; unconscious assumptions and attitudes, instincts, hereditary mental patterns, psychological patterns due to infantile experiences, emotional reflexes or programs, psychic perceptions.

Mercury

The Logos, articulation of truth; the mind, communication, logic and reasoning, the nervous system; physical dexterity, movement, transportation, routine travel; connecting, symbol-making, creation of images, of cognitive maps, and of correspondences, translation and transduction; restlessness (hunger for input); detail or facility of expression in the above.

Venus

(Yin.) Love, nonverbal expression of truth; intrinsic bonding from within, non-coercive grouping, spontaneous attractions; creation of harmony of higher wholes out of complementary elements, of beauty; social adeptness; unconditional 'mother-love' (along with the Moon); sexuality (complementarily with Mars).

Mars

(Yang.) Survival energy, extremely individualistic and self-centered, emphasizing differences; identification with entities believed to ensure survival; fight-or-flight reaction, aggression; masculinity, force, strength, vigor, athletes, the military; iron and steel, and workers with these; when Mars energy is blocked, irritations, inflammations, infections, fevers, operations, accidents; sexuality (complimentarily with Venus).

Jupiter

Expansion: (re)incorporation of the external world, physical and psychological growth, exploration and learning, gaining control and autonomy, increasing the scope of action and experience (but inattention to detail and routine), incorporation and digestion (with the Moon); parental encouragement; broad experience, long-range objectives, social consciousness.

Saturn

Reality as culturally defined; relationship to groups, consensus. Reality as structure and limitation; rules; the consequences of error. Too much actualized and too little potential left; aging, death. The father; learning a discipline, growing into a social role, learning the rules; schools, teachers, guides, bosses. Areas of life that need work. The limits of what can be perceived with the ordinary mind.

Uranus

Unexpected disruptions of Saturnine structures, the random element of creation, the lightning-flash of enlightenment or insight, the desire to break free, the unusual or eccentric. Impersonal disruptions of the social order: revolutions, natural disasters; innovative technologies, the sciences.

Neptune

The ultimately real, containing all polarities but no distinctions; Nirvana; mystical perception of divinity and truth; non-attachment. Maya (with Saturn). Artistic creativity (with Venus), imagination, the more abstract arts. Ideals; illusions of perfection; sacrifice for higher causes (both martyrs and victims); unreality, illusion, mystery, confusion, denial or defeat of the ego. Dishonest or covert activities, e.g. poisoning; (with other planets) withdrawal from life into alcohol, drugs, or insanity.

Pluto

Archetype of death and resurrection; complete breakdown of Saturnine reality, forcing one to build a new 'normal' reality; psychotic episodes; radical transformations of consciousness and being. Transcendental aspects of sexuality. Political power as a manifestation of historical processes. Agents of breakdown and decay, e.g. the underworld, organized crime, social malcontents, terrorists. Healers and therapists, teachers of self-transformation, gurus, religious leaders who emphasize life after death.

Other Points

Ascendant

A point of self-manifestation where energies of the self pass from the inner realm to the outer and are made manifest to the not-self. Governs one's effect or impression, or the kind of action one takes upon the outer world; hence, related to the personality and physical body.

Midheaven

The point of greatest self-externalization in the social world. Refers to social position, role, status, life direction and career in external terms. Helps define what one does rather than how one does it. Helps identify what one needs to do with one's life in order to grow.

Lunar Nodes

An axis of relationship. Connections with other people involving feelings, perhaps with qualities attributed to the Sun/Moon midpoint. When emphasized, there is a tendency to go and meet people. The two nodes are hard to distinguish except when there are conjunctions, but the North Node may have a joining quality, and may have characteristics similar to Jupiter, and the South Node may have a separating quality, and may be similar in some respects to Saturn. Some astrologers relate the lunar nodes to past incarnations.

Aries Point

Like the Ascendant-Descendant and North Node—South Node axes, the Aries axis has to do with relationships. Of the three, the Aries axis is the most impersonal: it indicates one's relationships with the larger world around one and is associated with fame and greater social significance.

ASPECTS

The Conjunction

The union of planetary energies. Effects may be obvious to others, but hard for the native to assess. A dynamic quality, patterns of action (events or changes) rather than passive states. Almost no coloring of its own, specific meaning derived from planetary compatibilities.

The Two-Series or 'Hard' Aspects

Events or changes at a definite point in time, with a clearly defined crisis demanding action, after which they pass away. Unstable energy patterns, they produce difficulty when the person or the environment resists the changes which they demand, but they are the only real means for creative change. Found prominent in the horoscopes of people who are very successful and talented, or very unsuccessful and unproductive.

Opposition (180°)

Analogous to the seventh house: polarity, strife, and conflict, but also partnership, cooperation, and consciousness. Conflicts develop when unrecognized parts of the self are projected; energy and growth in consciousness result when the projected parts are recognized and integrated.

Square (90°)

Energies working at cross-purposes, so that the achievement of one goal interferes with progress toward the other; a test of the validity of these goals. The mutual resistance of the two energies results in greater individuality; the resistance of material reality. The energies involved, and the relationship between them, are usually difficult to perceive clearly. The instability of the square leads to ongoing growth to new levels except when, because of the person's resistance, the conflict is repeated continually on the same level.

Semisquare (45°) and Sesquiquadrate (135°)

Similar to the square but not as intense. An unstable, dynamic linking of energies resulting in change. Incongruity and mutual resistance of two sets of goals challenges their validity.

The Three-Series or 'Soft' Aspects

Less dynamic and usually less harsh than the 'hard' aspects. Stable energy patterns that resist change, but not static: homeostasis ('dynamic equilibrium') with no *net* change. Chronic changes or events that arise slowly and persist over long periods of time with no definite crisis; ongoing states of being.

Trine (120°)

Ease of action, without difficulty when one chooses to act within a status quo and in accord with the natures of the energies combined. Restores homeostasis (balance) after a condition of imbalance. Passive or receptive participation in events, with optimism and minimal expenditure of effort as in the martial arts (at best), or stuck in a rut (at worst).

Sextile (60°)

The symbolism of two times three: the sextile is to the trine as the opposition is to the conjunction. It often results in increased awareness, and usually represents circumstances which require some exertion of energy to reap the benefit, hence 'opportunity.' Preserves homeostasis (balance), but not to so limiting an extent as the trine.

Semisextile (30°) and Quincunx (150°)

The symbolism of three times four: the passiveness of the three-series combined with the tension and unease of the square. Relationships between entities with no logical connection, without enough energy to change the relationship, as e.g. the second, sixth, eighth, and twelfth houses are related to the first house. Routine annoyances and tensions of life; but also illnesses and death. Entities related by these aspects operate in conflicting ways, but each as if the other did not even exist.

The Five-Series—Quintile, Biquintile, Decile

Quality similar to that associated with Pluto, with overtones of Venus and Mars: some kind of concrete creation or destruction is effected. Intellectual functions (not excluding emotion) and all especially human matters. Transformational change. The ability to express creative inspiration (due to other factors) in concrete creations.

The Seven-Series—Septile, Biseptile, Triseptile, Semiseptile

A Uranus-Neptune flavor, energy linkings not entirely of this world. Creative inspiration, but also mental and emotional difficulties and tenuous connectedness with the physical universe; religion.

The Nine-Series

The novile or nonile. Completions, endings; what life produces in the long run; needs and capacities in relationships and marriage.

Signs

Aries

Beginnings. Primitive (being first), crude (raw, undirected energy), willful in an unstable, changeable way. Can be asocial or antisocial; wants freedom from others' demands; not dependent upon social approval, hence pioneering; but also not concerned with being reasonable, prudent, timely, practical, or even effective, hence abstract in a self-centered way. Emotions are primarily enthusiasm, assertiveness, and short-lived anger; often impatient, and lacking in persistence and stamina, but a high energy level may compensate. Inherently frank. A vitalizing influence.

Taurus

A vessel or matrix which manifests the energies of Aries in tangible form; a fecund creativity, developing energies which it receives and shapes, and imposing its own style. Stable, constant, persistent, limiting and contractive; earthy and sensual; not particularly social. A slow, deliberative influence.

Gemini

Rapid mental exploration, understanding quickly but without empathy, learning quickly but without deep understanding, curious about the environment but not evaluating it in personal terms; sociable, but resists deeper attachments as confining; adaptable, not confrontative, but also inconsistent and inconstant. Fond of games and trickery. A quickening influence that raises planetary energies to a higher, more abstract level.

Cancer

Feeling part of something; emotional relationships, particularly to the past, childhood, family, mother, community, or homeland. A need for emotional security, an emotionally supportive environment, and nurturing personal relationships;if satisfied, this need is transferred to others so that Cancer, in giving these benefits to others, contributes in vital ways to social cohesion; but if this emotional need is not satisfied, the person may become fearful, grasping and possessive in an infantile way, smothering rather than nurturing others, substituting material possessions for the missing emotional support. An emotional, protective, nurturing influence.

Leo

Developed ego and self-confidence, with a strong need for self-expression, for the admiration of others, and for uncompromising personal integrity, arising from fascination with self and a desire that others be similarly fascinated. A need for personal recognition, to be impressive, to control one's destiny, to be a person of genuine significance, with honor. Image is the king or the Sun, source of energy and inspiration to others. May be arrogant if these basic needs are not met. Persistent and stubborn. A stabilizing influence.

Virgo

The completed ego coming to terms simultaneously with the physical and the social universes as obstacles to which one must adapt, as frameworks for learning to be effective, and as realities that must be served. Submissive, efficient, effective; needs recognition for the quality of its workmanship; conforming, somewhat cautious and perhaps fearful, as if chastened for the excesses of Leo. Honest and realistic, seeks perfection or at least success in effecting changes through self-criticism and self-analysis. Bothered by the unreliability of the physical world; attempts to achieve control by concentrating on details, letting nothing escape its notice. High esthetic standards, but does not appreciate beauty without function; the sign of crafts. An influence of precision and care.

Libra

The first and most simple social relationship, the one-to-one dyad; intimate confrontation. Deft in dealing with others, takes the initiative while appearing to give in. Cannot conceive of self in a vacuum, but only in connection with another; needs intimate relationships for self-understanding and self-realization. Loves beauty and harmony and needs art, but may not appreciate or tolerate strong emotional content in art. A lighter and less serious influence, and a socializing influence through relationships.

Scorpio

Ego death and transformation through emotional merger of egos. Mystical, seeing the power of transformation at work in ordinary reality. Transcendent elements of sexuality. Profoundly relativistic, seeing no difference between good and evil, embracing death experiences for the sake of the resurrection that follows. Fond of living intensely; dramatic, loves emotion, loves mystery. Usually not prepossessing or dramatic in appearance, but enjoys confrontation and fighting. Often misunderstood because perceptions and feelings are difficult to analyze and communicate; may blame self for this and compensate by secretiveness. An emotionally intense influence for transformation.

Sagittarius

Learning to understand one's social context and to express one's will in it, in terms of abstract principles and general patterns rather than details of implementation. The first type is idealistic and freedom-loving, desiring self-expression and social reform. Reluctant to be tied down in relationships or tradition. The second type is successfully integrated into the social order and desires to be socially useful and to act as spokesman for social cohesion; attracted to science, philosophy, religion, or other disciplines by which to study and discover the interrelatedness of all things; prefers wisdom to mere knowledge; more consistent and more willing to grapple with details of implementation than the first type. An influence for increased freedom.

Capricorn

Strong social orientation: most at home with social consensus about what is real, important and acceptable. Strongly influenced by authority figures. Needs to be in control, and effective in practical terms. As a representative of the social order, concerned with detailed, practical implementation of the consensus reality, rather than the abstract principles themselves. Over-serious, justifies play and rationalizes enjoyment by its social contributions; wry, self-deprecating humor. An influence for achievement in conformity with consensus reality.

Aquarius

Completes the socialization of the various aspects of self built up through preceding signs. The individual as a cooperative member of the group; gregarious, enjoys social interactions, values friendships, respects collective effort; needs social interaction to define self, but then tends to dominate the group; derives sense of ego from identification with group or social needs. Freedom-loving, in the sense of freedom to change society to fit its fixed ideals and ideas of perfection. More at home with friendship than with love. A social, mentally active, but emotionally dry influence.

Pisces

In the advanced type: transcendence of ego, subordination to the universe and to that which it embodies, surrender of the soul to God. In the primitive type: the embryonic stage prior to a new beginning. Ego and reality system not clearly defined, hence highly imaginative, and less self-assertive as something particular. Extremely receptive to influence from others: a passive victim unwilling to take responsibility (primitive type), or a seeker for truth at a deep spiritual level, possibly a martyr for truth (advanced type). May perceive alternate realities; primitive type will be confused by these. Apt to take refuge in an aloof, private inner world, which may be mere fantasy in the primitive type. Often drawn to social service; primitive types may maintain covert egotism by ensuring that their wards remain dependent. An influence that reduces forcefulness but enhances receptivity and empathy.

Houses

Internal	Relational	External
FIRST		
Persona (mask), the interface mediating between self and world; one's self-image, and one's image presented to others.	Personality; physical appearance. The sense of being polarized with respect to something or someone external; oneself as active agent.	We vs. They; one's group or 'side' (but only in relation to an external group).
SECOND		
The part of the ego that desires to flow beyond the boundaries of the body to attach itself to external entities, making them part of one's being.	Attitudes toward possessions and attachments; one's valuing and its expression in behavior. Mine vs. yours. Awareness and experience of attachment vs. detachment.	Wealth, physical possessions and resources; the actual objects to which one is attached.
THIRD		
The part of the mind that makes consciously learned mental and physical functions operate automatically. The unconscious basis of the fundamental mindset that most influences one's experience of everyday reality. The psychological processes (patterning of psychic energy) that occur when a habit is operating.	The 'automatic pilot' mind, which maintains one's relationship with the everday world, e.g. through speech and routine communications. Expression of attitudes and basic behavioral programs; experience of attitudes and behavioral programs of others in the immediate environment.	People, places, and situations that are closely involved in one's intimate, personal world: brothers, sisters, other relatives, neighbors, the neighborhood supermarket, etc. Short journeys, and other ways of making routine connections in one's personal world.
FOURTH		
Psychic functions that connect one to the rest of life, with feelings of belonging, being at home in, and being connected; one's line to the collective unconscious. Inherited psychological structures.	One's most supportive and nurturing relationships, the most personal and intimate aspects of one's social existence. Infant and prenatal experiences, with their unconscious behavioral consequences.	The nurturing parent, and others with whom one has supportive and nurturing relationships (both giving and receiving support); one's house, home, childhood and adult family, community, home town, nation, and so on.
FIFTH		
Those aspects of the psyche that wish to express the nature of the self; the drive to play out one's chosen role, or to create, giving one a feeling of being alive and unique.	Relationships that are formed mainly for pleasure or for self-expression; love affairs. Relationships with the products of one's spontaneous creative activity; childbearing.	Places of amusement, gambling, and speculation. One's experience of one's children in terms of self-expression and creativity.

Internal	Relational	External

SIXTH

Aspects of the psyche that make deferred gratification possible. The part of the unconscious mind that incorporates energies and influences from conscious experience into the psyche. One's attitudes toward necessity and service.

Necessities that have their origin in external circumstances; work, and other activities not pursued for the sake of self-expression. Relationships of subservience, or relationships formed out of necessity, duty, or responsibility.

One's experience of employers an employees. Actual day-to-day tas of one's profession. One's job if it only a means of support, and do not fulfill one's life purpose. Illness (due to energies being incorporat that are difficult for the mind body to handle).

SEVENTH

Aspects of oneself that manifest during close confrontations with the outer world, coloring one's experience of or one's reactions to what appears to be external reality. Using relationships with others to define oneself to oneself.

One-to-one encounter, and one's manner of reaching out to others to form close I-thou relationships.

One's experience of one's mari partner, business partner, enemi or competitors. They vs. We (in rect we-they encounters).

EIGHTH

Inner energies that want to reach out and experience the world, which compel one to shed any attachments that impede them, and which thus force one ahead toward growth and change.

Encounters with outer circumstances reflecting one's inner dynamic toward change. Intense relationships; orgasm and other death/rebirth experiences. One's ability to use experience as a guide for change.

One's experience of events and c cumstances in which one must de with transformation, or with the a tachments of oneself or others to th which is transformed: the death others; breakdown, decay, an rebirth; other people's money an resources, i.e. other people attachments.

NINTH

Energies of the conscious mind reaching out to experience and perceive as much of the world as possible and to understand what it perceives. Psychological patterns (philosophy, worldview, or reality system) that modify and influence one's perceptions. Greatest possible consciousness of the not-self.

One's relationship to the world in experiences that shape one's views of reality, particularly consciousness-expanding travel and other experiences that place one in an unfamiliar setting.

Whatever seems remote from ever day experience: foreign countri philosophies, religions, and ways life; foreigners or people with a ve different lifestyle and worldvie Teachers in the sense of gurus.

TENTH

Energies of the conscious mind reaching out to act in the external world. Concerned with the questions 'Who am I,?' 'What am I doing?' and 'Where am I going?' in one's social setting. The internalization of previously external energies, e.g. fathering; the Freudian super-ego. Greatest possible consciousness of the self.

Relationships of inequality between oneself and another, in which the dominant person teaches or guides the other.

One's experience of guide figures, a thority figures, disciplinarians, b ses, employers, government officia etc., derived from one's experience fathering in early life.

Internal	Relational	External

ELEVENTH

One's need to reach out, establish contacts with others, and become integrated into a group. Shared ideals and aspirations. One's ability to identify with others, and to make the identity of the group part of one's own identity.

Friendships, group membership, and other relationships that are lighter than those of the seventh house.

People to whom one relates, and groups with which one identifies.

TWELFTH

Energies that one has actually put out into the world. If these were sources of early-life defeats and were unintegrated with the conscious self, they may seem to work against one as evils or as weaknesses which one fears. Resolution may come by the ego sacrificing itself in symbolically appropriate ways.

The projection of hidden aspects of oneself onto intimate relationships. Relationships of devoted service, transcending the ego.

Social circumstances and situations that are difficult because one finds them undermining. Also, social entities and circumstances that assist one in overcoming the consequences of one's twelfth-house energies: hospitals and other such institutions, teachers and spiritual undertakings.

READING LIST

Reading List

Here are some further readings on the topics discussed in this book.

Addey, John M. *The Discrimination of Birth-Types in Relation to Disease.* Green Bay, WI: Cambridge Circle, 1974.
A pamphlet outlining some of Addey's early work on harmonics.
———, compiler. *Harmonic Anthology.* Green Bay, WI: Cambridge Circle, 1976.
Selections from the writings of Addey and others showing the development of harmonic theory over the years.
———. *Harmonics in Astrology: An Introductory Textbook to the New Understanding of an Old Science.* Green Bay, WI: Cambridge Circle, 1976.
A systematic treatment of Addey's ideas in the late 1970s.
The American Ephemeris, 1931 to 1980, and Book of Tables. Compiled and programed by Neil F. Michelsen. Pelham, NY: Astro Computing Services, 1976.
Besides containing both true and mean positions of the lunar nodes, the most complete and accurate current astrological ephemeris. Includes declinations, timed aspectarian, Moon positions every twelve hours, excellent instructions for erecting a horoscope, and many useful tables. Other volumes for other timespans are available, as is an abbreviated version giving longitudes only.
Arroyo, Stephen. *Astrology, Psychology, and the Four Elements.* Davis, CA: CCRCS Publications, 1975.
Half this book is a brilliant discussion of the meaning of fire, earth, air, and water in the horoscope, though I differ with Arroyo's seeing all astrological symbolism, including houses and aspects, as springing from the elements. The other half of the book is a plea for not fitting astrology into the straitjacket of science, and an affirmation of astrology's value as a system of psychology that helps people.

Bach, Eleanor, and Climlas, George. *Asteroid Ephemeris*. Brooklyn, NY: Celestial Communications, Inc., 1973.

This, the first asteroid ephemeris, has been superseded by the more accurate and complete *Asteroid Ephemeris* of Zipporah Dobyns et al., but it contains Bach's ground-breaking introduction on the meaning of Ceres, Pallas, Juno, and Vesta, with examples from the charts of the famous.

Dean, Geoffrey, and Mather, Arthur, compilers. *Recent Advances in Natal Astrology: A Critical Review, 1900-1976*. Subiaco, Western Australia: Analogic, 1977.

A comprehensive and exhaustively documented compilation of viewpoints and research on all the major issues of astrology (houses, orbs, signs, etc.). Flawed by short-sighted evaluations of various ideas, but nevertheless a unique and extremely valuable guide for thinking about the validity of various astrological principles. Soon to be revised and enlarged.

deVore, Nicholas. *Encyclopedia of Astrology*. New York: Philosophical Library, 1947. Paperback reprint: Totowa, NJ: Littlefield, Adams, 1977.

Not complete, but still a goldmine of information.

Digicomp Research Corporation. *True Lunar Nodes, 1850-2000*. Ithaca, NY: Digicomp, 1975.

Informative preface and introduction. Ephemeris gives daily positions. Early editions are one day off, however: if the position given for January 1, 2000 is 3 Leo 54 instead of 3 Leo 58, read the position for one day earlier than the day desired.

Dobyns, Zipporah Pottenger. *The Asteroid Ephemeris, 1883-1999*. Preface by Eleanor Bach, programing by Rique Pottenger, computations by Neil Michelsen. Los Angeles: TIA Publications, 1977.

The most complete and up-to-date ephemeris of Ceres, Pallas, Juno, and Vesta, with longitudes every day and declinations at four-day intervals. Bach's preface is brief. Dobyn's introduction is much longer and presents her views and research on the asteroids.

———. *The Node Book*. Rev. ed. Computer programing by Mark Pottenger and Rique Pottenger. Los Angeles: TIA Publications, 1979.

Dobyns favors the geocentric nodes of the planets. Besides ephemerides of these nodes, there is much introductory material on the meanings and astronomical basis of nodes, and a discussion of the nodes of the asteroids and Moon.

Donath, Emma Belle. *Asteroids in the Birth Chart*. Distributed by A.F.A.: Gemini Institute, 1976.

A well-regarded discussion of the meanings of Ceres, Pallas, Juno, and Vesta.

Ebertin, Reinhold. *Applied Cosmobiology*. Translated by Heidi Langman and Jim ten Hove and edited by Charles Harvey. Aalen, West Germany: Ebertin-Verlag, 1972.
> 90° dial techniques and case studies by the founder of the Cosmobiology school.

———. *The Combination of Stellar Influences*. Translated by Alfred Roosedale and Linda Kratzsch. Aalen, West Germany: 1972.
> Brief, to-the-point delineations of all three-factor combinations in the horoscope make this an invaluable reference tool. Be wary, however, of the negative tone of the Neptune and Pluto delineations. Includes North Node, Midheaven, and Ascendant, material on medical manifestations of planetary energies, and an introduction to general principles of Cosmobiology.

Fagan, Cyril. *Astrological Origins*. St. Paul, MN: Llewellyn Publications, 1971.
> Fagan is the father of the modern sidereal movement in astrology. This and the next two volumes set forth his reasoning and procedures.

———. *The Solunars Handbook*. Tucson, AZ: Clancy Publications, 1976.

———. *Zodiacs Old and New*. London: Anscombe, 1951.

Gauquelin, Michel. *The Cosmic Clocks: From Astrology to a Modern Science*. Foreword by Frank A. Brown, Jr. Chicago: Regnery, 1967.
> The first Gauquelin work to be widely read in America. A popular presentation of his earlier research.

———. *Cosmic Influences on Human Behavior*. Translated by Joyce E. Clemow. New York: Stein & Day, 1973.
> A popular presentation of Gauquelin's more recent findings.

Hawkins, John Robert. *Transpluto: Or Should We Call Him Bacchus, The Ruler of Taurus?* Dallas: Hawkins Enterprising Publications, 1976.
> Challenging thoughts on the hypothetical planet put forward by the Ebertins and Theodor Landscheidt. Contains Ebertin-style delineations of Transpluto aspects and midpoints.

Holden, Ralph William. *The Elements of House Division*. Romford, Essex: L.N. Fowler, 1977.
> One of several good books explaining the differences between the various house systems.

Hutcheon, Roger. *Planetary Pictures in Declination*. Cambridge, MA: ATS Press, 1976.
> How to use a dial to work with declinations.

Jacobson, Roger A. *The Language of Uranian Astrology*. Franksville, WI: Uranian Publications, 1975.
> A well-written introduction to the methods of the Uranian school, with good delineations of the Uranian hypothetical planets.

Jayne, Charles A. *Parallels: Their Hidden Meaning.* Monroe, NY: Astrological Bureau, 1978.

Declinations explained by an authority.

———. *The Unknown Planets, with Ephemerides.* Monroe, NY: Astrological Bureau, 1974.

Ephemerides of the hypothetical planets Pan, Isis, Hermes, Osiris, Midas, and Lion, with evidence for their validity and a discussion of their meaning. Also discusses other hypothetical planets, including Vulcan, Rex, Sigma, Jason, Isis, Morya, and those of the Uranian school.

Jung, Carl G. *Psychological Types.* Translated by H.G. Baynes and revised by R.F.C. Hull. Vol. 6 in The Collected Works of C.G. Jung. Princeton, NJ: Princeton University Press, 1971.

The classification of human personalities into sensation, thinking, feeling, and intuition types that has lured astrologers into proposing parallels with the four astrological elements and left them debating to this day.

Lorenz, Dona Marie. *Tools of Astrology: Houses.* Topanga, CA: Eomega Grove Press, 1973.

A generally accurate and readable explanation of various house systems. Computer programing errors mar some of the tables, however.

Manilius. *The Five Books of M. Manilius.* London, 1697. Reprint. Washington, DC: National Astrological Library, 1953.

A seventeenth-century English translation of Manilius's *Astronomicon.*

Morinus. *Astrosynthesis: The Rational System of Horoscope Interpretation according to Morin de Villefranche.* Translated by Lucy Little, with an introduction by Zoltan Mason. New York: Emerald Books, 1974.

A small part of the works of this great Renaissance astrologer lovingly published by one of his modern proponents.

Neely, James, and Tarkington, Eric. *Ephemeris of Chiron, 1890-2000.* Edited by Malcolm Dean, with EDP support by Michael Campbell and introduction by Tony Joseph. Toronto: Phenomena Publications, 1978.

An elegant and accurate ephemeris published shortly after the planetoid's discovery. Tony Joseph's suggestions on what this new body might mean are drawn from the Greek myths about Chiron.

Nelson, John H. *Cosmic Patterns: Their Influence on Man and His Communication.* Washington, DC: American Federation of Astrologers, 1974.

Nelson's story of how, when working for RCA, he came to use heliocentric planetary aspects to predict interruptions in short-wave radio transmission. Some of the most convincing evidence for the astrological effect.

————. *The Propagation Wizard's Handbook: Coping with Our Occult Sun and Its Meddlesome Satellites.* Peterborough, NH: 73 Inc., 1978.
Nelson's more recent research.

Ptolemy. *Tetrabiblos.* Edited and translated into English by F.E. Robbins. In *Manetho; Ptolemy* volume of Loeb Classical Library. Cambridge, MA: Harvard University Press, 1940.
The best edition of Ptolemy's *Tetrabiblos,* with the original Greek text facing an annotated translation.

Robson, Vivian E. *The Fixed Stars and Constellations in Astrology,* 1923. Reprint. New York: Samuel Weiser, 1969.
A compilation of traditional lore on 111 fixed stars.

Tobey, Carl Payne. *Astrology of Inner Space.* Tucson, AZ: Omen Press, 1972.
A grab-bag of nontraditional but well-reasoned ideas on nodes, rulerships, clockwise signs, and many other topics.

Wilson, James. *A Complete Dictionary of Astrology.* London, 1819. Reprint. New York: Samuel Weiser, 1969.
Subtitled "In which every technical and abstruse term belonging to the science is minutely and correctly explained and the various systems and opinions of the most approved authors...divested of their extravagance, contradictions, and absurdities," which sums it up well. Still an invaluable source.

Witte, Alfred, and Lefeldt, Hermann. *Rules for Planetary Pictures: The Astrology of Tomorrow.* 5th ed. Translated by Curt Knupfer. Hamburg: Ludwig Rudolph/Witte-Verlag, 1974.
Brief delineations of all three-factor combinations in the horoscope including the known planets, the Uranian hypothetical planets, the Ascendant, Midheaven, North Node, and Aries Point. Contains an explanatory introduction.

Witte, Alfred, and Niggemann, Hans. *Rules for Planetary Pictures (Uranian System), Adapted from the Teachings of Alfred Witte as originally Dictated to His Students, of Whom the Author had the Honor and Privilege of Being One.* Rev. and enl. ed. New York: Hans Niggemann, 1959.
Essentially the same delineations as the Witte-Lefeldt version given above.

INDEX

Index

AFTERWORDS

Robert Hand and Para Research

Late in 1974 Robert Hand was giving a talk at a meeting of the National Council for Geocosmic Research on the use of sophisticated calculators for casting horoscopes. Among his listeners was Frank Molinski, owner and President of Para Research, a small but growing computer horoscope service that was just breaking into publishing.

After the lecture the two men met for the first time, and explored the exciting prospect of creating delineation texts to be assembled for specific horoscopes by computer. They realized from the outset that this material should be published simultaneously in book form. Robert Pelletier's *Planets in Aspect* had been published by Para Research earlier that same year and was doing well, but the publishing division of the company was far from profitable. Most of the company's income still came from its computer horoscope services. They knew the combination of books and computer horoscopes would be unbeatable, and an important contribution to astrology.

The first book to emerge from the new working partnership was *Planets in Composite*, released in 1975, which provided the text for the Astral Composite. In this book, Robert Hand drew upon his knowledge of midpoints in astrology to create the definitive text on this very important type of relationship horoscope. For the first time, in the Astral Composite, the lay public had easy access to the depth of insight that astrology can bring to human relationships.

Planets in Transit, begun in the spring of 1975, was also finished in one year. This was a year of some of the most intense writing of Robert Hand's life. *Planets in Transit* has become the authoritative text on transits, and one of Para Research's most successful books. Like the earlier books, it was considered from the outset to be both a book and the basis for a computer horoscope product. Brief summaries written at the same time as *Planets in Transit* were programed to be printed in calendar format. This convenient display of daily transits over an entire twelve-month sequence was made available to the public as the Astral Guide.

Planets in Youth was begun in 1976 and was published in 1977, making this the third Robert Hand book in as many years. This book is specifically written for interpreting the horoscopes of children, with their unique perspectives, needs, and level of experience. Now astrologers have expert help in 'translating' the delineation of a horoscope into terms appropriate for a child's experience of life. Robert Hand's ability to offer insight without being patronizing, which is so very important with children, is made available to parents who are not astrologers through the Youth Portrait, latest of the growing line of Para Research computer horoscope products.

Robert Hand's fourth book was begun in 1977, with the working title *Planets in Synthesis.* This was the first Para Research/Robert Hand proposal planned entirely as a book, with no accompanying computer horoscope product. *Planets in Synthesis* was to tell readers how to put all the information in a horoscope together into a coherent delineation. It was expected to be completed in 1978, but the effort required for this work was underestimated.

One difficulty was that Robert Hand no longer had as much time available for uninterrupted writing. He had many more speaking engagements and lecture tours. Also, he was helping to form Astro-Graphics Services, and developing his own astrological software (programs) for microcomputers.

As work progressed, the new book was becoming encyclopedic in size and scope, and readers and booksellers were clamoring for copies. Late in 1979, with the second part still not finished, Para Research and Robert Hand decided it had grown too large for one volume. Robert Hand had, in fact, been working concurrently on not one but two related projects: astrological symbolism and astrological synthesis.

You are holding in your hands the first of these two studies, *Horoscope Symbols.* This book examines and re-evaluates in radical depth the major symbol systems of western astrology. It integrates what is sound and essential in the astrological tradition with Robert Hand's incisive interpretation and evaluation of the latest in astrological research. It provides the foundations for integrating and synthesizing the enormous quantity and diversity of information that a horoscope makes available to the astrologer.

Robert Hand's next book, *Horoscope Synthesis,* will focus on the all-important task of integration and synthesis; it will be published in the near future. Not since Alan Leo has so mammoth a task been undertaken by one so qualified to fulfill it. Robert Hand has assimilated and incorporated into his writing the new astrological, psychological, astronomical and other scientific research that has developed since Alan Leo's time, and integrated it with the wealth of astrological tradition that came before.

Astro-Graphics Services

During the time he was writing this book, Rob Hand was involved in creating Astro-Graphics Services. The seeds of this enterprise were sown in March, 1976, when Rob became one of the first astrologers to acquire a microcomputer. Sensing the potential in the new technology of small computers and becoming fascinated with programing them, he conceived of starting a business that would improve the tools available to astrologers, foster new techniques and further the re-thinking of astrological principles while it supported a community of astrologers near his home on Cape Cod. Astro-Graphics Services is now a reality, consisting of five astrologers of diverse viewpoints, seven computers, two telescopes, a large library of astrological, psychological, computer, and other scientific books and journals, and an organic vegetable garden, all in the small town of Orleans, Massachusetts.

Aside from Rob himself, one of the five astrologers is A.H. Blackwell, a widely respected siderealist and researcher on *in mundo* positions. A.H. has pioneered in developing horoscope formats that represent the sky realistically, as in a map projection. He is also a meticulous scholar, specializing in the history of astrology and in documenting birth data.

Another founder is Steven M. Blake, who has been an innovator in applying meditation methods to astrological counseling in a psychological-humanistic approach. He is a popular lecturer on this and on local space astrology. He was the first president of the Cape Cod Chapter of the National Council for Geocosmic Research, and a faculty member (along with Gary Christen, Michael Munkasey, Rob Hand and A.H. Blackwell) of its master classes in spherical astronomy and alternative forms of astrology, which were held in September of 1980 and 1981.

Gary Christen is one of those rare people with a degree in astrology (B.A., Rutgers, 1974). A well-known Uranian astrologer, Gary is the inventor of the paran wheel and the difference sort, and is producer of highly accurate Uranian and Cosmobiology 360° and 90° dials. With his skills at the light table and drafting board, he is a lot of the 'graphics' in

Astro-Graphics. He was co-editor of NCGR's *Geocosmic News* (with Pat White), and edited a revised version of the *Key to Uranian Astrology* published by Hans Niggemann. He has been instrumental in the effort to make available in English the untranslated articles of Alfred Witte.

Patricia White is a free-lance writer and editor, and sat on the board of directors of the National Council for Geocosmic Research as director of publications, managing editor of the *Journal of Geocosmic Research* and co-editor of *Geocosmic News*. She edited this book, and writes much of the material that comes out of Astro-Graphics Services.

At present Astro-Graphics provides astrological programs for two of the most popular home computers, the Apple II and the TRS-80, and also for CP/M - based systems. AGS provides a variety of individualized services, including cheerful help by telephone. Customers are entitled to updated programs free, and upgraded programs at cost. AGS instruction manuals are exceptionally clear, with foolproof input routines.

AGS software for professional astrologers is accurate within plus or minus one minute of arc for planets and one second of arc for the Sun. The Moon's position is usually this accurate but occasionally deviates up to three seconds of arc, adequate accuracy for lunar returns with house cusps accurate to one minute of arc. These progams include:

AGS-1 Natal Horoscope Package This program has tropical and sidereal zodiacs, seven house systems (Placidus, Koch, Campanus, Meridian, Equal, Regiomontanus, and Topocentric), and a built-in two-century ephemeris (1800-2000), with other centuries on separate disks. This program produces a two-page printout in spoked wheel format with planets proportionally spaced in the houses to suggest true zodiacal positions (with glyphs for some printers), room for up to seven planets in a house, and space on the side for additional planets that don't fit in a house. The easy-to-read aspectarian includes ten planets, Node, Ascendant, Midheaven, Vertex, East Point, and Part of Fortune; the usual major and minor aspects plus the fifth, seventh, ninth and sixteenth harmonics; degrees and minutes from partile (exact aspect) and whether aspects are applying or separating. It also lists longitudes and latitudes (both geocentric and heliocentric), retrogrades, right ascension and declination, daily motion, dignities, mutual receptions, and weighted scores of planets in elements and crosses. Three lines of text can be customized (free of charge) with your name and address. AGS-1 lets you store any horoscope on disk for further processing using many of the other programs available from Astro-Graphics.

AGS-2 Relationship Package The synastry routine prints all the inter-house planetary relationships and aspects between two horoscopes.

The package also includes two composite horoscope routines, one for the midpoint in space (Hand type), and the other for the midpoint in time and space (Davison-Shapiro type); both of these print out in wheel format.

AGS-3 Heliocentric Horoscope This routine prints more detailed information than AGS-1, including: heliocentric longitudes and latitudes, perihelia, nodes, and radius vectors, with a complete helio aspectarian and midpoint list.

AGS-4 Harmonics and Arc Transforms The harmonic horoscope routine casts an Addey-style chart for any harmonic, using wheel-with-aspectarian format with equal houses from the Ascendant or Midheaven. The arc transform routine casts a similar chart for any arc. The harmonic listing routine lists any consecutive 25 harmonic positions for all planets.

AGS-5 Progressed Horoscope This routine prints a day-for-a-year progressed horoscope in wheel-with-aspectarian format using any one of seven house systems, as in AGS-1. Angles may be progressed by mean solar arc on the equator (3m56s of sidereal time per year), true solar arc on the equator ('solar arc'), or quotidian rate (24h3m56.5s of sidereal time per year). The program also does converse progressions.

AGS-6 Horoscope In Mundo This program projects natal positions onto planes other than the ecliptic: Campanus projection onto the prime vertical, Regiomontanus oblique projection onto the equator, or Erlewine-style local-space projection onto the horizon (which also allows projection of any point on Earth onto the local horizon). The printed output is in list format with an aspectarian.

AGS-7 Parans This program locates all parans within a five-degree orb, lists RAMC for times when bodies will be on the angles at a given locality, sorts them in order of time to make parans apparent, and prints a paran aspectarian.

AGS-8 Midpoints This program tabulates zodiacal positions of all midpoints (including Ascendant, Midheaven, mean Node, Vertex and Aries Point), then sorts midpoints in any desired modulus (45°, 22.5°, 72° etc.).

AGS-9 Solar Returns This program prints tropical, precession-corrected tropical, or sidereal solar returns in wheel-with-aspectarian format. You can also do returns to any harmonic (i.e. demi-, quarti-, quinti-solars, etc.) and converse (or prenatal) solar returns. The Sun routine in this program makes these the most accurate solar returns you can cast.

AGS-10 Lunar Returns This program produces lunar returns similar to AGS-9 solar returns, with houses accurate to the nearest minute of arc.

AGS-11 Solar Arcs This program prints a lifetime table of solar arc lengths at three-month intervals, with precision adjustable to the nearest minute or second of arc.

AGS-12 Astro-Mapping This program prints all longitudes and latitudes on Earth where natal planets would be angular (i.e. on the horizon or meridian) so that you can plot them on a map; parans are where lines intersect. Useful for determining where on Earth natal planets would be strongest, and for relocation astrology.

AGS-13 House Comparison with Relocation This program prints cusps in up to seven different house systems, or instantly relocates house cusps for any new longitude and latitude coordinates.

AGS-14 Transit Package This program prints date and time of transiting aspects to natal positions over a given period not only in geocentric longitude, but also in declination and heliocentric longitude if desired. It also enables you to make ephemerides on disk. (Requires two disk drives.)

AGS-15 Progression Package This program prints the date of progressed mutual aspects and aspects to natal points in geocentric longitude, with heliocentric longitude and declination if desired, and with a variety of rates for progressing angles. (Requires two disk drives.)

In its Electronic Astrologer™ Series, AGS also offers programs that delineate the horoscope as well as cast it.

001 Astro-Scope™ The Electronic Astrologer™ This program gives positions of planets and house cusps accurate to the tenth of a degree, and then provides a text of fifteen hundred words or more based on planetary positions in sign, house, and aspect. The text by Steve Blake and Robert Hand is concise, yet captures the essence of the symbols and covers a great deal of ground. Each disk comes with an attractive booklet with full instructions and an introduction to astrological terms and concepts. Program 001 gives screen output only; a version that gives a nicely formatted printer output and the same accuracy as AGS-1 is available as AGS-16. The printout version requires two disk drives.

002 Sex-O-Scope™ The Private-Life Horoscope™ This program is similar to Astro-Scope™, but it is oriented toward relationships and sexual needs. The text, by John Townley, author of *Planets in Love* and a former editor of *Sexology Today*, treats a wide range of sexual behavior in a witty and tolerant style. The printout version of 002 is known as AGS-17.

Astro-Graphics Services offers a chart-casting service for high-accuracy horoscopes from AD 1470 to 2103 in your choice of house system and zodiac. Included are heliocentric charts, harmonics, progressions, quotidians, solar arcs, returns, relocation and local space charts, astro-mapping, synastry, composites, parans and midpoints. Phone orders are accepted, and fast service is assured.

AGS Graphic Ephemerides (transit graphs) allow you to see a whole year of hard-aspect transits at a glance. Date and degree scales on both margins make it easy to locate any date and degree with a straightedge, leaving ample margins for planet notations. Full instructions for the 45° modulus are included with each pad of twenty-five.

Valliere's Graphic Almanac tells you when transiting planets are angular, using Jim Valliere's award-winning Kinetic Mundascope™ graphs. Each twelve-month volume includes instructions, Jim Valliere's mundane forecast for the year, and other useful information on personal and business planning by cosmic cycles.

The *Astro-Graphics Sidereal Ephemeris, 1981-1985* is an inexpensive, handy-sized daily midnight listing of helio longitudes and latitudes, with Moon positions given every twelve hours, and the synetic vernal point given every month. The Sun is accurate to 1″ of arc, Moon to 6″, Mercury through Mars to 3″, and Jupiter through Pluto to 1′ or better. There is a technical introduction by A.H. Blackwell, an article on the starting point of the sidereal zodiac by Cyril Fagan, and a second-difference interpolation table explained by Robert Hand.

The *Astro-Graphics Heliocentric Ephemeris, 1981-1990* gives daily heliocentric longitudes and latitudes for Mercury through Mars, and five-day positions for Jupiter through Pluto, based on data more recent than that given by the U.S. Naval Observatory. Planets are computed to seconds of arc and rounded to the nearest minute. Sign notation is used for the convenience of astrologers.

The 360° and 90° dials offered by AGS are the ultimate in Uranian Cosmobiology wheels: precision-drawn by computer for 15′ accuracy on the 360°dial and 2′ accuracy on the 90° wheel. These dials have a pinhole center, and are durably laminated in plastic with a marproof matte finish.

Astro-Graphics dry transfer symbols give a finished, professional look to charts, art work and publications. Unlike other rub-on sheets, this includes asteroids, Uranian planets and Chiron, plus other useful symbols. Each sheet contains more than twelve hundred symbols, making this a very economical method of working.

Details on prices and on other products as they become available may be obtained from Astro-Graphics Services, Box 28, Orleans, MA 02653, telephone (617)255-0510.

Para Research Publications

NUMEROLOGY AND THE DIVINE TRIANGLE
by Faith Javane & Dusty Bunker

At last a truly comprehensive and authoritative text on numerology! *Numerology and the Divine Triangle* embodies the life work of Faith Javane, one of America's most respected writers and teachers of numerology, and her student and co-author, Dusty Bunker, a teacher and columnist on metaphysical topics.

Part I is a complete introduction to esoteric numerology and includes a section on the life of Edgar Cayce as a case study of numerology in action.

Part II includes extensive delineations of each of the numbers 1 to 78 and, for the first time in book form, a synthesis of numerology, astrology and the Tarot. Each of the Tarot cards is illustrated. *Numerology and the Divine Triangle* is number one in its field, the book to which all books on the subject will be compared from now on. Paper, $9.95.

NUMEROLOGY AND YOUR FUTURE
by Dusty Bunker

In her second book, Dusty Bunker stresses the predictive side of numerology. Personal periods, including yearly, monthly and even daily cycles, are explored as the author presents new techniques for revealing future developments. The numerological significance of decades is analysed with emphasis on the particular importance of the 1980's. Looking toward the future, the author presents a series of examples from the past, particularly the historical order of American presidents in relation to keys from the Tarot, to illustrate the power of numbers. This book is for everyone; it is easy, instructive and fun to read. Illustrated. Paper, $8.95.

GRAPHOLOGY HANDBOOK
by Curtis Casewit

This authoritative text spells out the fundamentals of graphology and illustrates them with over one hundred handwriting samples ranging from presidential proclamations to notes jotted down by ordinary people. The author, who currently teaches graphology at the University of Colorado, has studied with the leading graphologists of Europe and the United States. He presents the science of handwriting as a means to discover undeveloped talents, diagnose health conditions, screen prospective employees, understand friends and family, and reveal your own personality. Paper, $6.95.

ASTROLOGY INSIDE OUT
by Bruce Nevin

This is an excellent introduction to astrology and much more. Its theoretical framework, integrating esoteric tradition with modern harmonic research in astrology and recent developments in physics and psychology, will interest every astrological reader. Through its many ingenious visualization and meditation exercises, even seasoned astrologers will learn new ways to recognize and interpret astrological patterning from the 'inside out. Paper, $9.95

COMPLETE RELAXATION
by Steve Kravette

Complete Relaxation is unique in its field because, unlike most relaxation books, it takes a completely relaxed approach to its subject. Interspersed with text and beautifully drawn illustrations you will find a series of poetic explorations designed to put you in closer touch with yourself and the people around you. *Complete Relaxation* is written for all of you: your body, your mind, your emotions, your spirituality, your sexuality—the whole person you are and are meant to be. As you read this book, you will begin to feel yourself entering a way of life more completely relaxed than you ever thought possible, because *Complete Relaxation* speaks directly to the inner you. Paper, $8.95.

HUNA: A BEGINNER'S GUIDE
by Enid Hoffman

Centuries ago, the Kahuna, the ancient Hawaiian miracle workers, discovered the fundamental pattern of energy-flow in the universe. Their secrets of psychic and intra-psychic communication, refined and enriched by modern scientific research, are now revealed in this practical, readable book. Paper, $4.50.

ASTROLOGY, NUTRITION & HEALTH
by Robert Karl Jansky

Explains how to use the natal horoscope to foresee and prevent health problems. This concern is as old as Hippocrates and Ptolemy, but there are few books on the subject written for the layman. The author, a professional astrologer trained in biochemistry, demonstrates, in readable nontechnical language, how a knowledge of astrology can help the reader understand the components of metabolism and health. Paper, $6.95.

JOURNEYS into the BRIGHT WORLD
by Marcia Moore and Howard Sunny Alltounian, MD

Pioneering a new path to higher consciousness: A personal account by the extraordinary couple who risked everything to learn its secrets. Why did they do it? Why did Marcia Moore, the celebrated yoga teacher, astrologer and author, and Howard Sunny Alltounian, MD, a successful and respected anesthesiologist, risk their health, their careers and their sanity? This is the intimate personal story of their life, their love and their explorations into forbidden zones of higher consciousness. Here is tape-recorded evidence of the struggles they endured, the past lives they relived and the joy that they found—under the guidance of the goddess Ketamine. It's an inner-space adventure story, more exciting and more profound than any novel. And every word of it is true. Paper, $5.95.

To Order Books: Send purchase price plus fifty cents for each book to cover shipping and handling to Para Research, Dept. HS, Rockport, MA 01966. Massachusetts residents add 5% sales tax. Prices subject to change without notice.

PLANETS IN ASPECT: Understanding Your Inner Dynamics
by Robert Pelletier

Explores aspects, the planetary relationships that describe our individual energy patterns, and how we can integrate them into our lives. Undoubtedly the most thorough in-depth study of planetary aspects ever published. Every major aspect—conjunction, sextile, square, trine, opposition and inconjunct—is covered: 314 aspects in all. Cloth, $16.00; paper, $10.95.

PLANETS IN COMPOSITE: Analyzing Human Relationships
by Robert Hand

The definitive work on the astrology of human relationships. Explains the technique of the composite chart, combining two individuals' charts to create a third chart of the relationship itself, and how to interpret it. Case studies plus twelve chapters of delineations of composite Sun, Moon and planets in all houses and major aspects. Paper, $12.95.

PLANETS IN TRANSIT: Life Cycles for Living
by Robert Hand

A psychological approach to astrological prediction. Delineations of the Sun, Moon and each planet transiting each natal house and forming each aspect to the natal Sun, Moon, planets, Ascendant and Midheaven. The definitive book on transits. Includes introductory chapters on the theory and applications of transits. Paper, $18.95.

PLANETS IN YOUTH: Patterns of Early Development
by Robert Hand

A major astrological thinker looks at children and childhood. Parents can use it to help their children cope with the complexities of growing up, and readers of all ages can use it to understand themselves and their own patterns of early development. Introductory chapters discuss parent-child relationships and planetary energies in children's charts. All important horoscope factors delineated stressing possibilities rather than certainties. Cloth, $16.00.

PLANETS IN LOVE: Exploring Your Emotional and Sexual Needs
by John Townley

The first astrology book to take an unabashed look at human sexuality and the different kinds of relationships that people form to meet their various emotional and sexual needs. An intimate astrological analysis of sex and love, with 550 interpretations of each planet in every possible sign, house and aspect. Discusses sexual behavior according to mental, emotional and spiritual areas of development. Cloth, $16.00.

PLANETS IN HOUSES: Experiencing Your Environment
by Robert Pelletier

Brings the ancient art of natal horoscope interpretation into a new era of accuracy, concreteness and richness of detail. Pelletier delineates the meaning of each planet as derived by counting from each of the twelve houses and in relation to the other houses with which it forms trines, sextiles, squares and oppositions, inconjuncts and semisextiles. Seventeen different house relationships delineated for each planet in each house, 2184 delineations in all! Paper, $10.95.

ASTROLOGICAL INSIGHTS INTO PERSONALITY
by Betty Lundsted

This book combines principle and practice. The first section introduces the author's basic concepts in a clear and readable way. The second and largest section discusses each of the major planetary aspects as a context for personality development. The third section presents the author's approach to chart analysis and synthesis and uses two case histories to illustrate how you can use the material in this book.

Betty Lundsted says that the symbols in your natal chart paint a picture of your early childhood environment which influences you for the rest of your life. She presents a unique approach to understanding how this effects your expectations, relationships, self-esteem and sexuality.

Betty Lundsted applies her training in metaphysics and eastern philosophy and her interest in psychological motivation to her astrological investigations. In this book she shares the interdisciplinary approach she has developed in years of counseling and teaching. The reader with a grasp of the fundamentals of astrology will use this book to grow as an astrologer and as a person. 352 pages, paper, $9.95.

THE ONLY WAY TO LEARN ASTROLOGY
by Marion March & Joan McEvers.

A success in its earlier typewritten version, *The Only Way to Learn Astrology* is now available in a completely revised, redesigned and re-typeset edition. This new edition is more compact, clearer and easier to read. If you are looking for a comprehensive basic astrology book, *The Only Way...* is the ideal text for beginning self-study. It is also an excellent basic reference book because each planet is completely delineated in each sign and house position, and in each of the major aspects.

The book, developed over many years of successful teaching, is based on Marion March and Joan McEver's tested course outline. Now, with the republication of *The Only Way to Learn Astrology*, this proven method of learning astrology is available to everyone. 320 pages, paper, $9.95.

BASIC ASTROLOGY: A Guide for Teachers and Students
by Joan Negus

This basic astrology text offers a systematic, introductory method for beginners; it is also a good manual for teachers who want to know what to teach and when and how to teach it.

Step by step, Joan Negus covers the basics, with simplicity and directness, emphasizing the principles of astrology more than the complex details of chart interpretation.

One of the outstanding features of this text is the carefully conceived program of homework assignments at the end of each lesson. These homework assignments, and the charts, tables and other references needed to do them, are all reproduced in the accompanying large-format Workbook.

If followed diligently, this book will give the student a solid foundation for dynamic and imaginative chart interpretation. 124 pages, paper, $4.95; Workbook, 60 pages, paper, $2.95.

Para Research's
Computer Horoscopes

Three computer horoscope products developed together with astrology books by Robert Hand are available through Para Research: the *Astral Composite*, the *Youth Portrait* and the *Astral Guide*. Other Para Research computer horoscope products were developed in collaboration with other authors.

The *Astral Composite* was developed with *Planets in Composite*. A ten-thousand-word, personally unique text is compiled from computer files written by Robert Hand. Because it is based on midpoints, this is not synastry, which is the relationship of two charts to one another, but a chart of the relationship itself. In addition, it includes a horoscope of each of the two individuals in the relationship, accurate to the nearest minute of arc.

The *Youth Portrait* was developed with *Planets in Youth* to reformulate horoscope delineation so as to address the realities of life from a child's point of view. It turns out that adults, too, are delighted with their *Youth Portraits*, because it gives them an enlightening view of the child within, and awakens many stimulating and rewarding memories of their own growing-up years.

The *Astral Guide*, written at the same time as *Planets in Transit*, gives succinct day-by-day forecasts based upon transits to the natal horoscope. Each *Astral Guide* is printed on 16 x 22 calendar pages for the year beginning at any specified month.

All Para Research computer horoscope products other than the *Astral Guide* are handbound, ten-thousand-word, twenty-five page books, designed to be retained as personal references for many years. More complete descriptions and ordering information for these special computer services may be found on the following pages.

To receive our complete horoscope catalog with information about other Para Research computer horoscope products, write to: Para Research, Rockport, MA 01966

How To Order Your Para Research Horoscopes
Use the coupon or, if you prefer, use another piece of paper.
For each Astral Composite or Youth Portrait that you order,
send $20 plus 1.50 to cover postage and handling, to Para
Research, Dept. HS, Rockport, Massachusetts 01966. The price
is subject to change.

Name, Address, City, State, Zip Code
The address to which the horoscope should be sent.

Time of Birth
Accuracy to the minute is important. Don't rely on parent's
memory. Consult hospital records or birth certificate. Midnight
and noon are neither A.M. nor P.M.; A.M. is between midnight
and noon; P.M. is between noon and midnight. To avoid confusion, if you are submitting a noon birthtime, please write
"noon." If you are submitting a midnight birthtime, please write
"midnight" and two dates: the day that was ending and the day
that was beginning. For example: "June 19/20, 1947, 12:00 midnight."

Please do not convert from daylight saving time to standard
time. Just send us local clock time and we will convert. Or if
you cannot do this, please explain. If you do not send birthtime,
we will use 12:00 noon.

Date of Birth
Month, day and year.

Place of Birth
If you were born in a small town that may not be on our maps,
please give us the name of the nearest city.

Please Print Clearly
Keep a copy of the birth information you send us for comparison with the computer printout. Notify us in case of error.

Guarantee
Para Research guarantees every horoscope. If for any reason,
you are dissatisfied, please return the Astral Composite or
Youth Portrait for a full refund.

Free Catalogs
Catalogs of Para Research book and horoscope publications will
be sent with your horoscope. If you are not ordering a
horoscope but would like the catalogs, please request them from
Para Research, Dept. HS, Rockport, MA 01966

Now there's a horoscope for the two of you

It takes more than love to make a relationship work. It takes understanding. And understanding comes from knowing. Do you really *know* the one you love?

By combining new astrology techniques with humanistic psychology, scientific analysis, and computer accuracy, Para Research has developed a new way of looking at a relationship.

Now there is a horoscope for the two of you. It's the Astral Composite, the world's first computerized *composite* horoscope. This 10,000-word report takes a look at your relationship by actually casting a horoscope of the relationship itself.

Until now astrologers have compared two people's horoscopes by superimposing one on the other. Such a comparison views the people as individuals who happen to be involved in a relationship. This is helpful to a point, but misleading and incomplete.

The Astral Composite is different from comparison horoscopes. As its name implies, it is a *composite* of the two natal charts. With this method a third chart is created, a chart of the relationship itself. When two people come together to form a relationship, something new emerges. They are still the same two people, of course, but together they are something else as well. Together they are the relationship. This is what the Astral Composite is all about.

This method of analyzing human relationships was developed about 30 years ago. Today most astrologers still adhere to the old comparison method. One astrologer, Robert Hand, has further developed the composite technique for a new kind of horoscope. The result of his work is the first complete text on composite horoscopes in any language. It is now available to you as the Astral Composite from

Para Research, America's leading producer of computer horoscopes.

What does the Astral Composite consist of? An Astral Composite is three charts in one. First the computer calculates the natal charts of the two people involved. Next these two charts are combined to form a third chart, the chart of the relationship. One plus one equals three. This is followed by a reading of the chart, describing the potentialities of the relationship. All the factors of love, money, and friendship are taken into account. This helps point out the kind of relationship that works best for the two of you. You may be great together as lovers, but when it comes to a more lasting commitment you may be heading for trouble. Better to be prepared than to fall into a situation unknowingly.

The Astral Composite not only points out the strengths and weaknesses in your relationship, it also offers astrological advice on how to improve the relationship. Even the most difficult planetary combinations in the composite chart can be turned into positive forces. With your Astral Composite you will be able to enrich your relationship to the fullest degree.

Specifically, this is what you get when you order your Astral Com-

posite at the remarkable inexpensive price of $20.

• Three charts: a natal chart of each person plus the composite.

• An introduction describing the meaning of each planet.

• Planets in the houses: divisions of the horoscope describing different areas of the relationship. The positions of the Sun and Moon show the main emphasis of the relationship.

• All major planetary aspects: these are important to understanding the dynamics of the relationship. Conjunctions, sextiles, squares, trines and oppositions are included as well as aspects to the Ascendant.

• Accurate calculations: an IBM computer is used to provide accuracy to the nearest minute of arc. (Our accuracy depends on accurate birth data. See coupon below.)

• Text by Robert Hand: Mr. Hand is a specialist in the field of astrology for relationships. He is the first and only astrologer to write an extensive work on composite charts.

• Approximately 10,000 words and 25 pages in easy-to-read, beautifully bound book format.

• Money-back guarantee: the Astral Composite is unconditionally guaranteed by Para Research. If unsatisfied, simply return the horoscope for a full refund.

We would like to emphasize that this is a full-dimensional analysis of a relationship. There is no other horoscope in the world that can compare to the Astral Composite. It represent the most exciting development in astrology since the invention of the computer. It is truly unique.

You are invited to partake in what we feel will be a revealing experience for the two of you... and your relationship.

The new horoscope for children that grown-ups love

To understand your children and how you can help them solve the problems they face growing up, order their Youth Portraits.

Your growing child faces many possibilities but few certainties in the exciting, challenging process of becoming an adult. A child never stops learning, trying new ways of acting and forming new attitudes that foreshadow success or failure later on.

You Can Help Your guidance can make all the difference in the way a child grows up and copes with the complexities of life in the 20th and 21st centuries. Computer horoscopes written for adults, like our own Astral Portrait, discuss marriage, career and other matters of importance to adults, but they do not offer children and their parents the kinds of information they need.

Youth Portrait Every word of every Youth Portrait, our new computer horoscope, is written with a school-age child in mind and speaks directly to that child without talking down. Every page of every Youth Portrait offers you and your child insight into the child's character and personality: strengths, weaknesses, needs, fears, abilities and talents that the child may be unable to tell you about. Every Youth Portrait contains:

•Complete natal horoscope calculations based on date, time and place of birth.

•Time, longitude and latitude of birth researched by hand before being input to the computer.

•Sign positions of all the planets and house cusps to the nearest minute.

•All planetary aspects with orbs and intensities to the nearest minute.

10,000 Words of Text Every Youth Portrait contains text explaining the meaning of:

•The sign position of the Sun, Moon and planets, plus the Ascendant (the rising sign).

•The house position of the Sun, Moon and each of the planets.

•All significant planetary aspects in the child's chart.

All of the text has been written by Robert Hand, an authority on child psychology from an astrological point of view and author of *Planets in Youth*, the definitive work on the subject.

Adults Love It As we were developing the Youth Portrait program, we tested it on adults as well as children. We found, to our surprise, that there is nothing childish about the Youth Portrait! Many adults say it is more revealing of their inner selves than any other horoscope they have ever read. Having interviewed many adults who say they got great value out of their Youth Portraits, we now think we understand why.

To understand your childhood and the problems you faced growing, up order your own Youth Portrait.

It is a truism that unresolved experiences influence your adult life. When you read your Youth Portrait you will experience much more than nostalgia. However, old or young you are, you will gain a new perspective on your present inner life.

The Child You Were You will recognize the child you were years ago. You will remember happy times and sad ones. You will recognize the child you were still inside the adult you are today. And understanding the child inside you will help you live a more fully satisfying life as an adult now.

Your Parents Your Youth Portrait will give you new insights into your relationship with the adults who brought you up. You will see yourself as they saw you. You can't change the past, and maybe you wouldn't want to if you could. But by understanding the past you can make your present and future better.

Money-Back Guarantee Every Youth Portrait is a twenty-five-page, ten-thousand-word, permanently bound document that you can keep and read again and again for years If you are not satisfied with your Youth Portrait, you may return it at any time and get a full refund.

Order Now Your child's Youth Portrait or your own may be the most important book you will ever read. Don't put off ordering it and risk forgetting. Fill in the coupon below and send it to the address shown with $20. Do it now.

©*Para Research, Inc.*

How To Order Your Astral Guide

Use the coupon or, if you prefer, use
another piece of paper. Send the following information plus $24
for each Astral Guide plus 1.50 to cover postage and handling
to Para Research, Dept. HS, Rockport, Massachusetts 01966.
The price is subject to change.

Name, Address, City, State, Zip Code

The address to which the Astral Guide(s) should be sent.

Time of Birth

Accuracy to the minute is important. Don't rely on parent's
memory. Consult hospital records or birth certificate. Midnight
and noon are neither A.M. nor P.M.; A.M. is between midnight
and noon; P.M. is between noon and midnight. To avoid confusion, if you are submitting a noon birthtime, please write
"noon." If you are submitting a midnight birthtime, please write
"midnight" and two dates: the day that was ending and the day
that was beginning. For example: "June 19/20, 1947, 12:00 midnight."

Please do not convert from daylight saving time to standard
time. Just send us local clock time and we will convert. Or if
you cannot do this, please explain. If you do not send birthtime,
we will use 12:00 noon.

Date of Birth

Month, day and year.

Place of Birth

If you were born in a small town that may not be on our maps,
please give us the name of the nearest city.

Please Print Clearly

Keep a copy of the birth information you send us for comparison with the computer printout. Notify us in case of error.

Guarantee

Para Research guarantees every horoscope. If for any reason,
you are dissatisfied, please return the Astral Guide for a full
refund.

Free Catalogs

Catalogs of Para Research book and horoscope publications will
be sent with your Astral Guide. If you are not ordering a
horoscope but would like the catalogs, please request them from
Para Research, Dept. HS, Rockport, MA 01966

Want to know when your luck is going to change?

This personal calendar of transits, based on the exact time and place of your birth, forecasts your best days and helps you make the most of them.

In many ways you are a different person every day of your life. You know that from experience. You know that some days are good for getting things done. Other days, every little task is a struggle. Some days you get along with everyone easily and pleasantly, especially the opposite sex. Other days, no one will give you anything you want. Some days are great for bargains. Other days, you shouldn't buy anything.

The Future Wouldn't it be wonderful to be able to look into the future, to know what kinds of days are coming for you and when? In astrology, cycles of psychophysical energy in your life are represented by aspects (angles) from the positions of the planets at a given time in your life to the positions of the planets at the time of your birth. These aspects are called transits. And transits are the most fundamental and reliable tool of astrological forecasting.

Transits Here's an example. At fifty-eight minutes after midnight EST on September 7, 1980, Venus will enter the sign Leo. If you were born with Venus in Leo, then sometime during the following twenty-seven days—the exact time depends on your time of birth—transiting Venus will be conjunct (in the same position as) your natal Venus. This transit marks a favorable time for you to begin a new relationship or renew an old one.

But if Venus is not in Leo in your birth chart, you will not have that transit then. (You'll have others, and you'll have Venus conjunct Venus some other time during the year.) Some transits, like Venus conjunct Venus, happen once a year or more. Others happen only once in a lifetime. Some transits are fleeting and subtle. Others are long-lasting and profound in their psychological consequences. But whether you know it or not, the moving planets are forming one transit or another to your natal planets *every two or three days!*

Forecasting You owe it to yourself to find out in advance what your transits are going to be. But to find out on your own, you need to consult astronomical tables and find the positions of each of the transiting planets every day and compare them mathematically to the positions of the planets at the time of your birth.

The Astral Guide Luckily, you don't have to do that. Our IBM 370-155 computer is programmed to do the thousands of calculations for you and provide you with a personal calendar of transits based on your exact time and place of birth. This unique calendar will have twelve poster-sized pages, sixteen by twenty-two inches, with your name and birth information printed at the bottom of every page. It will forecast every significant transit to your natal planets that will occur during a twelve month period and explain the meaning of each transit for your life

Astrophoto Your transits for each month of your Astral Guide will be superimposed on an astro-photograph of the Great Nebula in Andromeda against the heavenly blue of deep space. Our new Astral Guide format, created by one of America's leading designers. is so handsome you can hang it in any room in your home.

Cost Before we developed the Astral Guide, only the very rich could afford to have their transits calculated and interpreted daily by professional astrologers. Now you can have the same kind of advice whenever you want it. and it won't cost you thousands or even hundreds of dollars. Many people would consider twenty-four dollars a month a bargain price for a personal transit calendar. But you can have your Astral Guide for much less than twenty-four dollars a month. To find out how and why, read on.

High Speed Printing Your Astral Guide calendar of transits is the result of years of astrological research and computer programming. But since all of that work is now complete you don't have to pay for it. Your Astral Guide will be produced by a computer-driven high-speed printer that prints hundreds of lines per minute. High speed and high volume lower the cost of each Astral Guide tremendously.

Because of this, we are able to offer you your Astral Guide not for twenty-four dollars a month but for twenty-four dollars a year. That's only *$2.00 a month!*

Order Now Your Astral Guide will come to you with an unconditional money-back guarantee. Processing and delivery can take up to three weeks. Fill out the coupon below and send it with $24 today. Your future is waiting for you.